GW00568321

The Double Game

THE DOUBLE GAME

*The Demise of America's First Missile
Defense System and the Rise of Strategic
Arms Limitation*

James Cameron

OXFORD
UNIVERSITY PRESS

Oxford University Press is a department of the University of Oxford. It furthers
the University's objective of excellence in research, scholarship, and education
by publishing worldwide. Oxford is a registered trade mark of Oxford University
Press in the UK and certain other countries.

Published in the United States of America by Oxford University Press
198 Madison Avenue, New York, NY 10016, United States of America.

Library of Congress Cataloging-in-Publication Data
Names: Cameron, James (Assistant professor), author.
Title: The double game : the demise of America's first missile defense system
    and the rise of strategic arms limitation / James Cameron.
Description: New York, NY : Oxford University Press, 2017. |
    Includes bibliographical references and index.
Identifiers: LCCN 2017016890 (print) | LCCN 2017039708 (ebook) |
    ISBN 9780190459932 (Updf) | ISBN 9780190459949 (Epub) |
    ISBN 9780190459925 (hardcover : alk. paper)
Subjects: LCSH: Ballistic missile defenses—United States—History—20th century. |
    National security—United States—History—20th century.
Classification: LCC UG743 (ebook) | LCC UG743 .C36 2017 (print) |
    DDC 358.4/309730904—dc23
LC record available at https://lccn.loc.gov/2017016890

9 8 7 6 5 4 3 2 1

Printed by Sheridan Books, Inc., United States of America

For Catarina

CONTENTS

Acknowledgments   *ix*
Abbreviations   *xi*

Introduction   *1*
1. Rational Superiority, Crises, and Arms Control, 1961–1963   *12*
2. The Great Society and the Politics of Assured Destruction, 1963–1966   *49*
3. First Steps toward SALT, 1966–1969   *79*
4. Collapse of the Consensus and the Struggle for Coherence, 1969–1970   *107*
5. Reconciliation with Necessity and the Race to the Summit, 1971–1972   *136*
Conclusion: The Double Game   *161*

Notes   *171*
Sources   *207*
Index   *219*

ACKNOWLEDGMENTS

I have accumulated a vast number of debts over the course of this project.

The American History Subject Group at Cambridge provided the ideal environment in which to develop as a historian, both through the supportive camaraderie of the Graduate Workshop and the inspiration of Tony Badger's American History Seminar. I would like to thank Thomas Tunstall Allcock, Patricia Boulhosa, Christopher Burlinson, Andrew David, Kristal Enter, Zach Fredman, Adam Gilbert, John Heavens, Simon Jackson, Alice Kelly, Stella Krepp, Hannah Higgin, Charlie Laderman, Ceri Law, Asa McKercher, David Mislin, Zoe Petkanas, Neil Rogachevsky, Lucy Razzall, Mike Sewell, Olivia Sohns, Danica Summerlin, John Thompson, Hanna Weibye, and Waseem Yaqoob for their good fellowship. Andrew Preston and Matthew Jones gave invaluable advice on how to convert the PhD into a book. Louise Hopper gave me the encouragement I needed to go back to school.

I was lucky enough to spend two formative years at Yale University. I am deeply grateful to Joseph and Alison Fox, and the Brady-Johnson Program in Grand Strategy, for making those years possible. Julia Adams, John Lewis Gaddis, and Elizabeth Bradley provided great academic leadership of the programs of which I was a part. John Negroponte and Bruce Russett both gave their time to talk with me about their lives in the Cold War. William Attwell, Amanda Behm, Chris Dietrich, Andrés Hincapié, Ryan Irwin, Ian Johnson, Nathan Kurz, Christine Leah, Rebecca Lissner, Chris Miller, and Eva-Maria Muschik were wonderful colleagues. James Graham Wilson kindly read and reread the manuscript during this period. Special thanks are due to Paul Kennedy, whose deep generosity and hospitality made New Haven feel like home.

Stanford's Center for International Security and Cooperation provided the perfect setting to rewrite the manuscript. David Holloway was an invaluable source of advice and support during this process. Lynn Eden

and Scott Sagan were instrumental in fostering the community of scholars from which I learned so much, while Brad Roberts and Alain Enthoven
helped me understand the dilemmas of real-world policymaking. Marc
Trachtenberg sat down with me one sunny day and generously subjected
my argument to a forensic analysis. I am very grateful for the comments,
suggestions, and company of Daniel Altman, Larry Brandt, Benjamin
Buch, Malfrid Braut-Hegghammer, Edward Geist, Steven Glinert, Martin
Hellman, Jonathan Hunt, Mark and Athena Howard, Jackie Kerr, Elaine
Korzak, Andreas Kuehn, Christopher Lawrence, Neil Narang, Megan
Palmer, Benoît Pelopidas, Niccolò Petrelli, Robert Rakove, Jason Reinhardt,
Kurt, Naomi, and Basia Schendzielos, Rebecca Slayton, Magda Stawkowski,
David Traven, Gil-li Vardi, Casey Wilke, and Benjamin Wilson. Thank you to
Amir Weiner for inviting me to the Russian History *kruzhok* to be grilled by
Soviet specialists and to Frank Gavin for the many enlightening conversa-
tions during the rewriting period. I am deeply grateful to the Stanton and
MacArthur Foundations, both for supporting my two years at Stanford and
the vital work they do to foster a new generation of policy-relevant scholar-
ship in the field of nuclear security.

Without the United Kingdom Arts and Humanities Research Council
and the Parry Dutton Fund of Sidney Sussex College, Cambridge, this book
would not have been written. Thanks to the staffs of the National Archives
and Records Administration, the John F. Kennedy, Lyndon B. Johnson,
and Richard Nixon presidential libraries, and the Library of Congress
Manuscripts Division, I wanted for nothing in the archives.

Susan Ferber at Oxford University Press has been an extremely kind,
attentive, thorough, and patient editor, uncovering and expunging a variety of previously unknown writer's tics. I would like to thank OUP's two
anonymous reviewers, who challenged me to refine and rethink many
aspects of the manuscript. Jeremy Toynbee and Michael Stein have been a
great help in preparing the book for production.

I could not have hoped for a better academic mentor than David
Reynolds. Always available, intellectually rigorous, on time, and on target,
David is the model of the scholar and supervisor I would like to become.

There are debts that are very difficult to measure. My mother, Yvonne,
and my sister, Vita, both kept me grounded and committed—not only during this process, but long before that. Finally, my wife Catarina has spent
the entirety of our relationship with this project as a constant presence,
often keeping us apart. This book is for her.

ABBREVIATIONS

ABM	Antiballistic missile
ACDA	Arms Control and Disarmament Agency
AICBM	Anti-intercontinental ballistic missile
CIA	Central Intelligence Agency
DOD	Department of Defense
FBS	Forward-based systems
FRG	Federal Republic of Germany
FY	Fiscal Year
ICBM	Intercontinental ballistic missile
JCS	Joint Chiefs of Staff
MAD	Mutual assured destruction
MFA	Ministry of Foreign Affairs (Soviet)
NCA	National Command Authority
NIE	National Intelligence Estimate
LTBT	Limited Test Ban Treaty
MIRV	Multiple independently targetable reentry vehicle
NSSM	National Security Study Memorandum
NATO	North Atlantic Treaty Organization
NORAD	North American Air Defense Command
NPT	Nonproliferation Treaty
NSC	National Security Council
PPBS	Planning Programing Budgeting System
PRC	People's Republic of China
RAND	Research and Development Corporation
SALT	Strategic Arms Limitation Talks
SLBM	Submarine-launched ballistic missile
SSBN	Nuclear-powered ballistic missile submarine
USAF	United States Air Force
USIB	United States Intelligence Board

The Double Game

Introduction

On May 26, 1972, Richard Nixon sat down in St. Vladimir Hall of the Grand Kremlin Palace to sign the first treaty to permanently limit the United States' ability to field a major nuclear weapons program. The Antiballistic Missile (ABM) Treaty, unlike the Interim Agreement on the Limitation of Strategic Offensive Arms that Nixon also signed that day, was of indefinite duration. It restricted the United States and the Soviet Union to two ABM sites each, one protecting their capital cities and another around an offensive missile field, thereby outlawing a nationwide missile defense system for both superpowers.[1]

The Moscow Summit was the pinnacle of US–Soviet détente during Nixon's presidency. The ABM Treaty was the most concrete agreement to emerge from that summit, giving substance where there had only been vague expressions of goodwill at Nixon's previous meeting with Mao Zedong in Beijing. In this sense, the ABM Treaty has enjoyed the somewhat dubious honor of representing one of the principal foundations of US–Soviet détente in the 1970s.

Both its advocates and detractors deemed the ABM Treaty strategically significant because it represented the United States' acceptance of mutual assured destruction (MAD).[2] Without the protection afforded by an ABM system neither side could hope to launch a first strike to destroy the enemy's offensive nuclear forces, safe in the knowledge that a missile defense would be able to absorb the ragged retaliation by surviving units. With each side able to assure the destruction of the other after an initial blow, the treaty's supporters argued, the incentives to launch a preemptive attack were minimal. Such a situation would lower the chance of a nuclear war and promote a stable relationship between the two superpowers. It would also preclude a new arms race between defensive systems and new offensive weapons to overcome them. Such a competition would not only be extremely expensive, but also ratchet up tensions through increased suspicions on each side that the other was preparing a first strike capability.[3] By contrast, the ABM Treaty's detractors saw MAD as an act of strategic and moral folly. It was strategically senseless because the condition of assured suicide was nowhere near as stable as supporters' simplistic formulae made out, and it was morally contemptible because it predicated peace on mutual "genocide."[4] Critics also argued that the Soviet Union had not accepted the logic of stability based on mutual vulnerability implied by the treaty and instead was using strategic arms control as a means by which to further its military advantage.[5] The acronym MAD was coined in 1971 by one of these early detractors, defense analyst Donald Brennan, as a way to illustrate such misgivings.[6]

The intense and passionate debate between the supporters and detractors of MAD in the wake of the conclusion of the first Strategic Arms Limitation Talks (SALT I) has been a key factor in structuring the discussion of the nuclear-strategic competition prior to 1972. In established narratives, the American acceptance of MAD in the SALT accords emerged from the latest round of a debate among nuclear strategists and policymakers, which had proceeded along the following lines: As the Cold War deepened during the second half of the 1940s, the United States had a nuclear monopoly to hold off an attack by the Soviet Union's far larger conventional forces based in Eastern Europe. After the successful Soviet test of an atomic bomb in 1949 and the development of a long-range bomber fleet, however, the United States government realized that it required a more sophisticated strategy to fend off a Soviet conventional thrust into Western Europe under its new nuclear umbrella. This came in the form of Eisenhower's New Look, which raised the possibility of US nuclear use—dubbed by Secretary of State John Foster Dulles as "massive retaliation"—in response to Soviet encroachments at any level of warfare, both conventional and nuclear. The threat that the United States could opt to turn a conventional war in Europe into a nuclear war was a key element in this deterrence architecture. The credibility of this threat depended on maintaining a marked US superiority in strategic striking power.[7]

While several strategists raised concerns regarding the credibility of this posture of nuclear brinkmanship, the successful Soviet launch of the Sputnik satellite into orbit in October 1957 tipped the Eisenhower administration's strategy into a state of crisis. For the first time, the United States found itself on the back foot technologically and theoretically vulnerable to a Soviet first strike, raising the specter of a Soviet surprise attack on US nuclear forces in a way that fundamentally questioned the credibility of the American reliance on its strategic nuclear preponderance.[8] Rising to power on the back of the supposed missile gap that had developed to the United States' detriment under Eisenhower, John F. Kennedy and his secretary of defense, Robert S. McNamara, adopted a new strategy: flexible response. Utilizing the insights of a new generation of think-tank strategists, flexible response was designed to bolster the credibility of US security commitments. It required the United States, in concert with its allies, to be able to outmatch the Soviet Union at any level of warfare, from counterinsurgency in the global South, to a conventional war in Western Europe, to a superpower nuclear exchange. Finding itself outgunned at every turn, the Soviet Union would conclude that it could not use its military capabilities to revise the status quo in Europe or tip the superpower competition in its favor further afield. In addition to new counterinsurgency and conventional capabilities, this strategy necessitated a huge buildup in US offensive nuclear forces in order to provide the president with multiple attack options, as well as a more generously funded missile defense program than that which had existed under Eisenhower.[9]

Yet a number of developments during the 1960s placed the United States' nuclear strategy in jeopardy. While laboring under a great nuclear deficit during the first half of the decade, from the mid-1960s the Soviet Union began its own buildup of intercontinental ballistic missiles, encased in protected concrete silos, in order to catch up with the United States. At the same time, McNamara concluded that missile defense was extremely inefficient; the system was simply too unreliable and too expensive to offer an effective counter to the Soviet missile threat. In recognition of these facts, the Johnson administration developed a nuclear doctrine that emphasized the importance of nuclear forces able to survive a Soviet attack and retain the ability to annihilate the USSR, a criterion known as assured destruction. Measures to limit damage through attacks on Soviet nuclear forces or ballistic missile defenses were downplayed because they were unable to provide an effective counter to the Soviets' own assured destruction capability. In the face of failures to start arms control talks with the Soviets in order to enshrine these strategic insights in formal treaties, the administration was forced to announce the deployment of a limited ABM system in September 1967. Yet the United States had lost significant ground in the intervening years. Instead of an ability to cow the USSR at the highest of levels of conflict, the United States faced the prospect of a Soviet nuclear arsenal of equal or greater power while having no effective defense.[10]

With the 1972 SALT accords, the narrative concludes, the Nixon administration recognized the inevitable outcome of this situation: in the absence of an effective defense against ballistic missiles, the only way to ensure survival was strategic stability based on mutual vulnerability and approximate parity between the superpowers in numbers of offensive systems. Both the United States and the USSR should know that, in the event of a nuclear strike by the other, they could respond with a counterblow that would devastate their opponent's society. By banning missile defenses and freezing the race in nuclear missile launchers, it is argued, the agreements signed at Moscow signaled the United States' acceptance of MAD. Although domestic political factors occasionally play a role in this tale, the strategic interaction between the national security establishments of the two superpowers is the dominant dynamic in this story.[11]

During the 1970s and into the 1980s, some political scientists had begun to place greater emphasis on the way in which other factors—in particular, domestic and bureaucratic politics—perverted American strategic decision-making during this period. Scholar Desmond Ball charged that Kennedy's buildup in ICBMs was conditioned far more by bureaucratic and domestic politics than the true scale of the Soviet threat.[12] A former member of Johnson's Defense Department and Nixon's National Security Council, Morton Halperin, showed the importance of bureaucratic and domestic political bargaining in the Johnson administration's decision to proceed with an anti-Chinese ABM in September 1967. Political scientist Ernest Yanarella argued the ABM's development was the result of the "technological imperative": the institutionalized competition between American offensive and defensive technology within the Pentagon's own research and development programs.[13] SALT delegation members Gerard Smith and Raymond L. Garthoff wrote about the way in which the Nixon White House's attempts to gain the maximum domestic political credit for any agreement through backchannel negotiations, pressure for a US–Soviet summit before the presidential election of 1972, and the overselling of the SALT accords after Nixon's return from Moscow all had a negative effect on the quality and durability of strategic arms limitation as a policy.[14] However, despite these detours into domestic and bureaucratic politics, the emphasis remained on the fact that, through SALT I, the United States government had fundamentally accepted the reality of MAD.

The rise of MAD has thus remained at the heart of narratives about the development of arms control between the superpowers ever since the 1970s. Yet declassified records of conversations between Nixon and his advisors show that Nixon did not subscribe to MAD. He did not hold that the arms race lay at the root of US–Soviet tensions. Less than three years before the Moscow Summit, he had publicly excoriated those who, he claimed, naively believed that "if we would only reduce our forces . . . tensions would disappear and the chances for peace would brighten." To accept this reasoning, Nixon argued, "would be disastrous for our nation and the world."[15] Nixon privately hoped that he could convince the Soviets and the North Vietnamese that he was a "madman," who might use nuclear weapons in Southeast Asia in the absence of an acceptable settlement. Weeks before the Moscow Summit, Nixon lamented that the US nuclear edge was much diminished since the Cuban missile crisis in 1962, when "it had been 'no contest,' because we had a ten to one superiority." He returned to this theme even after he signed the SALT I agreements. Nixon also pushed forward with qualitative improvements to US forces and authorized the developments of plans for limited options designed to make nuclear weapons more usable.[16] For Nixon, the potential loss of credibility resulting from a nuclear retreat outweighed any notional benefits accruing from the decreased tensions associated with both superpowers' acceptance of MAD.

In Moscow, however, Nixon not only signed a treaty outlawing any conceivable defense against a Soviet attack, but coupled it with a five-year agreement that left the Soviet Union with a marked edge in the number of land-based intercontinental and submarine-launched ballistic missiles. In public, the president accepted the fundamental tenets of the strategic case for arms control. Both on his return home from Moscow and in his memoirs, Nixon adopted the logic of the arms controllers in his defense of the agreements. While assuring conservatives that the United States would continue with qualitative improvements to the US arsenal, in his address to a joint session of Congress on June 1, 1972, Nixon publicly accepted the fundamentals of MAD. The SALT accords, Nixon declared, had "enhanced the security of both sides" by "check[ing] the wasteful and dangerous spiral of nuclear arms. . . . We have begun to reduce the level of fear by reducing the causes of fear, for our two peoples and for all peoples in the world." The halt in the defensive race, Nixon later argued, made "permanent the concept of deterrence through 'mutual terror.'" Both superpowers, Nixon held, "therefore had an ultimate interest in preventing a war that could only be mutually destructive."[17] Nixon hated MAD, believed its logic was defeatist and naïve, yet he signed agreements that enshrined it at the heart of the United States' relations with the Soviet Union. This book explains why.

It also explains why Nixon's two predecessors, John F. Kennedy and Lyndon Baines Johnson, were not able sign a strategic arms limitation accord, despite considerable misgivings within both of their administrations regarding the utility of the US nuclear edge. Kennedy entered office ready to regain America's quantitative and qualitative lead in nuclear weapons. He also wanted to harness new developments in managerial and social sciences to rationalize both the procurement of nuclear weapons and the manipulation of the risk of nuclear war in a crisis. In doing so, Kennedy hoped to force the Soviet Union to conclude periodic superpower confrontations in hotspots such as Berlin on the United States' terms. The combination of overwhelming force and its procurement, structuring, and employment by reasonable statesmen constituted an overall approach to strategic issues, summarized here as rational superiority.

After the Cuban missile crisis, however, those at the top of the Kennedy administration understood that any benefits accruing from the United States' nuclear edge in terms of increased confidence during crises in the Caribbean and Central Europe were far outweighed by the risks entailed by the increased chance of a nuclear holocaust. In the wake of Cuba, Kennedy questioned the utility of US superiority on more than one occasion. The subsequent recollections of McGeorge Bundy, Kennedy's national security advisor, and McNamara substantiate the judgment that by 1962 Kennedy officials had accepted the essential features of MAD.[18] Both Bundy and McNamara brought these experiences with them into the Johnson administration.

If there was a general sense by the end of the Kennedy presidency that nuclear superiority was of limited strategic utility, behavior on the part of subsequent administrations is confusing to say the least. Kennedy planned to make the US nuclear edge a key issue in the 1964 presidential election, while Johnson lauded US military superiority in his public remarks. By McNamara's own admission, the number of US tactical nuclear weapons in Europe grew to 7,000 under his watch.[19] As well as continuing the huge nuclear buildup in nuclear missiles to levels far beyond what the Soviet Union possessed, the secretary of defense also authorized the deployment of multiple independently targetable reentry vehicles (MIRVs) on US land-based and submarine-launched missiles, as well as a limited missile defense system for the United States.[20] As with Nixon, there was a marked difference between officials' public behavior and their private anxieties.

The truth was that all three presidents—Kennedy, Johnson, and Nixon—engaged in a double game when it came to US nuclear strategy.[21] Publicly, they sought to present an image of strategic coherence in order to reassure those outside the administration, including the American public and Congress, that they had full control of the nuclear standoff between the two superpowers. Yet declassified transcripts and tape recordings of White House conversations show that the situation was far more complex and contradictory, with all three administrations struggling to reconcile their public commitments with their personal feelings regarding the reality of the nuclear balance, as well as a number of other competing domestic political and budgetary priorities. This double game, in which policymakers struggled to balance the demands of presenting a front of strategic coherence with the incoherent reality behind the scenes, provided an overarching dynamic through which the first US missile defense program met its demise and the United States government officially accepted the logic of mutual assured destruction.

As chapter 1 shows, when Kennedy attacked Eisenhower for the missile gap and propounded the logic of rational superiority, he was responding to a public craving security in the wake of Sputnik. Moving forward with ABM was part of this wider scheme of reassurance. After he found out that superiority did not give him the level of confidence he thought it would during the Berlin and Cuban crises, Kennedy began to question its utility. Yet Kennedy's advisors warned against changing course, for fear of the potential political consequences—particularly in view of the upcoming presidential election of 1964. Planning to use the US nuclear edge as a key plank of his reelection campaign, Kennedy bequeathed a significant gap between his rhetoric of superiority and the more complex reality to his successor.

For Johnson, the primary challenge was to maintain quantitative nuclear superiority without spending so much on it as to endanger his broader domestic agenda. When he entered office, Johnson was fundamentally focused on domestic issues and saw nuclear strategy as one tool in his wider attempt to reconcile spending on national security with his Great Society program. In order to get the Great Society moving, LBJ believed he had to reassure the United States that the country's international status would be maintained, including an explicit commitment to retaining the US nuclear edge. Chapter 2 tells the story of how McNamara, reaching the peak of his power, sought to reconcile this public commitment with LBJ's domestic priorities. McNamara's doctrine of "assured destruction," from which MAD would eventually derive the final two letters of its acronym, was the secretary of defense's attempt to cap the resources the United States would commit to nuclear arms while providing a strategic rationale that would maintain American nuclear preponderance. Rather than a justification for superpower nuclear parity, as it would become in the 1970s, MAD was initially conceived in the furnace of domestic politics and designed to provide a rationalization for why the Soviet Union would never aspire to nuclear equality with the United States. The Soviet Union, McNamara argued, would be satisfied with a numerically inferior offensive force that could nevertheless survive a first strike and ensure US destruction in a nuclear war. Such a situation—of assured destruction between the superpowers based on mutual vulnerability, but with Soviet quantitative nuclear inferiority—would keep the extremely expensive US ABM in research and development, thereby reconciling Johnson's budgetary and national security agenda.

Yet it became increasingly clear from 1965 that McNamara's assumptions regarding Soviet behavior were wrong. While the Kennedy administration had recognized in 1963 that effective nuclear superiority—the ability to deliver a first strike that eliminated the Soviet Union's offensive forces—was a thing of the past, the United States retained a quantitative edge in missile launchers. Johnson, however, had to face the reality of a Soviet buildup in intercontinental ballistic missiles at just the point that the country, weighed down by commitments in Vietnam, was increasingly unable to respond. Chapter 3 illustrates how Johnson and McNamara tried to maintain the increasingly untenable balance between retaining formal quantitative US nuclear superiority and ameliorating the arms race. They did so by attempting to persuade the Soviet leadership that banning antiballistic missiles and freezing the growth of offensive forces, leaving the USSR in a state of quantitative nuclear inferiority, would actually serve the interests of both superpowers. With the Soviets unable and unwilling to open a real dialogue on these terms, however, Johnson's presidency failed to make the breakthrough necessary to cement his reputation as the godfather of US–Soviet détente. Meanwhile, domestic pressure forced McNamara to authorize deployment of a limited ABM system for the United States.

While the Johnson administration had attempted to keep the lid on US strategic programs against domestic political pressure for deployment, for Nixon the problem was exactly the opposite. As Chapter 4 illustrates, in contrast to his predecessors, Nixon fully signed on to the idea that the United States should maintain a nuclear lead, and he hoped to use ABM as a bargaining chip with the Soviet Union in order to maintain as much of it as possible. Yet the domestic political situation had changed dramatically by 1969, with a significant and unprecedented spike in public and congressional opposition to new spending on strategic forces. Unprepared for the collapse in the public consensus regarding the necessity of nuclear superiority and the implicit trust in the authority of the presidency to decide existential matters of deterrence, the Nixon administration almost lost its first congressional test on a national security issue when its redesigned missile defense system passed the Senate by just one vote.

There was a signal change in the way in which the Nixon administration dealt with ABM, and strategic arms control more generally, thereafter. Seeing the domestic consensus behind the US nuclear edge collapse, the Nixon White House decided to make a virtue of necessity by pushing for an early summit meeting based on arms control. During 1970, Nixon and Kissinger attempted to get a top-level meeting with the Soviets in order to reap the domestic political rewards they believed would result, and they used an ABM ban as the main inducement. They did so at great cost to the United States' position at the formal Strategic Arms Limitation Talks, which had commenced in November 1969. Wishing to keep the details of their "backchannel" negotiations with Soviet Ambassador to the United States Anatoly Dobrynin secret from the arms-controllers in order to garner the maximum domestic political credit for Nixon personally, the White House committed major errors that vitiated much of the US ABM system's utility as a means to pressure the Soviets into accepting a cap on the growth of their offensive forces.

With little progress on other fronts, in particular "peace with honor" in Vietnam, by late 1970 Nixon needed something to show for his electoral pledge to enter an era of negotiation. Chapter 5 shows how, under domestic pressure for results, Nixon acceded to a deal that banned national ABM systems, but did not provide a strong limit on the number of Soviet ICBM and SLBM launchers. Instead, the Soviets led in both of these categories. In order to get the deal through Congress, Nixon employed the same rhetoric of stability through arms control that he had despised throughout his career and had publicly condemned as late as 1969 when making the case for a US ABM system. Thus Nixon, the nuclear hawk, became the arch proponent of agreements that would be the bane of other hawks until the United States' withdrawal from the ABM Treaty in 2002. Just as Kennedy and Johnson had bowed to domestic political pressure to maintain their rhetoric of strategic superiority, so too Nixon conceded to the country's changed mood and publicly accepted the fundamental logic of arms control based on mutual assured destruction.

As well as the political science literature on nuclear policymaking, this book builds on an increasingly rich new historiography that seeks to draw connections between nuclear strategy and other seemingly separate issues. Francis J. Gavin pointed to Nixon's deep misgivings regarding MAD. Other work by scholars, including Gavin, Marc Trachtenberg, and Matthew Jones, has shown how nuclear policies pursued by the US government in the 1960s and 1970s were in fact the product of a diverse range of influences, including the future of a divided Germany within Europe, American concerns regarding the nation's deteriorating balance of payments, and race. Bargaining over the future of Germany—the focus of much superpower anxiety regarding both nuclear proliferation and the long-term future of the postwar European settlement—was fundamental to the development of US–Soviet arms control and détente more broadly during the 1960s and early 1970s.[22] This book does not attempt to downplay the importance of European geopolitics. Instead, it adds another element to an already complex history—the perpetual presidential struggle throughout the period between 1961 and 1972 to reconcile public pronouncements regarding nuclear weapons with private doubts and competing domestic priorities, both political and budgetary.

In doing so, it adds further weight to the idea that superpower arms control, and US–Soviet détente in general, was a necessarily gradual process. The structural domestic political pressures on the three presidents meant that there were no missed chances for détente that a more competent pair of hands could have grasped. Tragic as it was, John F. Kennedy's assassination did not suddenly foreclose a potential blossoming of détente between the United States and the Soviet Union—the gap between Soviet aspirations to parity and Kennedy's entrapment in the rhetoric of superiority was just too wide for that. Similarly, though Johnson made major strides toward agreements with the Soviet Union on a number of issues, most notably through the 1968 Nonproliferation Treaty, he was never able to break free from the sense that superiority was a domestic political priority. It was only with the evident collapse of the domestic political consensus in 1969 during the ABM debate that superpower détente on the basis of strategic arms control became possible.

This story also speaks to contemporary concerns about how nuclear postures are adopted and strategy made. Debates that continue to preoccupy many in the strategic studies community, such as whether nuclear superiority confers increased resolve to the state that possesses it, played only a secondary role in presidential deliberations during the 1960s and early 1970s.[23] The renunciation of ABM and the adoption of MAD was not simply—or even primarily—the result of nuclear-strategic calculus. Kennedy had serious misgivings regarding the importance of US superiority, yet planned to press ahead with it in search of domestic political gain. Preoccupied with the Great Society and Vietnam, Johnson saw the nuclear balance almost entirely in domestic political and budgetary terms. While instinctively in favor of superiority, Nixon had little time for military or technical advice if it conflicted with his quest for a deal before the 1972 presidential election. As the following chapters will demonstrate, strategic debates within the executive branch on issues such as superiority were important, but they were not decisive.

The progress of ABM from military program to prohibition was not simply a question of bureaucratic or organizational politics. It is true that US nuclear strategy during this period was shaped as much by fights inside the Beltway as it was by the Soviet threat. Yet an exclusive focus on the relative power of various elements of the US national security bureaucracy does not account for change over time. The Joint Chiefs of Staff and the Pentagon were incredibly important during the Kennedy and Johnson years, yet their power waned considerably as the public mood turned against the cost of maintaining US nuclear superiority from the late 1960s onwards. The reasons for agencies' relative weight in decision making lay in the broader congressional and public milieu. All three presidents paid a great deal of attention to the evolution of congressional views on nuclear issues and tailored their nuclear rhetoric in order to fit with their—generally impressionistic—sense of the country's mood.

It is now clear that the United States wrote a number of checks during the 1960s that it could not cash simultaneously, including nuclear superiority with arms control and victory at an acceptable cost in Southeast Asia. The 2000s saw a similar rhetorical and strategic overstretch with perhaps even more deleterious consequences for the US position in the world than those which faced the country in the late 1960s and early 1970s. As the United States finds itself under new budgetary and strategic pressures across the globe, the gap between the rhetoric that much of the American public and Congress seemingly expect of its leadership and the United States' capabilities to stand behind those commitments is widening again. Regardless of the Obama administration's early advocacy of a world free of nuclear weapons, this credibility gap could once more be filled with the threat to use nuclear weapons in defense of areas that are indefensible through conventional means. This book shows how the way successive presidents have talked about and framed their strategies is as much the product of leaders' doubts, budgetary bargaining, and domestic political opportunism as strategic calculus. In doing so, it sheds light on the dynamics of a new period of nuclear deterrence.

CHAPTER 1

Rational Superiority, Crises, and Arms Control, 1961–1963

On January 20, 1961, John F. Kennedy stepped onto the rostrum in front of the Capitol Building to deliver his inaugural address. The soaring rhetoric of that speech seared itself into the memories of those present and the millions who watched or listened to it around the world. Kennedy delivered "a request" to the Soviet Union "that both sides begin anew the quest for peace, before the dark powers of destruction unleashed by science engulf all humanity in planned or accidental self-destruction." In his next breath, however, the president declared, "only when our arms are sufficient beyond doubt can we be certain beyond doubt that they will never be employed." Behind him, wearing an incongruous top hat foisted on him to placate Massachusetts milliners and bundled up against the freezing temperatures, was Secretary of Defense Robert S. McNamara. Over the next three years, Kennedy and McNamara would struggle to fulfill the president's dual pledge to "never negotiate out of fear," yet "never fear to negotiate."[1]

Like many of the finest lines of political rhetoric, this promise was far easier to articulate than to implement. Kennedy faced a multitude of problems, the most acute of which was the US–Soviet standoff over Berlin and the issues it raised regarding the relationship between nuclear deterrence, fear, and diplomacy. Unknown to Kennedy that January day, those issues would come to the fore even more dramatically during the Cuban missile crisis of October 1962. Throughout this period of intense superpower confrontation, the president and his secretary of defense would have to fulfill Kennedy's campaign trail promise to fashion a coherent, rational defense program that would regain ground that had been supposedly lost during the Eisenhower years.

On the surface, the Kennedy-McNamara partnership handled these dilemmas with an adroitness unmatched by future administrations. They built up US intercontinental strike capabilities in order to close the perceived "missile gap" that had opened under Kennedy's predecessor, Dwight D. Eisenhower, and thus left the United States in a position of substantial superiority over its superpower rival. They also rationalized defense procurement and the methods by which the United States' nuclear power could be used in a crisis, staving off Soviet challenges in Berlin and Cuba. At the same time, they negotiated the first permanent nuclear arms control agreement, the Limited Test Ban Treaty (LTBT), ensuring that the United States could have an accord that dampened the arms race without endangering its nuclear edge.

Despite their many achievements, the Kennedy administration failed to resolve—and, to some extent, exacerbated—fundamental tensions between US nuclear superiority and the demands of crisis management, and the new movement toward superpower détente. The United States' antiballistic missile (ABM) program played a minor role in these events. Yet, even at this early stage, ABM illustrated many of the contradictions inherent in Kennedy and McNamara's theory of defense management. Moreover, the strategic framework that the Kennedy administration left in place, and the contradictions within it, would shape the progress of the program for the rest of the 1960s.

CAMPAIGN RHETORIC AND STRATEGIC THEORY

Kennedy had used Americans' nuclear insecurity to his political advantage against President Dwight D. Eisenhower and his vice president, Richard M. Nixon. Spurred by the first successful Soviet test of the *Sputnik* satellite in October 1957, Kennedy's main charge was extremely simple. He accused the Eisenhower administration of allowing the Soviet Union to gain a quantitative advantage in the numbers of intercontinental ballistic missiles (ICBMs). This lead was so large, he claimed in a speech on the Senate floor in August 1958, "that by 1960 the United States will have lost . . . its superiority in nuclear striking power." This, he warned, would "make our exercises in brink of war diplomacy . . . infinitely less successful."[2] Kennedy repeated this "missile gap" charge during his presidential campaign. The phrase had such resonance that he began to talk about the "Nixon gap" between what his opponent said and did.[3]

The missile gap worked because it stuck in the guts of voters. ICBMs could be launched from the territory of the USSR to hit American cities with minimal warning and no means of defense. For the first time the prospect of a nuclear Pearl Harbor was real. However, in this case the entire American homeland would be at risk from a massive Soviet attack and any US "victory" after such a strike would hardly be worthy of the name. Soviet Premier Nikita Khrushchev was right to declare to the Soviet Presidium that he could make "main-street Americans . . . shake from fear for the first time in their lives."[4] Not for the first time, or the last, US citizens would feel defenseless in a way entirely new to them.

Yet the missile gap was not simply a charge of quantitative inferiority in weapons, but also qualitative inferiority in the way they had been acquired and managed. The Eisenhower administration, Kennedy charged, was not ready to confront the challenge of the missile gap. Eisenhower was a small-government conservative, perennially worried about the danger that Cold War demands would turn the United States into a garrison state. Kennedy accused him of putting "fiscal security ahead of national security." This claim played into a broader critique of Eisenhower's national security policy, which, Kennedy charged, lacked both a solid understanding of the new challenges facing the United States and the appropriate level of "vigor" for dealing with them. These ranged from communist subversion of decolonization to the deficiencies in the United States' conventional military capabilities. The missile gap was simply one aspect of this broader malaise. "The Soviet Union," Kennedy claimed on the campaign trail, had "decided . . . to go all out in missile development. But here in the United States we cut back our funds for missile development and in our race for outer space." Part of the solution was to "step up crash programs on the ultimate weapon [:] The Polaris submarine, the Minuteman missile, which will eventually close the missile gap."[5]

Kennedy sought to show the way forward by surrounding himself with advisors who exemplified this modern, rational approach to national security affairs.[6] A new breed of civilian "defense intellectuals," these men were based at research institutes dedicated to mastering nuclear weapons in a way that would cover the deficiencies of the Eisenhower defense program. The most famous of these was the Research and Development Corporation (RAND) in southern California. RAND had originally been set up by the US Air Force and in its early years relied on USAF contracts. Yet, based on the West Coast, RAND presented itself as daringly modern and free-thinking, seemingly detached from the internecine squabbling that was perceived to have engulfed the defense politics of Washington, DC. According to a glowing 1959 *Life* feature, RAND was "an idea factory," which was "removed from Pentagon red tape." Accompanied by pictures of young men emerging from rooms marked with mysterious signs such as "Sierra Control, No Eyes" and lounging on modernist furniture discussing American recovery from a nuclear holocaust, RAND appeared both highly technical and breathtakingly daring. According to *Life*, RAND had saved the Air Force a billion dollars by redesigning its basing system. Pointedly, the story described how RAND "once wrote a report which predicted the date of the first Russian Sputnik months in advance—but . . . no one in authority bothered to read it." The Corporation was everything it appeared Eisenhower was not and Kennedy wanted to be: contemporary, intellectually dynamic, and ready to master the imponderables of the missile age.[7]

After winning the election, Kennedy looked around for someone who could put these ideas into practice. Tellingly, he did not put one of the RAND intellectuals in charge of the overall effort. Although fluent in strategic theory, none of these men had held anything resembling a top-level executive position. The leader of this group, Albert Wohlstetter, had owned a prefab housing business before going into nuclear strategy, hardly on the scale of the Department of Defense (DoD).[8] Nor did Kennedy opt for somebody from the Democratic defense establishment. Senator Henry "Scoop" Jackson of Washington State, a noted Democratic defense hawk, suggested Paul H. Nitze, a Truman-era director of policy planning at the State Department. Jackson argued that with wartime service on the Strategic Bombing Survey and a stellar legal career behind him, Nitze had both the policymaking and business experience to make a great secretary of defense. According to Jackson, Truman's secretary of state, Dean Acheson, and Robert Lovett, a former secretary of defense, also backed Nitze's candidacy.[9] If Kennedy had wanted to look tough yet technocratic, Nitze would have been a good choice.

Yet it appears that Kennedy wanted somebody more independent—an experienced executive without links to the Democratic national-security establishment. At the same time that Jackson was giving the president-elect his views, Kennedy was reaching out to McNamara. President of the Ford Motor Company and a Republican, McNamara was very much a new face for the Kennedy team. JFK had never met him before he offered him the job of secretary of defense. McNamara could best Nitze for organizational talent, boasting a reputation as one of the fabled "Whiz Kids" who had been hired by Ford after their successful management of the logistics for the American strategic bombing campaigns in Europe and the Pacific during the Second World War. The Whiz Kids were famous for turning the company around by applying the quantitative methods they had learned in the military to the business of producing cars. McNamara had risen faster and higher than any of his peers. Independent, intellectually ambidextrous, and experienced at running one of the largest corporations in the world, McNamara was the perfect fit.[10]

David Halberstam's portrait of McNamara in *The Best and the Brightest* has served as the archetype against which all subsequent interpretations of the secretary of defense should be judged:

> If the body was tense and driven, the mind was mathematical, analytical, bringing order and reason out of chaos. Always reason. And reason supported by facts, by statistics—he could prove his rationality with facts, intimidate others. Once, sitting . . . for eight hours watching hundreds and hundreds of slides flashed across the screen showing what was in the pipeline to Vietnam and what was already there, he finally said, after seven hours, "Stop the projector. This slide, number 869, contradicts slide 11." Slide 11 was flashed back and he was right . . .[11]

This vision of McNamara as a human computer was fundamental to his relationship with subordinates and the wider American public. "We were zestful, moved by . . . vistas of the elimination of nuclear terror by means of systematic application of human reason," Tom J. Farer, a middle-ranking member of McNamara's Defense Department remembered. "We were true believers, and McNamara was our prophet."[12] McNamara exuded this technocratic approach, telling Arthur M. Schlesinger, Jr. in April 1964 that the "problems are very similar . . . whether one is administering . . . the Catholic Church, or a large industrial organization such as Ford Motor Company . . . or a government department."[13]

However there was another side to McNamara's character, often in tension with the cool technocrat, which was also captured by Halberstam:

> Sometimes, to those around him, he seemed too idealistic as to be innocent. He never talked about power and he did not seem to covet it. Yet the truth was quite different. He loved power and he sought it intensely, and he could be a ferocious infighter where the question of power was concerned. Nothing could come between him and a president of the United States. . . . For all his apparent innocence, he had triumphed in the ferocious jungle of Detroit automotive politics, he was acutely aware of how to gain and hold power.[14]

McNamara had dispatched rivals and subordinates at Ford ruthlessly after the famous failure of the Edsel model in 1958, leaving him with a clear run at the company's top ranks. In November 1960 he was the first non-Ford family member to become president. This rise sometimes required compromises with the rational cost effectiveness criteria that served as the bedrock of his public image. He allegedly manipulated the numbers to fit in with the preconceptions of his predecessor, Henry Ford II, and the company's chairman, Ernest R. Breech. Rationalization was an important concept to McNamara, but it was ultimately a tool to further his influence by centralizing operations under his control. At both Ford and the Department of Defense, he was deeply conscious that he served at the pleasure of a higher authority. If presented with a choice between compromising on cost effectiveness and alienating his boss, McNamara would always privilege the former over the latter.[15]

The rational side of McNamara's personality dominated as he reached out into the think-tank world for appropriate subordinates. The new secretary of defense had had no experience of military affairs since his demobilization. One of the few books he read on the subject was *The Economics of Defense in the Nuclear Age* by Charles Hitch, RAND's head of economics. In his belief that "*all* military problems . . . in one of their aspects, [are] economic problems," Hitch's organizational philosophy was very close to McNamara's. McNamara installed Hitch as the Department of Defense comptroller, in charge of establishing what later became known as the Planning Programming Budgeting System (PPBS). If McNamara was Kennedy's man to implement a thoroughgoing reform of Defense, then Hitch's PPBS was the main tool by which McNamara hoped to implement his managerial philosophy.[16]

The fundamental contention of PPBS was that the individual military services could not be trusted to set defense priorities. Under Eisenhower the budget had been divided among the services. Each service had then been left to allocate resources as it saw fit. In the minds of the civilian defense intellectuals, this approach lay at the heart of the Eisenhower administration's failings: nobody had a sufficiently broad overview of the defense program, nor the power with which to make it coherent. This had led to inefficient spending on many competing projects—for example, parallel efforts by the Army and the Air Force to develop ballistic missiles, contributing to the Soviets' development and testing of an ICBM before the United States.[17]

As Hitch's deputy Alain Enthoven later explained, the secretary of defense had to impose order on the services to make them conform to politically defined "national purposes." These national purposes would form the basis for all procurement across the services. Judgment of whether a program effectively contributed to national objectives would be decided through a method known as systems analysis, which had been pioneered at RAND during the 1950s. This method held that it was useless to look at each individual weapon in isolation. Instead, the weapon should be judged as a component in a larger "system"—for example, the "bomber system," comprising of other components such as airfields, supply, and logistics, which in turn could be seen as part of the larger "strategic offensive forces." This would effectively contribute to an overriding national objective—for example, the ability to destroy all major Soviet cities after absorbing a nuclear strike from the USSR. The analysis was conducted on the basis of cost effectiveness: that is, the contribution of a weapon to the system measured against dollar expenditure on its development, construction, and operation.[18]

In the strategists' view, a weapon's performance should be as susceptible to quantitative definition as its cost. Although Enthoven later denied that quantitative methods dominated the systems-analytical approach, McNamara summed up the attitude of DoD civilians when he told a journalist that although he was "sure that no significant military problem will ever be wholly susceptible to purely quantitative analysis . . . every piece of the total problem that can be quantitatively analyzed removes one more piece of uncertainty from our process of making a choice."[19] Numbers would be a major component in the effort to cut through the smoke and mirrors that had been thrown up by the services to protect their bureaucratic prerogatives, and would clear the way for more rational procurement decisions.

The RAND civilians' ideas regarding the national objectives that should be fulfilled by PPBS matched Kennedy's muscular election rhetoric. RAND consultants were instrumental in drafting the Military Aspects section of the administration's planned Basic National Security Policy, which pledged "to preclude, under all circumstances, U.S. military inferiority to an opponent or any potential enemies at any point during or after [a] war" by destroying Soviet capacity to strike back in such a way as "to conclude the war on terms acceptable to the U.S."[20]

The defense intellectuals were more ambitious in the way in which they thought such an outcome could be achieved. Deputy Assistant Secretary of Defense Henry S. Rowen, another RAND alumnus, explained to National Security Council (NSC) staffer Carl Kaysen that Eisenhower's strategy of Massive Retaliation had been a plan for "spasm war," which was clearly "ridiculous and unworkable . . . our general plan should be flexible and include a large variety of controlled responses."[21] This strategy, known as flexible response, called for the gradual escalation of violence by the United States during a confrontation in a way that would convince the Soviet Union that further military action was useless and would result in the USSR's destruction. Central control was an important component of this vision.[22] Even when the conflict escalated to the nuclear level, the

Military Aspects paper argued that the United States should be able to use nuclear weapons to "threaten" and "mislead" the Soviets, as well as "carry out demonstrations" of US force, and "monitor and enforce" terms for the conclusion of the war.[23] Nuclear superiority, rationally procured through cost effectiveness calculations, and deployed in crises through graduated escalation, was the basic element of the Kennedy administration's image of rational superiority.

IMPLEMENTING RATIONAL SUPERIORITY: THE DEFENSE BUDGET AND THE NUCLEAR BUILDUP

The new occupants of the Pentagon were keen to put their ideas into practice, and they did so in a way that would have a significant impact on the future of the US force posture. Amendments to the fiscal year (FY) 1961 and 1962 defense budgets were necessarily rushed attempts to patch the various holes that the new Kennedy team saw in Eisenhower's program. With the FY 1963 budget, however, the Kennedy administration was starting fresh. Indeed, as Deputy National Security Advisor Carl Kaysen emphasized in a memo to President Kennedy, the FY 1963 budget was important not only as the first over which the administration could exercise full control, but also as the one that, by setting priorities for FY 1963–1967, "will determine expenditures . . . for the whole of the rest of your administration."[24]

Hitch and Enthoven set about their task with alacrity, issuing a series of directives to the service secretaries on the new budgetary process. In May 1961, Hitch outlined the stages through which the budget would be drawn up: requirements would be set from May to June; programs would be set for those requirements from July to August; and the budget would be finalized in the time remaining. The second of the three phases, known as the "programming phase," would be the fulcrum on which the process would turn and where systems analysis would make the greatest impact. At this point, "statistical cost estimates" would evaluate the contribution of various weapons systems to the overarching national objectives, as articulated in the administration's planned Basic National Security Policy.[25] Hence, by the time the programming phase was over, the outline of the new American military establishment should have been clearly visible.

Yet the Basic National Security Policy document was not approved by the time the budget had to be drawn up. In order to maintain his freedom of maneuver, Kennedy ensured it never would be.[26] Despite this hiccup, most of its recommendations were integrated into the force planning for the FY 1963 budget. In his October submission to Kennedy, McNamara recommended a force that he believed could "limit the damage" done to the United States in a nuclear war by destroying Soviet offensive forces, as well as "hold in protected reserve forces capable of destroying Soviet urban society, if necessary, in a controlled and deliberate way." This was the bargaining chip inherent in a nuclear attack strategy that McNamara would later articulate as counterforce: the United States would eliminate Soviet nuclear forces and then hold Soviet cities hostage. If the Soviets did not agree to American terms of surrender immediately, the United States would set about destroying Soviet cities until the USSR submitted.[27]

The central elements of the offensive forces that McNamara set to achieve this mission were the 1,100 Minuteman ICBMs to be built by FY 1969, as well as 656 Polaris submarine-launched ballistic missiles (SLBMs) to be carried on forty-one boats.[28] If anything, Kaysen was too humble in his predictions for the FY 1963 budget: these numbers would approximate the US nuclear missile force not just for the Kennedy-Johnson years, but until the 1980s.[29]

On the face of it, everything was going according to plan. Many of Kennedy's subordinates praised the budget for bringing coherence to the smorgasbord of bureaucratic compromises that had characterized Eisenhower's defense spending. Maxwell D. Taylor, the president's military advisor, was "impressed" with the finished product, declaring that it was the first attempt to answer the question of "'How much is enough?' for these forces."[30] David Bell, director of the Bureau of the Budget, praised the "enormous advances in concept, clarity and logic" McNamara had "brought to the military planning budgeting process." According to Bell, the difference between the first full Kennedy budget and that left by the Eisenhower administration was "literally revolutionary." Despite some outstanding issues, Bell considered "the improvement in the degree of rationality" as "tremendous."[31]

Underneath the smooth presidential memoranda, however, the situation was not so clear-cut. This was particularly evident in the tortured reasoning behind the administration's position on the United States' ABM program.

ABM had a checkered history under the Eisenhower administration. The November 1957 Gaither Report, produced by a committee of experts and published in the immediate aftermath of the Soviet Union's first successful ICBM test, had recommended acceleration of US strategic programs on all fronts, including ABM. The committee recommended that the existing Nike-Hercules system be rolled out as early as possible around US bomber bases and augmented with an accelerated research and development program to resolve outstanding technical issues.[32]

Eisenhower resisted deployment, however. Indeed, it made very little military sense. As the committee had admitted in its report, the Nike-Hercules ABM program was far from perfect: it could only provide defense of a relatively small area and could intercept incoming warheads at very low altitudes—approximately 30,000 feet. At this height, the heat from the detonation of Nike-Hercules' nuclear-tipped interceptors would cause significant harm to any civilians out in the open during an attack.[33]

The president's scientific advisers backed Eisenhower's stance on ABM. The anti-ICBM (AICBM) Panel of the President's Science Advisory Committee described Nike-Zeus, the follow-on system to Nike-Hercules, as "appallingly complex" and extremely vulnerable to direct nuclear attack such that it was likely to be "of doubtful value" in the protection of military installations. Given these defects, the AICBM Panel recommended that the program be kept in research and development in order to find solutions to these outstanding problems before any major deployment be initiated.[34]

Little had changed by the time the Kennedy administration looked at the project in early 1961. In his February review of the Eisenhower defense budget, McNamara judged that no reliable missile defense system would be available to the United States "until the late 1960s, if then." The system was extremely expensive. Nike-Zeus would cost $14 billion at a time when the annual defense budget was approximately $50 billion. Even if it were built, McNamara noted that it was "far from clear that the system would be effective" against Soviet forces that would exist by the end of the decade.[35] In short, it was highly doubtful that ABM was a cost-effective option for the administration.

It is therefore surprising that the new secretary of defense recommended accelerating the deployment of Nike-Zeus by one year in his amendments to the FY 1961 and FY 1962 budgets by allocating funding for components that would take a long time to manufacture. For FY 1963, he advocated spending $110 million on preproduction funding for a system that would consist of twelve sites providing protection for major metropolitan areas and costing approximately $3.6 billion. As McNamara himself admitted to the president, "a purely technical appraisal would not lead to a recommendation for deployment of a weapon system with so limited an operational effectiveness."[36]

In justifying his decision, the secretary of defense showed the inherent tension between the psychology of deterrence and quantitative analysis that lay at the heart of rational superiority. By February 1961, the Americans had evidence that the Soviets were working on an ABM system. McNamara argued that regardless of its effectiveness, the Soviet ABM "could significantly reduce our deterrent power and perhaps more importantly the credibility of that deterrent in the eyes of our major allies, and even among some of our own citizens" if it were not countered with a similar American effort.[37] McNamara elaborated further on this point in his recommendations for the FY 1963 budget, arguing that "even with assurance from our technicians that our second strike force can penetrate such defenses, Soviet claims and demonstrations will have a major effect on the uninformed here and abroad and may have major political results."[38]

"Superiority matters," the scholar Robert Jervis has argued, "because others . . . think it matters."[39] In an open democratic system such as the United States, the "others" Kennedy and McNamara had to convince included members of the general public who had, at best, hazy notions of the elaborate cost effectiveness criteria that the secretary of defense was using to draw his conclusions about ABM. McNamara in effect conceded this point by noting that the perception of efficacy amongst those ignorant of nuclear strategy was more important than any "rational" calculations of cost effectiveness by his systems analysts.

Kennedy had expertly played on the gut feelings of Americans during the 1960 presidential election, but he was not the only one with this skill. Nuclear weapons, Chief of Staff of the United States Army General George H. Decker declared, were "more symbolic than utilitarian (sic)." This symbolism was very simple indeed: nuclear arms represented "advanced technological superiority" and hence "the ability of a nation to 'bat' in the 'major leagues' of world power politics."[40] In many respects, pre-game psychology was more important than real capabilities—especially if tough pre-match talk would ensure the opposition would not take to the field in the first place.

Taken to its extreme, this logic almost completely overturned the idea of cost-effectiveness as a criterion on which nuclear procurement should be based. As Jervis has noted, perceptions of resolve can be enhanced if states commit to accomplishing "hard and expensive tasks." Achieving relatively easy things, such as building yet another jet-powered bomber, provides little benefit because it is too easy; striving for something really difficult, Jervis argues, such as constructing a defensive system to protect against Soviet missile attack, can really give public morale a boost.[41] The Kennedy-era US military certainly agreed with this sentiment. "The important thing is to embark upon the Nike-Zeus production with enthusiasm and confidence," Kennedy's military aide Maxwell Taylor argued, while making the case for the ABM. "We have past expressions of pessimism to offset if we are to get a solid psychological return from the decision to go into production."[42] An inefficient weapons system might be more inspirational and therefore desirable than a cost-effective one, Taylor implied, as long as the administration expressed sufficient "confidence" in its ability to function.

Embarking on something as impossible as an ABM might increase the "psychological return" on investment, thereby bolstering public confidence and therefore deterrence to a greater extent than a more cost-effective and less inspirational weapons system. Perhaps the logic of weapons procurement could not be rationalized after all.

The Army in particular exerted a great deal of pressure to assure, at a minimum, that long lead time components of Zeus be appropriated for FY 1962, including a publicity campaign employing complimentary articles in two major defense publications, *Missiles and Rockets* and *Army Magazine*, as well as a study group chaired by Assistant Secretary of the Army Richard Morse.[43] This coverage did not go unnoticed, even by Kennedy, who needled General Decker over whether "the magazine which prepared the extensive 'sell' on the Nike/Zeus was his magazine" at one of his first meetings with the Joint Chiefs of Staff (JCS).[44] The Army was supported by a number of congressmen, including Daniel Flood (D-PA), John McCormack (D-MA), Overton Brooks (D-LA) and George Miller (D-CA), as well as senators Strom Thurmond (D-SC) and Karl Mundt (R-SD).[45] For the FY 1963 budget, the Army and North American Air Defense Command (NORAD) expanded their campaign beyond long lead time items, pushing for a far larger system than the one McNamara was proposing: a twenty-nine-city program costing $15 billion. In this context, the $3.6 billion system approved by McNamara was a considerable cut.[46]

This pro-ABM effort was part of a broader push by the armed services to make the most of Kennedy's pre-election rhetoric and public pressure for action by advocating for huge increases in appropriations for strategic forces. Service requests for general war offensive forces exceeded the secretary's recommendations by $1.46 billion in FY 1963 alone, and $9.69 billion over the life of the FY 1963–1967 defense program. This included a Minuteman ICBM force of 2,600—more than double the recommendation of the secretary of defense.[47] Deprived of a major stake in offensive forces after its role in intermediate-range ballistic missiles was curtailed in 1956, the Army wanted to push its own strategic niche: continental missile defense.[48] McNamara offered the Army a compromise, just as he offered the Air Force a compromise at 1,100 Minutemen. Kennedy's speechwriter and confidant Theodore Sorensen believed McNamara wanted to give the Army something on ABM "to avoid a major battle" over the service budgets.[49] Bureaucratic-political imperatives, not cost-effectiveness, therefore guided McNamara's decision.

In the end, the Bureau of the Budget struck down funding for early deployment of Nike-Zeus. Citing the system's manifest inadequacy to fulfill its tasks, director David Bell was instrumental in deleting appropriations for

Nike-Zeus for FY 1963. McNamara agreed that it was one of the elements that could be removed after Bell told him that cuts needed to be made in order to present a balanced budget to Congress.[50] Following a conversation on December 9 between Kennedy, Sorensen, and a third individual—most likely McGeorge Bundy, Kennedy's special assistant for national security affairs—Nike-Zeus appropriations were dropped from the FY 1963 request.[51]

The 1961 debate over Nike-Zeus illustrated the inherent limitations of PPBS as a means by which to rationalize the defense budget, given the weight of expectation on the new administration. In order to live up to his pre-election rhetoric, Kennedy had authorized a large buildup in American strategic arms out of all proportion with the picture of Soviet forces begin-ning to emerge as a result of better satellite reconnaissance. At the time of the modifications to the Eisenhower budgets, the administration was working from estimates that showed considerable near-term Soviet leads in land-based strategic missiles.[52] By September 1961, however, a new National Intelligence Estimate (NIE), representing the consensus within the US intelligence community, suggested that the Soviets had far fewer land-based missiles than had previously been thought. The US intelligence community concluded that the Soviets had no more than twenty-five operational liquid-fueled ICBMs, compared with the Americans' sixty-two Atlas ICBMs and eighty Polaris SLBMs.[53] Nevertheless, the administra-tion proceeded with plans to increase American strategic power to 1,100 Minuteman ICBMs and 656 Polarises.

This decision provoked some controversy within the administration. "Does not such a sharp increase [in strategic forces] have a high probabil-ity of provoking a response in kind by the Soviets?" questioned Kaysen, as he wrestled with the implications of the future gap in favor of the United States. Bundy had similar reservations. "One quite subtle point which may deserve some attention," Bundy noted, was "the effect of our own plans upon the plans of the enemy."[54] However, these misgivings were offset in part by domestic political considerations. U. Alexis Johnson, deputy undersecretary of state for political affairs at the Department of State, advised Secretary of State Dean Rusk that despite White House concerns that the US was com-mitting itself to too great a buildup of nuclear forces, McNamara felt "he could not go lower and still live with the Air Force and the Congress."[55]

THE BERLIN CRISIS

As well as being domestically unadvisable, Bundy's reflective stance did not fit the demands of the moment beyond America's shores. At the Vienna summit meeting with Kennedy on June 3-4, 1961, Soviet Premier Nikita Khrushchev had reprised his 1958 ultimatum to Eisenhower demanding that the three western powers—the United States, the United Kingdom and France—withdraw from the western sector of Berlin. Deep in the Soviet occupation zone, Berlin had been a recurrent thorn in the side of the USSR and the German Democratic Republic. The western half of the city was an island of capitalism through which thousands of East Germans had made their escape to the Federal Republic of Germany. Publicly, the Soviets argued that the western powers had forfeited their occupation rights by violating the Potsdam Agreement and other accords, which provided for the demilitarization of Germany and its treatment as an economic whole during four-power occupation. In June, Khrushchev upped the stakes: if the western powers did not withdraw by December 31, Khrushchev warned Kennedy, the Soviet Union would sign a separate peace treaty with the German Democratic Republic, thereby terminating current four-power arrangements regarding the city.[56]

Khrushchev's threats in early June focused American minds on the problem of how to defend Berlin in a way that would not escalate into a direct clash between the superpowers. The hawks, led by Truman's former secretary of state and dean of Democratic cold warriors, Dean Acheson, argued that the only way that the United States could display the "will" to defend the city would be to apply the full gamut of measures available to the president, including calling a national emergency, putting Strategic Air Command on a higher state of alert, and deploying more ground forces to Europe. If these moves did not deter the Soviets, Acheson advised, Kennedy should be prepared to use nuclear weapons in defense of Berlin.[57]

For Kennedy and his inner team of advisors, such moves ran an unacceptable risk of nuclear confrontation. Instead on July 25 the president announced a substantial increase in the Pentagon budget, which would be focused on strengthening American conventional forces, including boosting the US Army to one million men.[58] Yet Kennedy, fearing the consequences, stopped far short of the kind of national emergency combined with rapid deployment to Europe that Acheson had advocated.[59]

At the same time, the president consistently referred throughout his address to US commitments to "West Berlin," rather than the city as a whole. In the words of historian Campbell Craig, Kennedy's use of this terminology indicated that "the United States would not oppose a termination of its occupation status in East Berlin, whatever its sixteen-year-old rights were."[60] In this way, Kennedy began to engage in a tactic that would become a recurring theme in his crisis diplomacy: declarations of military strength that provided symbolic assurance that the United States had the will to contain the Soviets, but shorn of the level of confrontation suggested by his more hawkish advisors. It was a clever mix, and one that the president used repeatedly as he sought to balance the maintenance of credibility, both at home and abroad, with the search for compromise with the Soviet Union.

It did not take long for the Soviets to respond. Again, referring only to the western half of the city, Khrushchev pledged, "any blockade of West Berlin" was "entirely out of the question." Yet on August 13, with Khrushchev's permission, the East German authorities began constructing what would become the Berlin Wall, stemming the tide of refugees from the East and setting the division between the two halves of Europe for a generation.[61]

Although Kennedy was privately somewhat relieved that the Soviet Union had taken this step, which solidified the division between East and West Berlin that he had implied in his July 25 address, the public politics of the Cold War required a response in order to underline US resolve to maintain its position in the western half of the city. This need became even more acute after Khrushchev's speech to the Twenty-Second Congress of the Communist Party of the Soviet Union on October 17, in which he claimed that "the forces of socialism" were at that point "more powerful than the aggressive imperialist forces." While declaring that he would rescind his December 31 deadline, he coupled his claim regarding the balance of power with a pledge that a peace treaty that would settle the status of Berlin "must and will be signed." The speech implied that the West would bend to the Soviet Union's superior power by acceding to Khrushchev's demands.[62]

Now possessing sufficent intelligence regarding the extent of Soviet inferiority in intercontinental ballistic missiles, the Kennedy administration decided to go on the rhetorical offensive. On October 21, Deputy Secretary of Defense Roswell Gilpatric delivered a speech to a high-profile business association in which he revealed the full extent of American superiority over the Soviet Union. Gilpatric emphasized that the West's "real strength" in Berlin came from the American edge in nuclear weapons. He dismissed Soviet nuclear testing as a mere propaganda exercise, instead stressing the concrete measures the United States was taking: the acceleration of the Polaris and Minuteman programs, as well as longer-term improvements such as "missile defense" and new "penetration aids" that would keep the United States ahead of the USSR. "The destructive power which the United States could bring to bear even after a Soviet surprise attack upon our forces," Gilpatric stated, "would be as great as—perhaps greater than—the total undamaged force which the enemy can threaten to launch against the United States in a surprise attack." This was the first time that a Kennedy administration official had explicitly boasted of the extent of the American lead in nuclear weapons. Gilpatric made sure that both the American public and US allies knew, to borrow General Decker's imagery, who the heaviest hitter was. At the same time, the deputy secretary reassured his audience that the United States was "improving our ability to make swift, selective responses to enemy attacks on the free world" including future improvements to "'command and control' systems to assure a controlled response to any form of aggression."[63]

The Gilpatric speech emphasized the core messages of rational superiority that Kennedy had articulated on the campaign trail in a way designed to bolster US credibility. Yet the private history of this period shows how complex the interaction between US military capabilities and resolve really was. In early September 1961, Carl Kaysen presented Kennedy's military advisor, Maxwell Taylor, with a report that suggested the United States had the capability to launch a limited disarming first strike on the Soviet Union. By hitting eighty-eight targets with as few as fifty-five bombers, Kaysen argued, the USAF would be able to disable the Soviet Union's capability to retaliate directly against the United States. Even with these favorable odds Kennedy did not appear convinced that such an advantage translated into anything operationally meaningful. He sent a list of questions to the Joint Chiefs of Staff that underlined his concerns regarding the ability to "control" a first strike after it was underway, including the possibility of recalling the bombers launched if it was subsequently discovered that the Soviet attack was a "false alarm." McNamara and Rusk elaborated further military and diplomatic concerns regarding a first strike at an NSC meeting on October 10. While his subordinate, Paul Nitze, was more optimistic that the United States "could be in some real sense victorious" if it struck first, McNamara pointed to the military uncertainties. "Neither side could be sure of winning," McNamara noted—rather "the consequences to both sides of a strategic exchange would be so devastating that both sides had a very high interest in avoiding such a result." Rusk pointed to the opprobrium that the United States would likely receive "from the rest of the world" if it were "the first side to use nuclear weapons."[64]

This private skepticism regarding the tangible reality of US superiority in military and diplomatic terms, combined with the countervailing fear of looking weak, was reflected in the mixture of tough rhetoric and private conciliation that the United States pursued. The White House directly oversaw the preparation of Gilpatric's address, but left its delivery to someone several rungs down the bureaucratic ladder. This reflected real worries regarding the risk of humiliating the Soviets, even from the author of the first strike study. Daniel Ellsberg, who drafted the speech, asked

Kaysen why Kennedy did not deliver the same message, complete with US intelligence backing it up, to Khrushchev via a private channel. "John Kennedy isn't going to talk that way to Khrushchev," Kaysen responded.[65] While the administration felt tough public talk was necessary, private compromise was Kennedy's aim. The president sent Attorney General Robert Kennedy to negotiate a backchannel deal that defused the military stand-off that erupted in Berlin when US and Soviet tanks confronted each other on October 27 at Friedrichstrasse checkpoint.[66] The White House also felt that such a direct leader-to-leader confrontation, even behind closed doors, would, in Kennedy's words "sound too belligerent," spurring the USSR toward greater efforts to rectify the strategic balance.[67] As developments in Cuba and in the Soviet strategic weapons program would illustrate, however, the subcontracting of statements on superiority to subordinates was not enough to obviate this risk.

Indeed, there are indications that, as the first year of his presidency closed—even as the theoretical US military edge over the Soviet Union was peaking—Kennedy had lost confidence in nuclear superiority as anything but a way to give him political cover for necessary concessions. Once the danger over Berlin receded, the president convened his top national-security team for a meeting on January 18, 1962, designed to give him the opportunity to communicate his view of American foreign and defense objectives in broad outline. A talking-points note, most likely written by Bundy, urged JFK to tell the meeting that he did "not subscribe to the doctrine of long-term 'nuclear superiority'" and that "in the long run" the United States was "headed for a nuclear stalemate." Yet other considerations played a role. "Sentiment for more missiles and more nuclear weapons" in Congress was still "pretty strong," the memo argued, although it was difficult to see how "this sentiment could be rationally defended." The United States would therefore "plan to keep ahead—as far ahead as it makes any sense to try to be, in the thermonuclear age."[68] The note argued, essentially, that nuclear superiority was more important for instilling confidence in external audiences than giving the same assurance to the commander-in-chief.

It is hard to believe that, given their controversial implications, Kennedy's staffers would have written these words without fair confidence that the president shared them. Nevertheless, the summary record of the meeting suggests that Kennedy refused to go so far, confining himself to the observation that "because Soviet nuclear strength [was] developing," the United States should place greater emphasis on bolstering its conventional forces, in particular their ability to resist Soviet attempts to take advantage of national liberation movements.[69] Whatever private doubts Kennedy may have had regarding the importance of the US nuclear edge, he kept them to himself and a few extremely close aides and was unwilling to share them even in the relatively closed setting of the National Security Council.

THE CUBAN MISSILE CRISIS

It took another major crisis in which Kennedy stared nuclear war in the face to bring these sentiments to the surface. Sparked by the American discovery, on October 15, 1962, that the Soviet Union was clandestinely deploying medium- and intermediate-range ballistic missiles to the island, the Cuban missile crisis was perhaps the most dangerous moment of the Cold War. In accordance with claims made by surviving participants in later years—though, significantly, not at the time—there is little evidence to suggest that Kennedy drew confidence from the United States' overwhelming strategic nuclear superiority over the Soviet Union during the crisis.[70] There is much, however, to indicate that, in historian Marc Trachtenberg's words, "the fear of escalation" canceled out any notional edge the United States would enjoy in a nuclear exchange between the superpowers. Indeed, evidence from the ExComm tapes reinforces the claim that Kennedy's extreme aversion to confrontation indicates the president did not believe "the Soviets were outgunned and would simply have to back down."[71] At two points in the crisis at least, hawks confronted Kennedy with arguments that relied on the relative confidence conferred by the American military advantage; in both instances, the president pushed back by articulating his fear of unintended escalation and the undifferentiated carnage that would result.

The first occasion was a meeting with the Joint Chiefs of Staff on October 19. After his initial anger regarding Soviet emplacement of missiles on Cuba had subsided, Kennedy was leaning toward the imposition of a blockade of the island. Yet Maxwell Taylor, by then chairman of the JCS, opened the meeting by stating flatly that the chiefs were unanimous in recommending military action against Cuba in order to "eliminate or neutralize the missiles there and prevent any others coming in."[72] The second confrontation came during a heated conversation with senior members of Congress on October 22, just hours before Kennedy would go on network television to announce the US discovery of the missiles and his decision to impose a "quarantine" of Cuba—itself a euphemism for blockade, which was an act of war. During that meeting, Senator Richard Russell (D-GA), chairman of the Senate Armed Services Committee, vociferously attacked Kennedy's decision, telling the president he "could not . . . live with" himself unless he expressed his view that the situation "required stronger steps" than those Kennedy proposed. The action Kennedy took, Russell warned, would determine whether the United States was "a first class power, or . . . not."[73]

For both the JCS and Russell, the benefits of action from a position of strength outweighed the risks of attacking the missiles. Russell asserted that he did not "believe" Khrushchev would "launch a nuclear war over Cuba." Far riskier, in Russell's view, was the possibility that Khrushchev, emboldened by US inaction, would "convince himself that we are afraid to make any real movement and to really fight." Russell believed it would be far better to confront Khrushchev now, rather than when the United States was in a less advantageous strategic position, asserting that he did not "see how we are going to get any stronger or get into any better position to meet this threat." At some point in the near future, Russell warned, the United States was "going to have to take this gamble . . . for the nuclear war."[74] The JCS made essentially the same points. Chief of Staff of the Air Force General Curtis LeMay asserted that an attack on Cuba would not raise the risk of a confrontation, but on balance decrease it. "If we don't do anything to Cuba, then they're going to push on Berlin and push *real hard* because they've got us on the run," LeMay told Kennedy. Chief of Naval Operations George Anderson concurred "with General LeMay that this will escalate and then we will be required to take other military action at greater disadvantage to the United States, to our military forces, and probably would suffer far greater casualties within the United States if these fanatics do indeed intend to fire any missiles."[75]

However, in both confrontations Kennedy expressed his view that aggressive action could lead to a chain of uncontrolled escalation—a risk he considered greater than taking action later when at a military disadvantage. To the JCS, the president highlighted the likelihood that the Soviets would respond to an air strike by "just going in and taking Berlin by force at some point. Which leaves me only one alternative, which is to fire nuclear weapons—which is a hell of an alternative—and begin a nuclear exchange, with all this happening."[76] Kennedy responded along similar lines to Russell. "Our war plan [if the Soviets seize Berlin]," Kennedy pointed out to the senator from Georgia, "has been to fire our nuclear weapons at them." In deciding for an air strike, Kennedy pointed out, "We have to all realize that we are taking a chance that these missiles, which are ready to fire, won't be fired. So that's a gamble we should take. In any case we are preparing to take it. I think that is one hell of a gamble."[77]

In both cases, the president rejected the certainty of both the JCS and Russell that the Soviets would back down in the face of US resolve. To LeMay's argument, Kennedy responded that the Soviets "can't let us just take out, after all their statements, take out [sic] their missiles, kill a lot of Russians and not do anything."[78] In the case of an air strike, Kennedy told the congressional leadership, "You'd have those bombs go off and blow up fifteen cities in the United States."[79] The potential benefits of diplomacy in the form of averting any kind of war, Kennedy implied, were greater than accepting the inevitability of a clash and attempting to limit the destruction of the United States through a surprise attack on Cuba. Instead, as scholar Sheldon M. Stern has argued, "the president persistently measured each move and countermove with an eye toward averting a nuclear exchange."[80]

Yet Kennedy went further in his meeting with the JCS by highlighting the fact that eliminating the Soviet missiles on Cuba would not, as far as he was concerned, lead to a significant change in the military balance between the two superpowers. "The existence of these missiles," Kennedy argued, "does add to the danger but doesn't create it. The danger is right here now." Despite their relative lack of sophistication compared to the US arsenal, Kennedy pointed out that Soviet strategic forces had the potential to inflict tens of millions of American casualties, "especially if [the Soviets] concentrate on the cities." The president was arguing, in effect, that the risk of *any* retaliatory strike on US urban areas was sufficient to stay his hand: "I don't think this [the Cuban deployment] adds particularly to our danger," Kennedy stated, "Our danger is the use of nuclear weapons [*unclear*] anyway."[81] The relative balance of damage, therefore, was insignificant in that it did not materially add to the president's confidence when assessing the choice between a blockade of Cuba or an air strike. The benefit of US superiority, through its potential to limit destruction through a preemptive strike, was of little value.

After the president had left the JCS meeting, General David Shoup, commandant of the US Marine Corps, vented his frustration with Kennedy's aversion to any move that might provoke military escalation. "I heard him say *escalation*," Shoup seethed to his colleagues, "That's the only goddamn thing that's in the whole trick. It's been there in Laos; it's been in every goddamn one [of these crises]. When he says *escalation*, that's it." The chiefs agreed that Kennedy was deterred by the possibility that an attack on Cuba would draw the US into a wider war over Berlin. "He equates the two," LeMay opined. "If we smear Castro, Khrushchev smears [Mayor of Berlin] Willy Brandt," Chief of Staff of the Army Earle Wheeler concurred.[82]

Not only was Kennedy deterred more than his military chiefs and hawkish senators, but also to a greater extent than his civilian advisors. This was the case even—arguably especially—during periods of acute stress. The crisis probably entered its most dangerous phase on Saturday, October 27. That day, the United States was confronted by a public Soviet call to remove US missiles from Turkey in exchange for Soviet withdrawal from Cuba, going far beyond the demands contained in a private letter that Khrushchev had sent the previous day. Later, a U-2 reconnaissance aircraft was shot down over the island. Before reports of the U-2 downing reached him, JFK was, in Trachtenberg's words, "the strongest advocate" of accepting Khrushchev's public offer to remove the Jupiters.[83] He took this stance against the advice of almost all of his principal advisors, including Bundy; Rusk; McNamara; the head of the CIA, John McCone; his brother, Robert; and former US ambassador to the Soviet Union, Llewellyn Thompson. Again, despite the nuclear edge possessed by the United States, the fear of escalation played into JFK's thinking. "Today it sounds great to reject it [the Turkey offer], but it's not going to after we do something!" the president declared. Even after receiving reports about the U-2, the president held firm against McNamara's calls for military action, stating that the United States would announce that it would provide security for future reconnaissance missions, but that afterwards the group would "go back to what we're gonna do about the Turks and NATO."[84] On the same day, Robert Kennedy offered Dobrynin a private understanding that the United States would remove the Jupiter intermediate-range ballistic missiles from Turkey, thereby moving the crisis to a less acute phase.

Even faced with further bluster from Khrushchev, combined with the death of an American serviceman, Kennedy resisted huge pressure from his senior advisors to take military action that he believed could spark a worldwide conflagration.[85] Thus the tapes add even more weight to Trachtenberg's conclusion that during the Cuban missile crisis, "the fear of escalation . . . went a long way toward neutralizing whatever advantages might have accrued to the United States by virtue of its 'strategic superiority.' "[86] This was particularly true in the case of the ultimate decision-maker, John F. Kennedy.

THE CONSEQUENCES OF THE CRISIS

The events of October 1962 had a profound impact on the Kennedy administration. First, the crisis served to widen the gap between Kennedy's views on nuclear superiority and those of outside strategists who believed in the utility of the manipulation of nuclear risk from a position of strength during a crisis. In the summer of 1962, Chairman of the State Department Policy Planning Council Walt Rostow contracted Thomas C. Schelling, renowned nuclear strategist and professor of economics at Harvard, to head a study group on the implications of Soviet developments in strategic forces for US foreign policy in the 1970s. Published on the eve of the crisis, Schelling's report predicted that growing parity in nuclear weapons between the United States and the USSR and their development of secure second-strike forces would lead to increasing interest from the superpowers in developing doctrines for "the conduct of controlled warfare." Schelling speculated that, as a result, "the sharp distinction usually drawn between general war and limited war" might "dissolve," leading to a situation where nuclear weapons could be seen as legitimate instruments to secure military aims less than total destruction of the enemy. Schelling emphasized that such developments were "just a possibility." Nevertheless, he and his panel believed that superpower parity could make limited nuclear war between the superpowers war more, not less, likely.[87]

The contrast between the tense desperation of the thirteen days of October and the apparent insouciance regarding the use of nuclear weapons implied by Schelling's prediction could not have been greater. Outside the seminar room, the cool attitude exhibited by nuclear strategists toward the manipulation of the risk of an intercontinental exchange melted. Kennedy was shaken by his experience. Reflecting with McNamara and Taylor a few weeks afterwards, he declared that, "Even what they had in Cuba alone would have been a substantial deterrent to me."[88] The numerous close calls during the confrontation—in particular the shooting down of a U-2 over Cuba and the straying of another into Soviet airspace—showed that it was extremely difficult for those at the heart of a vast military machine to manipulate risk effectively. Events could very easily spiral beyond leaders' ability to control them. Most importantly, October 1962 exposed the central fallacy of the nuclear strategists' pretentions to rationalize the conduct of nuclear war: the fear of total annihilation meant even playing with the possibility of killing millions in order to secure marginal geopolitical advantage could never be a rational act.[89]

While his advice during the crisis was more hawkish than he would subsequently recall, McNamara adopted this skepticism regarding the utility of nuclear superiority into his subsequent force planning.[90] In his ABM recommendations for the FY 1964 budget, drafted in November 1962, the secretary noted the contribution that the system could make to deterrence by raising Soviet uncertainty regarding US capabilities. However, McNamara also argued that there were equally cogent interpretations of Soviet behavior that augured against deployment of a missile defense for the United States. For the first time, McNamara introduced the notion that the Soviet reaction in the form of "a penetration aids program, an increase in the number of missiles, or the deployment of very large yield weapons" would have negative consequences for the United States. The previous year's memorandum had noted that ABM deployment could lead to a new arms race, but had portrayed this as beneficial because it would sap Soviet resources. By the end of 1962, McNamara argued that a Soviet reaction of this type was a potentially negative development. It appears that the secretary of defense no longer saw increased Soviet uncertainty regarding US capabilities during a nuclear war as an unaugmented good.[91] This attitude suggested a far less sanguine approach to the manipulation of risk in a crisis: Soviet insecurity might not result in the USSR backing down over a flashpoint. It could instead act recklessly, increasing the risk of the situation spiraling out of control.

The previous year, the secretary of defense had deemed it prudent to advocate a compromise that would push forward with an ABM deployment—albeit on a far smaller scale than the Army wished. Now, McNamara continued to split the difference, but in a way that postponed any production decision far into the future. Rejecting any chance of producing Nike-Zeus, he advocated a high-priority research and development program for a successor system, Nike-X. The chiefs, with one dissenting vote from the Air Force, wanted to proceed immediately with a commitment to build Nike-Zeus, augmenting it with Nike-X when it became available in 1969. By contrast, McNamara advocated Nike-X deployment stretching from 1969 to 1972 or 1973, leaving the United States with no protection until the end of the decade.[92]

McNamara claimed that the greatest weight of his argument rested on the technological shortcomings of Nike-Zeus. "During the past year," the secretary argued, "we have gained a much broader understanding of the problems of ballistic missile defense."[93] It was true that the system had undergone full testing during 1962 on the Kwajalein missile range in Hawaii.[94] In addition, some of the US aboveground explosions that year had explored aspects of missile defense. However, there does not appear to have been a change in the secretary of defense's assessment of the system between the FY 1963 and 1964 budget recommendations commensurate with his shift from recommending deployment to postponement. He had judged it technologically insufficient in October 1961, and he did so again in November 1962. The major change was the secretary's shift toward a more studied ambiguity regarding Soviet strategy, underpinned by a greater sense of the unintended consequences of nuclear confrontation.

The November 1962 budget memorandum on offensive forces also exhibited a greater humility regarding the extent to which nuclear weapons could be used as effective instruments in international policy. The secretary of defense downgraded the United States' capability to destroy Soviet nuclear forces to a secondary objective for US nuclear forces behind the capability to attack Soviet cities in a second strike. In both his scaling back of the tasks for US offensive forces and movement away from missile defense, McNamara exhibited a loss of confidence in how nuclear war from a position of strength might be manipulated, as the BNSP had aspired, "to conclude [a] war on terms acceptable to the U.S."[95] In doing so, he struck at the intellectual roots of RAND's pretensions to a rational nuclear posture and controlled crisis management.

This points to a gap between the private feelings of the president regarding the importance of the US nuclear edge and the public image that he projected as he sought to make the most of his triumph. In line with his earlier strategy of public toughness coupled with private concessions, Kennedy's understanding with Khrushchev regarding Turkey was kept secret, reinforcing the myth that he had deftly played his hand and optimized gains for the United States. The *New York Herald Tribune* described Kennedy's performance as "a demonstration of American will and power that has impressed both friends and foes." "A firm stand and a resolute will are what the Kremlin respect," intoned *The Philadelphia Inquirer*.[96] One commentator proclaimed that Kennedy had learned the lesson of his anti-appeasement book, *Why England Slept*: "He has studied Khrushchev's record and sees that [an] audacious gambler can be faced down by cold realism."[97]

In the eyes of the media, Kennedy's cool head under pressure had both saved the day and expurgated earlier sins of his administration and the Democratic Party. Prior to the crisis, Kennedy had been the target of domestic criticism regarding his policy toward Cuba, in particular from congressional Republicans and Southern Democrats.[98] As *The New York Times* noted, the administration's successful performance during October 1962 "in all probability will transcend in the public mind the Cuban 'Fiasco' of 1961—the botched Bay of Pigs invasion," while at the same time blunting a common Republican attack that the Democrats were soft on communism. "Having gone as near the brink of war as . . . Dwight D. Eisenhower ever did, with dramatic results, Mr. Kennedy and his party should have gone a long way toward scotching this recurrent issue against them"—just in time for the November congressional elections.[99] At the point at which those at the top of the Kennedy administration were stepping further away from the tenets of rational superiority, the strategy became one of the White House's greatest domestic political assets.

Yet there was another side to that asset: the domestic political battle that would ensue if anything were said that might contradict it. This danger was underlined by the public reaction to McNamara's attempts to float the idea that greater certainty on the part of the USSR regarding its retaliatory capabilities might lead to a state of mutual deterrence. He did so first in an interview with journalist Stewart Alsop, published in early December 1962. McNamara suggested that a "balance of terror" in which "both sides have a second strike capability" could be "more stable" than a situation in which one side was vulnerable to a first strike. Despite making what he admitted was "a rather subtle" and counterintuitive point that a more capable and protected Soviet force could actually be better for US security, McNamara was not making an argument for numerical parity with the USSR. The secretary of defense reassured Alsop that any "margin of error" regarding US intelligence estimates of Soviet forces was "much less than the margin of [US] superiority." In the article accompanying the interview, McNamara's subordinates and associates underlined to Alsop that numerical superiority was still necessary to give the United States the flexibility to be able to choose from a range of options during a nuclear exchange.[100]

After the interview's publication the secretary of defense recalled that "all hell broke loose."[101] In fact, reaction to McNamara's position was not entirely negative, with the *Washington Post* commending the secretary of defense for his "blunt appraisal" that "neither side [had] the power to preclude a devastating retaliatory blow by the other side."[102] Yet despite McNamara's explicit statements to the contrary, military publications effectively accused the secretary of defense of "conceding to the Soviet Union a nuclear war-making power matching that of the United States." The Air Force Association's in-house magazine, *Air Force Space Digest*, charged that McNamara's strategy betrayed the United States' "deliberate intention to replace the necessary strategic superiority with strategic stalemate," an interpretation, it claimed, that was shared by every individual service chief.[103] Throughout 1963, McNamara thus continued to tread a careful line. While maintaining that both superpowers had the capability to destroy the other, thus making "the relative value" of superiority less than it was, McNamara also continued to assure external audiences that the United States maintained a clear quantitative lead in nuclear weapons.[104] A major step away from a policy predicated on quantitative edge for the United States would ensure a bruising domestic political battle with the armed forces.

In addition to being a domestic imperative, quantitative nuclear superiority was central to the Kennedy administration's policy toward Western Europe. On May 5, 1962, five months before the Cuban crisis, McNamara had delivered a speech to the North Atlantic Council in Athens, Greece, an address that he repeated in unclassified form to the graduating class of the University of Michigan at Ann Arbor, on June 16. The Secretary of Defense advocated centralization of NATO's nuclear forces under the control of the United States. To do so, he argued, would facilitate unified targeting that would provide the best basis for managing a nuclear conflict through destroying the enemy's nuclear forces, with reserves sufficient to eliminate Soviet cities if the USSR refused to submit. Western Europe, McNamara maintained, should concentrate on conventional militaries because no single country had the economic resources to underwrite a full nuclear deterrent capable of implementing a strategy of the kind the secretary was suggesting—one explicitly based on maintaining superiority over the Soviet Union. In augmenting their conventional forces, the Europeans would increase the length of time NATO could hold out against a Soviet invasion without resorting to nuclear weapons. This speech had a far broader agenda than nuclear strategy alone: the Kennedy administration hoped that it would help stem proliferation in Europe by warning the French and the West Germans away from pursuing independent nuclear forces, as well as easing the economic burden of keeping US troops in Europe.[105] McNamara implied that the United States not only had the economic but also the intellectual means to implement a counterforce strategy; he emphasized "unity of planning, executive authority, and central direction" as the "vital attributes" of his new approach.[106] Yet by January 1963, chastened by Cuba, he sought to step back from counterforce. In the words of journalist Fred Kaplan, "McNamara instructed his staff that they were no longer to cite counterforce as the official Pentagon strategic concept."[107] However, to repudiate the image of rational superiority fully and explicitly could have undermined European—particularly West German—confidence in the American nuclear umbrella, with potentially disastrous consequences for nuclear proliferation and the relaxation of tensions with the Soviet Union.

The tension between public rhetoric and private doubts recast the relationship between nuclear strategy and US defense policy. The rationalization of superiority promised by the nuclear strategists was proving quite difficult to implement—from the bureaucratic bargaining inherent in the procurement of Nike-Zeus and Nike-X, though to their employment in an integrated system that would maximize the gains for the United States both in crisis situations and war. Instead of becoming the basis on which the US defense posture could be streamlined, RAND's prescriptions were taking the role of a presentational tool to convince the American public, Congress, and West Europeans that the administration had the nuclear competition under control. This role was vital because it provided reassurance in a conflict that was as much about confidence as military potential.[108] Yet far from subordinating nuclear weapons to reason, rational superiority was simply becoming a rationalization of the mixture of bureaucratic and political expediency underwritten by an all-consuming fear of nuclear confrontation that characterized the Kennedy administration's approach to nuclear weapons.

In the wake of Cuba, the Kennedy administration moved expeditiously to conclude a test ban treaty with the Soviet Union. The Limited Test Ban Treaty was signed by the US, USSR, and Britain in August 1963. By prohibiting tests in the atmosphere, the administration scored a huge success. Kennedy's handling of the LTBT showed his great skill at reconciling this first step toward arms control with the requirements of rational superiority. In moving beyond the Test Ban, however, rational superiority limited the extent to which the Kennedy administration could proceed with arms control as a foundation of détente.

Missile defense had been central to internal administration debates over the military-technical utility of nuclear testing since the Soviet resumption of tests in 1961. As Carl Kaysen emphasized to Kennedy, "the strongest arguments" in favor of the resumption of tests lay with those who advocated them in terms of improving the United States' knowledge of ABM's potential.[109] The relationship between the science and politics of testing was complex, however, with both sides being able to deploy scientific experts in support of their positions.

When Kennedy entered office, the United States had not detonated a nuclear weapon for experimental purposes since Eisenhower's moratorium on testing took effect in October 1958. In mid-1961, the Department of Defense and Atomic Energy Commission indicated that the improvements they could make to the design of offensive and defensive systems were being impaired by the lack of test data. The development of the best possible defensive system relied on knowledge regarding phenomena relating to the detonation of warheads known as "weapons effects." In particular, the range of possible interceptor missiles had not been determined with accuracy because American scientists did not have a full picture of the maximum radius at which a nuclear detonation could neutralize an incoming warhead. This was due to insufficient data regarding the range of X-rays and neutrons released by a nuclear explosion above the atmosphere. The wider the range, the more effective the interceptor could be. The ABM radars used to detect an attack and guide interceptors to their targets were also vulnerable to "radar blackout." The radiation released from a nuclear detonation by the enemy, or even the defense's own interceptors, would effectively blind the ABM radar for a number of minutes, thereby impairing its ability to deal with a large-scale attack. More data were required on the extent and nature of this phenomenon to ensure that radars could be positioned in appropriate quantities and locations to provide full coverage, even if some were temporarily blinded. The Department of Defense and Atomic Energy

Commission argued that the nature of these effects and potential solutions could not be identified without further testing.[110]

Arguments favoring testing on military-technical grounds were underpinned by RAND's assumptions regarding the utility of nuclear superiority. As the director of defense research and engineering, Harold Brown, eloquently explained in December 1961, the United States could not hope to secure a first-strike capability if it resumed testing, nor would it become vulnerable to a disarming Soviet attack if it did not. Instead, Soviet estimates of victory in war and hence the strength of the US deterrent would depend on nuclear postures along "a broad spectrum of intermediate situations between pure minimal deterrence and a full first-strike capability." Destruction would be great in any event, but relative damage and hence deterrence depended on "the quality of the nuclear weapons as well as the delivery systems on each side." Testing was therefore necessary to improve the quality of US nuclear weaponry, thereby pushing the balance of relative damage in the United States' favor and strengthening deterrence.[111]

These relative damage estimates were now contingent on the contest between offensive and defensive forces, the technical efficacy of which required further testing—particularly in the case of ballistic missile defense. The Joint Chiefs of Staff could rely on a group of scientists to support this view, including the hydrogen bomb pioneers Stanislaw Ulam and Edward Teller, who collaborated with a number of others on an Air Force report that made the scientific case for testing. Nuclear technology, the report warned, "can be stopped by the hand of man as little as the advance of weaving machinery could be stopped by the Luddite mobs."[112] The United States had to exert maximum effort in all fields of nuclear research; otherwise it risked being at a grievous technological and psychological disadvantage.

By contrast, the Ad Hoc Panel on Nuclear Testing chaired by Wolfgang Panofsky, noted physicist and director of the Stanford Linear Accelerator Center, rejected the notion that nuclear testing could make a significant contribution to solving the difficulties encountered by the US ABM program. The panel accepted that such tests would be impossible under a test ban, but concluded that "the present U.S. Nike-Zeus AICBM system is not limited by nuclear warhead performance or lack of knowledge on nuclear kill mechanisms but rather by the highly unfavorable exchange ratio of the cost of Nike-Zeus vs. increased number of enemy ICBMs, especially if the enemy employs decoys."[113] The offense could always overwhelm the defense, the panel argued, regardless of how accurate or effective the interceptors were, because the system was much more expensive than building more missiles or fitting them with objects that would look like additional warheads on radar.

The Panofsky Panel dismissed the view that resumption of testing was critical to maintaining American nuclear superiority over the Soviet Union. It advised that "none of the specific weapons tests now discussed" were of "such urgency" to exert a major influence on whether to resume nuclear testing. This meant that discussion on this issue could "be governed primarily by non-technical considerations."[114] Underlying this was the view that the kind of marginal differences in damage assessments cited by Brown would have little impact on Soviet calculations of risk in times of crisis. Deterrence could be preserved without testing.

Both Kennedy and McNamara's views on testing appeared to change after Cuba. Before the crisis, Kennedy subscribed to the Brown-Teller-Ulam view that testing was essential for deterrence. In early September 1961, Kennedy complained that the first US underground test planned in response to Soviet resumption was smaller than the USSR's first test. According to the chairman of the Atomic Energy Commission, Glenn Seaborg, "he was concerned that the disparity . . . would invite such adverse comment as to be unacceptable. He wanted a larger test, if possible." The aesthetics of testing were as important to Kennedy as the scientific data gained from such experiments. Faith in the West's technological superiority required testing to demonstrate that the United States was not falling behind in emerging areas of the arms race such as missile defense.[115] As Kennedy declared in his announcement of a new round of tests on November 2, 1961, referring to his administration's nuclear buildup, "We have taken major steps in the past year to protect our lead—and we do not propose to lose it."[116]

If anything, McNamara was ahead of Kennedy on the merits of testing. Even before the Soviet Union announced its test series in September 1961, the secretary of defense backed the chiefs in calling for resumption of detonations, arguing "that he felt the gross advantage to the U.S. from a resumption of testing was substantial . . . it was possible, although it could not be guaranteed, that an effective anti-ICBM weapon could be developed if testing were resumed."[117] He pushed the military-technical case for aboveground testing after the Soviet announcement, arguing in February 1962 that the United States must "neither fall behind nor appear to fall behind" the Soviet Union and would only favor cessation of testing after the current round of experiments. Though skeptical of the chances of success, McNamara claimed that testing was "highly important" to see if the United States could "redesign the Nike-Zeus system for anti-missile defense to overcome its present weaknesses."[118]

By the summer of 1963, however, McNamara was pushing the public case for a test ban by arguing further ABM experimentation was unnecessary.[119] Yet the 1962 round of tests provided no clear answer to the question of ABM's effectiveness. Kaysen believed that while "the information learned from the tests has been of moderate importance . . . it has little prospect of affecting the strategic balance one way or the other."[120] In its preparations for the 1962 tests, the DoD stated that the series "by no means satisfies the total needs" for this kind of research, suggesting that the tests scheduled for that year could not have filled the gap in knowledge sufficiently to justify the secretary's change in position. The DoD had advocated further weapons effects testing as central to the development of an effective anti-ballistic missile system, arguing that theoretical analysis of current data would become "sterile" in the absence of "experimental confirmation and guidance." The document concluded, "We are now at a point in important areas of such research where full scale experiments are absolutely essential to any further progress."[121] No progress had been made, yet the secretary of defense no longer saw the need for further testing.[122]

The truth was that the administration's concern to pass the test ban was more pressing than its desire for further progress on ABM.[123] In pushing for a test ban after Cuba, the administration advocated an amelioration of the arms race between the superpowers and the stemming of proliferation by raising the barriers to entry for countries with nuclear aspirations. In doing so, it hoped to assuage Soviet anxieties regarding a nuclear West Germany, thereby decreasing the possibility that the United States would have to display its commitment to the security of Europe in another Berlin crisis. For the United States, perhaps most importantly, the treaty had the potential to retard the progress of the People's Republic of China toward a nuclear capability. As Kennedy himself argued in public, the United States wanted to do everything possible "to lessen [the] prospect" that "a future president" would have to deal with a nuclear-armed China.[124]

This change was also in part due to scientific conclusions regarding the contribution of the Soviet testing program to furthering the USSR's knowledge of ABM effects. Administration experts believed that, although the USSR's 1962 round of tests had contributed to their capability to field a small warhead suitable for an ABM interceptor, they had "no evidence" to suggest that the Soviets had overcome major technical hurdles to fielding a missile defense.[125] This assessment appears to have been shared by the Soviets. "Such were these problems," the principal Russian historian of the Soviet ABM effort has noted, that by the end of the Soviet testing round, it was clear that "the construction of a defense against a massive, saturating missile strike was impossible."[126] The consensus, although neither side knew it, was that, at the current state of technology, missile defense faced fundamental hurdles that would make it extremely difficult to significantly affect the strategic balance.

Yet the administration did not come clean regarding the inability of aboveground testing to solve ABM's problems. Instead, McNamara pushed the Limited Test Ban Treaty as a textbook case of rational superiority in his testimony to the Senate Foreign Relations Committee. Despite the inconclusive nature of the 1962 tests, he made a strong technical case that missile defense research would not be adversely affected by the conclusion of the LTBT. In doing so, he endorsed Nike-X in the strongest terms:

> The ABM system which we are now designing will provide us with a high confidence of achieving low-miss distances. The ABM warhead designs which we now have or can develop through underground testing will provide a high probability of killing Soviet warheads even if they incorporate advanced technology far beyond what now exists.[127]

The secretary now maintained that no more aboveground testing would be needed because all further development could be conducted underground, despite his frequent private statements to the contrary over the preceding two years.

Strangely, Kennedy himself contradicted these assertions. "The problem of developing a defense," Kennedy averred to journalists, was "beyond us and beyond the Soviets technically." Nor did the president hold out much hope, nothing that "those who work the longest are not particularly optimistic that a scientific breakthrough can be made."[128] The idea of a rational nuclear strategy based on technical appraisals of what was required to fulfill national security objectives was nothing more than a public façade—and one that occasionally slipped as the administration argued, on the one hand, that no more testing was required because the fundamental issues had been solved, and, on the other, that no further tests were necessary because the problems facing missile defense were fundamentally unsolvable.

The most important issue, however, was to reassure the Senate that the treaty would not leave the Soviets with a commanding technical lead in any aspect of nuclear weaponry. Whatever the reality, the external image of cool rationality under pressure was central to Kennedy's post-Cuba reputation, both at home and abroad, as an effective crisis manager and dependable cold warrior. This image was a central element in neutralizing criticism from domestic hardliners that, in making a deal with the Soviet Union, the Democrats were being soft on communism. For their part, the LTBT's opponents such as Edward Teller publicly testified that an ABM system could not be built without further testing.[129] "The real problem," regarding the LTBT's ratification, Senate Minority Leader Everett Dirksen (R-IL) told the president, was the "overriding fear" of hawkish senators such as Richard Russell and John Stennis (D-MS) that the United States would "be disadvantaged by the Soviets in the nuclear field."[130]

In this context, it is clear why the central tenet of the administration's public advocacy for the test ban was that the treaty would maintain, and perhaps even extend, the life of the American edge in nuclear weapons. McNamara claimed that "by limiting Soviet testing to the underground environment, where testing is more difficult and more expensive, and where the United States has substantially more experience," the United States could "at least retard Soviet progress and prolong the duration of [its] technological superiority."[131] Presentation of the ABM in such favorable terms was part of this wider strategy, the centerpiece of which was a presidential letter confirming the United States' readiness to resume aboveground testing in the event of the treaty's abrogation by the USSR, as well as an affirmation that the treaty "in no way limits the authority of the commander-in-chief to use nuclear weapons for the defense of the United States and its allies."[132] Overall, as Kennedy underlined to journalists, "the test ban is a source of strength to us."[133]

Liberal senatorial advocates of the LTBT, such as George McGovern (D-SD) and Hubert Humphrey (D-MN), echoed the administration's line on superiority. "We now have clear-cut superiority over any other nation," stated McGovern, "Far from adding to our nuclear superiority, continued testing . . . could clear the way for our rivals to narrow our present nuclear lead." Even Hiram Fong, Republican of Hawaii, whose constituents were naturally "acutely sensitive" to the issue of fallout in the Pacific, affirmed that Hawaii's residents were also "acutely mindful that American superiority in thermonuclear weapons and delivery systems has successfully deterred nuclear war" and they "strongly support[ed] the president and the Congress in their determination to maintain nuclear superiority."[134]

The commitment to nuclear superiority was also crucial for maintaining consensus within the administration. The Joint Chiefs of Staff had been sidelined during discussions with the Soviets over the treaty. The head negotiator Averell Harriman's telegrams from Moscow were kept from the chiefs, with Kennedy fending off their requests for a review of the treaty text before it was agreed with the Soviets. When the text was finalized, the president confronted the military with a bureaucratic consensus favoring their consent, thereby presenting them with as close to a fait accompli as he could manage.[135] In exchange for changing their military opinion that the treaty was not beneficial to the United States, the JCS extracted a commitment from the White House for maximum effort in the research, development, and deployment of new types of nuclear weapons. The chiefs endorsed the treaty, but only on condition that the United States "continue underground testing at a rate to insure continued progress in nuclear technology" backed by "a clear intent to maintain and improve the military posture of the West."[136] With its reliance on miniaturized nuclear warheads and the as-yet poorly understood use of X-rays to destroy reentry vehicles in the vacuum of space, missile defense was one of the principal beneficiaries of such an underground testing program. Continuation of the American ABM program was therefore vital in order for the White House to substantiate its commitment to the nuclear superiority the JCS demanded as a price for changing their position on a test ban.

Commitment to superiority was also important for winning over European skeptics. Chief among these was Konrad Adenauer, chancellor of the Federal Republic of Germany, who may have maintained aspirations for the FRG to have its own nuclear capability—an effort that could be drastically retarded if the FRG acceded to an aboveground test ban. The White House had kept Adenauer out of the negotiations and on August 2 McNamara went to see the chancellor to talk him around. Adenauer worried that an atmosphere of détente would lead other West European countries to relax their guard. During the conversation it became clear that Adenauer was concerned that the treaty could impair defense preparedness, including the maintenance of unquestioned American nuclear superiority. The chancellor charged that "the treaty would serve to handicap the United States in the development of an anti-missile missile." McNamara assured him that the United States was "ahead of the Soviets" in ABM technology and such advantages would be locked in in by the LTBT, the same commitment he had given to the Senate Foreign Relations Committee.[137] Kennedy followed up on McNamara's mission with a letter expressing renewed resolve to defend the FRG, reiterating that the LTBT had been as much the product of "strength and resolution as ... the process of negotiation."[138] West Germany signed the treaty on August 18, 1963, but keeping Adenauer in line required the Americans to reemphasize their commitment to Central Europe through the maintenance of their preponderance in nuclear weapons.

Kennedy's handling of the Limited Test Ban Treaty was extremely deft, fashioning a consensus not only between the two superpowers, but also among the majority of America's NATO allies, as well as within the administration and the Senate. The administration's approach left a number of unresolved problems, however. Not least of these was the gap between McNamara's public stance and his private convictions. Before Harriman had left for Moscow, the secretary of defense had urged him to explore limitations on missile defenses with the Soviets because continued efforts in this area "would be increasingly expensive as time went on, with no end in sight."[139] This view was at odds with that expressed in his public testimony. The secretary had gone on record strongly endorsing Nike-X. This left him in a weak position if, as his comments to Harriman suggest, he wanted to scrap it as a waste of money. It also spoke to an attitude completely antithetical to the commitment the Kennedy White House had made to the Joint Chiefs. The administration pledged to maintain American predominance in nuclear weapons, no matter what the cost. It accepted that the arms race would continue and that the US government would spend all that was required to secure superiority so that the United States could display resolve if superpower relations deteriorated to confrontation. McNamara's comments to Harriman suggest that he was looking to the long-term cost of an unrestrained competition between offensive and defensive arms and questioning whether parity through a ban or agreed limitations on missile defenses could ameliorate this burden. Yet there was no room for such thinking in the Kennedy administration's public case for the test ban.

By banning aboveground testing, the Kennedy administration had also fundamentally changed the nature of debates over nuclear weapons development. In removing the possibility of full systems testing for Nike-Zeus or Nike-X, the White House had ensured that scientific judgments regarding the system's performance would become even more contingent on paper studies and removed from experimental results. As the debate over testing from 1961 to 1963 illustrated, and DoD had admitted, this theoretical work became "sterile" without resort to full systems testing, leaving a vacuum that was filled with conclusions informed more by scientists' conceptions of international politics than experimental data. In the long term, this added a new level of politicized abstraction to the debates over the deployment of missile defense. This was not a major issue in 1963. The fact that McNamara's constantly shifting military-technical rationales regarding the effectiveness of missile defense were left unchallenged illustrates the extent to which the executive branch's word was taken for granted during the early 1960s. It became a major problem, however, in the late 1960s, as executive primacy over national security policy and, with it, the fundamental assumptions underpinning nuclear superiority began to crumble under the pressure of the Vietnam War.

THE GAP BETWEEN RHETORIC AND REALITY

On November 22, 1963, the day of his assassination, John F. Kennedy was planning to make rational superiority a key plank in his pitch for reelection.

In a departure from his caution since assuming office regarding direct comparisons between the Soviet and US military power, he would have rattled off statistics on the US strategic buildup in order to support his claim that he had followed through on his 1960 promise "to build a national defense which was second to none . . . not 'first, but,' not 'first, if,' not 'first, when,' but first—period." Yet, he would also have stressed that raw force was not enough: "In a world of complex and continuing problems, in a world full of frustrations and irritations, America's leadership must be guided by the lights of learning and reason or else those who confuse rhetoric with reality and the plausible with the possible will gain the popular ascendancy with their seemingly swift and simple solutions to every world problem."[140]

The problem was that rational superiority had become nothing but "rhetoric." Kennedy and his closest advisors weighed the truth in an NSC meeting on September 12, 1963. Increases in the survivability of Soviet forces meant that a meaningful US edge over the Soviet Union that could be used in a disarming first strike was now in the past. In response to a question from the president, Chief of Staff of the Army General Harold Johnson admitted that "even if" the United States conducted a first strike, "surviving Soviet capacity [would be] sufficient to produce an unacceptable loss in the U.S." The conclusion reached was that the two superpowers were in "in a period of nuclear stalemate." General Johnson "acknowledged that it would be impossible for [the U.S.] to achieve nuclear superiority."[141] This conclusion built on the president's existing doubts. "We have an awful lot of megatonnage to put on the Soviets [that is] sufficient to deter them from ever using nuclear weapons," Kennedy reflected in December 1962, "Otherwise, what good are they? I don't—you can't use them as a first weapon yourself, so they're only good for deterring . . . I don't see quite why we're building as many as we're building . . . " McNamara's response belied the claims to cool rationalism associated with his public persona: "take the requirement and double it and buy it. Because I don't believe we can, under any circumstances, run the risk of having too few here. So I, in my own mind, I just say, 'Well, we ought to buy twice what any reasonable person would say is required for strategic forces.'"[142]

Even as its doubts deepened regarding quantitative nuclear superiority's military utility in an age in which both superpowers had the capability to strike back after a first blow, the Kennedy administration continued to use public rhetoric that emphasized its importance. As Bundy noted years later, "Kennedy was well aware" that in the future there would be a "stalemate" between US and Soviet nuclear forces, "but that was not what he chose to emphasize in public in what was already the beginning of an election year." As his draft remarks on November 22, 1963 show, Kennedy was not simply eliding the issue of nuclear superiority, but would have actively used it as an example of his administration's achievements in his campaign for reelection.[143] As well as politically useful, rational superiority had also been a successful device for the Kennedy administration in charting a course through recurrent crises toward the Limited Test Ban Treaty. In the nuclear age the will of the United States was the vital ingredient; if the president made the country feel secure and able to face any threat, then it would be secure.[144] Kennedy had guided the United States away from the crisis of confidence that had characterized the post-Sputnik period. At the same time, he had used his country's newfound strength and the resultant political capital to conclude one of the landmark arms control treaties of the nuclear age. In this sense therefore, rational superiority was a political masterpiece, just not in the way the denizens of RAND would have preferred.

The contrast between public confidence and private doubts left the United States in a dilemma on the eve of Kennedy's death. There were fundamental limits to arms control in 1963, imposed by the Kennedy administration's strategy and the domestic political climate it was tailored to. Glenn Seaborg's account of the LTBT negotiations suggests that, had Kennedy lived, the new era of détente would have led to yet more arms control agreements.[145] The scholar David Kaiser has gone so far to suggest that Kennedy could have "scored some of the successes achieved by Richard Nixon."[146] Yet chances for further steps in bilateral arms control between the superpowers were slim. Meaningful superiority may have been over for those few who endured the crushing tension of the Cuban missile crisis, but it was not over for the American and West European publics, or for the Soviets. The president and his secretary of defense were unhappy with a continued arms race, but believed it was necessary in order to maintain support for their tentative steps toward bilateral superpower arms control.

"Détente," as historian Andrew Preston argues, was indeed "predicated on confrontation," but not only in relation to showing resolve in geographically peripheral areas such as Vietnam.[147] In its advocacy for the Test Ban, the Kennedy administration had effectively committed the United States to doing whatever it took to ensure the maintenance of American nuclear predominance at the highest, most abstract, and in many ways peripheral levels of state violence. This represented the broad public consensus as well as the cornerstone of the American commitment to NATO. If anything, in committing the United States further to the defense of a nonnuclear West Germany, the LTBT had made nuclear superiority more important, not less. The administration was afraid of the consequences of reversal. As McNamara advised Kennedy in December 1962, the United States might be able to deemphasize superiority "someday," but could not "change it today without seriously weakening the [NATO] alliance."[148]

Commitment to superiority was also necessary to keep the military on the administration's side. "The same emotionally biased people" who had charged Eisenhower with the missile gap "exist in the Pentagon today," McNamara warned Kennedy. "I don't mean to say that Curtis [LeMay] is emotionally biased, but he is beginning to say that the program I am presenting is endangering the national security and he believes it. . . . We have to say our policy is maintaining nuclear superiority." Indeed, the Joint Chiefs of Staff continued to push for further weapons building in September 1963, even as they admitted privately that a first strike was out of the question. For General Johnson, the key was the ability to limit damage even in the absence of a US ability to conduct a completely successful first strike. This, in the general's view, necessitated "more US missiles and more accurate US missiles," as well as a US ABM system.[149]

Far from being the dawn of a new US–Soviet détente based on arms control, the situation at the end of the Kennedy administration was replete with difficulties. On the one hand, the administration had decided that the rhetoric of rational superiority was the winning position from a domestic political standpoint. On the other, the White House harbored serious doubts regarding its utility in crisis situations, reinforced by the closing of the window in which the United States could have potentially conducted a successful disarming first strike on the Soviet Union. These tensions—latent in November 1963—would come to the fore as the Johnson administration struggled to reconcile the commitment to the US nuclear edge with the requirements of détente on the basis of superpower arms control. Far from being Johnson's creation, they were his unenviable inheritance.

CHAPTER 2

The Great Society and the Politics of Assured Destruction, 1963–1966

Lyndon Johnson's first and overriding aim on November 22, 1963 was to assure the American people of the continued integrity of executive power. The new president was sworn in less than two hours after John F. Kennedy was pronounced dead. Johnson traveled back to Washington with Kennedy's casket on Air Force One, awkwardly treading the line between respect for the assassinated president and assertion of his new powers.[1]

Johnson took possession of the suitcase of nuclear codes known as "the football" before he was officially sworn in. With the government fearing an invasion or coup, American nuclear forces went on alert. Yet despite the thousands of megatons at his disposal Kennedy had been assassinated with nothing more powerful than a 1930s-vintage Italian bolt-action rifle. If there was any point the American people needed reassurance of their security, it was this moment. As his biographer has noted, Robert McNamara was "a physical symbol of confidence and continuity," prominently greeting Johnson in front of the press after Air Force One touched down at Andrews Air Force Base outside Washington, DC.[2]

Despite his pressing need to reassure the American people they were secure from external threats, in the hours after Kennedy's death Johnson's attention was already shifting elsewhere. Over a number of evenings in late November, the new president huddled with his advisors, "filling yellow legal tablets with legislative proposals" on civil rights, urban renewal, the environment, higher education, and immigration. "Halting, limited, constrained," as they were, the package of measures that would become known as the Great Society would nevertheless be a major attack on racial, economic, and social injustice in the United States. For Johnson the politics of national security and the Great Society were inextricably intertwined. Only by maintaining confidence in the United States' ability to pursue militarized containment of the Soviet Union would Johnson be able to achieve his domestic legislative agenda. Reassuring a joint session of Congress that the United States would "keep its commitments from South Vietnam to Berlin," Johnson knew he had to convince the legislative branch and the broader public that he would protect the country by maintaining its military strength. His twin impulses to transform the United States domestically while upholding continuity in the cornerstones of containment defined Johnson's presidency.[3] Robert McNamara would be his willing accomplice in that mission.

The Johnson-McNamara partnership's imperative to ensure both national and social security was no clearer than in the case of nuclear forces. Johnson did not want to spend more on defense than was absolutely necessary because it cut into what he could devote to the Great Society. To this end he and McNamara worked together to limit the growth in the US nuclear arsenal. McNamara remained committed to scaling back the ambition of the objectives set for American nuclear forces and provided the strategic justifications to legitimize Johnson's choices in conformity with rational superiority. This included an attempt to postpone, perhaps indefinitely, the deployment of an antiballistic missile system for the United States.

Together the president and his secretary of defense struggled to reconcile their desire to cap military spending and ameliorate the arms race with the necessity, as they perceived it, of maintaining the American lead in the number and quality of nuclear weapons. Both the achievements and shortcomings of their efforts are clearly illustrated by the United States' ballistic missile defense program.

DOMESTIC POLITICS AND THE PRIMACY OF RATIONAL SUPERIORITY

Johnson and McNamara quickly established a close relationship in the early months of LBJ's presidency, forged through McNamara's demonstrated ability to fulfill Johnson's immediate needs. These were primarily budgetary and electoral. The FY 1965 budget was a headache for Johnson, who had to reconcile his predecessor's commitment to an $11 billion tax cut with the opposition of fiscal conservatives in Congress to larger deficits. It would be difficult to forsake Kennedy's promised tax cut in an election year with the associated drop in employment and growth, yet there was strong congressional opposition, most significantly from Harry Byrd (D-VA), chairman of the Senate Finance Committee, to any budget that crossed the symbolic $100 billion mark. A conservative Democrat, the chairman "measured his success as senator not by what he passed, but what he stopped from passing," according to his congressional colleague Russell Long. Johnson also feared that Southern Democrats like Byrd would hold up the tax bill in order to kill any chance of successful passage of civil rights legislation in 1964. Byrd used his prerogatives as chairman ruthlessly by deploying every single procedural trick in the book to delay passage of the tax cut. A long and experienced interlocutor with Byrd, Johnson ordered his economic team to shave billions off the federal budget, otherwise "you won't pee one drop."[4]

McNamara was eager to ingratiate himself with the new president. The secretary of defense saw himself as there to provide the rationalizations the president needed to get what he wanted done. This meant reconciling rational superiority with Johnson's other political requirements. On December 7, the secretary of defense publicly outlined measures that, he claimed, would shave $1.5 billion off the DoD budget.[5] The same day he told Johnson that he could get the defense budget to the president's required "figure of $51.4 billion—the one you're carrying around in your pocket." Importantly, McNamara told the president that he had not informed the Joint Chiefs of the ceiling: "they'll know exactly the number of dollars, but they won't know that I set the dollar limit first." The strategic rationales would all lead to this figure and McNamara would square the chiefs as long as Johnson kept their secret quiet.[6] The president was thereby able to announce a reduction in defense spending "while maintaining our position of strength," and Johnson's administrative budget managed to slip in $2.1 billion under Byrd's requirement.[7] For this effort McNamara occupied a special place in Johnson's esteem. The secretary of defense, Johnson told his Texas business associate, Robert B. Anderson, was "the only guy" who was "really trying to help" him get the budget down.[8]

By early 1964, Johnson's confidence in his secretary of defense was sealed. "Is this my 'can do' man?" the president greeted McNamara just after the new year.[9] "I'm the first president that ever cut it down!" he bragged later to Dallas Morning News columnist Dick West, "Kennedy had a budget of 103 billion 800 million, 5 billion over last year. I cut the son of a bitch down to 97.9!"[10] He rewarded the secretary of defense by clearly articulating his primacy over the Joint Chiefs of Staff. Johnson told McNamara the importance he attached to "team play" between the chiefs, the secretary of defense, and the president. "When the ball goes the right side of the line, we [all] go the right side of the line," Johnson assured McNamara. This was the kind of "team play" McNamara liked: deference to the Office of the Secretary of Defense and his political master. McNamara thanked Johnson for telling the chiefs of the importance of unity because "it sort of freezes [the Joint Chiefs] into that position." Johnson agreed: "I hope you go home and brag on yourself to your wife."[11]

Johnson was determined to keep the US nuclear establishment in check as part of his campaign to balance budgetary probity and domestic reform. The president told the chairman of the Council of Economic Advisors, Walter Heller, that he would not hesitate to cut training facilities for obsolete nuclear bombers "in order to help grandma or somebody in West Virginia [or] Tennessee that's not eating now." While committed to modernizing US nuclear forces, Johnson knew an arms race had the potential to divert resources from his domestic spending priorities. "We're not going to make more atomic bombs than we need because that makes Russia make more," the president told Heller, vowing that his administration was not going "to operate a WPA project for atomic bombs . . . We may lose 300 workers, but we'll put them to work on poverty."[12]

Such instincts dovetailed well with McNamara's campaign to scale back the aims and structure of US strategic nuclear forces, which was already in motion by the time of Kennedy's assassination. The centerpiece of this effort was his division of the nuclear establishment's mission into two. This was first articulated in McNamara's FY 1965 draft presidential memoranda on offensive and defensive forces of late 1963. According to McNamara, the US military should be able ride out a first strike by the Soviet Union, retaining the ability "to destroy . . . the Soviet government and military controls, plus a large percentage of their population and economy." This McNamara set at "30 percent of [the Soviet] population, 50 percent of their industrial capacity and 150 of their cities." He named damage limitation as the second objective—that is, to minimize the level of harm inflicted on the United States' population, industry, and military through a combination of offensive strikes against Soviet nuclear forces and defensive measures, including but not limited to hardening of missile silos, the construction of fallout shelters, air defense, and missile defense.[13]

McNamara deemed the assured destruction mission to be "essential." As he argued in December 1963, the buildup over which Kennedy had presided had rendered a force more than adequate to fulfill this task. To illustrate this point, McNamara took a hypothetical scenario in five years' time in which all the Minuteman missiles—the cornerstone of the Kennedy-era arms buildup—would be rendered inoperable. After a Soviet first strike on the remaining forces, the United States would have the capability to respond with 1,200 megatons, resulting in the deaths of "approximately 115 million people," or 50 percent of the USSR's population, and the destruction of "57 percent of the Soviet industrial floorspace."[14] Even if Minuteman had never been deployed, the United States still had the capability to inflict losses in a matter of hours that would dwarf those suffered by the USSR during the Great Patriotic War and well above McNamara's baseline requirement.

McNamara couched the utility of damage limitation in far more oblique terms, describing how further forces "may be justified," but only if they "could further reduce the damage to the U.S. . . . by an amount sufficient to justify their added costs."[15] In McNamara's view, current measures had not met this standard. The secretary of defense compared US defensive preparations "to a building with fragile walls and no roof or foundation." The secretary of defense estimated that a mere fifty missiles "would kill more than 30 million people and a 200-missile attack would kill most of [the United States'] urban population." In his view defensive measures had been a budgetary sinkhole. The billions spent on active bomber defenses in the 1950s had been wasted: they were of dubious effectiveness against a mass attack by Soviet aircraft and completely useless against ballistic missiles. At the same time, additional missiles above those required for assured destruction were not a cost-effective method by which to blunt a Soviet attack. The United States could not hope to achieve a first-strike capability through which it could save the American population by preemptively destroying Soviet offensive forces. US anti-submarine warfare capabilities were not sufficient to deal with the USSR's seaborne deterrent, while hardening and dispersal of land-based Soviet missile silos would protect them against preemptive attack. Even under the most favorable conditions, a US president opting for a first strike on the Soviet Union would be choosing to condemn 28 million of his fellow citizens and 60 million West Europeans.[16]

Other members of the Johnson administration suspected McNamara's strategic schema was an attempt to impose a framework on American nuclear forces in a way that, while not explicitly discrediting the buildup achieved under Kennedy, would place definite limits on the further expansion of the US nuclear arsenal. Carl Kaysen of the National Security Council staff pointed to the fact that the offensive forces McNamara budgeted for bore only a tangential relationship to his strategic concept. The ambition of significantly blunting Soviet offensive forces had been thrown out, and with it the requirement for ever-greater numbers of weapons to match growing Soviet airfields and missile sites. However, the numbers McNamara asked for did not shrink to match these far more modest ambitions. As Kaysen remarked drily, this "might indicate that it is McNamara's judgment that these numbers are the minimum the services will accept."[17] Given Johnson's clear emphasis on fiscal restraint combined with maintenance of a clear nuclear edge, the minimum the services would accept indeed appears to have been the aim. While McNamara projected 1,200 Minutemen in his FY 1965 budget, the Chief of Staff of the Air Force Curtis LeMay asked for 1,950, and Secretary of the Air Force Eugene Zuckert 1,400.[18] By the time of his FY 1966 memorandum in December 1964, McNamara brought this figure down to 1,000.[19] The imperative was to cap the growth of America's arsenal, an aim that aligned with Johnson's fiscal requirements; the justification in the language of systems analysis and cost-effectiveness was shaped by the need to ensure consistency with Kennedy's policy of rational superiority.

This dovetailing of budgetary and strategic rationales doomed ABM. As Deputy DoD Comptroller Alain Enthoven explained to his State Department colleagues during discussion of the Pentagon's FY 65 spending plans, the "considerable pressure" from both the White House and Congress "not to go on increasing the DoD budget" meant that the United States had to grapple with "a real question of priorities" when it came to approving funds for big new weapons systems, such as missile defense. Enthoven informed his colleagues that an ABM system as part of a big effort to limit damage to the United States in the event of a nuclear attack was just not worth cuts to other important areas of the defense budget, such as conventional forces.[20]

Strategically, the secretary of defense managed to tear apart the ABM's central rationale while praising the technological achievements of the Nike-Zeus and the Nike-X research and development programs. McNamara declared that, "developments in recent years have removed the specter of impossibility from ballistic missile defense." However, the objectives for such a system were scaled back radically. McNamara's evaluation of the system's effectiveness indicated that it would not provide any significant defense against a Soviet intercontinental strike, but would instead be useful only in the case of an accident or in the event of a small attack by a third country.[21] The chiefs pushed against this judgment with increasing vehemence throughout the mid-1960s.

Yet McNamara could only go so far in paring back the expansion of US nuclear forces. There were strong domestic political pressures on the Johnson administration militating against any move away from a clear margin of US superiority, not least in Congress. Although much diminished since the height of their influence in the 1950s, as a result of the senatorial seniority system that rewarded long service with key chairmanships, Southern Democrats still dominated major defense committees in both houses. Senator Richard Russell ruled the Senate Armed Services Committee and was reinforced by a number of other Southerners, as well as defense hawks such as Henry M. Jackson (D-WA) and Stuart Symington (D-MO). A strong advocate of defense preparedness, Russell was not even the most hawkish on the Armed Services Committee, having to muster his parliamentary skills to defeat an amendment proposed by his committee colleague, Senator Strom Thurmond (D-SC) to fund the Nike-Zeus ABM system in the FY 1964 budget against the administration's wishes. The two most senior Democrats on the House Armed Services Committee, Carl Vinson (D-GA) and Mendel Rivers (D-SC), were cut from similar cloth.[22]

Often there was a direct link between maintaining a strong line on defense and passing key pieces of domestic legislation at the committee level. The same defense hawks were also fiscally conservative members of key appropriations committees. The chairman of the Senate Finance Committee, Harry Byrd, for example, was also the second most senior Democrat on the Senate Armed Services Committee. On other issues, such as Civil Rights, where the Southern Democrats knew they did not have the votes to oppose Johnson, they still attempted to offer a quid-pro-quo on defense. A staunch segregationist, Russell realized that Johnson's legislative skills would make opposition to civil rights and voting rights legislation a lost cause. Nevertheless, he attempted to maintain some leverage with the president. In late November 1964, a few months after his failed last-ditch attempt to derail the Civil Rights Act, Russell met with Johnson to discuss foreign and domestic affairs. Questioned on their recent clashes over civil rights after the meeting, Russell told reporters that, as chairman of the Senate Armed Services Committee, he wanted to work with the president to resist the "communist enslavement" of the United States.[23] The threat was clear: Russell would concede Johnson his domestic agenda, but backtracking on militarized containment would be too much. Even if Johnson had wanted to, challenging Southern Democrats on this issue while attempting to push through the Great Society would have been more than the congressional traffic could bear.

American popular attitudes toward US–Soviet relations reinforced the difficulties for any president who thought of reversing Kennedy's emphasis on nuclear superiority over the Soviet Union—let alone the domestically focused Johnson. In their study *The Political Beliefs of Americans*, based on polling conducted in October 1964, Lloyd Free and Hadley Cantril found that, although often "abysmally ignorant" regarding the details of national security, Americans had clear convictions regarding the "grand of objectives of foreign policy." Free and Cantril found that 61 percent of Americans thought that the United States "should take a firmer stand" against the

Soviet Union, with a majority of "all groups"—liberal or conservative, internationalist or isolationist—taking this view. Only 4 percent of respondents favored a reduction in the United States' defense preparedness, as opposed to 31 percent who wanted it increased and 52 percent who believed it was "about right." At the same time, however, only 20 percent favored a policy of rollback against the Soviet Union, while 85 percent supported talks with the USSR, including 80 percent of those who favored a stronger US stance against the Soviet Union. Concerned with the Cold War, though not necessarily well informed on its finer points, most Americans appeared to favor talks with the USSR from a position of strength—that is, the position that the Kennedy administration had pursued and most recently advocated when pushing for the Limited Test Ban Treaty.[24] Congressional and public opinion appeared to have little tolerance for a change in course.

These domestic political imperatives were reinforced by the fact that Johnson was vulnerable to charges of weakness in a presidential election year. As NSC staffer William Smith argued to Bundy, the FY 65 budget represented "an across the board cutback," with total obligational authority for strategic offensive forces cut by 42 percent and defensive forces by 18 percent since FY 62. If these numbers were combined with evidence that the administration had become wary of the utility of nuclear weapons for defending NATO, the consequences could be fatal for Johnson's presidency. By prioritizing assured destruction, Smith argued that the country's nuclear forces would be transformed from a "sword" capable of preemptive attacks against Soviet installations into a "shield" that could only retaliate against a Soviet first strike. Conventional forces were to take the place of Eisenhower's nuclear commitment, but without stronger European participation this would result in a conventional defense of Europe that was as weak as in the 1950s. Unlike Eisenhower however, the US government of the 1960s could not be certain that the US would retain the assurance that had been the product of America's 1950s predominance in nuclear striking power. The shift to the purely retaliatory stance implied by any move to numerical parity could therefore set off a further crisis in West European confidence in the US commitment to strike first in NATO's defense. This, worried Smith, could stoke "domestic political fires. . . . What all this adds up to is that the coming year is not a good time either at home or abroad to launch forth on educating the world in our new military thinking."[25] Although he believed McNamara's recommended forces considerably overshot those necessary, Carl Kaysen was similarly reticent in recommending a downward revision for fear of "presenting a target to Goldwaterism on this issue"—a reference to Barry Goldwater, an extreme nuclear hawk and then-prospective Republican nominee.[26] As the presidential election approached, Johnson could not afford to be seen as stepping away from numerical superiority as the touchstone of American commitment to the defense of the free world.

The image of a rational finger on the nuclear button was also useful against Goldwater, Johnson's Republican opponent in the presidential election of 1964. Johnson struck a public pose of reasonableness and calm against Goldwater's calls to "lob [a nuclear weapon] into the men's room of the Kremlin" and pledges to delegate use to NATO field commanders. Responding to Goldwater's rhetoric, Johnson lectured that "the control of nuclear weapons is one of the most solemn responsibilities of the president of the United States—the man who is president can never forget it." Johnson's rationality compared to Goldwater's insanity was the subtext of one of the most infamous attack ads of all time, in which a girl picked flowers while counting up to ten, before a sinister countdown commenced and the view of a mushroom cloud appeared through her eye. Concluding with a call to "vote for President Johnson on November 3. The stakes are too high for you to stay home," it ran only once, but left a searing impression on the public. As historian Robert Dallek has argued, the "Daisy" advert and others "destroyed any slight hope Goldwater might have had of overcoming Johnson's lead." The president was thrilled with the positive reaction to the ad, ruthlessly channeling the spirit of the cool-headed Kennedy to dazzling effect.[27] After Goldwater claimed that Johnson had authorized the use of nuclear weapons during the Gulf of Tonkin incident in August, the president privately assured *Washington Post* journalist Chalmers Roberts that he "fully embraced" the nuclear release procedures that had been "spelled out by Eisenhower" and "carefully looked at . . . by Kennedy."[28] In the domestic political realm, the continuity embodied by rational superiority was the winning position.

However, Johnson's concern with Goldwater was not simply political one-upmanship. The president was genuinely concerned that the Republican nominee's penchant for rabble-rousing on nuclear weapons could be a serious threat to global peace if he were elected. Johnson was appalled by Goldwater's reference to NATO commanders being given the authority to use, as the Republican put it, "small conventional nuclear weapons." "Goldwater's had two serious nervous breakdowns. . . . He'll say small conventional weapons in the morning and then he'll say, 'Well, I didn't mean that'. . . . He's not a stable person," Johnson told Dick West.[29] Johnson wanted to beat Goldwater and skillfully used rational superiority to help him get there, but this partly stemmed from a deep unease with the possible consequences of having someone he considered mentally unstable with his finger on the button.

McNamara's strategic goals of assured destruction and damage limitation thus satisfied Johnson's needs by at once imposing a unilateral cap on American offensive and defensive forces and keeping faith with rational superiority. This framework, imposing strong cost-effectiveness constraints on missile defense, was designed to keep ABM in research and development almost indefinitely in a way that would satisfy both the need for strategic strength and budgetary prudence. In late 1964 and early 1965 both the president and his secretary of defense publicly walked this tightrope in order to build the budgetary case for Johnson's social programs. In December 1964, McNamara boasted to reporters about how the administration had secured "further economies" in the Pentagon "while continuing to increase our military strength." In late 1964 Johnson repeated his 1963 boast that he had kept the federal budget under $100 billion, telling newsmen that he wanted "to save every penny we can every place we can so that we may have some much needed funds to fill unfilled needs—educational needs, health needs, poverty needs, needs generally." In his State of the Union message on January 4, 1965, Johnson declared that although international events would "continue to call upon our energy and courage," the United States could "turn increased attention to the character of American life." Building on the theme of "the Great Society," which he had announced the previous year, Johnson proceeded to outline his major reforms to education, health, voting rights, and urban development. This shift from the foreign to the domestic was based, Johnson argued, on the fact that the United States possessed "military power strong enough to meet any threat and destroy any adversary. And that superiority will continue to grow so long as this office is mine—and you sit on Capitol Hill." Johnson reprised this theme in a special communication to Congress two weeks later, days before submitting the FY 1966 budget. The United States' "indisputable margin of superiority," as Johnson put it, would allow the United States to level off defense spending, thereby allowing "an ever-larger share of our expanding national wealth" to be spent on "other vital needs, both public and private." As historian Randall Woods has noted, LBJ used the "rhetoric of consensus" in order to get his hugely ambitious social reforms through Congress.[30] That included the Kennedy-era consensus regarding nuclear superiority.

With hindsight it is clear that Johnson's posture of strength had already set in motion events that would undermine his efforts to marry militarized containment of communism with the Great Society—and thus his entire presidency. In part as a way to respond to Republican charges of weakness, as well as reports of North Vietnamese attacks on US Navy vessels sailing close to the coastline, in early August 1964 Johnson launched retaliatory airstrikes on North Vietnam and pressed Congress for permission to prosecute further military action. Passed on August 7, the Tonkin Gulf Resolution authorized the president to take "all necessary measures" in response "to further aggression" against US forces in the region. With further political and military setbacks over the subsequent months, the White House rejected calls for talks without a halt to communist military operations in South Vietnam. On March 2, 1965, the United States initiated Operation Rolling Thunder, the continuous bombardment of North Vietnam from the air. US Marines landed at Da Nang six days later, marking the decisive escalation that would eventually see over 500,000 American troops committed to the defense of the South Vietnamese government.[31]

As the American commitment to South Vietnam deepened, McNamara's skill at juggling figures in the defense budget became increasingly important—indeed central—to the Johnson administration's attempts to stave off both fiscal and political pressure for cuts in its domestic programs. McNamara informed Johnson on December 1, 1965 that the Pentagon would need $11 billion in supplemental funding in order to pay for the war through mid-1966, with severe increases in costs to come through FY 1967.[32] Against this background, Johnson was faced an unenviable dilemma: make unrealistic budgetary assumptions as to the likely length—and therefore cost—of the war, or sacrifice his domestic agenda at the feet of budgetary austerity. The president believed he could not secure a tax hike from Congress to pay for the war and the administration's domestic programs. "I can't get one, I just know I cannot get it," he told McNamara. Instead, Johnson and McNamara decided to cap the FY 1967 defense budget at $57 billion by assuming that the American commitment would be over by June 1967, thereby postponing further appropriations. If they failed to do that, McNamara advised Johnson, "Your Great Society's going to be gutted." Johnson and McNamara were committed to doing everything they could in order to minimize the defense budget. Extra funding for strategic nuclear forces and missile defense was out of the question. "You try to write the best presentation you can on the [$] 57 [billion]," Johnson told McNamara, "showing that you're not doing anything abnormal [on Vietnam] except something that you can't possibly predict. Make it look as good as you can."[33]

McNamara's planning for nuclear forces was thus deeply embedded within Johnson's broader domestic and international agenda. Yet, despite the patina of systems analysis, McNamara's strategic prescriptions rested on a series of deeply impressionistic assumptions that would come under increasing attack in the coming years, to the point where he and Johnson were forced to look again at missile defense.

SHELTERS AND THE DOMESTIC POLITICS OF
A "BALANCED DEFENSE"

The strongest element of McNamara's argument against ABM was his insistence on a "balanced defense." The secretary of defense insisted that no element of a damage-limiting program should go ahead without concomitant efforts on all fronts, principally missile defense, continental air defense, and shelters. McNamara argued from a strategic standpoint that without one element of this defensive triad, the others would be open to circumvention by Soviet forces. He presented compelling evidence that showed any effective damage limitation program had to have a full fallout and blast shelter effort at its heart. Without shelters, the Soviets could simply detonate nuclear weapons upwind of US cities and rely on the resulting fallout to kill Americans. There was no point, McNamara stated, in deploying a missile defense until a shelter system had been built.[34]

McNamara's rhetoric was based on the military-technical shortcomings of an ABM without fallout shelter protection, but his argument also had profound domestic political implications for missile defense. McNamara succeeded in lashing the ABM to one of the most toxic issues in the domestic politics of American nuclear strategy.[35] Neglected under Eisenhower, the American civil defense program had received strong rhetorical support from Kennedy during the Berlin crisis. In his July 25, 1961 speech on Berlin, Kennedy had announced an extra $207 million for civil defense, to be spent on the appropriation of shelter spaces in existing structures, stocking them with appropriate supplies, and improving the fallout detection system.[36] However, by 1962 congressional enthusiasm was faltering: the administration requested $757 million for civil defense, but received $128 million.[37] Overall, US civil defense policy was marked by strong rhetoric, but little action. In the words of one prominent historian of the American program, "at the height of Cold War tensions Americans *talked* a great deal about fallout shelters, but relatively few Americans actually *built* fallout shelters."[38]

At the congressional level, McNamara was helped by the fact that fallout shelters were opposed on fiscal grounds by many of the same congressional defense hawks who favored an ABM system. These included Henry Jackson, who chaired the Senate appropriations subcommittee through which civil defense spending had to pass. In March 1964, Jackson refused to approve funding for Kennedy's Shelter Incentive Program, which would have provided federal subsidies for shelter construction, on the basis that it could not be afforded at a time when Johnson had declared a period of restraint in government spending. Indeed, despite the pleas of the assistant secretary of defense for civil defense, Steuart L. Pittman, neither the

White House nor McNamara was willing to intervene. As scholar Edward Geist has argued, "congressional budgetary politics" therefore doomed federal subsidization of civil defense. Even pro-ABM figures such as Jackson were not willing to go to the mat for civil defense in order to secure a missile defense system.[39]

Shelters were extremely expensive for individual families, costing approximately half a year's average earnings. More importantly, there was an intense debate over whether they would actually work. Fallout shelters would be useless if they were caught near the fireball of a Soviet detonation, against which residents would require a far deeper and more expensive blast shelter to have any hope of survival. At the same time, fallout shelters were neither conducive to American urban ways of life, nor certain prejudices regarding who would be saved and who would not. The best preexisting shelter spaces were in the center of cities. With the migration of the white middle class to the suburbs, this meant that, according to Representative Marsha Griffiths, "if the bombs fell at night, you would save nobody but skid row characters, drunks, a few people in hospitals and maybe the night shift on the local newspapers." Even in central areas most buildings could not be evacuated in the short period between detection of Soviet launch and impact. The only hope was to burrow into the earth.[40] The very fabric of American life would have to change if citizens were to have any hope of surviving a nuclear attack.

In this context it is clear that these practical issues were underpinned by an extreme aversion among the majority of Americans to changing their civilian lifestyles to suit military requirements. The idea of altering the Manhattan skyline in order to gain a slim chance of surviving a nuclear war smacked of a Fortress America mentality that was deeply alien to a population that had prevailed during in the Second World War with only minimal impact on civilians' lifestyles. As Kennedy had admitted in his Berlin address in July 1961, "in contrast to our friends in Europe, the need for this kind of protection is new to our shores."[41] There was a deep concern that hiding in a shelter was in some way unpatriotic—a notion that would have confounded residents of London, Berlin, Moscow or Hanoi. While the free security of the pre-nuclear age had dissipated, the thought of changing established cityscapes by burrowing deep underground gained no traction with the majority of Americans. American aversion to civil defense made ABM a political nonstarter if a fallout shelter system were the precondition for its construction.

In arguing for the indispensability of a civil defense effort for an effective missile defense, McNamara masterfully hobbled America's ABM program by associating it with a deeply unpopular policy that had breached the limits of American tolerance for civilian concessions to Cold War military needs. In this, he proved far more adept than the Joint Chiefs, who were left floundering in conferences with Johnson. When the president challenged JCS Chairman General Earle Wheeler in December 1964 over how a 40 percent hole in the civil defense budget would be funded, the chairman "stated that it would have to be furnished by the individual states." LBJ was "unconvinced" by this answer, noting flatly that the states were unlikely to spend the money, and in any case the cost might eventually be borne by the federal government because "the states claim that they must receive a portion of federal tax receipts in order to cover their current costs."[42] Such ignorance of domestic restraints could not have endeared the chiefs to a president who had made economy in federal spending a touchstone of his campaign to push the Great Society through Congress. McNamara understood Johnson far better, and he prevailed.

The JCS resisted McNamara's recommendations, but in an uncoordinated way. Wheeler pushed Johnson for "stronger leadership" on fallout shelters. This came to no avail in the face of the significant domestic political capital that would have had to be sunk into such an effort. In the absence of presidential support for a further push in this direction, the chief of staff of the Army urged the president to forge ahead with missile defense in the hope that civil defense would follow in its wake. Without support from the chairman however, this appeal fell on deaf ears.[43] McNamara cleverly dovetailed ABM's technical limitations with those imposed by domestic politics in order to weigh down progress toward deployment.

THE SOVIET UNION: RATIONAL AND MODERN

In addition to his case for the indispensability of a serious civil defense program, McNamara's argument regarding assured destruction and damage limitation also rested on more contentious and ultimately less enduring foundations. Just as assured destruction had become an American strategic goal in the wake of the Cuban missile crisis, so McNamara assumed that the Soviet Union had drawn the same lessons from Cuba regarding the limited utility of nuclear weapons and would therefore pursue a small force that would not challenge American superiority in numbers of launchers.

On the offensive side of the equation, McNamara expressed Soviet development of an assured destruction force in terms of the superpowers' equal capabilities. As he noted in his 1963 memorandum on offensive forces, "the same means by which we are developing an 'assured destruction' capability are also available to the Soviets." It appeared that, intentionally or not, the USSR was moving toward a secure force capable of riding out a second strike on the American model.[44] In this, the Soviet Union represented the United States' sole peer as well as its sole rival. McNamara predicted that the Soviets would "harden and disperse" their ICBMs and increase their number of ballistic missile submarines.[45] McNamara projected the Soviet Union to have between 400 and 700 hardened ICBMs by 1969. By McNamara's calculations, the Soviet Union would possess between 185 and 236 SLBMs, as well as 168 to 258 submarine-launched cruise missiles by mid-1969. The United States could not destroy all of these in a preemptive attack.[46] In McNamara's mind, the United States and the Soviet Union stood alone as the only countries with the capability to develop an assured destruction force of this size, and he assumed they both would do so.

It was in the context of missile defense that McNamara's framework moved from a community of capability into a community of interest. In arguing against an ABM deployment in 1963, the secretary posited that it would be "almost unbelievable that the Soviets would not react" to a US missile defense in order to protect the USSR's ability to destroy American society. In this, the numbers were on the Soviets'—and McNamara's—side. The secretary of defense cited studies that indicated that the Soviet Union would only have to spend an extra dollar for every three dollars the United States spent on a missile defense to protect 80 percent of its population from Soviet retaliation after a US first strike.[47] If, as McNamara argued, the Soviets saw the utility of their nuclear forces primarily through the prism of assured destruction, they would have to spend far less to overcome any defensive system built by the United States.

Such assumptions also underpinned American projections of Soviet force development, thereby helping McNamara's campaign to constrain US offensive as well as defensive forces. National Intelligence Estimates (NIEs) represented the consensus view of the intelligence agencies on the United States Intelligence Board (USIB) and were the source of McNamara's projections for the future of the USSR's nuclear striking power. In the wake of their gross overestimation of the number of operational Soviet ICBMs during the late 1950s and early 1960s, analysts cut their projections: the 1962 NIE, Soviet Capabilities for Long-Range Attack, estimated that the USSR would have 300 to 600 ICBMs by mid-1967; in 1963 this was downgraded to 400 to 700 by mid-1969. The 1964 NIE concluded that, "the Soviets are not likely to acquire as many as 700 operational ICBM launchers before 1970." Importantly, the NIEs now assumed that the USSR would aim for an ICBM force considerably smaller than that of the United States, but large enough to guarantee that the USSR could respond to any attack by destroying American society.[48]

The axiom of Soviet commitment to assured destruction and the numbers of missiles it produced were extremely convenient for McNamara, for they allowed the United States to maintain quantitative superiority—even if it froze its own missile buildup. Under this scenario, the United States would retain the edge needed to assure its own domestic public and Western Europe of its ability to defend NATO, while the Soviets would forego numerical parity in order to get a survivable second-strike capability, which was all, in McNamara's view, a responsible nuclear power really required. Strategic stability would be assured without the United States ceding superiority or a further escalation in the arms race through the deployment of ABM.

In postulating such a community of interest, McNamara took sides in the ongoing debate over the nature and future of Soviet society. From the early 1950s a group of sociologists had sought to challenge the idea of the USSR as a totalitarian state in which citizens led atomized lives under the aegis of an all-powerful government. Talcott Parsons of Harvard, one of the early prophets of modernization theory, was an enthusiastic proponent of integrating the Soviet Union into the universal trajectory toward a modern industrial society epitomized by the United States. Parsons and other social theorists such as Alex Inkeles and Barrington Moore, Jr., constituted a highly influential group that propounded their views in everything from Air Force reports to congressional committee rooms. The USSR, Parsons believed, was simply at "an earlier stage" of modernization. As the Soviet Union moved further toward modernity it would lose the irrational elements of its ideological perspective and increasingly share the same rational assumptions that guided American policy. Experts were key to the removal of ideology, as Parsons saw it, from the Soviet Union. Expertise required greater understanding of the objective facts of a particular field and thereby a more rational outlook. As the USSR developed a strong cadre of expert professionals, so the Soviet Union would lose its ideological bent, becoming more rational—that is, more American—in its perspective.[49]

Although not explicitly articulated, McNamara and the intelligence community's post-Cuba strategic prescriptions seemed to assume just such a technocratic elite guiding policy in the Soviet Union. The US intelligence community believed that the Soviets had recognized the slowdown in economic growth stemmed from an overcommitment of resources to the push to match the United States' strategic strike capabilities. Such a conclusion was driven by economic fundamentals. Soviet defense spending had increased by 40 percent since 1958, the USIB estimated, most of which had gone to long-range nuclear forces, leading to a Soviet defense budget almost as large as the Pentagon's, despite an economy "roughly half the size" of that of the United States. Such outlays were even more burdensome, the USIB indicated, because the push to match US techno-logical capabilities put an undue burden on highly educated personnel and "scarce" electronic components. The Soviet response had appar-ently been to shift resources away from the military to civilian sectors of the economy and move toward détente with the West. This, analysts believed, represented a qualified victory for civilian interest groups over the military "in a period of increasingly severe competition for resources among the various sectors of [the Soviet] economy." In order to achieve a diversified, modern economy, the USIB assumed the Soviet leadership had recognized that economic growth should be prioritized over raw mil-itary power. This domestic situation, the USIB judged, would probably manifest itself in "a recognition of . . . the general balance of power which emerged in the Cuban crisis"—that is, Soviet quantitative inferiority in strategic arms.[50]

McNamara increasingly adopted this idea of civilian versus military interest groups in the Soviet Union. Prior to 1963, the secretary of defense's memoranda had assumed a unitary totalitarian state. In his 1962 Senate budget testimony, McNamara outlined a vague threat from an expansive communist bloc that would be "quick to take advantage of a breakdown of law and order in any part of the world."[51] In 1964, however, he portrayed a Soviet leadership struggling to balance civilian and military needs against the background of a slowing economy. "The significant point," the secre-tary of defense declared, was that "the competing demands on the Soviet budget" would act "as a restraint on the size of the military forces." These difficulties and the resulting need for financing from Western countries could, McNamara speculated, "serve as a brake on Soviet troublemaking proclivities."[52]

These ideas were seemingly vindicated by developments in relations between the superpowers during the mid-1960s. McNamara's projected caps on the growth of US forces came at the same time as a series of steps in US–Soviet relations that seemed to show a broad commonality of out-look on major issues. The Johnson administration scored a number of suc-cesses, including reductions in the production of fissionable material on a unilateral basis by both superpowers in 1964 and the Outer Space Treaty in 1967.[53] Negotiations for the Nuclear Non-Proliferation Treaty were well advanced by this point, a process in which both powers actively sought to secure their mutual aim of restraining aspirant states from acquiring nuclear weapons in order to secure a superpower nuclear-backed condo-minium in both Western Europe and East Asia. A growing community of interest on this front was even more evident to both American and Soviet policymakers as they looked nervously toward the newest entrant to the nuclear club, the People's Republic of China (PRC).

THE PEOPLE'S REPUBLIC OF CHINA: IRRATIONAL AND PRIMITIVE

The PRC detonated its first device in October 1964, becoming the first Asian power to possess nuclear weapons. For the majority of the American bureaucracy this was a challenge of the first order to the balance of power in East Asia. McNamara found the Chinese test particularly chilling, but he used the American anxieties aroused by this development to redirect American energies on the ABM away from the Soviets and toward the PRC.[54] In doing so, he hoped to defer American missile defense deployment until well into the next decade.

McNamara's "China card" had a long pedigree. From 1963 the secretary of defense had argued that, given its limited capabilities, Nike-X could be profitably deployed against an attack from a "minor power." The Soviets possessed too many high-quality weapons to be stopped by any technologically conceivable US ABM system, whereas a less capable nuclear state with a narrower military-industrial base would only be able to field a few ICBMs without decoys or multiple warheads.[55] After the Chinese test, McNamara began to cite the PRC as the most likely target of any ABM, describing such a system as "very valuable" if the Chinese developed an ICBM force of "several hundred missiles."[56] Behind this assertion lay the assumption that the People's Republic of China would be willing to threaten the United States with a highly inferior ICBM force in order to gain the upper hand in a crisis, perhaps in Southeast Asia or over Taiwan, thereby inviting the obliteration of the Mainland in a preemptive or retaliatory American nuclear strike.

In contrast to his optimism regarding the Soviets, McNamara took an extremely pessimistic reading of Chinese intentions. The secretary's argument was based on the premise that the Chinese government was fanatical enough to risk huge destruction in order to force the United States into concessions in East Asia. This would be a huge gamble: McNamara estimated that the United States had the ability to kill half of Chinese city-dwellers while still maintaining an assured destruction capability against the Soviet Union.[57] By advocating a Chinese-oriented ABM, he was implying that such power could be insufficient to deter the PRC from nuclear use, or threats of use, against the US homeland. McNamara thereby assumed that Beijing would be willing to run risks that the Soviets, with their vastly larger and more capable nuclear deterrent tempered by a rational commitment to assured destruction, never would.[58]

There was some evidence to back this interpretation of Chinese intentions. The Chinese leadership's indifference toward human suffering was manifest as untold numbers of its own citizens perished in the Great Leap Forward of the late 1950s. CIA estimates of the mid-1960s noted the increasingly hostile rhetoric emanating from Beijing in the wake of the Sino-Soviet split. This had been accompanied by a purge of the top military leadership. From the late 1950s Chairman Mao Zedong had replaced experienced officers bloodied in the Korean War with older individuals more highly regarded for their ideological purity than military competence. The new minister of defense, Marshal Lin Biao, was described as "a chronic invalid," but one whose "writings on such subjects as the importance of indoctrinated soldiers over weapons are said to be 'creative developments' of Mao's own thinking, and are used for indoctrination purposes."[59] Analysts characterized the Chinese leadership as comprised of "dedicated, even fanatic, communists."[60]

Chinese expansionism was a subject of consensus during both Kennedy and Johnson's terms in the White House.[61] The PRC's first priority, according to contemporary NIEs, was "to eject the West, especially the U.S. from Asia and to diminish U.S. and Western influence throughout the world." This would be achieved through a doctrine of "revolutionary war" that emphasized confrontation over negotiation with adversaries. An outgrowth of the guerrilla tactics that had brought the communists to power in 1949, the revolutionary war concept involved constant harassment of the enemy in order to undermine his overextended positions throughout the world, wearing them down in a long war of attrition that would inevitably lead to final victory. In prosecuting this strategy in Vietnam, the Chinese openly denigrated the importance of US military capabilities and nuclear power in particular. Chinese diplomats boasted that the Mainland could ride out a strike and criticized the Soviets for allegedly bowing to US pressure over the conflict in Southeast Asia.[62]

However, intelligence analysts were skeptical of the notion that the Chinese would use, or threaten to use, nuclear weapons against the United States. Indeed, the PRC's pursuit of the revolutionary war concept was predicated on the notion that direct confrontation with the United States over areas of contention such as Taiwan carried unacceptable risks, while fear of the reaction from global and domestic publics would deter the United States from using nuclear weapons in small wars. China's peripheral strategy was therefore designed to minimize the chances of a US attack on the Mainland while maximizing the pressure that Beijing could bring to bear on American positions throughout Asia. Chinese denigration of US nuclear power was based as much on a perception of its unwieldiness in limited conflict, CIA analysts concluded, as the belief that the PRC could really withstand a nuclear attack.[63] In this context, Chinese first use, even in a third country such as Vietnam, was considered so unlikely as to be not "worth serious consideration."[64] In arguing that Beijing would contemplate a first strike against the United States, McNamara was well outside the mainstream of analytical opinion.

The secretary of defense married this position on Chinese intentions with their limited capabilities to keep the American ABM in research and development for the better part of a decade. In arguing for primitive Chinese nuclear forces, McNamara slipped back into the received wisdom emanating from Langley. CIA analysts described with scarcely concealed awe that "never before has a nation as industrially backward and so near the margin of bare subsistence attempted such an ambitious advanced weapons program."[65] This would place severe limits on Beijing's ability to develop a force capable of posing a significant threat to the United States. The Chinese had a small number of medium-range bombers and were developing a missile intended for use in East Asia. Yet a Chinese ICBM force was deemed highly unlikely before the 1970s.[66] This technological primitiveness was perfect for McNamara. As he argued in conference with Johnson and the chiefs in December 1964, China could develop "an inferior" but "very dangerous" ICBM force between 1972 and 1985, but given this long horizon "the United States [did] not require an antiballistic missile at this time."[67] Even then it could be far cheaper than an anti-Soviet system, given the smaller number of Chinese missiles.

McNamara's position on China was not simply bureaucratic gamesmanship. It appears that the secretary of defense was on the pessimistic end of the spectrum when it came to assessments of Chinese intentions. As historian Matthew Jones has noted, McNamara characterized the PRC as the new opponent of an American-dominated status quo in Asia and thereby the world as a whole. In this, he made a conscious division between the PRC in the 1960s and "the USSR in 1947," implying that the Soviet challenge was primarily in the past, not the present. Such views influenced his advice on more pressing issues as well, most notably his determination to draw the line in South Vietnam.[68] However, the combination of aggressive intentions and limited capabilities also served his purposes on missile defense by putting off even a limited deployment far into the future. If ABM needed an outlet in the form of an enemy, it was far better for McNamara's budgetary goals that it be the irrational, primitive Chinese than the rational, modern Soviets. As the foundations of his edifice for unilateral restraint in

US nuclear forces began to crack, McNamara must have fingered the China card in his pocket, wondering when he would have to use it.

THE SOVIET RESPONSE

Soviet strategic behavior proved the undoing of McNamara's framework. Initially the gap between the secretary of defense's predictions and Soviet conduct was relatively small, but by 1966 it provided sufficient ammunition for the military to challenge McNamara's belief in the Soviet commitment to assured destruction.

Soviet ABM policy was a persistent chink in McNamara's armor. The secretary could never reconcile evidence of a high-priority Soviet missile defense program with his framework for assured destruction. The Soviet air defense forces had been building prototype ABM systems since 1960. Such deployments, mainly around Moscow but intermittently near Leningrad, as well as the accompanying bluster from Khrushchev regarding the Soviet ability to "hit a fly in space," had produced occasional panics within the Kennedy and Johnson administrations before Soviet work unexpectedly ceased, only to start up again at a later date.[69]

The stop-start activity that the Americans observed was the product of the Soviet Union's own bureaucratic intrigues. Khrushchev, faced with the considerable technical shortcomings of the original Soviet ABM, codenamed "System A," and unable to admit that it was impossible for the Soviet Union to build an ABM that could defend its entire territory, embarked on a new project sponsored by a rival designer, Vladimir N. Chelomey. Chelomey declared that his system, codenamed "Taran," could not only defend the USSR against a full intercontinental assault from the United States, but also attacks from medium- and short-range, as well as satellite-based weapons. All this was supposedly to be achieved at a considerably lower price than System A. Despite the considerable skepticism from within the Soviet scientific establishment, Khrushchev's enthusiasm for Taran was such that the Kremlin proceeded with Chelomey's project, appointing him the head designer. During 1963 to 1964 work on System A slowed. With a decisive shift toward Taran, the Soviet government halted construction of System A in June 1964. After Khrushchev's ouster in October 1964, however, Chelomey was faced with the loss of his most important patron, as well as the huge gap between his original claims and the technical difficulties that dogged all ABM efforts. As a result, he was sidelined in the search for a full ABM system. The Soviet leadership reassigned priority to System A and restarted construction around Moscow.[70]

The CIA was therefore right to conclude that, despite the considerable technical difficulties the Soviets were encountering, "the magnitude of R&D and the probable early deployment activity point to a strong Soviet desire to obtain ABM defenses rapidly."[71] This was completely at odds with McNamara's universal logic that posited that no rational being would deploy a missile defense due to its cost ineffectiveness. In order to respond to this conflicting data, McNamara was forced to insert caveats into his memoranda that otherwise attested to the predominance of the Soviets' assured-destruction mentality. He implied that the Soviets could have made a mistake in their calculations, stating in 1963 that missile defense "as of now appears uneconomic to us, but . . . may be attractive to them."[72] Had the Soviets run their numbers correctly, McNamara implied, they would not have decided on this course.

Nevertheless, with Soviet ABM deployment proceeding, the US military spotted this wound in McNamara's side and consistently attempted to open it further through their intelligence assessments of the USSR's ABM capabilities. They argued strongly that there was not merely one ABM complex but two. The second stretched along the Baltic coast and became known in Washington as the Tallinn Line. The Air Force, Army, and Defense Intelligence Agency believed this system to be an ABM, whereas the CIA was the principal advocate for Tallinn's status as a high-altitude air defense system. The evidence was inconclusive and so initially posed only a small threat to McNamara's assured destruction thesis. This inconsistency only grew into a crisis as the Soviets neared completion of their ABM complex around Moscow. McNamara, probably fearing that the information would get out, confirmed that the Soviets were indeed deploying a missile defense system in November 1966.[73] This in itself may not have been fatal for the secretary's framework, were it not for contemporaneous developments in Soviet offensive forces.

In May 1965 the Office of National Estimates at the CIA noted an upward trend in Soviet ICBM construction. Nevertheless, the subsequent NIE later that year prevaricated over the trend's significance. Analysts argued that it was too early to judge whether the USSR was engaging in a buildup larger than that estimated in the past, given past stop-start behavior in Soviet strategic deployment programs. As a result, the upper estimate for 1970 was only increased from seven hundred to eight hundred launchers.[74] By 1966, however, the change in pace was irrefutable. That year's estimate projected that the Soviet Union would equal the US ICBM force of 1,056 launchers by 1969. The NIE concluded that, "on the same basis, the Soviet force could be as high as 1,600 operational launchers by mid-1971, and more than 3,000 by mid-1976." This assessment was considered so politically damaging to the administration's strategic arms policy that Director of Central Intelligence Richard Helms placed an extra note on the cover communicating Johnson's desire that there be "no revelation of [the estimate's] existence to unauthorized persons" because of "the extreme sensitivity of the information therein."[75]

Helms's caution was well advised. This estimate, combined with Soviet ABM deployment around Moscow, shattered the optimistic assumptions that McNamara had used to underpin his case against missile defense. The Soviets could no longer be considered as seeking an assured destruction capability comfortably below numerical parity with the United States, but were instead pushing for equality, if not superiority, in numbers of ICBMs. This was clear to Secretary of State Dean Rusk. Writing to the secretary of defense, Rusk implied McNamara might be guilty of identifying excessively with the Soviet strategic predicament. While admitting that he did "not think the situation of mutual deterrence has changed fundamentally" as a result of the recent buildup, he did "think we ought to consider whether the Soviets will assess the situation as we do." Rusk also recognized the damage that the announcement of a Soviet ABM deployment had done to the administration's policy of a unilateral freeze on new weapons systems. This revelation had served to "place the matter in a new perspective," because it would increase "congressional and public pressures to begin an ABM deployment ourselves."[76]

If McNamara's assumptions had been fundamentally undermined by the Soviet buildup, Moscow's deployment of an ABM represented the immediate symbolic challenge to American superiority, to which the United States would be under increasing pressure to respond. Deputy Secretary of Defense Cyrus Vance concurred, writing to Johnson that "the first reaction of most Americans will be in favor of an immediate start on deployment, if for no other reason than the Soviets are deploying an ABM system."[77]

Congressional pressure was building, helped by increasingly public interventions from the JCS. In 1965 the chiefs moved toward a position in favor of ABM deployment by pushing in Congress for advanced preparation for full production of the system.[78] As evidence of the Soviet buildup began to mount in 1965, Senator Strom Thurmond (R-SC) pilloried the Johnson administration for pursuing a cost-conscious nuclear strategy on the assumption that the Soviet Union would not challenge American nuclear superiority, derisively renaming the administration's approach "How to succeed in military preparedness without really trying."[79] As the Soviet buildup continued, the Republicans began warning of a new "ABM gap"—a charge that could be used to underscore how the Democrats' faulty assumptions regarding the Soviet Union had put the country in danger, much as Kennedy had done with Eisenhower in 1960. The Republican National Committee had produced a research paper, which Nathaniel Davis of the NSC staff feared "could provide valuable background for a more slashing political attack." According to Republican research, the "cost-accounting" rationale against missile defense was just a facade for the real problem: Kennedy's ill-advised conclusion of the LTBT meant that the United States could not know if ABM warheads would work because they could not be detonated in the atmosphere. The Soviets, the paper argued, could have already finished these tests in the early sixties and be well ahead. The "nuclear détente" between the superpowers, the GOP held, was a product of wishful thinking, not hardheaded analysis, and had put American security in jeopardy.[80] In this way, missile defense had the potential to be used as a tool for a more wide-ranging attack on the Kennedy-Johnson post-1963 nuclear agenda, not least because its charge of excessive optimism was broadly on target.

Whereas another individual may have conceded the fallacy of his strategic framework, McNamara dug in. Rather than reexamine his assumptions, McNamara responded to the Soviet challenge by deepening his identification with the USSR's dilemma as he saw it. Defending his force postures in his November 1966 budget memorandum on nuclear forces, he not only assumed Soviet commitment to assured destruction, but actively argued from both the American and the Soviet point of view. Under increasing pressure from the chiefs for further augmentation of US offensive and defensive measures, McNamara claimed that projected Soviet forces might not even be capable of a truly convincing assured destruction capability against the US threat if one was "evaluating the Soviet assured destruction capability with extreme conservatism, as a Soviet planner might do"—in other words, as a Soviet McNamara might do. If the Soviets operated under significant budgetary constraints and wanted to maintain their assured destruction capability through hardening, dispersal, or mobile ICBMs, then "they would have to reduce their spending on ABM" or multiple warheads and so could not develop a significant first-strike threat to American forces.[81] In arguing for maintaining the cap on American forces in the face of growing evidence that the assumptions underpinning his argument had been wrong, the secretary of defense looked across the gulf between the two superpowers and saw a Soviet McNamara looking back at him. After he failed to secure a unilateral cap on American arms, the secretary of defense would try to reach out to this hypothetical figure in order to halt the deployment of an American missile defense system.

The Soviet buildup and ABM deployment came at an extremely difficult time for the secretary of defense as he wrestled with the military
over the wisdom of continued aerial bombardment of North Vietnam.[82]
Regardless of the sincerity of the Johnson administration's bombing
pause lasting from December 25, 1965 to January 31, 1966, its failure,
combined with additional disputes over the wisdom of bombing North
Vietnamese fuel depots, further cemented the chiefs' belief that, despite
the elegance of his analyses, McNamara's military judgment was poor.
The men in uniform sincerely worried that just as McNamara's dovish
assumptions regarding the North Vietnamese could lose them South
Vietnam, so his assured destruction thesis could cede military advantage
to the Soviets. In the words of McNamara's biographer Deborah Shapley,
"by the fall of 1966 . . . the military's drive for ABM deployment became a
litmus test of whether men in uniform could ever win against 'monarch'
McNamara."[83]

In order to do so, the chiefs went to Congress, forming a united position in favor of the deployment of a $20 billion anti-Soviet ABM defense.
In this they enjoyed the support of Richard Russell, who led the charge
for ABM by securing "strong backing in the Armed Services Committees
of both houses." The House and the Senate voted $167.9 million to speed
up research and procure components, thereby cutting the time needed to
deploy a missile defense by a year. Faced with criticisms from Republicans,
key Democratic defense hawks, and the Joint Chiefs regarding the administration's strategic defense policy, the onus was on Johnson and McNamara
to react.[84]

Matters came to a head in early December 1966 during a meeting at the
LBJ Ranch on the FY 1968 defense budget. Chairman of the Joint Chiefs
Earle Wheeler postulated that ABM deployment was preferable to doing
nothing because Soviet reactions could not be predicted, an argument
borne out by erroneous intelligence assessments. Instead, Wheeler argued,
it was best to assume the worst. Employing the Kennedy administration's
rhetoric of superiority against its successor, Wheeler argued that with
ABM the United States would be able "to maintain the kind of favorable
power environment which helped us during the Cuba [sic] missile crisis."
Given the extent to which the Democrats' credibility as nuclear custodi-
ans had been burnished by the crisis, this threat had clear implications for
Johnson. The international repercussions, the chiefs argued, could be just
as calamitous. Chief of Staff of the Air Force General John McConnell put
the chiefs' position regarding the Soviets in the crudest terms: "General

McConnell said he can't forget that we are dealing with the descendants of Genghis Khan. They only understand force."[85]

In the face of military pressure McNamara fell back on previously prepared positions. The chiefs were pushing for a 25-city defense against the Soviet Union. In response, McNamara and his deputy, Cyrus Vance, suggested a system primarily directed against China. Instead of arguing for the Chinese rationale as a means to postpone deployment, they now presented it as a low-cost alternative to a full anti-Soviet ABM. A Chinese ABM geared toward shielding American cities would cost $4–5 billion.[86] This was less than half of the chiefs' very optimistic estimate for their preferred system and considerably below the $20 to 40 billion that McNamara told Johnson it would eventually cost as the program gained momentum.[87] The anti-China ABM would also have a secondary function of protecting a portion of American Minuteman missiles from a Soviet strike; there would even be a very "limited" period when it could save 20 or 30 million Americans from Soviet attack. Thus, Vance argued, a small system "would draw the teeth of much of the argument that the Soviets have a defense and we do not." While there was a "substantial majority" in Congress in favor of deployment, Vance told Johnson, there was not a clear consensus on what kind of system the United States should build. A system primarily directed against China but with a limited anti-Soviet capability, Vance argued, could be an acceptable compromise between doing nothing, leaving Johnson open to charges of an ABM gap, and expending vast resources on an anti-Soviet missile defense.[88]

At the same time, the civilian leadership at Defense held out the prospect of arms control through bilateral agreement. Deployment of an anti-Chinese system, Vance pressed, should be "coupled with talks with the Soviet Union, seeking to reach an understanding with respect to the further deployment of both ABMs and offensive missiles."[89] Having failed to impose a unilateral cap on American arms, McNamara and his deputy now advocated reaching out to the USSR.

McNamara and Vance were backed by a substantial sector of scientific opinion. At a January 1967 meeting, chairman of the President's Science Advisory Committee, and president of MIT, James Killian, endorsed the Defense Department's recommendation for a thin ABM as a "first step," but only if political considerations demanded it. Former PSAC member George Kistiakowsky was even more adamant, believing that the ABM should not be deployed at all, because any construction would mean "all hope would be lost" for arms control between the superpowers. All the scientists present recommended against deployment of a thick system preferred by the Joint Chiefs, because it would not work and would simply accelerate the arms race, while advocating "a diplomatic effort to persuade the Soviet Union to stand down" from its own ABM.[90]

Yet to stand pat by keeping ABM in research and development seemed domestically unsustainable. After their meeting with the science advisors, McNamara admitted to Johnson that "it would be a hell of a political crisis" if the president refused ABM deployment outright; the secretary of defense predicted that congressmen "would absolutely crucify" him and, as a result Johnson, if the secretary of defense went to the Hill "with nothing."[91] Johnson summed it up in his inimitable way. "I'm not defending this country from any Soviet missiles at all and [the Soviets] are deploying theirs already," Johnson told Federal Reserve Chairman William McChesney Martin, Jr., "and I don't believe you can live politically in this country if the people think you won't . . . make any plans to defend them."[92]

Johnson was certainly vulnerable to the "ABM gap" charge, but this was not the only issue on his mind. By this time it became increasingly likely that his decision to fund both the Great Society and Vietnam without a tax increase would spur inflation. In this context Johnson saw missile defense as unnecessary additional expenditure that he could well do without. "We've had the greatest increase nearly in budget history this year from [$] 99 [billion] last year to 113," Johnson complained to his old congressional colleague and chairman of the House Defense Appropriations Subcommittee, George Mahon (D-TX), in August 1966, "That's a hell of a jump." The optimism two years earlier regarding the United States' ability to sustain the defense of the free world without an adverse effect on domestic programs was now flagging. "Inflation is gonna go through this roof," Johnson predicted, if appropriations were not brought under control. "They say that of all the boondoggles," the president complained, ABM was "the most unexplainable."[93] These concerns continued to weigh on Johnson's mind as he made his final decision on ABM deployment in January 1967. "All the Joint Chiefs . . . say you've got to go all the way and the quicker the better and forty billion," Johnson griped to Senator Everett Dirksen (R-IL) after his meeting with his science advisors.[94]

As well as easing budgetary pressures, arms control also had the potential to galvanize his faltering support within the Democratic Party.[95] As the Vietnam War widened without any prospect of victory, a number of senior Democrats revolted, with J. William Fulbright, chairman of the Senate Foreign Relations Committee, denouncing the cornerstone of LBJ's foreign policy in televised hearings in February 1966.[96] Johnson had begun to sell Fulbright on a US–Soviet rapprochement in the autumn of that year, telling him he was pushing for a new round of diplomacy with the USSR to build on the consular agreement, signed in June 1964, and burgeoning nonproliferation negotiations. Johnson emphasized how he had told Soviet Foreign Minister Andrei Gromyko that: "I want to visit your country . . . I want to know your people. I'm not afraid of you and I don't think you ought to be afraid of me . . . there's no reason why we ought to keep all the world feeling that we're going to blow it up because I'm not going to—I don't think you're going to."[97] The president hoped that such an understanding could be used as the basis for more formal agreements that could rehabilitate his tarnished reputation.

It was not only dovish Democrats who saw Johnson going off the rails. Without referring to Vietnam by name, Henry Owen of the State Department Policy Planning Council wrote to Rostow in the summer of 1966 complaining of a general impression amongst academics, journalists, and politicians that the administration was in "a 'Cold War' rut, trying to defend indefensible positions." This was perceived as "a tired administration, lacking 'imagination' in foreign policy." Owen argued that the White House needed a new initiative "to dramatize our constructive goal—the building of a viable world order." Linking a great stride in this direction to Johnson's domestic reforms, Owen explained how "The genius of the Great Society was that it used positive domestic goals to replace waning fear of the Great Depression as the main motive in getting acceptance of domestic reforms. So, in the field of foreign policy, we must fix public attention on our constructive purposes, to replace a waning fear of external attack."[98]

While vulnerable to criticism from the right for weakness in the face of communist aggression, the administration in the wake of Vietnam was increasingly unable to rely on the Soviet threat as a way to galvanize liberals behind its national security policy.[99] Rostow reiterated this to Johnson. According to the national security advisor, the administration needed to hammer home that it was "on the way to solving great national and international problems" and "making progress." The overall message to the American people, Rostow argued, should be "let's stick together and see it through."[100] Arms control offered the prospect of a unifying theme for the Democrats that could result in tangible progress in international affairs and cut defense spending at a time when fiscal restraint was sorely needed. If handled correctly by preserving an American edge in nuclear arms, it would not necessarily denote weakness toward the Soviets.

MAD WAS A FACT AND A POLICY

By late 1966, Lyndon Johnson's partnership with his secretary of defense to slow the American buildup in nuclear arms was under severe pressure.

McNamara's political skills had been as central as Johnson's to this effort. The secretary of defense used his renowned facility with numbers to tie down the American missile defense program in a range of different ways. In doing so, he showed a keen grasp of politics—be it American budgetary conservatism, the widespread aversion to fallout shelters, or Sino-phobia.

The Johnson-McNamara partnership's policy toward ABM between 1963 and 1966 also sheds new light on the emergence of the doctrine of assured destruction, later pilloried as mutual assured destruction or MAD. During the 1970s, MAD was attacked by its opponents as an immoral and strategically flawed acceptance of superpower parity on behalf of the détente-era administrations; its proponents, including McNamara, responded that MAD "was not a policy at all," but "a grim fact of life"—a phrase famously picked up by Robert Jervis when he argued that "MAD is a fact, not a policy."[101] MAD was a fact—Kennedy's caution over Cuba the face of Soviet nuclear inferiority testified to that. But it was also a policy during the 1960s, inasmuch as it was developed and advocated by McNamara, in service of Johnson's domestic agenda, and against the US military's desire to move further with its offensive buildup and deploy an ABM system.

Unlike the 1970s, however, MAD was not initially an acceptance of numerical superpower parity. In pointing to the futility of further nuclear building after both sides secured a second strike capability, MAD was an argument that supported freezing the strategic status quo at any particular moment. In the mid-1960s that status quo was a formidable American superiority in the quantity and quality of nuclear weapons. McNamara instituted assured destruction in order to place caps on the deployment of new offensive and defensive missiles, but in a way that posited the Soviet acceptance of a permanently inferior status on the basis of its smaller economic potential to satisfy both military and consumer needs. In doing so, McNamara freed up resources for Johnson's Great Society programs and, increasingly, the war in Vietnam.

MAD was thus an instrument of Johnson's domestic as much as his international agenda. Unfortunately for both the president and his secretary of defense, McNamara's force structure was built on optimistic assumptions regarding Soviet strategic behavior that proved manifestly false within a few years of their promulgation. The Soviet Union's nuclear buildup undid McNamara's attempt to reconcile unilateral caps in nuclear spending with continued superiority.

Yet the Johnson-McNamara partnership still had one more card to play. Sensing the opportunity that arms negotiations offered, the president authorized an exploratory meeting on the topic between Ambassador Llewellyn Thompson and Soviet Ambassador to the United States Anatoly

Dobrynin, which took place on December 6, 1966.[102] In his January 1967 budget message, Johnson announced that he would pursue arms limitation talks with the Soviet Union. There would be "no action now" on ABM, but the president announced that he would put aside $375 million for deployment in case talks with the Soviets did not come to fruition.[103] All hopes now rested on persuading the Soviet Union of the logic of assured destruction. If it was convinced, the USSR would agree to an arms limitation accord that would enable the United States to forego a costly ABM deployment while at the same time hewing toward the strong domestic consensus behind the United States' nuclear edge.

CHAPTER 3

First Steps toward SALT, 1966–1969

From early December 1966, the United States government took the initiative to come to terms with the Soviet Union on a limit to both offensive and defensive nuclear weapons systems. This effort lasted right up until Lyndon Johnson's final days in office.

In one sense, Johnson's tentative efforts at bilateral arms control with the Soviet Union provides a counterbalance for a presidency that even today still struggles to emerge from the shadow of Vietnam. It is true that, through these early talks with the Soviets, as well as through the conclusion of the Non-Proliferation Treaty in 1968, Johnson bridged the period from the Limited Test Ban Treaty of 1963 to the Strategic Arms Limitation Talks (SALT) of the Nixon presidency. Without Johnson's attempts to come to terms on strategic arms, Nixon would never have been able to move so far, and so fast, with the Soviets.[1]

Yet there is another side to the Johnson-McNamara approach to nuclear arms control. In many ways, in its attempts to freeze US superiority in offensive forces, it was a reaction to the failure of existing policies in a way that attempted to salvage the strategic status quo.[2] Over the three years prior to initial soundings in December 1966, Robert McNamara had attempted to reconcile a unilateral cap on nuclear weapons with a commitment to rational superiority. By late 1966 McNamara's elaborate strategic framework had almost collapsed. The Soviets had shown themselves to be willing and able to make the sacrifices necessary to challenge US nuclear dominance in a way that upended McNamara's postulates regarding Soviet commitment to a small assured destruction force. At its heart, Johnson's attempts at a bilateral strategic arms accord sought to persuade the Soviets to halt their buildup, thereby preserving the American nuclear dominance that had been at the heart of containment since the late 1940s. This was not a completely new approach, but an attempt to freeze the existing balance that was quickly slipping into history.

In trying to find a new way to achieve arms control without jeopardizing rational superiority, Johnson's approach to the Soviets looked as much to past American predominance as to a new era of détente. It was an attempt to halt the arms race, but on terms that would salvage American nuclear superiority by freezing its predominance in launchers in place. In doing so, it embodied the assumptions that had underpinned McNamara's discredited strategic framework in which the smaller size of the USSR's economy would automatically translate into strategic nuclear inferiority. While Johnson's moves to open a bilateral dialogue on strategic weapons were a step forward, they therefore nevertheless reflected a commitment to upholding the existing order of globalized containment underwritten by American nuclear predominance.

The Johnson administration's approach to strategic arms limitation also illustrated the centrality of the domestic politics of rational superiority. Impelled to reach out to the Soviets to head off congressional pressure for an ABM system, American officials looked over their shoulders as they talked to the USSR, understanding that an agreement to freeze nuclear parity would be politically untenable. By the end of Johnson's presidency, the solid public and congressional consensus behind that policy was beginning to unravel, but not to the extent that would make a bilateral arms control accord on strategic offensive and defensive weapons possible. As with its commitment to South Vietnam, the Johnson administration found itself caught between two impulses: on the one hand, the desire to withdraw from an overextended position, in this case nuclear superiority, that was becoming increasingly untenable; on the other, the unwillingness to bear the domestic political costs of reaching a settlement on terms acceptable to the adversary.

ORIGINS

The Johnson administration's attempts to freeze American nuclear superiority through an arms control agreement stretched back to almost the beginning of LBJ's time in the White House. The president had called for "a verified freeze" on offensive and defensive arms as early as January 1964, in his address to the Eighteen Nation Disarmament Conference in Geneva.[3] In late 1963 US analysts predicted that by mid-1964 the Soviet

Union would have between 205 and 235 ICBMs, most of which would be located above ground on "soft" launching sites and therefore vulnerable to an American first strike. By contrast, the United States would boast six hundred Minutemen, all of which would be underground in concrete silos.[4] It was not immediately obvious to some of America's allies what could motivate the Soviets to freeze this vast disparity in strategic striking power. British Prime Minister Sir Alec Douglas-Home questioned the grounds on which the Soviets would agree to such an arrangement in a meeting with US Secretary of State Dean Rusk in February 1964.[5]

The reasoning behind American optimism regarding the possibility of a freeze was the same as that which supported McNamara's assured destruction thesis. Rusk responded that the Soviet Union would accept a numerically inferior assured destruction force because of "the expense" of an extended arms race with the United States.[6] The CIA judged that slowing economic growth would increase the pressure for diversion of capital away from military to civilian sectors of the economy. In the CIA's judgment, "the Kremlin leadership . . . [had] been trying to do too much with too few resources."[7] The Soviet Union could not challenge US strategic superiority if it wanted to raise the living standards of its population.

In the early years of the Johnson administration, American resources appeared limitless: in the opinion of the CIA Directorate of Intelligence, the United States could produce 1,000 Minutemen (the entire force eventually built) per year if the Soviet Union opted for a race to nuclear parity. In this context, the CIA argued, the Soviets were likely to see arms control as a golden opportunity to "deprive the United States of an important inherent advantage: greater [economic] *potential* for strengthening its military power."[8] Freeze negotiations would therefore be attractive to the USSR as a means by which to ensure the missile gap did not widen to its detriment. The Soviets would therefore choose an assured destruction force, safe in the knowledge that they would be able to obliterate American society in a second strike. Rusk pointed out to Sir Alec Douglas-Home in 1964 that "the Russians have a deterrent now."[9] Given the size of their economic base and the certainty that they would be able to kill millions of Americans in retaliation, the Soviet Union could afford to accept quantitative inferiority.

When the Johnson administration began to put out feelers for talks with Moscow at the end of 1966, the assumption that the Russians lacked the economic resources to compete with the United States and had therefore accepted the doctrine of assured destruction was under pressure. The upswing in Soviet ICBM construction suggested that the Kremlin would not simply concede the nuclear arms race of its own volition. There was mounting evidence that the Soviet leadership was willing to forego the benefits of increased consumption in order to realign the strategic balance, just at the point when the Johnson administration was struggling to reconcile the country's own military burden with its domestic agenda. By early 1967, the United States had 450,000 troops in South Vietnam, with calls for more. Despite McNamara's attempts to keep Pentagon outlays under control, the costs of Vietnam added to a significant jump in Great Society programs such as Medicaid, Medicare, Social Security, and federal aid to education, resulting in a deficit that climbed from $3.7 billion in FY 1966 to $8.64 billion in FY 1967. In the same budget message in which he proposed arms talks with the Soviets, LBJ put forward plans for a record-breaking $172.4 billion in federal government spending. This was up from $112.8 billion the previous year, to which had been added an additional $10 billion for Vietnam. While the midterm elections of November 1966 had not resulted in a complete wipeout for liberal Democrats, they had returned a significantly more conservative Congress that would be far more hostile to big increases in spending or a tax hike to pay for it.[10] Rather than the Soviet Union, it appeared that the United States was the country that was reaching breaking point under the twin demands for social and national security.

As their prior machinations regarding the budget illustrate, Johnson and McNamara had never been keen on testing their potential to produce one thousand Minutemen per year. Such instincts were now reinforced by the desire to contain military expenditures as the costs of the Vietnam War spiraled out of control. The balance of incentives that suggested the Soviets would agree to a freeze that codified their inferiority was shifting to the United States' disadvantage.

Nevertheless, most of Johnson's advisors believed that the offer of a freeze to the Russians was worth a shot. The alternative to negotiations was the immediate construction of an extremely expensive ABM system of dubious military effectiveness. Such a deployment would likely spark an arms race that would prove deleterious to both the United States' fiscal situation and US–Soviet relations. Nicholas Katzenbach, Rusk's deputy at the State Department, had "no substantial doubt" that the Soviet Union would respond to any US ABM deployment in order to reassert its ability to destroy American society in a second strike, a judgment that was shared by Rostow and the CIA.[11] Chances of an accord may have been slim, but it was far preferable to the immediate launch of a new round of the arms race.

Although the Soviet Union had made clear its intention to narrow the gap with the United States in intercontinental forces, some advisers still held out hope that an accommodation could be reached between the two superpowers that safeguarded American nuclear superiority. Despite recent developments in the strategic balance, Deputy Under Secretary of State

Foy D. Kohler reiterated the pre-buildup argument that the economic facts of life favored the United States. According to Kohler, this meant that "the Soviets would not necessarily seek parity in offensive forces." The USSR, Kohler pointed out, was struggling with a military budget four-fifths that of the Pentagon's while at the same time trying to provide a better standard of living for the general population, all on the basis of an economy just half that of the US. If the Americans were in economic difficulties, then the Soviets' problems were presumably even more acute.[12]

The Americans' reading of the post-Khrushchev collective leadership reinforced the belief that the Soviets might still be open to an accommodation. While the victory for civilian technocrats was not as decisive as had been inferred in 1964, the US intelligence community still judged that the Politburo was finely balanced between hardline supporters of Soviet military industry and civilian doves who wished to effect a shift of resources toward consumer goods. In finalizing the 1966 to 1970 five-year plan, the Kremlin had essentially pushed for a great increase in agricultural output, coupled with major economic reforms and a growth in Soviet military capability. The US intelligence community predicted that such a duality in Soviet economic policy would ultimately prove unsustainable, producing tension within the leadership.[13] Strangely, divisions in the Soviet government mirrored Johnson's own predicament as he sought to reconcile his domestic program with ballooning military expenditures. By reaching out to the Soviets, the CIA suggested that the Johnson administration could indirectly strengthen the possibility of future "internal liberalization" of the Soviet Union by heading off a new round of competition between military and civilian sectors of the USSR's command economy.[14]

INITIAL APPROACHES

Some Johnson administration officials believed themselves fortunate that their main Soviet interlocutor would be Chairman of the Council of Ministers Alexei Kosygin. Kosygin, as head of the Soviet government, was both a major instigator of managerial reform of the Soviet economy and formally responsible for foreign relations with capitalist states.[15] Johnson made an official approach to Kosygin on January 21, 1967, stating his desire to enter negotiations with the Soviet Union. From the outset the president attempted to make common cause with the chairman, explaining that he felt "great pressures from members of the Congress and from public opinion" to initiate deployment of an antiballistic missile system. Johnson underlined his understanding that were the United States to significantly augment its offensive forces, "you would in turn feel under compulsion to do likewise," with little gain in security for either side. The president highlighted the "colossal costs" of such a new arms race and urged dialogue to head it off.[16] The tone was one that emphasized the commonality of interest of two men who were far more interested in domestic economic development than the abstruse calculations of nuclear deterrence.

The Soviet reaction was not encouraging. In early February Kosygin visited London, where the British probed him on his views along lines sketched out by the White House. The Soviet premier reacted sharply to their questioning, describing McNamara's arguments regarding the cost effectiveness of missile defense as "obscurantism and misanthropy," questioning the value of a "philosophy . . . that concerned itself with killing people in the cheapest possible way." According to the British, Kosygin told them that "any child" knew that offensive weapons were cheaper than ABMs, but this was not a sufficient basis on which to devise a military strategy.[17] He repeated the essence of his private comments during a press conference, denouncing the idea that ABM could upset the nuclear balance and reiterating standard Soviet calls for total nuclear disarmament.[18]

When Johnson's newly appointed ambassador to the Soviet Union, Llewellyn "Tommy" Thompson, approached Kosygin directly, the Soviet premier reacted strongly to Thompson's framing of the issue in terms of the ruinous costs of missile defense. Repeating his accusations that the Americans wanted to approach the issue in terms of how "it is cheaper to kill," Kosygin emphasized that it would be "important to discuss the entire complex of [the] problem," though he did not make clear exactly what this meant.[19] In his oral response to Johnson's letter, Foreign Minister Andrei Gromyko argued that the two superpowers should "seek equally to ensure the security of each side rather than attempt to solidify such a correlation of forces as this or that party regards at a given moment to be advantageous to it."[20] Left implied was that the current "correlation of forces" favored the United States to an extent unacceptable to the Soviet Union. The Kremlin expressed a desire to continue exchanges by letter, but affirmed only that it did not explicitly rule out the possibility of direct negotiations on the issue at a future date.[21]

The Soviet government's attitude prompted those with most experience of the Eastern Bloc to voice their objections to the foreign-policy principals. Foy Kohler, recently returned from a stint in Moscow as US ambassador, told McNamara that in his view Kosygin's reaction was "perfectly predictable." The Soviet premier, Kohler pointed out, "was serving notice" on some important points of the USSR's policy, including their commitment to the Moscow ABM and the value they attached to readdressing the current strategic balance.[22] NSC staffer on Soviet and East European affairs Nathaniel Davis believed that Soviet dedication to a level approaching parity in nuclear arms made it "hard" for him "to believe that we could agree to reduce our offensive weapon advantage to the point necessary to achieve Soviet agreement." Johnson's Soviet experts were suggesting that the USSR's desire for nuclear parity could not be reconciled with the White House's avowed commitment to continued US superiority. Neither Kohler nor Davis advocated breaking off talks given the highly costly and ineffective alternative of ABM deployment. However, Davis warned that the United States "should go into this negotiation without illusions" regarding its likely success.[23] Kohler advocated the presentation of a concrete proposal to the Soviets in order to facilitate talks.[24]

Despite these misgivings at the working level, those at the top remained more optimistic regarding the reconciliation of American and Soviet worldviews. McNamara believed that the Soviets simply did not understand the consequences of their refusal to talk, telling Kohler that he entertained "some doubts that the Russians really understood what our offensive buildup would be like." He offered to go to Geneva to talk to Soviet arms control officials in the hope that he could convince them of the merits of his case.[25] In contrast to Davis and Kohler's preference for a concrete proposal, McNamara desired a meeting of minds during which he could persuade the Soviets of his views regarding the essential dynamics of the strategic arms race. This was a classic McNamara gambit: by indoctrinating the executive branch, Congress, and the American public into the world of systems analysis and cost-effectiveness, he had managed to guide American policy from a buildup to a unilateral freeze. Now he wanted to do the same to the Soviets.

GLASSBORO

McNamara's chance to press his case came in the immediate aftermath of the Six Day War between Israel, Egypt, Syria, and Jordan. Kosygin planned to make a speech to the United Nations in New York in support of the USSR's defeated Arab allies. Preparations for the US–Soviet meeting were hasty and the list of topics was both long and complex. Until the last minute Kosygin maintained publicly that he would only visit the UN and would not meet with the US president, which provoked Johnson's ire. "There's not gonna anything come [sic] from just two men talking unless both of them are willing to and ready to," the president complained to Senate Foreign Relations Committee Chairman J. William Fulbright. Johnson worried that the Americans were being too welcoming, leaving Kosygin with the idea that the president would do almost anything to meet with him. He was adamant that he would not stoop to going up to New York to meet with Kosygin. Comparing himself to a "girl" in a "red light district," Johnson suggested to Fulbright that he should play harder to get in order to entice the premier to meet him somewhere between Washington, DC, and New York.[26] Eventually the two sides settled on Glassboro State College in New Jersey.

Although the Americans were anxious for direct talks at the highest level, arms control was a distant third to two more immediately pressing issues: the Arab-Israeli conflict and Vietnam. Johnson was too realistic to believe that the two sides could come to overall agreements on so many issues at such short notice. Consequently, he tried to play down expectations. "I don't think that much is gonna come out of it," he told Senate Minority Leader Everett Dirksen. Yet Johnson also harbored the feeling that he could persuade Kosygin of American good intentions. "We're hoping that when he gets through talking to us, that he'll see that we're not going to gobble him up . . . now we don't know that that has any chance, but that's the best thing that has a chance from what [U.S. Ambassador] Thompson's been saying to him through the months." The president struck a characteristically optimistic note on the potential for personal chemistry between the two leaders. "I think I can get along with him all right," he told Fulbright, "I got along with Khrushchev all right."[27]

The American pitch to the Soviets on strategic arms combined Johnson's interpersonal skills with McNamara's analytical prowess. The president laid it on thick at the opening meeting, asking how many siblings Kosygin had. When the chairman answered that he had just one sister, Johnson "remarked that he was one of five children in his family." The United States and Soviet Union were like "the oldest brother . . . and the oldest sister" who had a responsibility "to avoid disputes and differences between them so as to set a good example to the other children in the family." One way they could do so would be to divert scarce resources away from the arms race, so that the "40 or 50 billion dollars on an ABM system" could be spent on "the peaceful development of our country."[28]

While Johnson handled the broad issues of war, peace, and economic development, he left his secretary of defense to tackle the military-technical specifics. Unfortunately for McNamara, who had prepared a detailed presentation of the issues, complete with classified charts, Johnson decided to broach the topic over lunch on the first day of the summit. The defense secretary had to launch into an impromptu exposition of the superpower arms race while the other guests tucked into their food.[29] Nevertheless, he managed to communicate his main points: missile defense was technologically inadequate and would simply push up the costs of the arms race, "which had already gone beyond all reason" to the superpowers' mutual detriment. Making his pitch for direct negotiations, McNamara told the chairman that he "hoped that this process could be stopped by discussing the entire range of problems whether in Moscow or in Washington or in both places."[30]

Neither Johnson's charisma nor McNamara's data appeared to make much headway with Kosygin. It is evident that the president and the chairman failed to connect. At one point, Johnson tried to lighten the mood by telling an anecdote about the writer Charles Lamb. Noting that Lamb could never dislike someone he knew, "the president expressed his view that . . . in getting to know each other better, they were also getting to like each other." Kosygin did not reciprocate such feelings of amity, instead repeating his views on the impossibility of halting arms shipments to the Middle East.[31] "Each time I mentioned missiles, Kosygin talked about Arabs and Israelis," Johnson complained in his memoirs.[32]

Kosygin gave little away in response to McNamara's presentation on strategic arms, but the Americans were unimpressed by what they heard. Kosygin questioned the utility of arms control negotiations, because McNamara "advocated a limitation of the development of defensive weapons while continuing the development of offensive weapons," despite the repeated assurances by the Americans present that they would negotiate on both.[33] More infuriating for the US side, it appeared that Kosygin failed to engage with the idea that defensive systems could upset the delicate balance of terror between the two superpowers. Kosygin maintained that Soviet ABMs were purely defensive and so posed no threat to the other side, at one point shouting, "Defense is moral, aggression is immoral!"[34] McNamara later dismissed Kosygin's remarks as "propagandistic."[35] In Rusk's view, Kosygin's attitude betrayed "the naiveté of the first look"—the chairman was simply ignorant of nuclear strategy.[36] Johnson was disappointed. "He just played the same old broken record in private that he did in public," he told Dwight D. Eisenhower. The president tried to put on a brave face. "I think that when he gets back he'll probably set a date [for talks], but he didn't assure me of that. . . . I think that he thinks we're not wild men." Eisenhower was not convinced: "They talk a little bit . . . but . . . I've seen no yielding yet."[37]

Part of the gap was indeed intellectual. As two senior Soviet arms control functionaries Aleksandr Savel'yev and Nikolai Detinov tell it, "notions such as 'strategic stability,' 'nuclear deterrence,' and so on, were, at that time, still foreign to the Soviet leadership." The Kremlin had not reached a firm view regarding the contribution that missile defense could make to the strategic balance. The roots of this were institutional: the Soviet military still dominated nuclear weapons policy to an extent that their counterparts in the United States would have envied. There were few civilian defense intellectuals in the Soviet Union. There was no bureaucracy dedicated to talks on the model of the United States' Arms Control and Disarmament Agency, and the Ministry of Foreign Affairs was barred from knowing most military secrets. The military-industrial complex was, according to Soviet defense thinker Georgii Arbatov, "a state within a state." From what has emerged since the end of the Cold War, it appears as though the military conceived of nuclear war as something to be "won," which served to justify far greater expenditure on antiaircraft and antimissile defenses.[38] This commitment was evident in the Soviet armed forces' structure and budget: The defense of the Soviet Union from aerial and missile attack had its own arm of service, the National Air Defense forces (*Protivovozdushnaia Oborona (PVO) Strany*). As McNamara told Johnson in December 1966, Soviet expenditure on defensive arms was "two or three times" that of the United States.[39]

Those few Soviets who attempted to break through the Soviet military's monopoly on national security questions were rebuffed. In the summer of 1967, just after the Glassboro Summit, Andrei Sakharov, a nuclear weapons researcher, wrote to Second Secretary Mikhail Suslov on behalf of a wider group of scientists in his institute, laying out the case against Soviet attempts to build a nationwide missile defense system and in favor of what he termed a "moratorium" on deployment. In terms very similar to those employed by McNamara, Sakharov argued that missile defense systems were prohibitively expensive, approximately "three to ten times" more than the equivalent offensive forces required to defeat them. He also disagreed with Kosygin's public statements that ABMs were defensive and not therefore destabilizing, pointing out that such systems could increase the incentives on the side that possessed them for a preventive strike, even if the belief that an ABM could protect the country might in fact be "an illusion." Permanent vulnerability through the prohibition of missile defenses would outlaw the potential for a preemptive strike by either side and thus "be a clear demonstration of [of the two superpowers'] willingness to coexist."[40]

Sakharov also appeared to accept the Americans' argument that the Soviet Union's economy could not sustain a competition in ABM technology. Not only was US economic per-capita output approximately two-and-a-half times larger than the USSR's, Sakharov posited, but "the output of electronic computers" in the United States was approximately "15 to 30" times greater than in the Soviet Union. Yet Sakharov went further. Given this situation, Sakharov argued, a new arms race in offensive and defensive technology could only be to the USSR's detriment and perhaps leave the Soviet Union "almost totally disarmed" if the United States combined significant first strike capabilities against Soviet nuclear forces with an effective ABM to absorb any retaliation. In order to prevent this, the Soviet Union would probably have to place great resources into its offensive at the expense of its defensive systems, thereby "acting unilaterally almost as if such an agreement [to ban ABMs] existed." Far better, Sakharov concluded, would be to work out a treaty prohibiting missile defenses for both superpowers.[41]

Other developments appeared to back up Sakharov's argument. In August 1967, the Soviet General Staff and Military Industrial Commission ordered a committee to examine the practicality of Soviet ABM systems then in prospect, which, unlike the Moscow system, were being developed to protect the entire country. In October, the commission concluded that it was impossible to defend the USSR against a US strike. However, for reasons unknown, these conclusions were not shared with the Politburo and the momentum toward prohibition of ABM languished.[42] Sakharov's request to Suslov that he be allowed to publish a sanitized version of his conclusions through an interview in *Literaturnaia Gazeta*, in order to stimulate discussion between Soviet and American scientists on the ABM issue, was also refused.[43]

Kosygin at Glassboro was therefore the mouthpiece of a collective leadership in which the drive for nuclear parity stood as a matter of strong consensus. The Soviet leadership had rejected the American contention that the USSR's smaller economic base predetermined an inherently inferior military superstructure. In fact in the wake of Nikita Khrushchev's ouster the USSR's collective leadership decided to drive for quantitative nuclear parity with the United States. As the foremost historian of Soviet nuclear forces has outlined, the drive for parity was "the single largest weapons effort in Soviet history and the most expensive"—even more costly than Stalin's push to build the first Soviet atomic bomb after the Second World War. At the peak of the construction program in 1967, the Soviet Strategic Rocket Forces consumed almost a fifth of the USSR's defense budget and employed 650,000 people. Given the need for both technologically sophisticated material inputs and highly educated technicians to build and operate the missiles, the burden on the Soviet economy was probably even greater than these figures imply.[44]

The Soviet effort was based on a rejection of the Khrushchev-era nuclear strategy that had relied on audacious threats, backed by a relatively small force of intercontinental ballistic missiles. At the meeting that deposed him in October 1964, Khrushchev's colleagues chided the general secretary for gambling with "people's fates" in "a risky enterprise" during the Cuban crisis with little to show for it.[45] No longer would the Soviet Union initiate confrontations in order to change the situation in Central Europe or elsewhere. Thus, at the Twenty-Third Congress of the Communist Party of the Soviet Union held in March and April 1966, his first as general secretary, Leonid I. Brezhnev ruled out a policy of military confrontation in place of class struggle.[46] In the immediate aftermath of the Six Day War, in Brezhnev's address to the Central Committee, he underlined the Politburo's determination that the Soviet Union would do everything it could to resist a confrontation with other nuclear powers that could turn into a global war.[47]

This strategy would be underpinned by military power that would dissuade capitalist states from initiating a standoff with the Soviet Union.[48] In its assumption that the Soviet Union would be happy with a smaller assured destruction force, the American side misjudged the way in which the events of October 1962 had shaken the Soviet military and civilian leadership. While Kennedy and McNamara had felt their hands tied by the vast preponderance of military power at their disposal, the Soviets perceived themselves to have withdrawn from Cuba under the crushing weight of American nuclear superiority. Consequently, the new Soviet leadership operated under the influence of what Savel'yev and Detinov describe as a "Cuban missile crisis syndrome." The primary lesson of the crisis was that the Soviet Union should never place itself in a position of such strategic overstretch and nuclear vulnerability again. Put at its simplest by Savel'yev and Detinov, "The development of the Soviet strategic force to great measure paralleled that of the United States on the principle that, 'if the Americans have something, we should have it as well . . .'" despite the huge economic costs that such an approach imposed.[49]

By the time Johnson and Kosygin met at Glassboro the Soviet Union was two years into a Five Year Plan that enshrined the drive for parity with the United States at its heart. The reorganization of Soviet economic planning since the fall of Khrushchev had both reflected and promoted the formation of a cohesive military-industrial interest group within the Kremlin. Many of the prime movers in Khrushchev's ouster had strong links to the Soviet military-industrial complex: Brezhnev had been Central Committee secretary for military industry in the late 1950s and early 1960s; other powerful cheerleaders for military programs included Dmitri Ustinov, Central Committee secretary for defense, and Marshal Andrei Grechko, the chief of the general staff. Moreover, the collective leadership centralized missile construction into a powerful new Ministry for General Machine-Building, ensuring that the missile industry would have a minister through whom it could press its interests.[50] With such political and bureaucratic momentum behind the decision to drive for parity, it would have been impossible for

Kosygin to turn Soviet policy around even if he had wanted to. The idea of a fine balance between hawks and doves in the collective leadership was an American illusion.

Johnson believed Kosygin was "just a cold-blooded, hard-hearted, straight strictly business executive that's a good administrator."[51] On the contrary, Kosygin knew what he was talking about when he chided the secretary of defense that he "was not a military man, even though he was engaged in dealing with military matters."[52] Underneath the exterior of a 1960s Soviet technocrat, Kosygin carried with him the scars left by two catastrophically destructive conflicts. He had joined the Red Army in 1919 and served throughout the Russian Civil War. At the beginning of the Great Patriotic War he had played a key role in the removal of Soviet industrial plants from the western Soviet Union before doing the same in Leningrad at the height of the siege in 1942.[53] A witness to the destruction that the USSR's unpreparedness in 1941 had wrought, Kosygin unsurprisingly conceived of defense as "a moral problem" and believed McNamara's "commercial approach" to nuclear weapons based on cost-effectiveness calculations "was by its very nature invalid."[54] The chairman's experiences were extreme, but typical of a generation of Soviet leaders who had endured horrors unimaginable to their American interlocutors. As a result, "there were no doves" in the Politburo—and certainly no McNamaras.[55]

This aversion to talks was also underlined by wariness of American actions as opposed to US rhetoric. The chairman's comments were more astute than the Americans realized. McNamara's assurances that the United States was willing to negotiate on offensive as well as defensive weapons were belied by his pronouncements to Congress and the American public. Even if the Soviets were simply relying on open sources, they would have been able to discern the introduction of two new missiles into the American arsenal: the Minuteman III ICBM and Poseidon submarine-launched ballistic missile (SLBM). Although the details of these weapons were not public knowledge, McNamara had confirmed the existence of "multiple nuclear warheads" in February 1967.[56]

This system of multiple independently targetable re-entry vehicles (MIRVs), to be introduced on Minuteman III and Poseidon, had a number of military-technical advantages. By placing up to twelve warheads on top of one missile, MIRV had the potential to expand the American targeting capacity exponentially. As the technology was developed, MIRV also became increasingly accurate, bringing the potential to hit hardened targets such as ICBM silos. The Air Force was an enthusiastic proponent of MIRV on this basis. McNamara liked it for different reasons. It was a relatively cheap way to build up American offensive capacity compared to restarting production of single-warhead ICBMs and SLBM submarines. Most importantly, by presenting a huge number of incoming vehicles to Soviet radars, MIRV could overwhelm any Soviet missile defense system on the technological horizon. There would certainly be too many different targets for the Soviets' Moscow ABM system to handle. McNamara could therefore argue that the Moscow ABM presented no threat to American assured destruction capability and hence there was no reason to go ahead with an ABM to protect US cities against a Soviet strike.[57] It is clear from his comments that McNamara did not believe MIRV was necessary to defeat the Moscow ABM system; the current American arsenal would be sufficient against a missile defense a full generation behind American technology. As he told Johnson in December 1966, by going ahead with MIRV, the United States "had overreacted" and the Soviet ABM "was not worth a damn." Yet it was a domestic political necessity: the secretary of defense could ease the pressure for a US ABM from the military and Congress if he gave them MIRV.[58]

The decision to go ahead with MIRV represented the dilemmas at the heart of the Johnson administration's arms control policy. While the American side could pledge to work with the Soviets on limiting offensive weapons, actions to maintain the American edge were domestically essential. Dobrynin complained privately to former national security advisor McGeorge Bundy that "McNamara's constant assertions of massive superiority" made it difficult for the Kremlin to come to an arms control agreement with the United States. Bundy responded that the Soviets would have to understand that McNamara's public statements on superiority were "a normal necessity in [US] society."[59] The politics of preparedness that both Kennedy and Johnson had used so effectively to enhance their fortunes from the late 1950s onwards were turning against the incumbent president. By the spring of 1967, the Republicans had begun to attack Johnson's nuclear strategy as likely to cede the American quantitative advantage in arms. Nathaniel Davis judged that while there were many methods by which to calculate the strategic balance, "the public understands the facts in essentially one way—a three to one US superiority in missiles." As such, Davis argued, "the political problem will be greater if we reach agreement with the Russians than if we don't." The United States felt it had to do everything it could to maintain an American advantage. While the USSR had a generational obsession with 1941, the Americans, particularly Democrats, were fixated on their interpretation of 1945. Even if the Johnson administration accepted a treaty that merely enshrined the current trends toward parity, Davis warned, Johnson's opponents would portray it as "a nuclear Yalta."[60]

Given the significant domestic costs of parity, the Johnson White House was treading a fine line between preparing the US Congress and the public for a reduction in the extent of the American nuclear edge and reassuring its domestic constituency that it was still committed to maintaining an advantage. In the spring of 1967, McNamara began to build the case that the then-current US advantage was in fact "overkill." Even admitting this much, however, posed significant political risks. As the *Washington Post* noted, in addition to the possibility of further Republican attacks, such a stance would "require down playing the significance of the Pentagon's own advertisements about US nuclear superiority." Given the delicate political situation, administration officials were hesitant to indicate whether the United States would be willing to go as low as a "two-to-one" edge over Soviet forces, let alone parity.[61]

Both at Glassboro and his letters to Kosygin, Johnson attempted to level with the Soviet premier regarding the domestic forces pushing him to respond to the USSR's buildup. The Soviets, however, took Johnson's explanation as "an ultimatum."[62] Johnson and McNamara, by contrast, tried to describe these pressures as detached from human agency unless both sides intervened to stop it. The Soviets did not see it that way: the United States had been the first to build a commanding lead in ICBMs in the early 1960s to which, in their view, the USSR was simply reacting. The "ultimatum" was conceived thus: the Soviet Union would never gain nuclear parity with the United States. Either the USSR could accept the status quo through an arms accord, or the two sides could continue spending, with the USSR constantly playing catch-up. McNamara half-admitted as much when he later told the historian Gregg Herken that he hoped "the Russians would come to their senses and stop deploying ABM—in which case we would not have deployed MIRV."[63] Under this scenario, the Americans would remain ahead in terms of nuclear launch vehicles. While couched in the language of assured destruction, the Americans implied that the Soviet Union would have to accept its status as the younger sibling in the family of nations.

The truth was that neither side could alter its positions to make further negotiations sufficiently "beneficial." On Vietnam and the Middle East, just as on strategic arms control, Johnson held out the possibility of talks with the Soviets or their allies. At Glassboro, the president offered his five principles as a way forward to a peaceful settlement in the Middle East in the wake of the Six Day War. The Soviets, reflecting the views of their Arab allies, rejected any negotiations that did not secure Israeli withdrawal from Sinai, the West Bank, and the Golan Heights as a precondition. This was an impossible demand for the president to meet. On Vietnam, Johnson held out the prospect of a bombing halt if the North Vietnamese ceased offensive operations against the South, followed by talks. Regardless of its wishes, the Soviet Union did not have the leverage over the North to do more than pass on the American initiative, which was rejected out of hand by Hanoi.[64] On all major issues—arms control, Vietnam, and the Middle East—there was simply not the domestic political space, or a coincidence of interests and capabilities, for the superpowers to make meaningful headway at Glassboro.

THE SAN FRANCISCO SPEECH

After the Soviet rebuff there was little McNamara could do to stem the pressure toward deployment of an American ABM system. The secretary of defense reached for his China card in order to minimize initial outlays and an escalation of the arms race. The White House understood how tenuous McNamara's justification for an anti-China defense was. The Chinese did not appear sufficiently threatening to warrant deployment of an ABM. Echoing the CIA's view, Rostow told Johnson that the Chinese had in fact been "extremely cautious in military operations and extremely respectful of U.S. military power, including our nuclear power." McNamara also knew China was a thin reed. The secretary of defense did not even believe that the Chinese would have an operational ICBM by the time the American ABM was built.[65] After hearing the news of the anti-Chinese gambit, Assistant Secretary of Defense for International Security Affairs Paul Warnke walked into McNamara's office with a sardonic question: "China bomb, Bob?" In historian Robert Divine's words, "McNamara looked down, shuffled some papers around on his desk and muttered, 'What else am I going to blame it on?'"[66]

Yet McNamara was determined to push ahead with an ABM deployment in order to protect the president politically. Many in the administration continued to advise deferral. NSC staffer Spurgeon Keeny argued that the announcement should not be made outside of the usual budgetary cycle because it would attract too much attention. Such an attempt to split the difference between a full anti-Soviet defense and no deployment, Keeny pointed out, would satisfy neither ABM supporters nor opponents. Nor would the anti-China rationale convince the Soviets. Instead, deployment "would reduce whatever small prospects there might otherwise be for such talks this year."[67] Under Secretary of State Nicholas Katzenbach advocated announcement of further research and development with a firmer commitment to deployment—in essence restating the administration's current position. The secretary of defense, however, rejected delay, arguing that deployment was now unavoidable. To put it off further, McNamara argued, would be "to place ammunition in the hands our critics, who will use it for partisan purposes."[68] Having failed to convince the Soviets to accept a freeze, McNamara was determined to protect his president from further Republican attacks.

McNamara's September 18 speech in San Francisco announcing the deployment of an ABM named Sentinel was a web of contradictions. It was at once an assertion of American nuclear superiority, yet couched in terms that questioned the fundamental assumptions that underpinned the necessity of US predominance. As such, it embodied the tortuous circumlocutions required to reconcile McNamara's private doubts with the public political consensus behind the American nuclear edge. The secretary of defense assured his audience that the US had "a superiority over the Soviet Union of at least three or four to one" and he pledged to "maintain a superiority . . . for as far ahead as we can realistically plan." Yet this edge was unnecessary, McNamara argued, because the Soviet Union had the capability to destroy the United States in a retaliatory strike in any case. After stating that the United States could be secure in its superiority but that superiority was essentially useless, McNamara then denied the Kennedy-Johnson nuclear buildup "had been unjustified" because the decision was taken under conditions of imperfect knowledge regarding Soviet plans for its nuclear forces. It was this cycle of uncertainty, suspicion, and overcompensation, or as McNamara termed it "the action-reaction phenomenon," that he wanted to stop.[69]

In many ways, the twisted logic McNamara's speech displayed was a fitting epitaph for his career as the custodian of the nation's nuclear arsenal. The logic of the "action-reaction phenomenon" clearly militated against deployment of an anti-China ABM. Yet in the final third of the speech, McNamara announced the deployment of a missile defense system around America's major metropolitan areas. This inclusion at the end of a speech that had emphasized the wasteful and self-defeating elements of the nuclear arms race struck observers as odd and disappointed those who supported assured destruction based on mutual vulnerability. British Defense Secretary Denis Healey considered it "a bloody good speech, except for the sentences on going ahead on an ABM."[70]

Nor did McNamara's account of the Kennedy administration's decisions regarding its ICBM buildup accord with reality. The Kennedy administration had continued extending the US lead despite intelligence that the Soviet missile force was far smaller than had been anticipated.[71] Moreover it had trumpeted its success in public. In order to reassure the country over the Limited Test Ban Treaty in August 1963, McNamara portrayed a situation "of existing and continuing United States nuclear superiority" and pledged that the Kennedy administration was committed to increasing American strike forces "both absolutely and relatively" to the Soviets'.[72]

The unstated dimension of McNamara's speech, and indeed of his tenure as secretary of defense after the Cuban missile crisis, was the need to reconcile the administration's private doubts regarding the utility of the American nuclear edge with the domestic political consensus behind rational superiority. In December 1962 when Kennedy questioned the wisdom of building more missiles, McNamara had cautioned against cutting back because "it will seriously weaken our position within this country and with our allies."[73] The Limited Test Ban Treaty had managed to reconcile the dual imperatives of dampening the nuclear arms race without jeopardizing the American nuclear edge. In his September 1967 ABM announcement, McNamara again attempted to reassure the American public of US nuclear superiority as a way to bolster the administration's credibility and thereby build a coalition behind new arms control initiatives. Yet in their drive for parity, the Soviets would never allow the Johnson administration to have both a clear nuclear superiority and a diplomatic agreement. US nuclear superiority could no longer coexist with bilateral arms control, but neither Johnson nor McNamara was willing to run the political risks inherent in choosing between these two imperatives.

The studied vagueness of McNamara's presentation was matched by the policy's implementation. The secretary of defense indicated that, in addition to its primary mission as protection of American cities against Chinese attack, Sentinel would also be able to defend some of the country's Minuteman fields. Yet in a heated confrontation with Healey over the merits of Sentinel at the NATO meeting in Ankara a few days later, McNamara asserted that he did not plan to deploy the short-range interceptors required for Minuteman defense immediately, but merely to preserve the option for the future. Nobody in the administration appeared to know whether the secretary of defense had blurted this out or had decided to quietly scale back the system. In Keeny's words, "confusion reigns supreme."[74]

MCNAMARA'S EXIT

McNamara's floundering over missile defense reflected and exacerbated a broader loss of control over the defense budget as a result of Vietnam. By late 1967, his Planning Programing Budgeting System was beginning to malfunction. Keeny complained to Rostow that the "confused budget situation" was "certainly without precedent in recent times." Attempts to cover appropriations for Vietnam had left the budget in such a state that it was "extremely difficult to determine the base on which FY 69 decisions must be made." No ceiling had been set for appropriations, leaving Keeny only able to suggest that the FY 69 budget was likely to exceed the previous year's by "several billions."[75] By January 1968, the White House put forward a budget for FY 1969 of $186.1 billion, running a deficit of $20 billion. With Johnson's credibility on budgetary forecasting shattered, Republicans claimed the gap between tax receipts and outlays would be nearly $35 billion. Fiscal conservatives looked as though they would finally get their long-sought cuts in domestic programs that would be imposed in exchange for the 10 percent tax surcharge needed to close the deficit, which after much foot-dragging Johnson had submitted to Congress in August the previous year.[76] Caps in nuclear forces had been part of a restraint in defense spending to make budgetary room for the Great Society. As a result of Vietnam, this strategy was now in tatters.

Vietnam tore the budget apart, but it also reflected broader conceptual failings manifest in the White House's approach to arms control. It appears that the Johnson administration as a whole could not fathom the depth of the differences between the United States and its opponents. At Glassboro National Security Advisor Walt Rostow had tried out some modernization theory on his lunch partner, KGB General Vladimir Volkov. Rostow argued that as the USSR continued to develop, its population would begin to "long for the distant horizons and for means of taking their families beyond those horizons." Such a law of development, Rostow argued, was "stronger than the laws of Marxism and even Newton's laws." Volkov laughed at him.[77] Some Soviets expressed their frustrations with this line of argument even more directly in private. Speaking at a Central Committee Plenum on the Prague Spring in April 1968, Petro Shelest, the hardline secretary of the Ukrainian communist party, denounced western "speechifying" regarding "the raising of the standard of living" and "the virtues of the American way of life" as simply a cover for the old imperialist aim of crushing socialism.[78]

Modernization in the sense of progress toward a consumer society was simply not the priority for either the Soviet Union or North Vietnam to the extent that Johnson's advisers assumed. Some, indeed, saw it as actively harmful to the kind of society they were trying to build. In either case, domestic plenty could be postponed or foregone in order to reach more pressing immediate goals: strategic nuclear parity in the case of the USSR, national unification for North Vietnam. The threat to cut off or retard the quickest route to a modern consumer society, through a new arms race in the case of the Soviet Union, or strategic bombing in the case of North Vietnam, did not represent the threat the Johnson administration thought it did. Negotiations that sought to preserve the American position in South Vietnam under the threat of further bombing and US nuclear primacy under the threat of another arms race were therefore doomed to failure.[79]

McNamara may have been approaching this realization, but he was trapped in an administration that was committed to preserving both the American nuclear edge and an independent South Vietnam. The secretary of defense was on the back foot on the latter as well as the former. In a further escalation of the bombing, American planes attacked Hanoi's power stations on May 9, 1967. On May 19, McNamara wrote to Johnson arguing that the American military campaign in Southeast Asia could not be expected to lead to the defeat of the North Vietnamese and the National Liberation Front. Instead, McNamara told Johnson, some form of neutral South Vietnam should be considered as a compromise between victory and total defeat. He was vigorously opposed by Rostow, who sided with the military in advocating a continuation of the bombing. On this, Rostow won and McNamara lost. With no further progress at Glassboro, the United States continued its aerial offensive on North Vietnam. McNamara visited South Vietnam in July, treading a fine line between the administration's optimism and his growing private doubts regarding the conduct of the war, hailing military and political developments, but stopping short of endorsing General William Westmoreland's judgment that the United States was "winning" the war. The only consolation for McNamara was Johnson's refusal of the military's request, backed by Rostow, for an additional 200,000 troops on top of the 500,000 already there.[80]

On August 25, 1967, McNamara testified before the Senate Armed Services Committee hearings chaired by Democratic hawk John C. Stennis (D-MS). To guard his domestic flank, Johnson waved through a request from the chiefs to destroy a number of targets that had previously been refused on grounds that they could provoke the Chinese. At the hearings McNamara broke his public silence, telling the Senate Armed Services Committee that bombing did not hold the key to winning the war. Instead of using batteries of facts to support the continued effort, he deployed them to eviscerate the case for punishment by strategic bombing. Although "our air attack has rendered inoperative about 85 percent of [North Vietnam's] electric generating capacity," McNamara told the committee, "it is important to note that the Pepco plant in Alexandria, VA generates five times the power produced by all of North Vietnam's power plants before the bombing." North Vietnam's industrial base was not sufficiently significant to its political leadership for its destruction to constitute a major sanction, nor did the bombing have a major impact on infiltration to the South. Yet under questioning from Senator Strom Thurmond (D-SC), McNamara maintained that the war was "not no-win," thereby doing just enough to keep his job.[81] As with the strategic balance, he continued to maintain that the status quo was viable while simultaneously disowning many of the assumptions that underpinned it. Disillusioned with both bombing and further augmentation of nuclear forces as a means to pressure North Vietnam and the Soviet Union, respectively, McNamara nevertheless continued to hold that negotiation could preserve the United States' original aims: nuclear superiority and an independent South Vietnam.

In early November, Johnson's patience with his defense secretary ran out. McNamara had sent him a memo in late October urging a cessation of bombing and Vietnamization of the entire campaign. This proved too much for the president, who engineered his exit to the World Bank soon afterwards. Vietnam and the arms race represented two failed attempts to preserve American aims by confrontation. In both cases the turn to negotiation represented a failure of existing policy without recognition of the unsustainability of existing political ends: the preservation of South Vietnam and American nuclear primacy. By late 1967, McNamara had apparently recognized that the United States could not secure these ends by confrontation. His exit meant he also failed to achieve them through negotiation.[82]

A FINAL PUSH

McNamara left the Department of Defense on February 29, 1968, as the Tet Offensive drew to a close. His credibility further dented by the battles that had raged throughout January and February in many of South Vietnam's major cities, Johnson announced that he would not run for a second term in office. In his address to the nation on March 31, the president expressed the hope that his decision would free him from the "personal partisan causes" that, he implied, had distracted him from the quest for "peace."[83] After Johnson's announcement, the administration launched a last-ditch effort to secure a settlement in Southeast Asia. At the same time, the Johnson administration pushed forward with arms control. Yet, as with Vietnam, the barriers to an end to the arms race were, if anything, made more intractable as the clock ticked down to Johnson's departure on January 20, 1969.

McNamara's exit from the administration brought a change to bureaucratic guidance of the arms control process. The new secretary of defense, Clark M. Clifford, was almost entirely consumed with Vietnam and so the State Department and the Arms Control and Disarmament Agency (ACDA) became the main advocates for missile talks.[84] This also brought a change in the style of the American approach that reflected Kohler and Davis' earlier preference for a concrete proposal rather than McNamara's predilection for a broad conceptual reconciliation with the Soviets. Instead of attempting to reach agreement on the dynamics of the arms race, State and ACDA focused on drawing up a technical proposal that could, Deputy Undersecretary of State and former ambassador to the Soviet Union Charles Bohlen argued, convince the Soviets that the Americans were truly serious about negotiations and "help remove doubts that, in proposing talks, we were merely bent on an intelligence fishing expedition."[85]

Despite this shift from Defense to State, the Department of Defense staff and the JCS retained an effective veto over any clauses they thought compromised American security. The JCS in particular resisted State's attempt to outline a full proposal through the Johnson-Kosygin correspondence, in which the United States would agree to an effective freeze of forces at current levels. According to the chiefs, such a course would pose "extreme risks" to American security. Johnson was cautious not to aggravate the chiefs at a time when he needed their acquiescence for peace feelers in Vietnam. Despite advice from Rostow and Rusk that he should override the JCS and send the message, Johnson issued a watered-down draft that struck all substantive clauses.[86] Rusk, who by this point had become a staunch advocate of arms control, was furious with JCS obstructionism, telling Johnson that starting talks would be "a sign to what General Eisenhower called the military-industrial complex that, goddamn it, getting an agreement to limit offensive and defensive missiles is the national policy of the United States." Bureaucratic obstructionism, Rusk argued, would simply lead to further "tens of billions of dollars" pouring into the "rat hole" of the arms race.[87]

Kosygin eventually agreed to talks in late June on the grounds that, in order to persuade non-nuclear powers to sign the Nuclear Nonproliferation Treaty, which was to be signed on July 1, it was vital to show them that the superpowers were serious about limiting strategic arms. At the same time, Rusk convened a working group to hammer out an arms control proposal between the interested agencies: ACDA, State, Defense, the Atomic Energy Commission, and CIA. Reflecting his more cautious approach to strategic arms talks, Clifford pushed for a less concrete proposal, until Rusk laid down the law, telling the meeting that "he did not feel we would be moving into the area of insecurity by the talks. Rather, a failure to control the arms race would decrease security." Nevertheless, the JCS was given a right of veto, with the proposal voted up or down in a final approval.[88]

Despite his frustrations, Rusk accepted the need to maintain consensus within the executive branch regarding arms control.[89] Perhaps cognizant of both the chiefs' opposition and the need to reach a quick consensus, the committee came out with a proposal that, according to Ambassador Thompson, would allow the United States "to continue with our own plans while restricting [the Soviets] in carrying out some of their own programs."[90] In offering a freeze of both ICBM and SLBM construction, the proposal left the United States with a commanding lead in submarine-launched ballistic missiles, the most survivable and capable of all American platforms. It did not include bombers, in which the Americans also enjoyed a significant quantitative edge. It also did nothing to limit the US MIRV program, which was on the verge of multiplying the American lead in deliverable warheads by three for ICBMs and twelve for SLBMs. On defensive weapons, the Americans offered a ceiling on ABM interceptor launchers at equal levels. The proposal required that either the Soviets divulge technical details or allow visits by American inspectors to surface-to-air missile sites along the Baltic coast, which the US military suspected of having some ABM capability. A lopsided offer and stringent inspection requirements was the cost of the chiefs' acquiescence. Given their fixation on parity and jealously guarded secrecy on strategic arms, it is very difficult to see how the Soviet leadership would have found such a framework acceptable.[91]

Johnson's quest for a summit was torpedoed by the Soviet invasion of Czechoslovakia on August 20, 1968. The Americans bitterly resented the fact that the Soviets issued the president a formal invitation to the USSR just a day before their troops crushed the Prague Spring. Rusk told Dobrynin that "the coincidence of the actions was like throwing a dead fish in the face of the President of the United States."[92] In reality, prospects for meaningful progress on substantive issues were slim.[93] Johnson's reaction to the Soviet move to crush the Prague Spring was indicative of the tightrope he was walking on arms control and a wider US–Soviet détente. On the night of the invasion, the president telephoned Republican presidential candidate Richard Nixon in order to inform him of the situation. Referring to the controversy over the Democratic platform regarding terms for a bombing halt in Vietnam, Johnson confided: "I think it shows you . . . the folly of professors trying to write into platforms strategy and tactics . . . What are these goddamn pink sympathizers going to say about these Russian troops . . . ?" At the same time, Johnson attempted to secure Nixon's assent that "politics stops at the water's edge," reminding him, somewhat selectively, that under Eisenhower his maxim as Senate majority leader was "wherever [the president] goes, he goes with the voice of the American people."[94] Johnson's tough talk to Nixon kept the prospects of a summit alive by appealing to the foreign policy consensus of peace through strength. Yet such a commitment to American military power diminished the chances of real progress toward an arms control agreement acceptable to the USSR.

As his comments to Nixon indicate, Johnson had not given up on the idea of a summit. However, in the wake of Czechoslovakia the administration felt it had to emphasize its intention to negotiate from a position of strength, thereby decreasing further the prospects of mutually productive talks in its final months. Clifford delivered a hard-hitting speech in September that committed the Johnson administration to building "the house of peace" on "the rock of power." He announced the exclusion of the Sentinel ABM from planned cuts to the administration's final defense budget and stated categorically that further US testing of MIRV would "not prejudice" arms control talks. For now, McNamara-style talk of two equally rational adversaries reaching out to stem the action-reaction phenomenon was jettisoned in favor of clear displays of American determination to prevail during the next round of the arms race.[95]

This was not simply public posturing. Clifford's tough stance reflected his more skeptical attitude toward arms control than his predecessor's, as well as anxiety that attempts to come to a settlement in Southeast Asia would be neglected in favor of a summit with the Soviets. Clifford later believed that both Johnson and McNamara saw progress on arms control as "a form of salvation for Vietnam." The secretary of defense's aides were wary that Johnson might give away too much in order to meet with the Soviet leadership and thereby leave office on a high note. "LBJ is so pro-Kosygin–LBJ Summit that he can't accept anything that will offend the Russians despite the overwhelming national interest involved," Clifford's special assistant, George Elsey, opined. The clear exception to this attitude in the Pentagon was Assistant Secretary of Defense Paul Warnke, who consistently lobbied his boss to talk to Johnson about reinitiating talks. Yet Clifford was concerned that Vietnam should take priority over any further east-west moves. Only when the South Vietnamese government agreed to attend the Paris peace talks after the presidential election did the defense secretary become more accommodating and begin adopting Warnke's recommendations regarding strategic arms control.[96]

The weeks after Nixon's election on November 5 saw an upsurge in activity regarding a possible US-Soviet summit. Rostow wrote to Johnson excitedly that "Moscow is ready to go—and eager—if you can work it out." Yet this was based less on any notion of concrete results and more on an emotional desire in Washington to get the process started. Johnson's team also sought to tie Nixon's hands, committing him to talks that they feared he would otherwise walk away from—to the detriment of both US security and prospects for détente. Yet the White House realized it could do little to put pressure on Nixon regarding a summit, except threaten to go ahead regardless of Nixon's wishes and "appeal to [his] statesmanship and self-interest."[97] Nixon could simply disavow anything that came out of such a meeting. The Soviets understood this, holding off on reissuing an invitation for Johnson to visit Leningrad. LBJ believed, correctly, that Nixon's team had warned the Soviets away, just as it had the South Vietnamese.[98]

With a meeting now out of reach, the White House engaged in an abortive effort to rework a Soviet-proposed summit communiqué into a statement of principles that would guide future negotiations. Defense placed firm limits on the extent to which it would bend to Johnson's desire to leave a final mark on the history of US–Soviet relations. Clifford was opposed to the Soviet suggestion that the talks be guided by the principle of "equal security," insisting that "equal" be struck from the text on the basis that it could be a pretext "to achieve numerical equality" between the superpowers' nuclear forces. Eventually State and DoD settled on the pledge that "security would be assured equally for both sides." This small change in wording, never published, masked the gulf between Soviet and American conceptions of the acceptable conditions for détente through arms control as Johnson's presidency drew to a close.[99]

THE UNBRIDGEABLE GAP

"Power?" Lyndon Johnson once joked, "The only power I've got is nuclear—and I can't use that." Made within earshot of *Time*'s White House correspondent, Hugh Sidey, this offhand remark nevertheless captures the essence of the thirty-seventh president's attitude toward nuclear weapons.[100] Not faced with the same kind of superpower crises that Kennedy had grappled with as president, Johnson never had to come to terms with the reality of wielding the United States' nuclear power in the same way as his predecessor. For LBJ, nuclear strategy was a more abstract question. Johnson's commitment to the US nuclear edge was grounded in his understanding of its relationship to his domestic agenda. Maintenance of the US nuclear edge within budgetary limits helped Johnson create the political and fiscal space he needed to pass the package of domestic legislation that made him one of the great reforming presidents of the twentieth century.[101] McNamara, who had played a far more central role in decision making over Berlin and Cuba than his new boss and consequently had far stronger views regarding the uselessness of nuclear superiority as a form of crisis bargaining, was happy to tailor his recommendations to Johnson's overarching agenda. This included placing the American ABM system in perpetual research and development, where it could be neither a danger to assured destruction nor the Great Society.

With the undoing of McNamara's optimistic assumptions regarding the Soviet commitment to an inferior assured destruction force, however, the White House reached out to the Soviets. Yet the domestic conditions for an agreement that would give due weight to the Soviet desire for parity in nuclear forces and political esteem were not present during LBJ's last few years in office. The politics of preparedness still dominated the American domestic scene in 1967 and 1968. McNamara told the president in December 1966 that 40 percent of the Senate favored an American ABM system, 25 percent ("the liberals") opposed it, and the rest were undecided.[102] Johnson and McNamara had pushed forward with an antiballistic missile system in September 1967 because they felt that to do otherwise was politically suicidal. Under these circumstances, the chances for ratification of a parity-enshrining arms control accord were slim.

The cracks in this solid public and congressional consensus in favor of nuclear superiority were already beginning to show in Johnson's final months in office. When he heard of McNamara's plan to emplace ABM batteries around American cities, Johnson's domestic aide Joseph Califano predicted that "all hell [was] likely to break loose from the liberals and the urbanists" because of the increased strain that ABM would place on the budget.[103] He was right. Disquieted by the imminent cuts to Johnson's domestic programs required for LBJ to get his tax hike, liberals in Congress were beginning to supplement their opposition to the Vietnam War with a campaign on a broader front to push back what they saw as both budgetary and political overstretch of the national security state. In June 1968 senators John Sherman Cooper (R-KY) and Philip Hart (D-MI) mustered thirty-four votes for an amendment to the military construction authorization bill to postpone ABM by one year. Johnson allegedly had to persuade eight liberal Democrats to vote against the amendment, according to Mike Manatos, his Senate liaison, on the grounds that he would bargain the system away at strategic arms talks.[104] By late 1968 local opposition groups were beginning to form in Seattle, Boston, and Chicago, the three cities where planning and construction of Sentinel was most advanced. By late 1968, the situation was so serious for Senator Henry Jackson of Washington State that he asked the Department of Defense to move the ABM battery away from the center of Seattle to somewhere more remote, a request that the administration granted.[105]

Yet these developments did little to dissuade the Johnson administration that a change in course was required. While not the only factor, the extent to which the Joint Chiefs retained a veto over any arms control proposals indicates that the White House remained convinced that the politics of military preparedness that had dominated the 1960s up to that point remained the norm.[106] The dominant mood in the Senate remained that of Chairman of the Armed Services Committee Richard B. Russell, who declared that the United States should "match [its] potential enemies missile for missile."[107] The American public's commitment to nuclear superiority remained an article of faith for the Johnson administration until the very end. By late 1968 the US body politic had not become sufficiently Balkanized over the question of nuclear superiority to create the political space necessary for an arms control accord that both satisfied domestic interest groups and Soviet security concerns.

Given the formidable obstacles to an agreement, it is difficult to see why the Johnson administration persevered with attempts to open talks as long as it did. Ignorance was not to blame. Midlevel experts such as Foy Kohler and Nathaniel Davis warned that the Russians would accept nothing less than nuclear parity. Despite his energetic advocacy of talks in 1968, Paul Warnke admitted that "no agreement with the Soviet Union can be expected to maintain US superiority."[108]

Such anxieties did not feature in deliberations between Johnson, McNamara, Clifford, and Rusk. There was a fair level of hypocrisy in the American position. In his analysis of the superpower nuclear competition as a product of the action-reaction phenomenon and the prescription of assured destruction as a cure, McNamara thought he had found the magic bullet that would solve the most costly arms race of modern history. Yet if McNamara had really believed in assured destruction, he would have accepted the logic that the American nuclear edge was unnecessary and should be dispensed with. Nothing in the Johnson administration's internal deliberations or public statements suggest that it had decided to do so.

Seen in this light, the Johnson-McNamara attempt to control the strategic arms race was yet another doomed attempt to reconcile the irreconcilable: guns with butter, the nuclear superiority bequeathed by Kennedy and McNamara with the next step in ending the arms race.[109] In this sense, historian John Dumbrell is right that Johnson's approach to arms control reflected his attachment to the "middle way."[110] Yet the middle way was the only way to sell an arms control accord domestically.

Pushing forward with superiority on this basis, the Johnson principals were reliant on the contention that the Soviet leadership would prove conducive to the logic of assured destruction and accept American predominance. Johnson and particularly McNamara approached negotiations with the Soviet leadership as a pedagogical exercise, assuming that disagreement simply reflected Kosygin's inability to grasp the relevant facts, rather than being the result of a differing values system that reflected alternative priorities. Such thinking proved wishful in the extreme.

Wishful thinking was one of the many strands that connected the Johnson administration's strategic arms control policy with the war in Southeast Asia. Johnson and his advisors may have seen their attempts to arrest the arms race as part of a process of "growing out of the Cold War."[111] Yet Johnson's approaches to the Soviets and his campaign in Southeast Asia reflected many of the same flawed assumptions. In both Vietnam and the arms race, the Johnson administration had pledged to hold on to American positions that in hindsight were fundamentally unsustainable. In both cases, the administration had assumed its adversaries would conform to American models that prized economic development over efforts to match the United States militarily. As these assumptions came unstuck, the administration clung to the ultimate aims of an independent South Vietnam and a margin of nuclear superiority. Yet with the threat to impede modernization failing to provide sufficient incentives to its opponents, and public opinion unprepared for something less than the status quo, the Johnson administration simply ran out of road.

CHAPTER 4

Collapse of the Consensus and the Struggle for Coherence, 1969–1970

First elected to Congress in 1946, Richard Milhous Nixon had lived his entire political life in the Cold War. By the time he assumed the presidency in January 1969, Nixon had been at various times one of the architects, manipulators, and victims of the fundamental totems that defined the American domestic politics of containment, one of which was the necessity of US nuclear superiority over the Soviet Union.[1] On the receiving end of Kennedy's "missile gap" charge in the presidential election of 1960, Nixon was profoundly aware of the domestic political cost of conceding numerical parity to the Soviet Union in strategic armaments. Eight years later, he ran on a platform criticizing the Johnson administration's laxity in retaining the US nuclear edge and rued its erosion in meetings with his White House advisors. Yet by the end of 1970, the Nixon administration was on the way to conceding not only parity to the Soviet Union, but also superiority in the number of land-based and sea-based missiles. This chapter explains how and why Nixon was brought to this point.

Nixon's strategy regarding arms control was a key part of his wider "structure of peace" to be constructed with the United States' communist adversaries—a concept that he presented in his first inaugural address on January 20, 1969 and that was manifested most clearly in Nixon's visits to Peking and Moscow in February and May 1972.[2] The conclusion of the first round of the Strategic Arms Limitation Talks during the latter summit, forming the substantive basis for US–Soviet détente, meant that arms control was arguably one of the most successful elements of Nixon's tenure in the White House. While other elements of Nixon's strategy, such as an acceptable end to the war in Vietnam, went off track, SALT could be seen as an area of consistent success.

Yet this seeming consistency masks the changing place of arms control in Nixon's strategy during the first three years of his administration. When he took office, Nixon saw arms control principally as a reward for Soviet efforts to help the United States find an acceptable solution to the war in Vietnam. This required that the United States hold out the prospect of a renewed arms race in front of the Soviets through deployment of multiple independently targetable reentry vehicles and an ABM system.[3] Faced with the prospect of competition on a new qualitative technological plane, Nixon and his advisers judged that the Soviets would be eager to come to terms with the United States on strategic arms and would facilitate talks to resolve the conflict in Southeast Asia in return.[4]

This gambit failed for two principal reasons. The first was the fundamental collapse in the US domestic political consensus regarding the importance of nuclear superiority over the Soviet Union, seen most clearly in the fractious debate over the future of the United States' antiballistic missile program. While highly cognizant of the surge in opposition to the Vietnam War, the Nixon administration initially underestimated the extent to which this antimilitary feeling had spread beyond American involvement in Southeast Asia. The ABM debate of 1969 was long and bitter, with opponents attacking both the administration's technical appraisal of Nixon's redesigned system, Safeguard, and the White House's estimation of the Soviet threat. In doing so, ABM oppositionists contested every assumption underpinning US nuclear superiority as a policy prescription, showing how each was based not on hard data but on deeply impressionistic assumptions regarding Soviet motivations and intentions. This collapse caught Nixon off guard. With both the notion of executive primacy on national security issues and the utility of the American nuclear edge over the USSR challenged by ABM opponents to an unprecedented extent, rational superiority was no longer the winning position it had been up until the end of Johnson's tenure.

The second factor contributing to the failure of Nixon's first arms control strategy was the administration's inability to integrate this new domestic political situation into its position at SALT, which opened in November 1969. Faced with such domestic political turmoil, Nixon responded by attempting to short-circuit democratic checks and balances, as well as the warring bureaucracy, by leaning heavily on the negotiating skills of his national security advisor, Henry Kissinger. In early 1970, and unbeknown to the US SALT delegation, Kissinger opened a backchannel negotiation on strategic arms with Soviet Ambassador Anatoly Dobrynin in order to come to an agreement.

However, Nixon and Kissinger failed to understand that the Soviet Union did not have such a backchannel arrangement; its position at the public talks accurately reflected its real stance on strategic arms. By neglecting the dynamic of the front-channel negotiations, therefore, Nixon and Kissinger allowed the American SALT delegation to give up one of its main bargaining chips—the US ABM program—with no concessions on offensive arms from the Soviet side. Far from circumventing domestic politics to reach a better agreement, the backchannel strategy exacerbated the difficulties of bringing the front-channel talks to an acceptable conclusion.

NIXON'S STRATEGY

No one was more immersed in the domestic politics of American nuclear strategy than Richard Nixon by the time of his 1968 presidential run against Johnson's vice president, Hubert Humphrey. He understood through bitter experience the damage that a perceived loss of the American nuclear edge could do to the domestic political fortunes of anyone associated with the administration on whose watch it occurred. In 1968 Nixon turned the charges of weakness that had dogged his 1960 campaign back on the Democrats, stressing the extent to which the United States had fallen behind the USSR in the rate of ICBM production and the need for American superiority. Within the Republican Party, Nixon's commitment to superiority had also helped reassure conservatives that he was an electable yet ideologically reliable alternative to Ronald Reagan. At the 1968 Republican National Convention in Miami, Nixon had headed off a last-minute challenge by the California governor by assuring Southern Republicans such as Strom Thurmond that he would maintain America's nuclear dominance.[5] Missile gap politics was second nature to Nixon; he was an expert both on the ways it could help and hinder his broader agenda.

This position was not merely a political pose. Nixon truly believed in nuclear superiority as the foundation of America's security commitments to its noncommunist allies, particularly in Western Europe—not in terms of its military utility, but rather for the signal it sent regarding the United States' commitment to fight on behalf of other states. The "fundamental" issue, Nixon noted in an early National Security Council meeting, was the "immense . . . political and psychological value" of breakthroughs in nuclear weaponry, a lesson that for him went "back to Sputnik." In order to protect America's nuclear credibility as well as his own political fortunes, Nixon wanted to ensure that the

United States was "moving forward adequately" in developing new weapons to foreclose the possibility of another Sputnik shock.[6]

However, the new president also realized that rapid Soviet advances were undermining the American commitment to the security of its allies in a way unprecedented since the dawn of the nuclear age. Between 1968 and 1969 alone, the Soviet Union added over 200 ICBMs to its forces and was well on the way to matching the United States in the number of land-based missile launchers.[7] Nixon reflected at an early NSC meeting that, as a result, the United States and the USSR had truly "reached a balance of terror." For the president, this meant that the US NATO "nuclear umbrella [was] no longer there." Nixon worried that the Soviets in reality had the edge because their superior conventional forces could overwhelm NATO, while nuclear parity could deter American escalation. Without nuclear superiority, the president believed, "flexible response [was] baloney."[8]

Fearing accusations that the United States had ceded parity to the USSR, Nixon moved quickly to give himself greater room for maneuver regarding his campaign promises. He stepped back from his pledge to superiority in his first press conference, arguing that the United States required "sufficient military power to defend our interests and to maintain [American] commitments."[9] The administration spent a great many hours attempting to draw up criteria to define this new doctrine of sufficiency, but as Deputy Secretary of Defense David Packard ill-advisedly told a journalist, "it doesn't mean a god-damned thing."[10] This was of course the entire point: by decoupling the American nuclear posture from the commitment to larger numbers in all metrics of the arms race Nixon increased his flexibility, both domestically and in view of potential arms negotiations with the Soviets. "We will call whatever option we choose sufficiency," White House aide Morton Halperin concluded dryly.[11] Realizing that claims to superiority might not stand up to subsequent events, Nixon moved away from the categorical guarantees that had both helped and hamstrung Kennedy and Johnson.

Yet as Nixon moved to widen his options in the event of talks, he also resisted pressure to initiate them immediately. The Soviet Union was eager to maintain the momentum toward negotiations that had marked Johnson's final months in office. Before Nixon's inauguration, the Soviets passed a message to Kissinger expressing their desire for talks.[12] On the day Nixon was sworn in, the Soviet Ministry of Foreign Affairs (MFA) issued a statement expressing its willingness to begin discussions.[13] Both publicly and privately, the Nixon administration held off, emphasizing that discussions on bilateral arms control would only be productive if movement were made on the regional conflicts, Nixon mentioning the Middle East in his open remarks and Kissinger talking about Vietnam behind closed doors.[14]

To an extent, this reaction reflected the president's personal cautiousness; he wanted to "get [his] ducks in a row" before agreeing to sit down with the Soviets.[15] However, the order for National Security Study Memorandum (NSSM) 28 dealing with strategic arms control was only issued on March 6, almost three months after the first such directive. This may have been due to Nixon's belief, in historian Francis J. Gavin's words, that "*geopolitical competition*, and not the arms race, remained the core driver of international politics."[16] Nixon repeated this argument in his first letter to Alexei Kosygin by noting that "military requirements depend, among other things, on the crises and dangers that confront us in the world. As the dangers recede, I am convinced so can the levels of arms in our arsenals."[17]

Nixon's slowness in initiating talks also had more prosaic roots. As pressing as the strategic situation was for Nixon, it paled in comparison with the political imperative to find a way out of Vietnam, the subject of the very first National Security Study Memorandum. Although the USSR MFA spokesman took pains to underline that the USSR was "not more interested [in an agreement] than the United States," the Soviets' seeming eagerness to make progress led Kissinger to conclude that the United States could use SALT "to induce [Moscow] to come to grips with the real sources of tension," namely regional conflicts.[18] Vietnam was at the top of that list. In the Nixon-Kissinger game of linkage, progress on arms control was seen as a second-order concern that could be used as a stick to prod the Soviets into helping the United States extricate itself from the defining national security debacle of the late 1960s. In a moment of candor, Kissinger told Anatoly Dobrynin, Soviet ambassador to Washington, that "everything depended on the war in Vietnam."[19]

Missile defense was an important part of Nixon's plan. The president summed up his reasoning succinctly in a scribbled note to Kissinger on the front of an ABM options memo: "1) [The Soviets] *have* closed the gap [in strategic nuclear weapons]—2) They continue to *increase*—3) They want to talk—4) We must see that the gap is not widened on the other side."[20] Nixon was adamant that the United States had to have an ABM deployment underway in order to match the Soviet Galosh system around Moscow. A missile defense deployment was an essential element in maintaining at least parity with the Soviet Union before talks opened. ABM, along with MIRV, was one of the few ongoing programs that the United States had to bargain with during any negotiations. For Nixon, the "leverage [was] real" on ABM: if the Soviets believed the United States would not go through with a system, then this would definitely impair the American opening position at SALT.[21] An ongoing ABM construction program would also maintain the pressure for talks, thereby increasing the chances that the Soviets would lean more heavily on their North Vietnamese allies.

ABM: GROWING DISSENT IN THE SENATE

Yet ABM was becoming the focus for growing congressional resistance to the executive on national security policy. There were many reasons for this. The June 1968 Senate amendment to postpone Sentinel by a year that had gained thirty-four votes in favor was a shot across the bow.[22] Worryingly for Nixon, the amendment had secured bipartisan sponsorship with the backing of twelve liberal Republicans, including one of the bill's sponsors, John Sherman Cooper of Kentucky, as well as Charles Percy of Illinois, Edward Brooke of Massachusetts, and George Aiken of Vermont.[23] This bipartisan liberal group was worried by the prospect of major cuts to domestic programs in the wake of Johnson's agreement to $6 billion in savings in exchange for his 10 percent surcharge. Congressional liberals wanted to see any cuts to the Great Society balanced by savings on non-Vietnam-related defense spending.[24] The numbers of congressional liberals appear to have been bolstered by the 1968 elections. Five freshman Democratic senators and one freshman Republican eventually voted against Nixon's system, whereas three of their predecessors had voted in support of Johnson's ABM and three had not voted at all.[25]

In addition to growing congressional dissent over the balance between domestic and national security priorities during a time of austerity, Nixon also labored under a partisan handicap. Some high-profile Democrats, including J. William Fulbright, stayed away from the 1968 vote—unable to bring themselves to vote for ABM or against a Democratic administration on a system that promised to defend the United States against nuclear attack.[26] The Democrat-majority Senate would not give Nixon the same courtesy. Tellingly, eight Democrats who had not cast a vote on Johnson's system ended up voting against Nixon's ABM a year later—the largest category of vote switchers between 1968 and 1969. To their number were added five Democratic senators who had voted in support of Johnson's ABM system the previous year.[27]

An outbreak of protests against the Army's designation of specific sites for the first round of antimissile installations drew further attention to ABM and reached its peak as the transition from Johnson to Nixon was taking place.[28] Although these protests did not have the same national resonance as those against the Vietnam War, they expressed many of the same themes and were sufficiently worrying to senators from the states involved to pressure the new administration to rethink.[29]

The specific locations of missile defense sites added political weight to the anti-ABM campaign. Protests near Boston received a major boost from Senator Edward M. Kennedy (D-MA), one of the high-profile Democratic nonvoters in 1968. As the most senior surviving member of the political dynasty, Kennedy was going after the administration on a range of issues in a push to raise his political profile in preparation for a presidential run in 1972. In response to protests in his home state and a personal letter from JFK's former presidential science advisor, Jerome Wiesner, Kennedy added the anti-ABM cause to this list, writing a letter to Secretary of Defense Melvin Laird demanding cessation of the program. On February 6, Laird halted Sentinel construction in order to review the system. This seeming chink in Nixon's political armor emboldened Kennedy's aides still further.[30]

Laird probably also made this move in order to reassure Nixon's congressional allies. Local protests had an impact on the pro-ABM camp, significant enough to worry a number of important Democratic and Republican senators who in previous years had put their full weight behind advocacy for the ABM. Senator Henry M. Jackson had previously lobbied the Johnson administration to move the Sentinel installation from Fort Lawton in the center of Seattle to somewhere more remote. The Army had moved it to Bainbridge Island, which hosted a naval shipyard, but also expensive homes.[31] Republican Senate minority leader, Everett Dirksen of Illinois, was so worried by the mail he was getting from around Chicago that, despite his enthusiastic advocacy in previous years, he refused to say whether he supported the system or not.[32]

Due to his lack of a majority in either house of Congress, Nixon relied on such figures. Jackson was one of the leading Democratic national security hawks in the Senate and was respected by his peers for his command of foreign policy. With a significant proportion of liberal Republicans opposing the system, Jackson was vital to whipping at least a portion of Democrats to vote with the president. Dirksen was Republican minority leader and so his vote was critical. He was also struggling to get Republicans on his side. In meetings with Nixon, Dirksen and other supporters told Nixon that they "hate[d] to be divided on this issue at this time," asking the president to find a solution that "will divide them just a little less."[33]

This clash between liberal opponents of increased defense spending and a number of senior senatorial figures was manifest in the faceoff between the Senate Foreign Relations and Armed Services Committees. For years, Armed Services had been the domain of Richard B. Russell (D-GA), during which time the committee had held almost unchallenged control over the passage of defense appropriations. In 1969, John Stennis (D-MS) took over the chairmanship of Armed Services and organized hearings on the impact of the 1968 Nonproliferation Treaty on US defense efforts. As an international agreement, the NPT was primarily the domain of Fulbright's committee. In retaliation, Fulbright called for hearings on the impact of missile defense on America's foreign policy by the Disarmament Subcommittee, chaired by Albert Gore, Sr. (D-TN). Thus the ABM debate became a divisive battle between liberal and conservative wings of the Democratic Party in the Senate, with the liberals seemingly in the ascendant.[34]

Two months into Nixon's tenure, therefore, the future of ABM was on a senatorial knife-edge. On March 10 Nixon's congressional liaison Bryce Harlow advised the president that "the ABM system advanced by LBJ [had] no chance whatsoever" in the Senate. Even Russell was skeptical that a modified system would get through the upper chamber and advised the administration to seek some kind of "prototype" rather than a full national rollout. Harlow predicted that the vote would be close, but averred that presidential weight behind a modified system could secure victory.[35]

FROM SENTINEL TO SAFEGUARD

Nixon decided to press ahead with missile defense, albeit in a modified form. On March 14 the president held a press conference at which he unveiled Safeguard, an ABM that, while maintaining some anti-Chinese capability, was designed primarily to defend the United States' land-based intercontinental ballistic missiles and bombers against a Soviet attack. This, the president maintained, shifted the focus of the system to the real Soviet threat as opposed to a hypothetical Chinese one.[36]

Nixon's performance at the press conference was in the best traditions of the Kennedy-Johnson period in which the appearance of executive rationality formed the bedrock of the White House case for nuclear programs. The president presented the new ABM as the middle ground between doing nothing and introducing a full defense of cities against a Soviet attack. Even the name, Safeguard, was designed to project an image of rational prudence. Defense of bombers and ICBMs as opposed to population was an easier technical task, Nixon argued, because the consequences of failure were far less catastrophic. Nixon thereby portrayed the shift in rationale as a consequence of external strategic concerns rather than the domestic political crisis that had blown up around Sentinel. The message was clear: the Pentagon and White House had weighed all of the alternatives and had found the most prudent, measured response to new strategic circumstances. However, the political bottom line was clearer still: Safeguard "does not provide defense of our cities," the president maintained, "and for that reason the sites have been moved away from our major cities."[37]

In reality the change was more aesthetic than military. Despite the shift in emphasis away from China and toward the Soviet Union, James Schlesinger, director of the Bureau of the Budget and RAND alumnus, warned Kissinger that the shift from Sentinel to Safeguard was "more of a change in rationale than in program."[38] Despite the obvious limitation of this reorientation, however, the administration pressed ahead.

In hindsight, much of the subsequent controversy might have been avoided had the administration placed greater emphasis on its desire to engage the Soviet Union in arms talks. The White House's chief speechwriter, Jim Keogh, in fact advocated such a course. Pushing the system on the basis of its military effectiveness, Keogh warned, "would inflame the opposition and do serious damage to our case." Instead, he offered a more conciliatory deployment announcement in which Nixon would declare, quoting Winston Churchill, "'We arm to parley.' We arm reluctantly, in the hope that by building new arms we sooner can lay them down."[39]

Nixon rejected the notion that the bargaining chip argument should be at the forefront of justifications for ABM. For the president, the Russians would be under greater pressure to talk if they believed that the United States was building the system to combat a real threat rather than simply to negotiate it away. Although Nixon believed Safeguard's negotiating "leverage [was] real," he also held that "talking about it would make it unreal"—a view with which Kissinger concurred. Instead, he wanted to say that Safeguard was not "simply a bargaining counter," but designed for a real military purpose.[40] As a result, the references to talks in Nixon's March 14 announcement were more ambiguous than Keogh would have liked. The president stated simply that the system would be reviewed on the basis of "any talks that we are having . . . or may be having, with regard to arms control," along with the evolution of the Soviet and Chinese threats and developments in defensive technology.[41]

In downplaying the possibility of arms talks, however, the Nixon administration overestimated the extent to which opposition would be dampened by moving ABM away from cities. It also underestimated the vigor with which informed critics would continue to pick apart a system that rested on fragile military-technical and strategic foundations.

CONFRONTATION

The weakness of Nixon's approach became apparent almost immediately. Senior Democrats met the administration's contention that the decision had been made on purely strategic grounds with derision. "Now, all of a sudden, apparently because of a commotion in Boston and Seattle, we're told that defense of the people in our cities is impractical and impossible," Albert Gore taunted Secretary of Defense Melvin Laird at the hearings on Safeguard before the Senate Foreign Relations Subcommittee for Disarmament.[42] Scientists called before Gore's committee, such as Wolfgang Panofsky, regarded the administration's decision to use the same equipment intended for city defense in order to protect missiles as technically unsound.[43] Jerome Wiesner told Gore's subcommittee the system would not be reliable against a Soviet strike. In particular, he drew attention to the software required to deal with the amount of data a Soviet attack would create. Wiesner claimed that it would be "the most sophisticated and intricate system that man has attempted to build" and unlikely to live up to expectations.[44]

Yet the most damaging of the charges leveled against the administration was of its own making. In his initial presentation on behalf of Safeguard, Laird stressed the threat that a new Soviet missile, the SS-9, posed to the survival of Minuteman. "The Soviets are going for a first-strike capability," the defense secretary announced, "there is no question about it."[45]

Nixon's domestic political aides, Assistant to the President for Congressional Relations Bryce Harlow, and Special Assistants Alexander Butterfield and Pat Buchanan, supported this confrontational stance— against the advice of Kissinger's NSC staff, which believed that it was too aggressive.[46] In contrast to later years, however, Kissinger and his assistants' role in selling Safeguard to the public was more operational than strategic: preparing fact sheets for other staffers, correcting the errors in White House mailings, talking to journalists, and lending expertise at presidential meetings on the subject. Butterfield and Harlow were in charge of the congressional salesmanship. At one of their meetings on Safeguard, Butterfield even instructed Kissinger not to speak unless he was asked a question by the president.[47]

After a few days, cracks began to appear in the administration's case on the SS-9, as information from unnamed intelligence sources began leaking into the public domain. By late May, it appeared that analysts from the CIA were talking to congressional opponents in a way that cast serious doubt on the basis of most of DoD's assertions. Laird had argued that "new evidence" required an upgrade of intelligence estimates of the SS-9's threat to Minuteman, but the CIA apparently told congressional figures that it had "no new intelligence information justifying Mr. Laird's extrapolation."[48]

Nixon was furious, telling Kissinger on June 12 that CIA Director Richard Helms had "fifteen minutes to decide which side he [was] on" in the ABM debate.[49] In mid-June, Laird and Helms testified together before the Senate Foreign Relations Committee, trying to present a united front.[50] However, the CIA director stood firm on his agency's assessment of the threat. A memorandum to holders maintained that the Soviets were only testing a multiple re-entry vehicle system, which did "not improve Soviet capabilities to attack individual targets" because the re-entry vehicles could not be targeted independently to hit different Minuteman silos. Only with a single large warhead would the SS-9 have the required combination of yield and accuracy to destroy a Minuteman. In that case, however, the Soviets would not have enough SS-9s to threaten the whole American ICBM force.[51]

The tenor of expert debate on ABM in 1969 is indicative of the problems faced by those who sought to "prove" the military-technical case for or against Safeguard. In response to scientific opposition the administration trotted out its own experts, most notably Albert Wohlstetter and Edward Teller, two seminal figures of early Cold War nuclear policy. While at RAND in the 1950s, Wohlstetter had used systems analysis to argue that Strategic Air Command's bomber force was highly vulnerable to a Soviet attack. In doing so, he had pressed for greater dispersal and protection of bomber bases to protect America's second-strike capability, a term he had coined. Preoccupied with strategic vulnerability ever since, Wohlstetter set out to prove that ABM opponents had played fast and loose with the figures when arguing that Minuteman would be safe from a Soviet first strike in the mid-1970s.[52] His primary target was George Rathjens, who had testified before the Senate that even if the Russians built 500 SS-9s and fitted them with highly accurate MIRVs, a quarter of the Minuteman force would survive without further protection. Wohlstetter claimed that in fact only five percent of Minuteman would survive. The difference between the two men was due to their varying assessments of three somewhat obscure metrics: the resistance of Minuteman silos to pressure from the blast of Soviet warheads, their nuclear yield, and Russian firing doctrine. Wohlstetter argued that Rathjens had overestimated Minuteman blast resistance by two-thirds and underestimated the explosive yield of the SS-9's warheads. Rathjens had also assumed that the Soviets would not be able to tell if some of their missiles failed on the launch pad and so would not retarget others to compensate. Wohlstetter's grounds for believing that Rathjens had erred was that he had not used the "official" estimates of all of these metrics, which meant those used by the Department of Defense.[53]

Rathjens responded in both classified form and an open letter to the *New York Times*, arguing that he had not used different numbers for hardness and accuracy of Soviet warheads, but had employed a composite figure that gave the probability of Minuteman destruction derived from public data released by DoD. He likewise argued that differences in yield were insignificant. Rathjens charged that the difference stemmed instead from Wohlstetter's erroneous belief that the Soviets had the means to determine which of their missiles had malfunctioned while their first strike was still underway. On the basis of this, Wohlstetter had assumed that the Soviets would be able to quickly reprogram their remaining forces to eliminate the surviving Minutemen in a manner that Rathjens argued was unrealistic.[54]

The Rathjens-Wohlstetter controversy showed how abstract and esoteric the military-technical debate over ABM had become, but also how difficult it would be to come to a consensus view given the deep levels of mistrust and antipathy that existed between the two sides. The two professors could not even agree which metrics they disagreed on, let alone attempt to reconcile them. Wohlstetter's "official" figures were the ones used by Laird— exactly the numbers that the opposition claimed were overly pessimistic regarding the Soviet threat. Fundamentally, all the figures used by both sides were merely estimates. As Wohlstetter admitted in his Senate testimony, "sizeable uncertainties [were] intrinsic" to the analysis of nuclear strategy.[55] The problem was that such uncertainties had become determining: the technical judgments such as the accuracy of Soviet warheads were so marginal that they could not be proved one way or the other, yet these variations made the difference between one in four Minutemen surviving a Soviet first strike, or one in twenty. The delicate balance of terror had instead, in historian Gregg Herken's telling phrase, become the delicate "balance of error."[56] Quantitative analysis, which during the relative consensus of the early 1960s had injected the appearance of cool-headed certainty into decisions regarding nuclear weapons programs, melted in the political heat of the 1969 ABM controversy.

The same was true of the two sides' varying assessments of Soviet intentions. Both pretended to have a special insight into the way the Soviet leadership thought about foreign and defense policy. Nixon claimed that the system did not aim to protect American cities from a Soviet retaliatory strike. The USSR, Nixon reasoned, would therefore not need to further augment its forces in order to maintain its ability to punish the United States— a move that would spark a further American reaction and a deepening of the arms race.[57] Opponents pointed out that military elites in the USSR would use Safeguard as a justification to continue the nuclear competition. Despite the system's manifest flaws, ABM critics maintained, Soviet officers would argue that they could not afford to take the chance and Moscow would devote yet more of the country's stretched resources to matching its estimate of the American threat. "To a much greater extent than either side would like to admit," wrote Soviet expert Marshall Shulman, "psychological apprehensions and bureaucratic politics tend to determine defense policies. Rational doctrine comes along as an afterthought."[58]

Both arguments rested on unprovable assumptions because hard evidence regarding the basis of Soviet strategic decision making did not exist, even for those with access to the best intelligence on Soviet intentions. At the same time that it was confidently putting forward the view that the Soviets would not react to ABM deployment, the administration was embroiled in a debate on exactly how the USSR thought about nuclear strategy. The problems were obvious at a meeting of the NSC's Review Group in May 1969. The experts were ambivalent on whether the USSR wanted parity with the United States or was really driving for superiority through a first-strike capability. On whether a further buildup in US forces could pressure the Soviets to negotiate, "Kissinger said he had seen strong arguments on both sides, i.e., that the Soviets were more conciliatory when scared or more conciliatory when not scared." Helmut Sonnenfeldt, an NSC staffer, admitted that the administration "just [didn't] know Soviet purposes," emphasizing that nobody could be certain of whether a position of strength would induce an acceleration in Soviet weapons programs or conciliation because "history provided examples for each view." Kissinger raised the possibility that the USSR might arm and negotiate at the same time, just as the Nixon administration was doing.[59]

In the words of Gregg Herken, "the ABM hearings had raised . . . all of the fundamental points in contention between the experts concerning Russian motives and the stability of deterrence—and resolved none of them."[60] In some sense, this was hardly surprising. Given the complexity of the arms race and lack of knowledge regarding Soviet motives, combined with the political divisiveness of foreign and defense policy in the late 1960s, it could be argued that the Nixon administration would have faced heavy attack from either side regardless of the position it took on ABM.

Yet the administration had erred by believing that it could rely solely on the authority of the executive branch to carry its side of the argument. With so many disillusioned liberal-leaning Kennedy and Johnson-era scientists out of office, the dispersal of expertise had rendered that impossible. Laird could no longer count on the monopoly of knowledge that had allowed McNamara to shift rationales under the screen of quantitative data. The truth was that McNamara's numbers had been no more plausible than Laird's. The image of cool-headed rationality that had underpinned the Kennedy-McNamara-Johnson approach to nuclear strategy had worked because of a fundamental trust that the executive would gather all the facts and make the right choice. The ABM debate in Congress showed that this was no longer the case among the political and expert class. This reflected a broader public skepticism regarding the costs of militarized containment of the Soviet Union. By July 1969, 53 percent of respondents to an American Institute for Public Opinion poll believed the United States was spending "too much" on defense.[61] In the wake of Vietnam, public trust in the executive's rationality was low, leaving the Nixon administration to struggle with the results.

In the face of these difficulties, however, the administration refused to change tack. Instead it placed even more presidential weight behind the program in a way that reverted to traditional arguments of peace through strength. On June 4, Nixon delivered the commencement address at the Air Force Academy in Colorado Springs where he made the big ideological case for maintaining levels of defense expenditure. Current controversies over levels of military spending and Vietnam were merely "a symptom of something far deeper," the president declared. He described a rising political group in American society that he labeled "the new isolationists." Their message of military retrenchment to save money was superficially appealing, Nixon argued, and a weak leader might "buy some popularity" by going along with them. Nixon, however, would not give in to "unilateral disarmament" because, he intimated, this group was un-American:

> My disagreement with the skeptics and the isolationists is fundamental. They have lost the vision indispensable to great leadership. They observe the problems that confront us; they measure our resources and then they despair. When the first vessels set out from Europe for the New World these men would have weighed the risks and they would have stayed behind.[62]

If the country listened to the new isolationists, Nixon argued, America would become "a dropout" and the rest of the world would "live in terror" of "the kind of peace that suffocated freedom in Czechoslovakia" in 1968.[63] Faced with objections to his administration's military-technical arguments that had brought the demise of the consensus of peace through strength into high relief, Nixon returned to the fundamental case: military spending was vital to maintaining American leadership in the defense of freedom. To listen to the Cassandras advocating retrenchment would be to leave the world open to its enemies in a way that would eventually endanger the security of the United States.

Nixon was delivering the established message in support of militarized containment of communism, but rather than bringing his opponents into line it polarized the debate further. The reaction of the press to the speech was generally negative and did little to win over his opponents, who hit back that Nixon's rhetoric belied his supposed transformation from anticommunist demagogue into a moderate. "It sounded like the old Nixon I used to know," Albert Gore told journalists: willing to tar his enemies with the communist brush in order to secure victory. As historian Rick Perlstein has noted, the president had indeed reprised one of his old leitmotifs—an attack on the "so-called best circles," as Nixon characterized them, who like alleged Soviet spy Alger Hiss would actually lead the country down the path to destruction.[64] *Time* described such a view as wrong-headed, pointing out that "Responsible critics . . . advocate neither unilateral disarmament nor withdrawal from foreign alliances. They merely raise questions of tactics and costs."[65] Nixon had attempted to reach out to the old public consensus in favor of nuclear strength, but it appeared to have evaporated.

NIXON'S STRATEGY IN DISARRAY

With Safeguard in major trouble in the Senate, Nixon and Kissinger realized that any leverage it could give them with the Soviet Union was eroding fast. The Soviets cooled noticeably to the idea of beginning talks. Kosygin waited for almost two months to reply to Nixon's letter intimating that progress should be made on the Middle East and Vietnam before negotiations could begin. When he finally did in late May, the Soviet premier explicitly rejected the notion of linkage, citing "the complexity of each of these problems by itself."[66] There was no indication that the USSR was keen to enter into negotiations in the near future. Kissinger attributed this to the Soviets "wanting to watch the outcome of our domestic debates to see whether we might be forced into unilateral 'restraint.'"[67] Far from gaining America leverage, the passionate and divisive debate over Safeguard gave the Soviets a clear view of how controversial further expenditure on nuclear weapons would be and raised the possibility that the Senate would scrap the ABM without the need for a bilateral agreement.

Nor was there much sign that postponing arms talks had facilitated progress on regional issues. In reality the level of pressure the Soviet Union could have brought to bear on its Southeast Asian and Middle Eastern clients was minimal. Dobrynin tried to explain to Kissinger that his government feared cutting off supplies to North Vietnam, lest the People's Republic of China fill the void and assume leadership of the communist world. Nor was there any meaningful progress toward talks that could lead to a resolution of the aftermath of the 1967 Six Day War between Israel and its Arab neighbors.[68] Nixon dropped the demand that talks be contingent on further steps in other areas. Rogers met with Dobrynin on June 11 and offered to start substantive arms control discussions on July 30 or 31.[69]

Nixon made the approach public on June 19, but to no avail.[70] The Kremlin held off on any acceptance until after the outcome of the Safeguard vote.

At the same time as it reversed its position on SALT the administration also re-examined its opposition to a compromise on ABM. One of the most promising deals was a proposed amendment by Senator Thomas McIntyre (D-NH), which authorized funds for building the radars at the two sites selected for construction in FY 1970, but held back money earmarked for the defensive missiles and purchase of further land. Nixon's domestic staff remained convinced, however, that talk of compromise was unnecessary and potentially dangerous. "We are on the threshold of breaking the opposition's back," Butterfield wrote to the president on the same day Rogers saw Dobrynin. "Why then should we now get out the white flag? . . . The mere knowledge of its existence will excite and energize the other side and seriously threaten a reversal." Nixon demurred on an open approach, ordering his aides to maintain a "*hard* line publicly" while exploring "a very careful explanatory line privately."[71]

Nixon was sufficiently worried to continue study of the McIntyre compromise as a last resort. Kissinger's staff approved it in late June, noting that there was "no missile silo construction . . . planned for FY 70 in any event," meaning that such an arrangement would not pose a significant setback to Safeguard's deployment.[72] By July 10, the administration was sufficiently uncertain that it would get the votes that Nixon instructed Kissinger, Harlow, and Klein to prepare the ground for a reversal by calling in friendly journalists to write a story depicting the McIntyre amendment as "exactly what he asked for in his original statement."[73]

A "CLOSE, ROUGH VICTORY"

Soon, Nixon's confidence returned. On July 14, Winston Prouty, junior senator from Vermont, announced that he would vote in favor of ABM despite voting against it in 1968. Declaring that Safeguard would give the president "an extra button" in the event of a nuclear attack, Prouty had been heavily leaned on by the Nixon White House through their contacts with the governor of Vermont. The administration had made clear that, if Prouty did not vote for Safeguard, he could expect very little support in his difficult 1970 reelection campaign.[74] With Prouty in the bag and the House of Representatives never in doubt, Nixon's team believed it could win. Even if Safeguard were marginally amended, the conference between the two houses of Congress was weighted firmly in favor of senior senators who backed the administration's program: Stennis, Russell, Jackson,

Thurmond, and John Tower (R-TX).[75] All the strategic and ideological arguments notwithstanding, Safeguard was won through old-fashioned arm twisting and horse-trading.

Opposition mistakes also made a contribution to the wafer-thin final vote. Edward Kennedy drove his car off a bridge in Chappaquiddick on July 19, killing Democratic Party worker Mary Jo Kopechne. This precipitated the scandal that ended his presidential ambitions for the foreseeable future and weakened his anti-ABM advocacy.[76] Most importantly, critics struggled to unite around a single Senate amendment. The majority, including John Sherman Cooper (R-KY) and Philip Hart (D-MI)—as in 1968, the two senatorial leaders of ABM opposition—were against deployment but in favor of research and development on Safeguard. Margaret Chase Smith of Connecticut was the most hardline, condemning spending for research and development on Safeguard as well as for construction. On August 5 she introduced an amendment that stripped all funds from Safeguard and missile defense programs, but it attracted only eleven votes. In an effort to get Smith's vote, Cooper and Hart backed a second Smith amendment on August 6 that authorized research and development for new systems, but not Safeguard. Safeguard came perilously close to defeat: fifty senators voted for the amendment, but a majority was needed to carry it. With Vice President Spiro Agnew casting his vote in favor, the final tally stood at 50–51. Remaining waverers, including Clinton P. Anderson (D-NM), and John Williams (R-DE), may have been swayed by the hastily drafted nature of the new language. Safeguard advocates attacked this last-minute amendment as "legislating in the dark." Smith then voted against the Cooper-Hart amendment that would have authorized research and development funds for Safeguard, leaving the count for Cooper-Hart at 49–50. Twenty-one Democrats voted with the Nixon administration, of which sixteen were from the South.[77]

Nixon was elated with his win on Safeguard. He saw it as evidence of the effectiveness of the "Nixon style" of executive-legislative relations. He ordered his staff to argue that ABM had passed as a result of the president's courageous leadership in the face of astounding odds and "against the advice of most of his senior advisers." The president believed his March 14 announcement had "turned the thing around and started us on the way up."[78]

Nixon claimed that "never was there any implication of arm-twisting, threats, etc." during the Safeguard campaign.[79] It would indeed have been wise for the White House to eschew such tactics. Many in Nixon's team, particularly Kissinger's NSC staff and some of his speechwriters, had argued that a confrontational approach to Safeguard would polarize opinion in a way that would weaken the administration's position. Yet Nixon had not only used "arm-twisting" tactics, most notably on Winston Prouty, but had also spurned many opportunities to reach a compromise with his opponents. He had even implied in his Air Force Academy speech that anyone who disagreed with him would never have made it to America in the first place. As the *Washington Post* editorialized, "There was plenty of room . . . for an accommodation . . . [But] The administration determined to go for a close, rough victory in the Senate."[80]

A "close, rough victory" was hardly the vote of confidence that Nixon had wished for to strengthen his hand at SALT. The president's initial attempts at linkage in 1969 had been unsuccessful for a number of reasons, most notably the administration's overestimation of the extent of Soviet influence over their third-world allies. Yet the contentious and close debate over ABM was surely another reason. Nixon had spurned the Soviets' offer of talks at the outset of his administration, yet by June it was he who had to approach the USSR. Seeing the trouble ABM was in, the Soviets waited Nixon out. Contrary to his initial instincts, the president now appeared to need an arms control agreement more than the Kremlin.

THE OPENING OF SALT

Despite the way in which the bruising domestic political battle of the summer had diminished optimism regarding linkage between SALT and Vietnam, initial soundings with the Soviets still gave the Nixon administration some hope regarding the utility of Safeguard as a bargaining chip at the negotiations themselves. Exploratory talks on strategic arms opened in Helsinki on November 17, 1969 and lasted until December 22. It soon became clear that the Soviet delegation had decided to disavow Kosygin's earlier argument, put to Johnson at Glassboro, that ABM posed no threat to stability because it was purely defensive. The chief Soviet negotiator, Vladimir Semenov, spent the vast majority of his allotted time at the November 28 plenary session addressing the ABM issue. He adopted McNamara's position that missile defenses would fuel the arms race because they threatened the other side's confidence in its retaliatory capability, thereby forcing the opponent to react.[81] The administration was gratified by the way that the Russians had shown their hand. Kissinger believed that, of all ongoing US strategic programs, the Soviets were "the most anxious to stop" Safeguard.[82]

Not only did the Soviet delegation express its anxiety over the US ABM program, but through informal channels it also suggested what kind of limitations it would favor. In his November 28 plenary speech, Semenov identified three possible levels for ABM under an agreement: zero, a system limited to capitals, and one covering the entire national territory of the two sides. In addition to their objections to nationwide systems, the Soviets made it known informally that, although a complete ban was possible, they would prefer to retain a limited number of ABM launchers in order to deal with the "third country problem"—by which they clearly meant communist China. Kissinger's staff speculated that it would be "doubtful that the Soviets, after all these years and efforts" would dismantle the Moscow ABM—a course that would "at the very least . . . provoke a major battle with the military."[83] By the time the talks concluded, therefore, the Americans understood that the Soviets favored limitations on ABM systems and that the Kremlin would likely prefer those limitations to include the existing defenses around Moscow.

While the administration appeared to be succeeding in using Safeguard as a means to put general pressure on the Soviets, it struggled to define the precise way in which ABM should be used to extract concessions from the USSR on offensive forces. Timing was not on the Americans' side. Nixon had pledged to review the deployment scheme for Safeguard in light of the progress at SALT. However at Helsinki the Soviets had moved resumption of talks back from February to mid-April 1970, meaning that decisions regarding the level of funding for Safeguard in FY 1971 had to be taken before any substantive negotiations took place.[84]

Bureaucratic rivalry exacerbated the situation. The Defense Department pushed for further deployment of Safeguard, which it argued would both put the onus on the USSR for concessions and provide a residual missile defense capability if talks failed. DoD initially advocated starting construction on two more sites, one near the coast in the Pacific Northwest and another to protect the Minuteman missiles at Whiteman Air Force Base, Missouri. At the same time, Defense urged the White House to select sites and begin survey work for three more installations: one on the Michigan-Ohio border; another near Washington, DC; and a third on a site site somewhere in the Northeast. DoD maintained that the Soviets would only agree to meaningful concessions on offensive weapons at SALT if the United States continued to display its capability to defend Minuteman in the absence of an agreement.[85]

This was not a view shared by the arms controllers. Gerard Smith, head of the SALT delegation and director of the Arms Control and Disarmament Agency, regarded such an expansive program as unnecessary. A new Safeguard phase, he believed, could be postponed while both sides talked. In Smith's view, congressional backing for the system in principle was more important for maintaining pressure on the Soviets than a concrete commitment to deployment. He predicted that keeping the system in research and development "likely would broaden somewhat support for Safeguard," thereby upping the Soviet imperative to negotiate meaningfully.[86] Wanting to continue to exert pressure on the Soviets, Nixon opted for DoD's recommendation to proceed with construction. However, he ordered another review of the specific deployment options, which settled on three alternatives: Whiteman Air Force Base and an unspecified site in the Pacific Northwest; Whiteman and Washington, DC; or Whiteman only.[87]

Despite rejecting Smith's arguments, the administration did take congressional pressure into account. Kissinger steeled Nixon for "another bloody fight on the Hill," and even the Joint Chiefs were chastened by the previous year's experience. JCS Chairman General Earle Wheeler was wary that the "heat from [the] localities" could potentially stiffen Senate opposition to Safeguard.[88] Henry Jackson, a staunch administration supporter, was also worried. He effectively doomed the Northwest site by opposing it on the grounds that he could not afford opposition at home in a year when he was facing reelection.[89]

Both Kissinger and Jackson also feared the backlash that a Washington, DC site would face in the Senate. This was based on anxiety over a reprise of the previous year's protests and reinforced by the politically toxic charge that a Washington, DC ABM would protect "politicians and generals, but not ordinary people."[90] The administration was intent on avoiding a repetition of the previous year's showdown in the Senate. At best this could further damage the American contention that Safeguard would proceed without an ABM agreement. At worst Safeguard could be defeated in the Senate, with disastrous consequences for the American position at SALT.

The final decision on Safeguard Phase II had all the hallmarks of a classic bureaucratic compromise. Phase II was geared more toward satisfying all constituencies within the US government and the administration's congressional anxieties than serving any coherent military-technical or diplomatic purpose.[91] Safeguard remained essentially a limited defense of Minuteman with no determination as to its final shape. The administration rejected the Pentagon's request for a site in the Northwest, opting for a single site at Whiteman Air Force Base to protect another wing of ICBMs. The White House also assented to preparatory work for five additional installations, including one near Washington, DC.[92] The administration had moved forward, but extremely cautiously. By expanding to one further site, the Nixon administration had done the absolute minimum necessary to maintain the momentum behind the program that DoD had argued was required to maintain pressure on the USSR at SALT and ensure the deterrent was protected in the event talks failed. At the same time, it had taken congressional opinion into account, as well as the need to keep all options on the table for SALT.

"A FIRST-CLASS BLUNDER"

The caution that the administration had shown regarding the domestic political implications of its congressional strategy, however, was completely thrown out when it came to developing the opening US position for the first substantive round of SALT, which commenced in April 1970 in Vienna. The Americans offered an almost perfect deal on ABM, from the Soviet perspective: a low level of missile defense limited to national capitals—in the jargon of SALT, National Command Authorities (NCAs).[93] This would allow the Soviets to keep their Moscow system, but leave the Nixon administration faced with the unenviable task of pushing a Washington, DC defense through Congress, a course it was extremely wary of. It would also cut the American program drastically, requiring the dismantling of both of the sites that Nixon had fought so hard for in 1969, as well as the additional site at Whiteman that was making an equally tortuous passage through the Senate. The Americans married this very favorable ABM proposal with a tough position on offensive weapons that would require either a ban on MIRVs coupled with intrusive on-site inspections of Soviet missiles, or ICBM reductions that would tilt the strategic balance in favor of the United States.[94] In response to this strange mixture, the Soviets accepted NCA "in principle" and rejected the offensive proposal, effectively depriving the United States of one of its major bargaining chips that it had to trade for a cap on Soviet offensive forces. As Kissinger later admitted in his memoirs, this opening position constituted "a first-class blunder," with the American side left with an ABM proposal "requiring us to dismantle what we had built and to build something we had not asked for," with no corresponding Soviet concessions on offensive weapons.[95]

Memoirists have put forward two competing explanations for this error. SALT delegation member Raymond L. Garthoff has ascribed it to Nixon and Kissinger's ignorance regarding the change in the Soviet negotiating position to one that favored limitations on missile defense. Believing that the Soviets still subscribed to the pro-ABM views Kosygin propounded to Johnson at Glassboro, Garthoff argues, Nixon and Kissinger calculated that the Soviets would reject the NCA option. This would give the administration political ammunition against the congressional anti-ABM movement by allowing it to say that it had negotiated for strong limitations in good faith, only to be rejected by the Soviets.[96] Kissinger, by contrast, blames the high level of bureaucratic infighting involved in hammering out the American opening position, which, he claims, blinded him to the question of how the disjuncture between the administration's congressional program and its stance at SALT would be reconciled.[97]

There is more evidence to support Kissinger's claim than Garthoff's. Contrary to Garthoff's assertion, it is clear that Nixon and Kissinger were well aware of the change in the Soviet ABM position. Reports from Helsinki highlighted the new Soviet view on missile defense. A Special National Intelligence Estimate prepared in the wake of the Helsinki talks emphasized the extent to which the Soviets had reversed their previous position.[98] Nixon was aware of this, underlining Kissinger's conclusion that the Soviets would probably prefer "a limited ABM system for protection against third country attacks," noting in the margin: "K[issinger]— this is what they will insist on."[99] If the White House had wanted to offer a position to propitiate Safeguard's critics that the Soviets would be sure to reject, it would have proposed a complete ban. Instead, it offered a limited system, which it knew to be within the range of potential Soviet preferences.

It is clear that the infighting between DoD, State, and ACDA over SALT was intense. The final evaluation report drawn up by Kissinger's staff, which outlined areas of difference between the agencies as well as potential types of agreement, ran to over 130 pages. ACDA and State supported any position that looked as if it would facilitate an agreement, while Defense did the opposite. The American capability to monitor any agreement on ABM and MIRV was a peg on which both sides hung many of their arguments. Overall, ACDA and State, supported by the CIA, took a far more optimistic view of the American ability to verify various forms of arms control agreements and downplayed the strategic significance of any Soviet cheating that could take place. Defense and the chiefs, by contrast, maintained a highly skeptical attitude toward American verification capabilities and were far more concerned with the strategic implications of any Soviet attempts to circumvent a treaty.[100]

At the heart of the argument lay a tradeoff between ABM and MIRV. MIRV, which gave US forces the capability to penetrate any conceivable clandestine Soviet ABM, could obviate the need for high confidence in verification of Soviet compliance with an ABM limitation. The JCS also held fast to MIRV because, they maintained, the rapid proliferation of Soviet military facilities meant that without MIRV the United States would not have enough warheads to destroy all necessary targets in the USSR or penetrate any possible secret Soviet ABM system.[101] Therefore, given the need to offer at least some limitations in the American SALT proposal, the Pentagon was willing to sacrifice Safeguard in order to save MIRV.

Given the military's priorities the Nixon administration opted to proceed with MIRV, albeit through a roundabout procedure. The White House initially proposed a MIRV ban at SALT, but couched it in a way that would almost certainly be unacceptable to Soviet negotiators. The ban required onsite visits by US inspectors to the USSR's operational ICBM launchers, which would surely be rejected by the Soviet military.[102] Unlike the ABM limitations, the Nixon administration proposed this insincere MIRV ban in order to propitiate congressional opinion. On April 9, the day the president made his decision on the SALT position, a sense of the Senate was passed that called on the White House to suspend deployment of both ABM and MIRV during the negotiation of a strategic arms accord. Although only an opinion of the Senate and not amounting to law, the resolution passed by 72–6, meaning that, in Kissinger's words, the White House would be "driven to discuss" a MIRV ban. Kissinger advised Nixon that by proposing limits on both ABM and MIRV, the president would be able to display his arms control credentials to skeptical senators.[103] To this offensive option, which was favored by senatorial doves, the White House added a second backed by hawks. The Department of Defense pushed for a proposal on offensive weapons that required a cap on ICBM and SLBM launchers of one thousand by January 1, 1978. This would be achieved through retiring ICBMs only. The proposal included special limits for the SS-9, a stipulation that would reduce the potential threat Soviet land-based missiles posed to the US ICBM force. This second proposal was highly unlikely to be acceptable to the Soviet Union because of the relative importance Moscow placed on its ICBMs compared to its ballistic missile submarines.[104] Thus, the White House integrated two alternative offensive proposals into its initial SALT position for Vienna—a MIRV ban and an ICBM reduction proposal— to satisfy doves and hawks respectively.

Kissinger is therefore correct that bureaucratic and domestic political considerations predominated in discussions over the US opening position at SALT, to the detriment of questions regarding Soviet reactions and negotiating tactics. Possible Soviet responses were not completely ignored, however. In his instructions to the delegation, Nixon emphasized that the USSR could not pick and choose parts of an option that it liked while bargaining over the rest. Each proposal, the president emphasized, had to be accepted or rejected as a whole package.[105]

Yet this is not what happened. On April 27, with the Vienna talks barely ten days old, the Soviets signaled that they would accept limitation of missile defense to national command authority levels while rejecting the American approach to offensive arms.[106] Despite this major upset, Washington did not authorize a new offer for over three months, leaving the US negotiators sitting on a position in favor of ABM limitations that gradually became entrenched with repetition.[107] While the initial lopsided American offer could plausibly be blamed on a focus on bureaucratic and domestic politics, the error of leaving the delegation sitting on an inadequate position has not been adequately explained.

THE BACKCHANNEL AND THE SEARCH FOR A SUMMIT

This neglect was the result of Nixon and Kissinger's concentration on secret backchannel efforts to reach an accommodation with the Soviet Union, which made the White House less invested in both the initial US proposal at SALT and the Soviet counteroffer. At the same time that the federal bureaucracy was becoming bogged down in the military-technical minutiae of the United States' opening SALT position, Kissinger secretly opened a second channel to Soviet Ambassador Anatoly Dobrynin. On February 18, 1970, Kissinger suggested that while "formal negotiations" took place in Vienna, he and Dobrynin could "deal with general principles" in one-on-one meetings.[108] On April 7, with the governmental infighting over SALT reaching a fever pitch, Kissinger reassured the ambassador of the White House's "willingness to settle a more limited agreement in this channel with him."[109] On April 9, the day Nixon made his final decision on the opening SALT position, Kissinger told the Soviet ambassador that, "[o]ne way" to reach an agreement "might be for a recess to be taken after a few months at Vienna, during which time the president and the Soviet prime minister could break a deadlock" through the backchannel.[110] It was important, Kissinger emphasized to Dobrynin, to keep knowledge of these talks secret from the Soviet Vienna delegation, because the US SALT team was "totally out of the loop regarding this aspect of the issue."[111] Thus even before the negotiations began, Nixon and Kissinger had established a scenario in which talks would grind to a halt, to be saved by communication between heads of government at the highest level.

This approach for a backchannel compact was impelled by Nixon's growing desire for a summit meeting. By the beginning of 1970, Nixon was under increasing pressure to make good on some aspect of his peace rhetoric. Despite promising on the campaign trail in 1968 to "end the war and win the peace" in Vietnam and his pledge to build a "structure of peace" in his inaugural address, the president had achieved very little of substance during his first year in office.[112] Initial approaches to the Chinese regarding a rapprochement had gone nowhere, nor had the Paris peace negotiations combined with intensified bombing of North Vietnamese sanctuaries in Cambodia produced progress toward a settlement in Southeast Asia. With congressional elections coming up in November, Nixon needed a foreign policy success.[113]

Faced with the daunting task of getting the opening SALT position through the interagency process, Nixon and Kissinger saw the backchannel as a way of reaching out over the heads of stakeholders in Washington to conclude a compact through what would become their preferred method of operation: secret negotiations with a powerful individual in the opposing camp.[114] As Nixon told the Soviet ambassador personally on June 10, the key was for the two sides to reach agreement on "matters of principle." The arms control machinery could finalize "the details," but the backchannel would allow the two sides "to get right to the point . . . without looking over one's shoulder at bureaucrats."[115]

Following the Soviet rejection of the initial American offer, Kissinger attempted to put this plan into practice. After meeting Nixon on June 10, Dobrynin agreed to Kissinger's proposal that the Vienna talks would be strung out for approximately "three weeks, during which time" the two would "agree on a general outline" of a US–Soviet SALT agreement. While the ambassador reiterated Soviet objections to the United States' Vienna proposals and proposed an unacceptable ABM-only agreement linked to "some general agreement about protection against provocative attacks," the two agreed to confer with their respective governments.[116] After the meeting Kissinger was bullish, informing Nixon that the White House was "in good shape" regarding the talks, and predicted that "they will be wound up one way or another." Kissinger told Nixon that the president could "have a SALT agreement anytime this year."[117] According to Kissinger, it looked as though the president could indeed outflank his opponents with a surprise SALT accord.

By June 1970, Nixon's domestic political situation had deteriorated sharply, increasing his need for a summit. In late April, American forces had invaded Cambodia, sparking protests across college campuses that culminated in the shootings at Kent State University on May 4. In Kissinger's words, the idea of a summit meeting, which had "started as a maneuver[,] reached a point of near obsession" for the president. In his memoirs, Kissinger claims that he "maintained grave doubts" regarding a meeting, because the Soviets had yet to show any significant interest in concessions on a range of national security issues. Moreover, Kissinger argues, "Our China initiative was still in the balance; it could be easily wrecked by the appearance of collusion with the Soviets."[118] In fact, the national security advisor stoked his president's ambitions, reminding Nixon of the way in which Kennedy had used the Limited Test Ban to enhance his political fortunes. Nixon agreed that a US–Soviet summit would help him domestically. In reference to the Johnson-Kosygin meeting of June 1967, Nixon said that he wanted to "get the glow of Glassboro" for "our boys"—presumably a reference to Republican candidates in the November 1970 congressional elections. The fact of an agreement at the summit was far more important to Nixon than its substance. "Whatever you agree to I am for," the president told his national security advisor, "I don't understand the details."[119]

With the bureaucratic formulation of a new proposal grinding on, the White House waited for a Soviet response via the backchannel. However, two weeks later the pressure from Smith for new instructions, as well as Nixon's desire for more information on the potential summit, was becoming unbearable. Kissinger went to see Dobrynin again on June 23 in an attempt to wring some details out of him, a tactic that predictably produced little in the way of results.[120] This lack of movement just made Nixon even more "cranked up," according to White House chief of staff, Bob Haldeman.[121] It was only in early July that the Soviet leadership responded, not with a new proposal, but a more detailed version of their position at Vienna, which included an unacceptable stipulation that the US side include its tactical aircraft deployed in Western Europe, or forward-based systems (FBS), in any offensive deal. They also offered an ABM-only agreement, combined with "measures for reducing the danger of missile-nuclear war between the USSR and the US resulting from accidental or unsanctioned use of nuclear weapons."[122]

While the Americans considered it essential to include both offensive and defensive weapons in any such deal, with this new ABM and accidental war agreement the Soviets were clearly pushing for a compact covering defensive systems only. Kissinger did not totally dismiss the idea of a separate missile defense agreement, telling Dobrynin he would come back to him after further consideration of the matter. That evening he informed Nixon that if he "want[ed] an agreement on SALT," then the United States could "sign at any level."[123] Perhaps he did not immediately grasp the implications of Dobrynin's proposal, or maybe he felt he had invested so much of his own personal prestige that he could not admit defeat so soon after Dobrynin's reply had scotched any prospect of a deal. Dobrynin himself surmised that Kissinger was under considerable pressure from Nixon to reach "even the most limited agreement" in time for the November congressional elections.[124]

Giving up the central American bargaining chip without reciprocal Soviet concessions on offensive forces, however, went too far. There was simply not enough in the proposal to entice the Americans. Had Kissinger attempted to force the issue, the resistance from all of the agencies involved in SALT would have been overwhelming. At a meeting on July 1, the Verification Panel in charge of formulating US SALT positions had "agreed" that "[t]here would be no advantage to the U.S. in an agreement limiting ABMs only." Informed of the Soviet proposal on July 4, Smith also rejected it on the basis that ABM was the United States' "strongest bargaining counter" and should not be forsaken for a quick deal.[125] Nixon needed some concessions on offensive forces if he was to conclude a SALT agreement. Kissinger informed Dobrynin of this on July 9.[126] The two sides were simply too far apart on offensive weapons to make significant headway. Although talk of some kind of US–Soviet summit in 1970 rumbled on until late September 1970, the chances of a quick SALT agreement that could have provided the substance for such a meeting died that day.[127]

Nixon and Kissinger's reliance on the backchannel to the exclusion of the formal SALT negotiations had serious ramifications for the American position at SALT. With the White House concentrating on a breakthrough in secret negotiations, it allowed NCA-level ABM to become the status-quo position at the Vienna talks. Nixon and Kissinger made a big mistake by believing that the Soviets saw the Kissinger-Dobrynin exchanges in the same light as they did: a way to circumvent the messy bureaucratic maneuverings that characterized doing business through Vienna. In fact, Soviet sources have confirmed that there was no "backchannel" as far as the USSR was concerned. Instead, information from both American channels was fed to a central commission on which all the relevant arms of the Soviet government were represented: the Party Central Committee, the Ministry of Defense, the Ministry of Foreign Affairs, the KGB, military industry, and even the Soviet Academy of Sciences. This commission was designed specifically, as two of the USSR's arms controllers put it, "to work out an integrated and coherent Soviet government position on specific issues."[128] The Soviet position at Vienna was therefore not a sham, but a full representation of the country's interests—as the American position at Vienna should ideally have been. Nixon and Kissinger expected an entirely new proposal; what they received was a more detailed version of the agreements already suggested at Vienna.

Contrary to the White House's expectations, the dynamic of negotiations in the front channel was the governing trend of the talks. This entrenched NCA-level ABM as the consensus view while Nixon and Kissinger waited for a new proposal via Dobrynin. In response to Smith's request for new instructions, the Verification Panel decided to attempt to extricate itself from the politically untenable position it had found itself in regarding defense of national capitals by proposing to ban ABMs entirely.[129] Yet while Kissinger had been talking, the delegation had been arguing in favor of the same position for such a long time that, as the JCS representative, Royal B. Allison, told his superiors, "to put forward for Soviet consideration at this stage an alternative of zero ABM . . . would invalidate many of our arguments and raise serious question[s] in [the] Soviet mind regarding our objectives and intentions."[130] The Americans tried it anyway, but the Soviets simply indicated that they had already agreed to NCA and would like to retain the original formulation.[131]

AN AVOIDABLE DILEMMA

The situation that the White House found itself in by the second half of 1970 was an unenviable one. When he assumed office in January 1969, Nixon was seriously concerned with the erosion of the US strategic position during the 1960s as a result of the Soviet race for parity. Despite this unpropitious backdrop, he had hoped that SALT could both halt the Soviet nuclear buildup and provide the leverage to extract concessions from the USSR on his number one foreign policy challenge, Vietnam.

The swift collapse of the congressional consensus behind new strategic programs, exacerbated by the administration's uncompromising approach, had made it impossible to hold off talks as a way to pressure the Soviets to help in Southeast Asia. Despite this, the opening round of talks in November 1969 had suggested that the Soviets still wished to halt the US ABM system, which could have given the Nixon administration the leverage it needed to extract concessions on the Soviet offensive buildup. Yet the White House frittered this advantage away through a combination of bureaucratic bungling and a misguided attempt to circumvent the formal negotiations in the search for an early domestic political win. By the fall of 1970, the administration had few bargaining chips left to play in its attempt to use SALT to stem the growth of Soviet nuclear forces.

The domestic climate of antimilitarism and the maddening obtuseness of the Washington arms control bureaucracy provided an unpropitious working environment, but Nixon and Kissinger must take much of the blame for this turn of events. It was Nixon's misjudgment of the domestic mood that had led to the debacle over Safeguard in 1969, while his desire for a quick agreement lay at the root of the administration's mishandling of the opening rounds of SALT. Kissinger, meanwhile, acted not as a strategic "architect," but instead had played the role of Nixon's "willing accomplice," scrambling to fulfill his political master's wishes in spite of any reservations he may have held regarding their strategic wisdom.[132]

This focus on domestic politics and their circumvention via the back-channel explains how the United States made the transition from an insistence on strong linkage between any ban on ABM and a cap on Soviet offensive weapons to a situation in late 1970 that left the Soviet and American delegations far nearer to a missile defense agreement than an accord on offensive forces. Domestic political imperatives would also frame the White House's approach to solving this dilemma.

CHAPTER 5

Reconciliation with Necessity and the Race to the Summit, 1971–1972

The final two years of Richard Nixon's first term witnessed a series of breakthroughs that defined his administration's foreign policy and the process of détente. For Nixon, his political fortunes "suddenly rebounded" in 1971, triumphing against the odds and beating his domestic critics through a host of successes "that carried right into the presidential election year of 1972."[1] Though not the most dramatic or important development of 1971, the May 20 framework agreement governing the final phase of the SALT I negotiations provided the first major foreign policy success of Nixon's first term. A year later, the ABM Treaty and Interim Agreement on Offensive Forces constituted the essential substance for Nixon's historic visit to Moscow.

Nixon and Kissinger portrayed the second half of Nixon's first term as the period in which they overcame the huge domestic political barriers to an arms control accord through backchannel diplomacy. Nixon believed that he had shown fortitude in his negotiation of the May 20 agreement in standing up to both the Soviets and his congressional critics, who urged him to strike an agreement on missile defense only. "To hell with the political consequences," Nixon recalled saying to Kissinger during the Moscow Summit, remembering that he was "determined not to allow either the Pentagon on the right or the Soviets on the left to drive [him] away from the position [he] believed was in the best interests of the country." For Kissinger, the White House accomplished the "breakthrough" at SALT through his own masterful handling of negotiations with Dobrynin, settling a number of issues—most importantly the linkage between offensive and defensive forces—in a manner favorable to the United States. This was "achieved . . . despite an obviously weak bargaining position" created by the fractious domestic politics of the period, thereby "confirming White House dominance in foreign affairs."[2]

The Nixon-Kissinger story papers over a much more complex interaction between domestic politics and the United States' national security strategy during these years. With Vietnam as intractable as ever, Nixon needed to capture what he termed "the peace issue" before the commencement of the presidential campaign of 1972.[3] "The peace issue" was the growing desire for an amelioration of Cold War burdens—be it in Southeast Asia or the arms race. The May 20 agreement's announcement was pure domestic political theater, designed to outflank Nixon's Democratic critics, who were themselves limbering up for the 1972 contest. Rather than linking offensive and defensive weapons, as Kissinger maintains in his memoirs, the agreement decoupled them, leaving the Soviets with a larger number of intercontinental delivery vehicles than the United States.[4]

The final settlement in Moscow was not a masterful diplomatic triumph, but a true reflection of the difficulties in which the administration found itself midway through Nixon's first term. By late 1970 and early 1971, ABM was a busted flush. An agreement was needed to stem the tide of domestic opinion flowing against further augmentation of American nuclear forces. As a result of congressional opposition, deployment of Safeguard crawled to near standstill in these years, depriving the United States of what little leverage it retained after the disastrous NCA offer of April 1970. In response, Nixon and Kissinger agreed to cut their losses by conceding a treaty on ABM in exchange for a far looser agreement on offensive forces. The May 20 Agreement represented this fundamental compromise.

Nixon and Kissinger did not transcend their domestic problems, but accommodated themselves to them in a way that diverges from their later recollections. By late 1970 the president had realized that satisfying "the peace issue" held the key to a successful first-term policy record that he could take into the November 1972 election. However, they did so to the best of their ability, given the circumstances. Faced with the choice between leaving the way open for the Soviets to pull further ahead in strategic arms and an imperfect agreement that could both place a temporary cap on offensive forces and serve to enhance his domestic political fortunes, Nixon chose the latter.

SOVIET SALVATION FOR A FALTERING GRAND DESIGN

As 1970 closed, the Nixon administration's achievements were far outweighed by its frustrations. The White House continued to push for a summit meeting with the Soviets. Nixon met with Soviet Foreign Minister Andrei Gromyko in October in a last-ditch attempt to secure Soviet consent to a summit that could be publicized before the congressional elections.[5] Gromyko expressed some interest in a preliminary announcement regarding one, but Moscow decided against a public statement.[6] The two sides were as far apart on SALT as ever, Nixon arguing that if an accord "dealt only with ABM [the U.S.] could not accept it. If it dealt only with offensive missiles, the Soviet Union would not accept it."[7] The Soviets shared this frustration, Gromyko cabling back to Moscow that Washington did "not anticipate any serious agreement on strategic weapons" in the foreseeable future.[8]

The mediocre congressional results of November 1970 were the product of far more than the administration's record on foreign relations, but they reflected the general lack of progress in all areas from Vietnam to the economy. The Republicans failed to gain control of either house, picking up only two seats in the Senate. "Of the thirty-six candidates in twenty-one states for whom Nixon personally stumped," historian Robert Mason notes, "two-thirds lost."[9]

The situation at the SALT talks reflected and reinforced this perceived lack of progress. The third round, beginning on November 3, 1970, had produced virtually nothing by way of concrete results. The Americans stuck to their insistence that there could be no separate ABM treaty, while the Soviets continued to stress the need for an understanding on American forward-based aircraft in Europe as a precondition for progress on offensive limitations. By December 5, NSC staffer Hal Sonnenfeldt had concluded that the negotiations were "stalemated"; the best that could be hoped for would be rhetorical sparring until the conclusion of the session in two weeks' time.[10]

However, on December 8 Semenov made a statement that proposed an "agreement" (soglashenie) regarding defensive weapons, coupled with an "understanding" (dogoverennost') on offensive arms.[11] Sonnenfeldt and the NSC's resident systems analyst, K. Wayne Smith, were wary regarding this new development. They considered it inadvisable "to get in last-minute temptations for deals whereby our programs are constrained explicitly 'by agreement' and theirs only tacitly 'by understanding.'" They counseled Kissinger to play it cool. The United States should wait for the Soviets to make the first move, putting them in the role of supplicant. "If the Soviets really want to make a deal," Smith and Sonnenfeldt argued, "they know our phone number."[12]

Such a position made diplomatic sense, but clashed with the growing desire in the White House for some form of foreign policy breakthrough at, as Nixon later described it, "the lowest point" of his presidency before Watergate.[13] There appeared to be scant possibilities for achievements in other areas. The prospects for peace in Southeast Asia were dim. While holding out hope for a settlement that would leave the South Vietnamese government with a chance of holding on the White House considered the total withdrawal of American combat troops. Electoral concerns were uppermost, Kissinger tempering Nixon's desire for a big announcement in 1971 because "trouble can start mounting in '72 that we won't be able to deal with and which we'll have to answer for at the elections." Peace with honor in this context appears to have meant peace with the maximum amount of political credit and minimal electoral blowback. Instead, Kissinger advised, it would be better to announce withdrawal by the end of 1972, thereby ensuring, in Haldeman's words, that the administration would not "have to deliver finally until after the elections and therefore can keep our flanks protected."[14] The Middle East proved no less intractable: both superpowers suspected the other of trying to undermine their influence in the region. The Soviets ramped up arms supplies to Egypt. Israel played on US anxieties by responding to American calls to reengage in UN peace negotiations with threats to talk directly to the Soviets about a future settlement.[15]

Absent unruly regional proxies and with a putative Soviet offer already on the table, SALT appeared a far better prospect for a quick agreement.[16] By late 1970, Kissinger was under pressure to deliver. He could not conceal his anxiety during his meeting with Dobrynin on December 22. According to Dobrynin's account, when the Soviet ambassador expressed his exasperation with Kissinger's "beloved global linkage theory," the national security advisor "began to make all sorts of excuses," suggesting that perhaps a separate ABM treaty might in fact be possible and asking for another meeting to discuss the matter further. It was the Soviet ambassador who presented the cold shoulder, arguing that it would be pointless to meet again if Kissinger was simply going to repeat the same "general observations." Kissinger promised to have a concrete proposal by their next meeting in early January.[17] The Soviets knew the White House phone number, but they never had to use it. Nixon and Kissinger were more than willing to play the supplicants in order to get an agreement.

If the style of Kissinger's approach confirms his critics' fears that he exposed the White House to domestic political manipulation by the Soviets, then the initial form of the Nixon-Kissinger proposal for an interim agreement was even worse. Far from emphasizing the linkage between offensive and defensive arms, Kissinger informed Dobrynin that the White House was "prepared to make an ABM agreement *only*," as long as there was agreement to halt missile construction on both sides while a more permanent offensive treaty was worked out. Kissinger also held open the possibility of a freeze on land-based ICBMs alone, leaving open the question of the rapid Soviet buildup in submarine-launched ballistic missiles (SLBMs).[18] In contrast to the administration's previous position, Kissinger perceived the agreement as a way to decouple offensive and defensive limitations. Dobrynin told his superiors that Kissinger underlined how, "in President Nixon's view, the main thing is to overcome the current impasse."[19] In essence, the White House was offering the Soviets almost everything Semenov had asked for on December 8 in the front channel, coupled with only the barest of pledges for further negotiations and a freeze that could potentially cover only one component of their offensive forces.

Yet by early 1971 such an offer was all Safeguard was worth. Further expansion of the system looked unlikely during that year's congressional debate for FY 72 appropriations, while the administration continued to grapple with the disjuncture between its SALT position and the program before Congress. The previous year, the White House had asked for minimal expansion of construction at another Minuteman missile field around Whiteman Air Force Base along with acquisition and preparation of five further installations, including one for Washington, DC. Congress granted Whiteman, but slashed the appropriation to cover land purchases for only one new site at Warren Air Force Base in Wyoming, safely away from any major cities.[20] By 1971, Defense acknowledged that domestic opposition made major progress on Safeguard hopeless, cutting its initial request to the White House for FY 72 to authorizing building at Warren and initial preparatory work for a site near Washington, DC.[21]

Even this looked unlikely. The mood was hardly supportive even among the administration's traditional conservative allies. Sonnenfeldt advised Kissinger that the key to the Safeguard lobby in the Senate, Henry Jackson, was against a defense for Washington, DC.[22] Aware that further construction at existing sites was far more likely to be passed by the Senate than the politically controversial NCA defense, the White House eventually asked for only the option to either build a further site at Warren or begin surveys around Washington, pending the outcome of SALT.[23] The administration did not get even this minimal expansion. In August 1971 the Senate Armed Services Committee authorized the procurement of complex components and "advance preparation" for Warren and Whiteman, but rejected the possibility of a defense around Washington, DC. Only the two original sites, at Grand Forks and Malmstrom, were approved for full construction.[24]

For arms control advocates, as Kissinger recounted in his memoirs, "the debate over the SALT position was beginning to merge with the almost religious annual opposition to the ABM." This was a situation for which, with its polarizing rhetoric on ABM in 1969, the administration had to take at least some of the blame. Details of the Soviet offer for an ABM-only agreement had begun to leak into the public and were supported by the *New York Times*, as well as Senator Frank Church, who was joined later by Hubert Humphrey, Harold Hughes, and George McGovern. In early March, Edmund Muskie took over the defeated Albert Gore's chairmanship of the Senate Foreign Relations Subcommittee on Arms Control and International Law and Organizations, which observers assumed he would use as a platform to attack the administration's arms control policies in preparation for an expected presidential run.[25] Originally intending to expand Safeguard on the basis of progress in arms control, the White House had effectively halted the program under congressional pressure with no commitment from the Soviets on offensive arms. Nixon summed it up succinctly to Kissinger and Haldeman in April 1971: "the reason we can't get the defense [appropriations] now is that the goddamn Congress won't give it to us."[26] In offering an ABM agreement with only limited controls on offensive forces, Nixon and Kissinger accepted that domestic political opposition now made Safeguard an almost useless bargaining chip at SALT.

The backchannel provided the best available option to maximize the credit the president could receive, capturing what Nixon called "the peace issue" from his Democratic critics.[27] Peace was not a word commonly associated with Nixon during this period. With no prospect of a settlement with Hanoi on acceptable terms, in February 1971 the United States supported South Vietnamese forces as they moved into Laos in order to disrupt the Ho Chi Minh Trail. It was a humiliation for the South Vietnamese military, which was outmaneuvered and outfought by its communist adversaries. Newspapers around the world published pictures of Saigon's troops clutching to departing helicopters in a bid to escape their opponents. In his memoirs, Kissinger argued that these experiences toughened the president to the point that he would "not to succumb to the human emotion of wanting the credit for the initiatives identified with peace."[28]

Nixon certainly did not have an emotional attachment to peace. "The American people are so peace-loving," he sneered, that "they think agreements solve everything." Yet polls were beginning to reflect public impatience with the lack of progress on Vietnam on Nixon's watch, with more against the administration's conduct of the war than approving. Nixon understood that the majority of Americans were tired of confrontation and saw the political benefits—albeit far short of a settlement in Vietnam—that could accrue from an arms control agreement that would beat his Democratic critics at their own game. He wanted to make the SALT agreement "for political reasons," agreeing with Kissinger's analysis that one of its main aims was "to break the back of this generation of Democratic leaders." With other aspects of the peace agenda embattled, Nixon needed to make the most of any progress in relations with the USSR. "If . . . this Soviet thing goes, we're not going to let these bastards take the credit for it," Nixon told Kissinger and Haldeman, "We've got to take the credit for it every time we turn around."[29] The focus was on getting one over on Nixon's opponents. "I'm not so sure the SALT thing is going to be all that important," the president told Kissinger on March 16, 1971, "I think it's basically what I'm placating the critics with." The national security advisor agreed. "Even if [a summit] gets a sort of half-baked SALT agreement," Kissinger hoped that at least it "would get us a few months of . . . quiet here."[30]

By then entering his ninth year as Soviet ambassador to the United States, Anatoly Dobrynin was an experienced and shrewd observer of American domestic politics. Yet even someone of considerably less political skill could have detected the extreme sensitivity of this particular president to his domestic predicament. On Christmas Eve 1970, Dobrynin received a phone call from Kissinger in which the national security advisor requested that senior members of the Politburo not receive Muskie during his planned visit to Moscow. In response to this blatant request to bolster the president's domestic political standing, Dobrynin advised his masters that the Kremlin "should play a certain game with Nixon," by showing him that they could affect his reelection prospects by holding up an agreement on key issues.[31] The Soviets were ready to play Nixon for all he was worth.

Dobrynin also understood the way in which the Soviets could manipulate the backchannel to their best advantage. He reported that Kissinger, "being highly ambitious," had a vested interest in "doing all he can to encourage" Nixon's desire for a summit in order to enhance his own power and prestige over that of the State Department. Most importantly, Dobrynin advised that this desire for a summit should be used "to exert additional pressure on the White House and bring about certain progress" on SALT. The Soviet ambassador also understood that secrecy made it difficult for Kissinger to juggle the technical details of the talks on his own, which was "undoubtedly leaving a considerable imprint on the current stage of the negotiations."[32] Dobrynin was unwilling to help Kissinger in that regard. The national security advisor complained of the "physical difficulty" of discussing SALT, Berlin, and the Middle East in the same channel. Dobrynin rejected his request to move the latter into another forum, thereby maximizing the potential for an American slipup.[33]

Perhaps emboldened by the rapidity with which Nixon and Kissinger had moved toward their position regarding a separate ABM treaty and the importance that Dobrynin had attached to the president's domestic need for a summit, the Soviets pressed for further concessions. Kissinger sent the Soviets a draft letter outlining the White House's offer of an ABM treaty coupled with an offensive freeze on February 22.[34] On March 12, the Kremlin insisted that negotiations on an offensive cap should wait until after the conclusion of an ABM treaty, which would thereby rob the United States of all leverage. It also reaffirmed the Soviet view that missile defense sites should be limited to capital cities, an unacceptable condition given the current state of Safeguard and the slim chance that such a system would be approved for Washington.[35] Kissinger responded four days later that the most the White House would accept was a commitment to focus on an ABM agreement in the first instance, while at the same time working out arrangements for a freeze in offensive arms that would enter into force simultaneously with an ABM treaty.[36]

During this period of stalemate, the Soviets remained committed to ensuring as loose a link as possible between the conclusion of defensive and offensive agreements. Until mid-May, the Kremlin shrugged off any attempt to insert language into the text of the understanding that would obligate even negotiation, let alone agreement, on offensive measures before an ABM treaty was signed. Kissinger was still insisting on a sentence in the letters formalizing the agreement that pledged that "the pertinent measures [for an offensive freeze] would be worked out while the agreement to limit ABMs is being negotiated."[37] Dobrynin refused to budge, maintaining that "he could assure [Kissinger] that the text was strong and clear and left no question about the intent" to sign simultaneous agreements, in the face of all evidence to the contrary.[38]

Under pressure from both the Soviets and Congress for an agreement on ABM, Nixon and Kissinger almost cracked. A Soviet attempt to nudge the White House into further concessions by initiating similar discussions in the front channel at Vienna in the first and second weeks of May led the White House to lash out at Dobrynin. Kissinger phoned the ambassador to tell him that the president was "furious" with the Soviets for authorizing an approach by Semenov to Gerard Smith, the head of the American SALT delegation. Kissinger accused the Soviets of bringing "pressure" on the White House by leaking a less favorable draft of the agreement in the front channel. "Do you want the president to think that after he turned [the offer] down you are then raising it with one of his diplomats to see if they will raise it?" Kissinger fumed.[39]

Dobrynin was clearly shocked by the tenor of his interlocutor's outburst and worried that he had pushed the White House too far. Fearing that Nixon had concluded the Kremlin was trying to undermine his reelection prospects by putting off an agreement, Dobrynin warned Moscow that "Nixon . . . is a very petty and distrustful man with a huge ego, who carries grudges." If the USSR held out much longer on an ABM agreement, these "personal traits," combined with the president's latent anticommunism, would soon lead to a deterioration of relations between the two countries.[40] Despite these fears, the Soviet ambassador held his nerve. The next day, May 12, Dobrynin dropped the Soviet insistence on ABMs limited to national capitals, but resisted a more specific definition of offensive-defensive linkage.[41]

THE IMPACT OF MAY 20

On May 20 Moscow and Washington issued a joint statement agreeing "to concentrate this year" on an ABM agreement and conclude "certain measures" on offensive forces.[42] This announcement succeeded in changing the tone of the American domestic debate over SALT in a way that both rendered short-term political dividends for the administration and relieved pressure for an immediate conclusion of an ABM-only agreement. Much of this stemmed from the formulation of the public statement that accompanied the secret understanding. Its brevity and vagueness made it perfect for spinning to both arms controllers and arms racers in ways that reassured both that their interests would be met.

The May 20 agreement allowed the president to capture "the peace issue" from the Democrats. For the editorial staff of the New York Times, Nixon was indeed transformed overnight from an inveterate warmonger into a peacemaker. Its editorial page praised the agreement as "a major forward step" that could pave the way for "the most important breakthrough toward nuclear arms control since the atomic test ban treaty of 1963."[43] This was particularly gratifying for Nixon, who had reveled in Kissinger's suggestion prior to May 20 that the president could secure an agreement that was "a lot better than the nuclear test ban."[44] Nixon was jubilant at how he had outmaneuvered the arms controllers by securing the prospect of an agreement on both defensive and offensive weapons when most of his critics believed only an ABM agreement was possible. "Henry, we are killing them," he told Kissinger as they pored over the New York Times coverage together on May 21. "There are senators out on limbs. Newspapers out on limbs."[45] Kissinger characteristically stoked the president's triumphalism, relaying how one of his journalistic contacts told him that the administration had "got the Democrats in an absolute stew because, every, every reasonable criticism has now been met . . . on SALT and only the nuts can oppose us."[46]

The May 20 agreement marked the beginning of the reconciliation between the White House and Democratic doves that intensified with Kissinger's trip to China in July and would last until Watergate. Previous antagonists suddenly became noticeably more cordial. Kissinger and J. William Fulbright began a friendly relationship over the telephone. Kissinger joked that he couldn't "afford" all the "publicity" Fulbright was giving him by praising the national security advisor's efforts, presumably because of the damage it was doing to his reputation with conservatives. Fulbright could give as good as he got. "I'm not as good a swinger as you," the senator responded, referencing Kissinger's allegedly wild love life, "but you are a hell of a lot younger."[47]

Kissinger agues in his memoirs that the exchange of letters between the two governments matched the public statement in its transformative impact on the negotiations:

> The Soviets had in effect accepted a freeze on new starts of strategic missiles; they had concluded a sublimit on heavy missiles; they had in effect dropped their claim that our aircraft based abroad be counted; and we had put them on notice that submarine-launched missiles would have to be limited or accounted for. In addition, we had managed to slide off our ill-advised NCA [ABM] proposal of the previous year.[48]

There is meager evidence in the letters exchanged between the two governments to substantiate Kissinger's expansive claims. The pertinent paragraph in the two-page American letter reads:

> To facilitate an agreement on limiting strategic offensive weapons, the United States government favors the idea of freezing strategic offensive weapons in principle and is prepared to reach a basic understanding on this point. The concrete details of this understanding, including such questions as the types of weapons to be frozen and the nature and dates of the freeze, would be discussed before the agreement to limit ABMs is completed. It is understood that the freeze on strategic offensive weapons would not preclude possible modernization and replacement.[49]

There is nothing in the letter that indicates Soviet acceptance of a sublimit on SS-9s. Indeed, by leaving the possibility of "modernization and replacement" open, the letter could indeed be considered as endorsing the substitution of older missile types for the Soviets' latest weapon. There is also no indication that the Soviets had been "put on notice" that SLBMs would be included; the most that can be said is that they had not been explicitly excluded.

Indeed, on the basis of Kissinger's conversations with Dobrynin, the Soviets could well have believed that the United States would go ahead with a freeze on ICBMs only. Kissinger had failed to clarify his position of early January regarding which weapons would be included in the offensive freeze. On January 28, Kissinger had confirmed Dobrynin's assertion that only "land-based missiles" would be frozen. On February 10, however, Kissinger had told the Soviet ambassador that the United States was prepared to conclude "either" an agreement covering ICBMs, or one that limited both ICBMs and SLBMs. Dobrynin for his part stated that the Kremlin was "prepared to discuss sea-based systems, but . . . preferred not to at this point." The best that can be said of the situation regarding the inclusion of SLBMs in the offensive freeze is that it was ambiguous. The Soviets could well have concluded that the United States was more flexible on the issue of SLBMs than turned out to be the case. This ambiguity would cause further problems for Nixon and Kissinger when they later sought to include SLBMs in the final offensive agreement.[50]

The status of Kissinger's claims regarding forward-based aircraft is also complex. By accepting a freeze, rather than reductions, the Soviets had implicitly conceded that forward-based aircraft would not be removed from Western Europe in order to confer parity in systems that could strike the homelands of the two superpowers—a position they had defended as recently as December 1970.[51] However, as Garthoff points out, in negotiations after the May 20 agreement the Soviets did not accept that FBS should be definitively excluded, but held the point in reserve for the future negotiations for a permanent agreement. On this point, therefore, Kissinger's claim that he had secured the exclusion of FBS from negotiations is only half true.[52]

Fundamentally, the American text only committed the two sides to talk about, not finalize, an agreement on an offensive freeze prior to the conclusion of an ABM treaty. This undermines Kissinger's claim that he had achieved his "main aim," which was "to link offensive and defensive limitations" in the text of the secret agreement.[53] If anything, the White House had conceded the primacy of ABM negotiations in exchange for a mere reaffirmation of the status quo on offensive discussions. This was a view Kissinger had previously shared when he wrote to Nixon commenting on a Soviet draft of late April that "only offered to discuss the idea of a freeze, not to conclude it." This was not "a concession" Kissinger had argued just weeks before the May 20 agreement, "since [the Soviets] were already obligated to discuss offensive limitations under the SALT agreement."[54] In the face of political pressure for an agreement both from the Soviets and Congress, Nixon and Kissinger had accepted the inevitability of a series of accords that did far more to satisfy Soviet anxieties regarding American ABM systems than US concerns with the USSR's offensive buildup.

Dobrynin claimed that the Kremlin's commitment to an offensive freeze "was covered" in the Russian text.[55] However, if anything, it was looser. While the American letter stated that the freeze "would be discussed before the agreement to limit ABMs is completed," the Soviet version could be interpreted to read, "the concrete details of such an understanding . . . *might be* discussed."[56] Helmut Sonnenfeldt, Kissinger's Russian-speaking assistant, provided a comparison of the Soviet and American letters on May 19, the day before the public announcement. Although Sonnenfeldt did not pick up on this key ambiguity, he did note that the Soviet version spoke of a "possible freeze" in offensive arms, rather than a firm commitment to one, thereby making the Soviet pledge more tenuous.[57] Even if he was not fully cognizant of the differences between the two texts, Kissinger was probably aware prior to the May 20 announcement that the language in the Soviet letter governing the linkage between offensive and defensive negotiations was even less watertight than that in the American version.

These differences would continue to dog the subsequent rounds of SALT in a way that weakened the American delegation's hand as they argued for simultaneity of negotiations on the basis of this document, the Russian version of which did not contain the guarantees the administration claimed.[58] Dobrynin already anticipated the future Soviet approach, advising the Kremlin that by delaying discussions on the offensive freeze until "the text of a separate ABM agreement was already mostly complete," the Soviets could dictate the pace of negotiations on an offensive freeze because "the Nixon administration would no longer find it so easy to walk away from what would essentially be a finished [ABM] agreement."[59] This was exactly what Moscow did over the next twelve months.

Such loose linkage between offensive and defensive agreements had to be concealed from Nixon's conservative allies in order to win their support. Nixon believed he needed what he described later as "the responsible right"—people like Henry Jackson and John Stennis—to go along with his arms control policy if he was to have a sufficiently wide coalition for a SALT agreement.[60] This required some significant liberties with the facts. The White House worried that in their effusive praise for the ABM aspect of the agreement, the *New York Times* and others might underplay the significance of the offensive limitations, which were essential to reassure conservatives.[61] On the day of the announcement, Kissinger phoned Jackson to secure his support by endorsing the senator's theory that the vague details of the agreement were designed to "save . . . a little face" for the Soviets. "We cannot say this publicly," the national security advisor assured the senator, but the Soviets could not consent to an open admission that there would be an agreement "on both offensive and defensive [weapons] because that would look like they were backing down." While this was a generous interpretation of the facts, what Kissinger said next was simply a lie. "We have an explicit understanding [on offensive-defensive linkage] which I don't want you to talk to anybody about," Kissinger said, thus securing both the senator's consent to the interim understanding as well as his silence. Jackson's consent was bought with a piece of supposed insider knowledge that was in fact false.[62] Kissinger was playing a dangerous game. Had Jackson gone public with the national security advisor's confidences, he could have been flatly contradicted by Soviet spokespeople, which would have destroyed his support for the agreement.

The White House recognized that it would be harder to convince hard-line conservatives of the agreement's soundness. Senator Strom Thurmond of South Carolina would not be placated, writing an opinion piece for the conservative journal *Human Events* in which he declared that "the Soviets have won their point for all practical purposes" by securing a pledge "that major attention would be given to the limitation of ABM systems first." While not explicitly attacking the administration, he noted that "The Soviets are seeking to encourage those elements within the American public who recoil from the harsh realities of the modern world and seek peace at nearly any price."[63] Thurmond was not the only one to fire a shot across the administration's bow. "If [Nixon] has an ace up his sleeve, the time to show it is soon," warned William F. Buckley, Jr., in the *National Review*, "If it isn't there, he will lose reelection, which is a minor consideration up against what he, his children, and his children's children stand to lose."[64]

The administration tried to placate these right-wing supporters-turned-critics. In an August 1971 meeting with representatives of major conservative organizations and publications, including *National Review* and *Human Events*, Kissinger pleaded for their understanding. Vietnam had led to a "collapse" in support for the basic premises of militarized containment, Kissinger argued. This meant that the administration was "in a daily fight for our lives with Congress, with the press, and with the bureaucracy" over strategic programs and arms control. Given this situation, Kissinger implied the May 20 agreement was the best that could be hoped for. On ABM, "The fact is that we cannot get either an adequate area defense or an adequate population defense," Kissinger concluded. With the Soviet buildup making a successful disarming first strike impossible, Kissinger argued that the United States' "advantage in ICBMs" that existed in the early 1960s could not "be resurrected." The attendees did not agree. Seemingly forgetting Nixon's unsuccessful intervention in the 1969 ABM debate, one participant called for "a direct personal appeal to the people" in order to bolster public support for the United States' strategic posture. Stan Evans of the *Indianapolis News* believed it was "a scandal" to leave the American public without an adequate defensive shield. "My conviction is that the *Washington Post* and the *New York Times* do not represent American public opinion," Evans shot back at Kissinger.[65]

Yet the administration thought it knew the state of public and congressional opinion better. This included the judgment that such conservative voices were in the minority. As Nixon explained to Gerard Smith months later, he considered "*Human Events, National Review*, and the rest" as "the nut right." If such people had their way, Nixon told Smith, he would never have a summit at all.[66] The White House ultimately felt that columnists such as Buckley were too extreme to make a mainstream impact. The country was heading in a dovish direction in 1971. Nixon and Kissinger saw people like Thurmond and Buckley as the remnants of Goldwaterism, not the harbinger of an emerging right-wing challenge to the entire détente project. When Buckley phoned Kissinger to inform him that he was going to "suspend" his endorsement of the administration over its opening to China, Kissinger told him that right-wing pushback would in fact assist the administration by providing a counterweight to the left's dominance in American domestic political discourse.[67] Nixon regarded those who questioned the details of the agreement as technical pedants who did not understand the bigger political picture. "Others will nitpick but we are going to have an agreement, Henry. Both you and I know that," Nixon told his national security advisor on the day after the May 20 announcement. "They will nitpick but there is going to be a deal."[68]

The May 20 agreement's main impact was to relieve some of the pressure from the American left to dispense with ABM before the end of SALT by showing progress toward a final settlement. Even in this regard however, it can only be seen as a partial success. Although much of the vituperative tone was removed from the domestic debate, the Senate's attitude toward Safeguard remained unchanged. In early August, the Senate Armed Services Committee reduced the White House's negotiating room by refusing its request for the option to build a site around Washington, DC.[69] The Soviets did their best to maintain this anti-administration mood in the upper chamber. In an attempt to push the Senate into even greater activism against Safeguard, Dobrynin told prominent ABM opponent John Sherman Cooper that, despite their protestations to the contrary, the White House had "never been serious about proposing zero ABM" at SALT, implying that Nixon had only done so in order to placate Cooper and other arms controllers.[70] The Soviets were attempting to maintain pressure in the Senate for greater American concessions.

As it had for the last two years, pressure from Congress served to undermine the notion of simultaneity between negotiations on offensive and defensive arms. In theory, under the terms of the May 20 agreement the SALT delegation could hold up progress on the ABM treaty if no Soviet concessions were forthcoming on offensive weapons. However, with the Senate slashing away at Safeguard even without a SALT agreement, the threat to proceed with the system was essentially worthless. Moreover, the Soviets continued to exploit American weakness regarding the Washington system in particular. The Soviets persisted in insisting on their interpretation of equality in ABMs, arguing that any deal must include the same number of missile defense sites for both sides. This, the Soviets maintained, should include a site around capital cities because one already existed around Moscow. By the end of the summer 1971 session of SALT in Helsinki, the US delegation had fallen back from demanding three ABM sites to protect US ICBMs in exchange for the Moscow system, to a position more in keeping with the current status quo in the Senate. The delegation now argued that the United States should be able to defend two Minuteman missile sites, while the USSR could have Moscow and one further site protecting an ICBM field. In such a truncated form, it is hard to disagree with Smith's judgment that by the end of the Helsinki session in September the US ABM position was "military nonsense and the White House and almost everyone else knew it."[71] Both as a weapons program and a bargaining chip, Safeguard as a form of meaningful leverage was all but dead.

The vagueness of the deal that Kissinger had struck with Dobrynin added further complications. The Soviets almost immediately began to play on the ambiguity surrounding the very concept of simultaneity as articulated in the letters. A few weeks before talks reopened at Helsinki in July, Dobrynin gave Kissinger a slip of paper on which he outlined "discrepancies" between the Soviet and American versions of the May 20 letters. On the basis of these, he told Kissinger that "it would be extremely helpful if [the US side] did not insist from the beginning that we talk about ABM and offensive weapons jointly."[72] Recognizing this, Kissinger initially agreed that the first few weeks of the Helsinki round could concentrate on ABM, but "after a while—he mentioned two to four weeks—the U.S. delegation would like to begin a parallel discussion of issues related to strategic offensive arms as well."[73] These discussions never materialized.

There was little the White House could do to provoke the Soviets into action, or even to agree to discuss offensive weapons before ABM talks concluded. When Kissinger pressed Dobrynin on the matter, the Soviet ambassador simply replied that since there had not been much progress on ABM, the Soviets could not consider taking up the matter of offensive weapons.[74] The Soviets doggedly stuck to their original offer. Nothing changed throughout the session in Helsinki during the summer of 1971. When the negotiations concluded in September, talks on offensive weapons had not even started.[75]

The most grievous feature of the May 20 agreement was Kissinger's implicit exclusion of SLBMs. With their focus almost exclusively on the issue of the heavy SS-9 ICBM the White House underestimated the strength of feeling within the federal bureaucracy regarding the inclusion of submarines in any temporary freeze.[76] Much of the post-May 20 press coverage suggested that there could be an ICBM-only freeze, indicating that this was the message given to journalists in background briefings.[77] According to the Soviet ambassador's notes, Kissinger initially assured Dobrynin that he would straighten out the bureaucracy by getting it to drop the question of SLBMs. Both the Pentagon and the ACDA were in favor of such limits "because the Soviet Union has been rapidly catching up to the U.S. in the number and quality of sea-based systems," Kissinger told Dobrynin, so "for the president himself to now directly oppose including them in the freeze would appear strange and incomprehensible." Yet the national security advisor assured the Soviet ambassador that "the White House will take steps to gradually return to the confidential agreement that has been reached." Kissinger simply advised Dobrynin to hold firm on SLBMs and the White House would instruct the delegation to drop the matter.[78]

That, however, proved impossible. The combined weight of ACDA, the Joint Chiefs of Staff, and the secretary of defense was just too much for the White House to contain. For Laird, the exclusion of SLBMs from the freeze was "intolerable," given the rate of Soviet ballistic missile submarine (SSBN) construction, concerns that were shared by the Joint Chiefs.[79] Kissinger attempted to put Laird off, but eventually the secretary wrote directly to the president, warning that the Soviet superiority in both land-based and sea-based systems would mean "serious international and domestic political problems. . . . We will reach an outcome which would be interpreted by our allies and the Congress as a sign of weakness and Soviet strength."[80] Smith agreed with Laird and the JCS that a SALT agreement that did not include SLBMs would leave the administration with "a bad public relation problem."[81]

With all the facts lining up behind Laird's conclusions, the White House knew it would have a political problem on its hands—especially given the current state of the American SLBM program. The United States was in the middle of converting its Polaris submarines to Poseidon launchers fitted with MIRVs. However, with all its dry dock capacity given over to this effort, it would be very difficult to produce a submarine to keep pace with the Soviet program. The United States was designing a new submarine-launched ballistic missile, Trident, but that would not be ready until the late 1970s at the earliest. Kissinger would be forced to enact a scheme to incorporate SLBMs in some form.[82]

THE CHINA GAMBIT

Negotiations with Moscow had not been the only piece of backchannel diplomacy in which Nixon and Kissinger had been engaged. The US invasion of Cambodia in May 1970 had put tentative US contacts with the People's Republic of China through the two countries' embassies in Warsaw on hold, but later that year communication had been re-established through Yahya Khan of Pakistan. The United States offered steps to normalize relations in October 1970, but the channel went dead in December. The Americans made a further gesture on March 15, 1971 when they abolished prohibitions on American travel to the PRC, to which Beijing reciprocated with the famous "ping pong diplomacy" visit of the US table tennis team in mid-April. It was only on April 27, however, that the Pakistani ambassador in Washington delivered a message in which the Chinese leadership offered to meet in Beijing with Nixon or a representative. Kissinger's visit, from July 9 to 11, concluded with agreement on a communiqué inviting Nixon to visit the PRC, which was released on July 15.[83]

The opening to China has traditionally been interpreted as putting further pressure on the USSR for substantive concessions.[84] The Soviets were indeed shocked and scrambled to address the possibility of a Sino-American alliance. Kissinger's announcement that he had visited China knocked Dobrynin sideways; the Soviet ambassador could hardly contain his surprise on the telephone on July 15, 1971 when Kissinger informed him of his visit to Beijing.[85] The Soviets issued an invitation for Nixon to visit Moscow on August 10. "The tone . . . changed dramatically," Kissinger argues in his memoirs, "coexistence . . . was coming about, not because of sudden moral insights but through the necessities of the international balance that we had helped to shape." The Soviets moved forward with an agreement on Berlin and a treaty on accidental war between the two superpowers.[86]

While the Soviets gave in on some issues, they held fast on strategic arms. There was little movement toward satisfying American concerns regarding simultaneous offensive-defensive negotiations and the limitation of ABMs to national capitals. The Soviets continued to refuse the opening of concrete discussions on offensive arms and still insisted that an NCA limitation on ABM would be "easier," despite Kissinger's complaint to Dobrynin that NCA "meant, in effect, zero for us and Moscow for them."[87]

Soviet levelheadedness in the face of the China announcement was one reason why the Americans were unable to gain more from Kissinger's visit to Beijing. As news of Kissinger's secret trip was flashed around the world, Dobrynin counseled the Kremlin to keep calm. The China announcement was clearly designed to exert pressure in "the invisible US-PRC-USSR triangle," Dobrynin wrote, but despite all the "ballyhoo" regarding a breakthrough in US–Chinese relations, fundamental differences between Beijing and Washington remained. Most importantly, the Soviet ambassador pointed out that Nixon's desire for great power summitry before the 1972 presidential election had led him to grasp for a meeting "straightaway" as soon as the Chinese had offered one. "There is no doubt," Dobrynin counseled, that Nixon "would act the same way if there were a similar turn of events with respect to his Moscow trip."[88]

The ambassador guessed correctly. The White House did not push the Kremlin into further concessions on SALT as a price for a summit and accepted the Soviet invitation for a meeting in Moscow just a week after it had been issued, on August 17. It appears that the chance of two summits in 1972 was too great a prospect to quibble over the details of strategic arms control. "The important thing," Nixon noted tellingly in his memoirs, "was that our patient preparation of linkage had paid off handsomely. We would have a Chinese trip and a Soviet summit as well." In the final analysis the trips themselves, rather than the agreements that would be achieved by them, had become the overriding issue for the Nixon administration.[89]

Not all leverage was thrown away in August 1971. Although they had gained a summit relatively easily, the Soviets were anxious regarding the content of Nixon's February 1972 discussions in Beijing. Kissinger took evident pleasure in drip-feeding Dobrynin information on the talks, although in one of those moments that proves Dean Acheson's comment regarding minute-takers never coming off second best, Dobrynin claimed Kissinger could not resist telling him everything that went on.[90] In order to be seen as the superior communist power, the Soviets had to come away from the summit with more than the series of platitudes that they discerned to have emerged from the Sino-American talks. In his assessment of Soviet policy in the wake of the Beijing summit, Dobrynin emphasized that in the context of the Beijing meeting, "the upcoming U.S.–Soviet summit in Moscow . . . takes on special significance."[91]

As he had in July 1971, however, the ambassador counseled patience. The Soviets, Dobrynin argued, had less invested in an arms control treaty than the United States. Dobrynin recognized the need for substance at the summit, but emphasized the importance of "constructive discussion" of the issues as opposed to "potential decisions" to resolve them. In the ambassador's estimation, "the US government attaches far greater practical significance to negotiations with the USSR, since the keys to resolving most world problems still lie in the capitals of these two great powers."[92] Moscow should not fret unduly: the Americans were keen for deals that went beyond the broad statements of the Beijing summit, while Moscow could live without an agreement as long as it looked as though talks had covered a greater range of concrete topics. Given the far more developed relations between the two superpowers, this was almost inevitable. In hindsight, it is clear that the opening to China had a far greater impact on the development of global politics in subsequent decades than it did on the tactical maneuverings between the United States and the Soviet Union between July 1971 and May 1972.[93]

SLBMS AT THE SUMMIT

The Soviets therefore contained themselves and allowed the administration to do most of the running toward an arms control accord. As they had with the May 20 agreement, Nixon and Kissinger remained focused on reaching fundamental deals directly with Moscow rather than at the SALT negotiations. Gerard Smith became increasingly worried that the White House was deliberately holding up talks in order to finalize the agreements at the summit. Nixon told Kissinger he believed that Smith, "want[ed] the final position on everything so he can negotiate a settlement"—a not unreasonable expectation given Smith's official role as the lead negotiator. "If [Edward] Kennedy were the president, the whole goddamn bureaucracy" would slow down negotiations so the White House could close the deal, Kissinger told Nixon, stoking the president's suspicions of Smith's political reliability. The two decided that Smith would be sidelined in the final phase of SALT, because, Kissinger argued, he was not the one "running for reelection."[94]

In mid-February 1972 Kissinger sought to pressure the Soviets into making concessions through the backchannel. He told Dobrynin that because the Soviets had been so intransigent on the issue of SLBMs, the United States would have no choice but to undertake a new construction program. Dobrynin held his ground, objecting that a freeze would simply hold the

Soviets back from deploying additional submarines while the United States designed its new fleet.[95] When on March 10, Kissinger offered that the Americans might allow the Soviets a total "as high as the middle 50's as against our 41" submarines, Dobrynin claimed not to understand why, if the Americans were ready to race the Soviets in SLBMs, they would want an agreement that would freeze Soviet superiority. At one point he confronted Kissinger directly with his suspicions that a freeze so lopsided in the Soviets' favor was some kind of fiendish American trick: "There must be some angle. What is it?"[96]

At this point, Nixon felt that he needed to spell out the domestic political stakes to the Soviet ambassador directly. According to the Soviet summary of this meeting—the American record does not describe it in detail—Nixon told Dobrynin the unvarnished truth: the White House believed that on balance, the arms control talks had "now become, at least in US public opinion, a kind of barometer for the future state of US–Soviet relations." There had to be high-profile agreements at Moscow, otherwise the American public would consider the summit a failure. On the other hand, the White House could not be seen as conceding too much, because it would be accused of selling out by the military and "certain vociferous Democratic [presidential] candidates." This was almost certainly Henry Jackson, who was running for the Democratic nomination and pledging a return to a policy of militarized containment of the Soviet Union.[97] The president of the United States was in effect asking Dobrynin to get the White House out of its domestic political predicament: with the summit public knowledge, anything less than an agreement was unacceptable; at the same time, the Soviets had to concede enough to satisfy conservative cold warriors. Nixon needed a deal and he was prepared to tell the Soviets exactly what he needed to get it.

Kissinger and Dobrynin pressed forward on resolving the SLBM issue, even as the prospect of a summit was thrown into doubt by Hanoi's launch of the Easter Offensive on March 30.[98] Even so, it was only during his late April 1972 visit to Moscow that Kissinger succeeded in gaining Brezhnev's assent to SLBM limits. Pressured by Nixon to address Vietnam as a priority, the national security advisor instead concentrated on smoothing out the remaining issues for the summit. Brezhnev toyed with Kissinger when he asked the general secretary about his views on submarines ("What can I say about them? They travel under water, we can't see them, they're silent") before giving Kissinger what he came for. The Soviets proposed that they would build sixty-two submarines if the United States froze theirs at forty-one. In compensation for their advantage in SLBMs, the Soviets would retire some of their obsolete ICBMs.[99] Kissinger was ecstatic, cabling Nixon that "Moscow agrees to include SLBMs at a time when it looked almost certain that we would have to drop this aspect . . . *if the summit meeting takes place, you will be able to sign the most important arms control agreement ever concluded.*"[100] He was as optimistic with his Soviet interlocutors. "I frankly think we will settle [SALT] next week," he told Gromyko, "I will have to browbeat our military, but it will take a week."[101]

Kissinger did indeed "browbeat the military" when he got back to Washington. The figures the Soviets were offering were higher than the "middle 50s" the national security advisor had offered Dobrynin just a few weeks previously.[102] Yet Admiral Thomas Moorer, whom the White House was considering sacking after his first term as chairman of the Joint Chiefs if he did not toe the line on SALT, backed the administration's tenuous contention that without an agreement the Soviets would be able to build up to eighty nuclear missile submarines over the five-year duration of the freeze. This made the 41-62 disparity look good by comparison.[103] With the Joint Chiefs on his side, Kissinger was half way to making his plan stick.

With his focus on the defense establishment and his haste to get results, however, Kissinger had neglected the possibility that other members of the bureaucracy could disagree with the tack he had taken in Moscow. Almost totally excluded from backchannel negotiations, Secretary of State William Rogers and Gerard Smith pressed on Kissinger a range of objections, both political and military, during a series of meetings in late April and early May. There were diplomatic problems with the proposal. The Soviets had insisted that their totals be seen as compensation for the nuclear forces of France and Britain as well as the United States, thereby violating the American prohibition on negotiating over their allies' deterrents—an issue that Kissinger had mentioned, but not resolved, in Moscow. Even more detrimental to the cohesion of the West, the Soviets demanded that the next round of SALT would include negotiations over the future of US submarine bases in Europe. Militarily, Smith and Rogers argued that the ballistic missile submarine total was overly lopsided in favor of the Soviet Union.[104] The president flew into a rage after a May 1 NSC meeting on the Soviet proposal. "What the Christ is Rogers talking about?" he asked Kissinger. Nixon "just thought, 'Oh, shit'" when Smith delivered a list of objections. He then turned on his national security advisor: "maybe the Brezhnev thing is a bad deal. . . . Is it as bad as [Rogers] says?"[105]

Kissinger needed to clean up the mess. The "substance" of the agreement—forty-one US to sixty-two Soviet SSBNs—could remain, he told Dobrynin, but the United States could not agree to terms that covered the nuclear forces of its allies or US bases on their territory.[106] Kissinger also suggested that certain "cosmetic touches" be made in order to ensure congressional support. The national security advisor proposed that, in addition to withdrawing some old ICBMs to compensate for their SLBM advantage, the Soviets retire some of their obsolescent early SSBNs at the same time as they introduced new ballistic missile submarines, in order to make it look as though they were trading in old models for new. Kissinger also sought to gain Soviet assent not to mention the exact numbers of offensive weapons that would be frozen in the text of the final agreement, proposing instead that the accord refer to the date on which forces would be capped. Although making the agreement more difficult to understand, Kissinger posited that such an arrangement would avoid the perception that the accord left the Soviets with a quantitative "advantage." In this way, Dobrynin recorded, "Kissinger . . . believes the substance of such an understanding on ballistic missile submarines could be camouflaged."[107] The national security advisor was, in effect, asking for Soviet help in hiding the extent of their numerical superiority in submarine-launched ballistic missiles from the American public and Congress.

It was only after Nixon arrived in Moscow on May 22, 1972 that the Soviets finally gave in by acceding to Kissinger's offer that they trade in their obsolete Hotel-class ballistic missile submarines for modern SSBNs. Once Nixon was in Moscow, negotiating personally on the final issues with the expectation of an agreement, the onus was as much, if not more, on the Kremlin than the White House to make the final deal.[108] In a series of late-night sessions, the Soviets seemed prepared to wait the administration out, refusing to budge on trade-ins, and it looked for a moment as if the entire deal might fall through. SALT probably came closest to failure on May 24, when the New York Times published a story sourced from Representative John M. Ashbrook, one of Nixon's principal right-wing Republican rivals, quoting the trade-in deal as well as comparative numbers for US and Soviet ICBM and SLBM totals. Ashbrook denounced the scheme for "doom[ing] the United States to nuclear inferiority" and called on the administration to reject it.[109] Perhaps spurred by the possibility that Nixon would take fright, the Soviets finally accepted a trade-in agreement that required them to retire their Hotel-class SSBNs.[110]

THE FINAL RECKONING

In his memoirs, Kissinger portrayed these last-minute concessions as a great victory for American diplomacy.[111] The numbers, however, did not look good. Under the terms of the Protocol to the Interim Agreement, the United States in theory could build 710 SLBM launchers on forty-four ballistic missile submarines. This comprised the 656 SLBMs it already had, with the option to build an additional fifty-four SLBMs if the United States retired its older Titan ICBMs. The Soviets could have up to sixty-two modern ballistic missile submarines, counted as 950 launchers, as long as they retired obsolete SS-7 and SS-8 ICBMs. Otherwise, the Soviets were limited to 740 SLBMs, including Hotel-class boats. Land-based ICBMs were frozen at current levels: 1,054 for the United States and approximately 1,618 for the Soviet Union.[112]

Leonid Brezhnev, by contrast, was able to use the numerical results of the negotiations to his own advantage when pressing the case for the SALT agreements. In his speech to the Central Committee on the eve of Nixon's visit, Brezhnev had outlined all the ways in which the agreements favored the Soviet Union. "The Americans know—and recognize in the negotiations," Brezhnev declared, "that we have a more intercontinental ballistic missiles than they do." The Americans had also recognized, according to Brezhnev, that the Soviet Union needed more ballistic missile submarines because of the United States' overseas basing. This had happened, Brezhnev opined, because the United States had "been convinced of the senselessness of attempting to attain superiority over the USSR and dictate to us from a position of strength."[113] Brezhnev convincingly argued that the Interim Agreement represented a break with the inferiority under which the Soviet Union had labored since the dawn of the nuclear age.

This was not what Nixon had hoped for, but in reality it was the best the United States could get. Laird argued that Safeguard was the United States' best counter at the talks, but the fact was that the administration had conceded ABM without any meaningful concessions on the Soviet side. ABM had been virtually useless as a way to pressure the Soviets during negotiations over the offensive freeze.[114] Even when Soviet negotiators began to talk about offensive weapons at the final Vienna session in the winter of 1971, they refused to budge on the fundamental defensive problem: their insistence on absolute equality in ABM systems, which would include the politically impossible Washington, DC defense. It was only at the final round in Helsinki in early May 1972, under the pressure of a looming summit, that the United States conceded that one of the two defensive systems for each side would be based around national capitals, thereby consigning the United States to a permanent inequality in the number of sites, if—as seemed likely given its previous opposition—Congress refused to fund a defense of the capital.[115]

Wary of criticism from the right that the Soviets had gained the upper hand, White House briefers played up the American superiority in MIRVs after the summit, claiming that even with the disparity in launchers the

United States would enjoy a 3,200 lead in deliverable warheads after the conclusion of the freeze.[116] At the same time, the administration underlined how much worse the situation would have been without an agreement, predicting that the Soviets would have had eighty SSBNs, the same contentious figure that had been agreed with Moorer.[117] The USSR's "willingness to negotiate . . . is directly related to America's strength," Nixon argued, assuring Republican lawmakers that the United States would press on with qualitative improvements, including not just MIRV, but also the new B-1 bomber and Trident.[118] Indeed, Laird publicly declared that his support for the SALT accords was contingent on Congress funding these new programs, leading some to charge that the administration was attempting to maintain qualitative superiority while employing the rhetoric of mutual deterrence through assured destruction.[119]

Such pledges did not assuage some hawkish critics, however. Most prominent of these was Henry Jackson, who argued that the American technological lead in warhead design would undoubtedly be eroded in the coming years. Once the Soviets caught up, they would have an advantage because their larger missiles would be able to carry more MIRVs than Minuteman. Added to the strategic concerns was a sense of personal betrayal. Jackson had defended Safeguard tenaciously on Nixon's behalf. The secret offensive-defensive linkage Kissinger had promised Jackson in the aftermath of the May 20 agreement had not been as strong as Kissinger made out. "Jackson," his biographer argues, "felt Nixon and Kissinger had let him down."[120]

Yet there was little Jackson and his small number of allies could do. The hawks were weak at a time of gross national fatigue with the Cold War.[121] Nixon played on this during his address to a joint session of Congress after his return to the United States on June 1. The president posited that the signing of the SALT accords in Moscow signified "the beginning of the end of that era which began in 1945." In doing so, he borrowed language that sounded a lot like McNamara's September 1967 warning of a "mad momentum" in the strategic competition between the two superpowers. The ABM Treaty and Interim Agreement, Nixon claimed, had "forestall[ed] a major spiraling of the arms race," which was "wasteful and dangerous." Three years earlier, Nixon had privately worried that nuclear parity would undermine US commitments around the globe. Now he argued in public that American forces were "sufficient" because "No power on earth is stronger than the United States today. And none will be . . . in the future."[122] Assured destruction was back in its familiar role as a justification for the nuclear status quo, except the balance was far less favorable to the United States in 1972 than it had been in the mid-1960s when McNamara had first proposed it.

Yet peace was the word in 1972 and "the reasonable right," in Nixon's phrase, could not oppose the Interim Agreement outright. Instead, Jackson tacked an amendment on to the joint resolution endorsing it, demanding that any further limitations on strategic arms would be concluded on the principle of "equality" between the two powers—a sideswipe at SALT that would grow in importance in subsequent years, but was hardly fatal for the Interim Agreement.[123] The ABM Treaty was even less controversial. It passed the Senate on August 3 with only two dissenting votes: one from William Buckley's brother, James L. Buckley of New York, and another from James B. Allen of Alabama. Buckley defended his vote on the grounds that he had "strong misgivings as to both the prudence and ultimate morality of denying for ourselves for all time . . . the right to protect our civilian populations from nuclear devastation."[124] It is a testament to the importance of American domestic politics in shaping views of the strategic balance that this moral argument, considered part of a lunatic fringe by Nixon and his advisors, became the basis for Ronald Reagan's Strategic Defense Initiative in the 1980s, despite the minimal change in the state of defensive technology.[125]

For the moment, it was détente and not confrontation that captured the national mood. ABM was the principal victim in Nixon's desire for a breakthrough that could carry "the peace issue." Nixon proceeded to make the most of his new image. As Kissinger noted distastefully in his memoirs, 1972 witnessed an escalation of peace rhetoric. The president started cautiously, suggesting that the United States was at "the beginning of a process that can lead to a lasting peace." Warming to the theme as the presidential election approached, he talked of peace lasting a generation, and finally a "century of peace."[126]

This was a far cry from Nixon's warning of June 1969 that collapsing support for military programs like Safeguard would doom Americans "to live in terror" of "the kind of peace that suffocated freedom in Czechoslovakia."[127] It was Nixon's fate to preside over the collapse of the public consensus supporting the president as the custodian of American superiority, a role that Nixon had been acculturated into since his earliest days in politics. By May 1972, he had accepted he could no longer fight the cratering of support for maintaining an uncontested edge for the United States in all metrics of the nuclear arms race, regardless of the cost. Despite Nixon's personal misgivings, the US ABM system was thus transformed from a symbol of confrontation to conciliation between the United States and the Soviet Union in an era of emerging superpower détente.

Conclusion

The Double Game

"The presidents of the nuclear age have a mixed record in seeking and telling the truth about our nuclear predicament," McGeorge Bundy, national security advisor to both Kennedy and Johnson, reflected in *Danger and Survival*, his 1988 book on the nuclear age. Faulting his former bosses for their failure to come clean regarding their real feelings of nuclear vulnerability and the senselessness of US superiority in the quantity of nuclear arms, he urged future administrations to "abandon the policy of selective truth telling" regarding the "complex realities of nuclear weapons."[1]

In private correspondence with Robert McNamara during preparation of his book, however, Bundy recognized how difficult it had been to speak the truth during his time in office almost twenty years earlier. McNamara, then engaged with Bundy in a campaign against Ronald Reagan's nuclear buildup, wrote to his former colleague that he felt "ashamed" that he had not taken on the arguments against nuclear superiority "more directly" when he was at the Pentagon.[2] Yet Bundy underlined to McNamara the centrality of domestic considerations. The "problem of explaining" the reality of mutual superpower vulnerability during the Kennedy and Johnson years was central to the dilemma both administrations found themselves in, Bundy admitted. This difficulty was primarily due to the difficulty of "swimming upstream on the basic issues" against "the congressional mood," which, Bundy implied, favored superiority.[3] Now a safe distance from events, Bundy wrote his former colleague, it did "no underlying harm to admit the incompleteness of both our understanding and our exposition [of the nuclear problem] in earlier years."[4]

The story of the rise and demise of the US ABM program, and the United States' move from nuclear superiority to parity in offensive forces that went with it, reflected this tension between top policymakers' personal doubts and their sense of what was demanded of them publicly as representatives of the executive power. The progress of the United States' first ABM system from research and development, to deployment, and finally to prohibition, was the product of a double game that policymakers played in an attempt to reconcile their perceptions of what Congress and the public would bear with their own private feelings regarding nuclear weapons and their place within each administration's broader strategy.

While all three presidents felt some tension between their public claims regarding the nuclear balance and their private misgivings, the specific mix of domestic political and budgetary priorities with which they had to grapple varied across administrations. The gap between Kennedy's experience of superiority and his basic domestic political instincts was the sharpest. Having profited from the missile gap in 1960, Kennedy increasingly questioned the necessity of US nuclear superiority with his closest advisers in the wake of the Berlin and Cuba crises, yet planned to use the US nuclear buildup as a central plank of his reelection campaign. Never facing the same kind of nuclear confrontations as his predecessor, focused on the Great Society and increasingly Vietnam, Johnson was more agnostic regarding the utility of superiority in a direct superpower clash. Yet he understood the basic fact that conservatives could endanger his domestic agenda if he stepped back from maintenance of the US nuclear edge—an understanding that ultimately doomed major progress on superpower arms limitation during his administration. Nixon believed in nuclear superiority, yet increasingly bent to domestic political pressure to shift his stance. In 1971, with the May 20 agreement, Nixon pivoted toward using SALT as the primary means by which to achieve US–Soviet détente and thereby enhance his own reelection prospects.

This dynamic between the public and the private, as well as the competing national security and domestic priorities, reflects a broader tradition in which "electoral, ideological, partisan, and institutional" pressures have shaped the evolution of US national security strategy.[5] Nuclear issues were hardly the only, or even the most important, national security dilemmas of the 1960s in which domestic politics played a fundamental role. The US campaign in Vietnam—from Kennedy's studied ambivalence in balancing the dangers of escalation against the domestic political costs of withdrawal, to Johnson's belief that an increased US commitment was expected by the broader national security consensus, and finally to Nixon's retreat from a politically untenable position under the cover of "peace of with honor"—illustrates the same dilemma of balancing domestic and international imperatives. The parallels between the problems successive administrations faced in Southeast Asia and those relating to nuclear strategy were hardly coincidental. The war in Vietnam had a major impact on the evolution of the nuclear force, primarily as the main factor that precipitated the collapse in the domestic will to bear the costs of the Cold War during the late 1960s. The story of the US shift to nuclear parity, therefore, reflects a broader problem with studies that treat the foreign and domestic as separate spheres, particularly at the highest level. As scholar Adam Quinn has recently noted, for the White House—then, as now—"Domestic, political and ideological constraints are no less real . . . than the external realities with which strategists must contend."[6]

While the confluence of domestic and external imperatives is not unique to US nuclear strategy, its highly abstract nature exacerbated the problem. Given the situation in which the arsenals on both sides had the capacity to end all life on earth many times over, the consequent detachment between military capability and usable power, and the increasing technological complexity of the military balance, nuclear-strategic rhetoric could define reality in a way unlike other realms of national security policy. The challenge for successive US administrations during the middle years of the Cold War was to articulate a strategy that would instill confidence in their ability to manage the superpower nuclear standoff in a way that would protect US and allied interests, yet forestall Armageddon. To adopt Robert Jervis's terminology, this theoretically placed the US government in the position of being a "reality maker," in the sense that if it issued statements claiming that it was confident in its declared strategy, then it was more likely that both the US public and external allies—the "reality takers"—would be more confident as well. Yet the story of the US shift from superiority to mutual assured destruction between 1961 and 1972 shows that such a clean division between makers and takers does not reflect the way policymakers saw the situation at the time. The supposed reality makers in the executive branch consistently perceived themselves as dependent on the evolving public and congressional consensus of what constituted a credible nuclear posture, hostage to the perceptions of the supposed reality takers. "Because credibility exists in the eye of the beholder," Jervis notes, "the beliefs of others not only measure but determine whether a stance or threat is credible."[7]

Skeptical regarding the utility of superiority, officials in the Kennedy and Johnson administrations pressed on with ABM, partly out of fear of the domestic political consequences if they did not. They were not entirely blameless for this state of affairs, since they had contributed to the public perception that superiority was necessary by consistently reaffirming the US nuclear edge in successive statements.[8] However, the raucous ABM debates of 1969 made it clear that the executive's ability to control the evolution of public perceptions was limited. The change in public and particularly congressional views was crucial in this. Once the public debate shifted dramatically away from a belief that US superiority was worth the cost, and Congress signaled its intention to cut funding on this basis, even Richard Nixon—a dyed-in-the-wool defender of militarized containment on the basis of US nuclear superiority—adapted rapidly.

To do otherwise than try to tack toward the middle ground of public debate—in other words, to tell the truth regarding presidential perceptions of nuclear weapons—could have had catastrophic consequences. The potential "harm," as Bundy later put it, which could have befallen the Kennedy, Johnson, and Nixon administrations if they had been too honest regarding their private skepticism of public wisdom could have come in numerous different forms. With a general understanding that public audiences would accept nothing less than superiority, the Kennedy and Johnson administrations ran the risk of precipitating a collapse in public confidence regarding the United States' ability to stand behind its security commitments. It would have been similarly dangerous for Nixon to voice his private doubts regarding American credibility in an era of superpower parity at a time when Congress was determined to deny him the funds for a major nuclear buildup. Executive responsibility for nuclear procurement and use, theoretically the source of world-ending power, fundamentally constrained US presidents as they engaged in a double game to reconcile their own views of the nuclear danger with those prevailing outside the walls of the White House.

This story places contemporary academic security studies debates over the necessity for nuclear superiority in a different light. First, it questions the persistent focus in the recent literature on the utility of nuclear weapons during crises.[9] It is commonly held that, with the advent of the nuclear age, "the nuclear crisis became the primary arena in which nuclear-armed states settled important international disputes."[10] While the Berlin and Cuban crises certainly marked a watershed in superpower relations, they did not resolve major issues between the United States and Soviet Union in and of themselves. It took almost a decade from the conclusion of the Cuban missile crisis to move to a situation in which the two superpowers could come together to conclude bilateral agreements that explicitly limited their nuclear arsenals. The circuitous way in which this was achieved had much to do with a far broader range of political changes that went beyond the direct superpower confrontations of 1958–1962. While crises were important, the shift from superpower nuclear confrontation to arms control agreements was the product of forces far beyond these discrete moments around which much of the security studies literature currently turns. An important part of this was the changing nature of US policymakers' perceptions of what the American public and Congress would bear in terms of a shift away from the clear nuclear edge that had been the United States' inheritance as the pioneer of the nuclear age.

Second, the story complicates the relationship between superiority and a state's resolve. The evidence strongly suggests that the Kennedy White House did not take much comfort from its nuclear edge during the Cuban Missile Crisis. Yet the public perception of its significance during October 1962 meant that the Kennedy and Johnson administrations behaved as if superiority mattered throughout the next six years. McNamara felt as though he had to continue to advocate superiority in public, even as he strove to keep the defense budget under control and reach out to the Soviets for arms control talks. Unfortunately for McNamara, the Kremlin had determined that it had to eliminate the notional American advantage—a fatal mix for Johnson's dream of a broader détente with the USSR based on arms control. By contrast, Nixon's understanding of nuclear weapons' importance in determining the global balance of power, which partly drew on the Kennedy administration's public portrayal of its deft handling of the nuclear edge in October 1962, was fundamentally challenged by the collapse in the congressional consensus behind superiority. Scholar and policymaker Philip Zelikow's conclusion that, "U.S. nuclear superiority mattered. And, at some level, it also didn't," is a clear-eyed assessment of its role in political life.[11] Superiority mattered in signaling resolve between 1961 and 1968, when the White House believed the public and Congress thought it mattered; when the congressional and public mood appeared to turn against maintaining the American nuclear edge in the late 1960s Nixon changed course, despite his reservations, signaling resolve by publicly articulating his satisfaction with nuclear parity.

THE DOMESTIC POLITICS OF US NUCLEAR STRATEGY AFTER 1972

Nixon's public embrace of mutual vulnerability and approximate parity in numbers of delivery vehicles did not mark the final resolution of this intense domestic political debate over the US nuclear posture. In fact, as the 1970s progressed a number of trends combined to make the debate over US nuclear strategy even more complex and ideological than it had been during the previous decade. The cumulative effect of these developments was, in the words of historian Lawrence Freedman, to "undermine the established liberal consensus," dominant since the 1969 ABM debate, in favor of arms limitation on the basis of parity, "but not to present a new consensus to take its place."[12]

By signing the SALT accords on the basis of approximate parity and an assured retaliation capability, the Nixon administration did not succeed in healing the ideological rift between arms controllers and Cold War conservatives. Instead, the White House made itself the target for new attacks from its erstwhile friends such as Senator Henry Jackson, who felt betrayed by the way in which they had been used by the administration to push for programs such as ABM, only to have them bargained away in exchange for what they perceived as inadequate Soviet concessions on offensive arms. The American debate was split primarily between two warring camps—conservative anti-SALT hawks and liberal arms-controllers—which broadly mapped onto the increasingly fraught contest over the wisdom of US–Soviet détente as a whole. Conservative opponents were flipped into opposition for a variety of reasons—SALT, Nixon's opening to China, the administration's conduct during the Yom Kippur War of October 1973, and the final American defeat in Vietnam. However, they all shared a conviction that the United States had gone too far in placating the communist world, principally the Soviet Union. The central contention of the critics was that proponents of détente had overestimated the extent to which the Soviet Union had changed from a revolutionary into a status-quo power. In nuclear strategy, this manifest itself in wishful thinking regarding the nature of Soviet motives for SALT, which, they argued, was being used to secure and deepen the USSR's long-term lead in key metrics of the arms race. This nuclear edge, they held, would embolden the Soviet Union to greater geopolitical adventurism by placing the credibility of extended deterrence in question. Some even suggested that the Soviet leadership might launch a war on the assumption it could win a nuclear exchange with the United States.[13]

Qualitative improvements in nuclear forces that the Nixon administration pursued, among them high-accuracy MIRVs and cruise missiles of various types, as well as the increasingly complex intelligence capabilities and countermeasures developed by both superpowers, facilitated this shift to an ideological plane by making it even more difficult to come to consensus on the state of the nuclear balance. The Rathjens-Wohlstetter debate over Minuteman's vulnerability to the heavy Soviet ICBM force, which the Nixon administration had attempted to use to its political advantage in 1969 in arguing the case for Safeguard, became a liability as the Soviets continued their buildup by developing MIRVs for their heavy ICBM force that could eventually, critics projected, destroy US land-based missiles in a first strike. To this, critics added further evidence of vulnerability, including the development of a new Soviet bomber, the Backfire, which had an aerial refueling capability that made it capable of striking the United States. In a hypothetical doomsday scenario, SALT's enemies, such as Jackson, maintained that the Soviet Union could eliminate the United States' ICBM force with sufficient reserves to hold US cities hostage. Faced with the choice of retaliating against Soviet cities in the knowledge that the Soviets would reply with a devastating second attack on the American homeland, critics argued, the United States could well concede World War III to the USSR.[14]

The admitted difficulty of accurately measuring the physical nuclear balance made the understanding of psychology even more important. Was there ever any evidence that an advantage in the number of MIRVs the Soviets could put on target emboldened them to greater adventurism, liberal skeptics asked? Pointing to US setbacks in the extra-European world, critics of arms control charged that it was indeed so, because the Soviets knew that they could ultimately prevail in a nuclear as well as a conventional war. Defenders of the status quo shot back that by questioning the nuclear balance, critics were themselves undermining the credibility of the US deterrent by questioning its sufficiency.[15] The fact that both of these arguments could be correct did nothing to help the resolve the debate.

This psychological dimension fed back naturally into the ideological debate over the nature and purposes of Soviet power, thereby creating a closed loop that was almost impossible to break—and merely increased in intensity during the Nixon, Ford, and Carter administrations. The great irony of this process was that, in their arguments stressing the importance of new Soviet military developments, the SALT critics were unconsciously echoing many of Nixon's private anxieties. Yet in public the Nixon and Ford administrations continued to defend the importance of SALT. This was because, whatever their real feelings regarding the cogency of their opponents' arguments, Nixon- and Ford-era officials knew that there was no countervailing consensus behind greater military spending in the comparatively cash-strapped 1970s. As the decade progressed, the White House was attacked by a resurgent right with which at least some partially agreed, but was unable to garner the congressional votes for a new defense program.[16]

While the Nixon and Ford administrations had been increasingly caught between the crosscutting imperatives of conservative fear of parity and liberal opposition to more defense spending, the Carter White House found itself on the opposite side of this dilemma—in favor of arms control by instinct, yet under increasingly effective assault from anti-détente forces. In his inaugural address of January 20, 1977, Carter had declared his aim to be "the elimination of all nuclear weapons from this Earth." He pressed forward with the SALT II negotiations and moved to eliminate nuclear programs such as the B-1 strategic bomber.[17] Yet by the end of his term in office, Carter had withdrawn SALT II from consideration by Congress, while the administration presided over a new strategic buildup, including deployment of the new heavy MX ICBM, and the promulgation of a new nuclear war-fighting doctrine in the form of Presidential Directive (PD)-59.[18]

It was the curious luck of Ronald Reagan, with a great deal of help from outside forces, to be able to at once embody all of these contradictions and yet fashion them into a coherent policy in a way his predecessors had not. A firm believer in the evil of nuclear weapons, Reagan was nevertheless the advocate of a huge strategic arms buildup, including the reinstatement of the B-1 bomber, the acceleration of the Trident SLBM program, and space-based missile defenses known as the Strategic Defense Initiative (SDI). The target of a vigorous domestic and international antinuclear movement on the basis of his hawkish positions, Reagan floated the idea of abolition of nuclear weapons with Soviet General Secretary Mikhail Gorbachev at the 1986 Reykjavik summit.[19] He went on to leverage his tough reputation to conclude the Intermediate-Range Nuclear Forces (INF) Treaty, eliminating an entire generation of theater nuclear weapons in Europe and laying the groundwork for the rapid completion of the two Strategic Arms Reduction Treaties in 1991 and 1992.

In a sense, Reagan was saved from resolution of these contradictions by the epochal changes in the USSR's foreign and defense policy under his Soviet opposite number. Gorbachev's acceptance of previously inadmissible terms for arms control—including dealing with Reagan despite the president's attachment to SDI, the elimination of all intermediate-range ballistic missiles across both European and Asian regions of the USSR, and onsite inspection for strategic arms reduction agreements—facilitated the huge progress in talks during the 1980s and early 1990s, as did the collapse of the Soviet Union, which Gorbachev's policies unwittingly brought about. Ironically, Bundy's call to "tell the truth" about nuclear weapons came just as Gorbachev's new thinking on international security obviated the need to do so. Gorbachev's precipitous concessions made it appear as though, at a minimum, the United States could have technological superiority and arms control at once or, at the maximum, could compel adversaries into unilateral reverses through its nuclear strength.[20] While hugely positive in manifold ways, the transformative international environment of the Cold War's final phase nevertheless obscured the dilemma between private doubts and public demands with which successive administrations had grappled for decades.

More than forty-five years after the 1972 Moscow Summit, the fundamental questions that animated much of the national security debate during the Kennedy, Johnson, and Nixon presidencies still resonate and indeed, are becoming more relevant. Reagan's policies appeared hugely successful in the short term but, implemented in extraordinary times, they helped to elide the difficult choices that normally face nuclear policymakers when grappling with Bundy's challenge to "tell the truth" regarding nuclear weapons. These tensions generally lay dormant during the post-Cold War period—the result of a uniquely favorable great-power environment. Indeed, the United States' withdrawal from the ABM Treaty in 2002 was justified on the basis that the Russian Federation was "not an enemy" and therefore the US missile defense program should turn to address threats from rogue states armed with small but deadly nuclear arsenals. In pronouncing the death of superpower competition in nuclear arms, the assessment also implied that the difficult tradeoffs that had accompanied the era of Cold War arms control were moot.[21] However, with Russia and China both emerging as significant nuclear-armed opponents to US security orders in Europe and Asia, it is now clear that this era was but a temporary respite.[22] At the same time as regional challengers are reemerging, the United States faces the prospect of an extremely expensive nuclear modernization program in an era of growing budgetary constraints.

The resurgence of these dilemmas is reflected in the mystery of the two Barack Obamas: the younger Obama who, like Carter, declared a world free of nuclear weapons as his aim in Prague in 2009, and the elder, who set in train the most expensive nuclear modernization program in the United States' history. In the relatively benign great power environment of 2009, which had persisted since the implosion of the Soviet Union almost eighteen years previously, Obama aired his skepticism regarding the utility of military force, and nuclear force in particular. While promising to maintain a "safe, secure and effective arsenal" in a nuclear-armed world, the new president nevertheless characterized "the existence of thousands of nuclear weapons," as "the most dangerous legacy of the Cold War," and pledged "to reduce" their prominence in upholding the United States' commitments around the globe, with a long-term view to their total elimination.[23] Obama's record at the end of his second term was more mixed. The president signed the New START Treaty with Russia and concluded a nuclear accord with Iran. Yet faced with a return to great-power rivalry presaged by the 2014 Russian annexation of Crimea and increasing Chinese assertiveness, Obama also deferred to congressional and military support for the full modernization of the nuclear triad, despite the long-term budgetary challenges that such a program will face as spending peaks during the 2020s.[24] Like Kennedy, Johnson, and Nixon, Obama struggled to reconcile his true feelings—in this case, skepticism—regarding the utility of US nuclear forces with the public demands of his office.

The story of US nuclear policy during the 1960s and early 1970s is suggestive of the dynamics we could encounter in the coming decades. If geopolitical rivalries between the United States and its regional challengers intensify further, then the salience of nuclear weapons as a factor in American domestic politics is again likely to grow. If nuclear weapons return as a central issue in the US domestic debate, then we are likely to witness increased pressure on future occupants of the Oval Office to conform to public and congressional expectations on the appropriate level of nuclear forces, regardless of their own preferences. Given the instability of contemporary American politics, as well as the difficulty of knowing from open sources what presidents really believe about nuclear weapons, it is hard to predict exactly how future administrations will play the double game. Suffice to say there is a fair chance it will return.

NOTES

AF	Agency File
APP	American Presidency Project, University of California, Santa Barbara
CF	Country File
CF/A	Country File, Addendum
D&A	Departments and Agencies File
DI	Directorate of Intelligence
DNSA	Digital National Security Archive
FOIA	Freedom of Information Act
FRUS	*Foreign Relations of the United States*
FWR	Files of Walt W. Rostow
JFKL	John F. Kennedy Presidential Library
LBJL	Lyndon Baines Johnson Presidential Library
NIE	National Intelligence Estimate
NPL	Richard Nixon Presidential Library
NSAEBB	*National Security Archive Electronic Briefing Book*
NSF	National Security File/s
OSD/JS	Office of the Secretary of Defense and Joint Staff
PCC	Papers of Clark Clifford
PMH	Papers of Morton H. Halperin
PNO	Program Number
POF	President's Office Files
RTCM	Recordings and Transcripts of Conferences and Meetings
SMOF	Staff Member and Office Files
Telcon	Telephone conversation
USNH	*US Nuclear History: Nuclear Arms and Politics in the Missile Age*
WHSF	White House Special Files

INTRODUCTION

1. "Treaty Between the United States of America and the Union of Soviet Socialist Republics on the Limitation of Anti-Ballistic Missile Systems," May 26, 1972, in *Foreign Relations of the United States, 1969–1976, Volume XXXII, SALT I, 1969–1972*, ed. Erin R. Mahan (Washington, DC: United States Government Printing Office, 2010), 908–913.

2. Francis J. Gavin, *Nuclear Statecraft: History and Strategy in America's Atomic Age* (Ithaca, NY: Cornell University Press, 2012), 120–133.

3. Raymond L. Garthoff, *Détente and Confrontation: American-Soviet Relations from Nixon to Reagan*, 2nd ed. (Washington, DC: Brookings Institution, 1994), 213–216, 335–337; Gerard C. Smith, *Doubletalk: The Story of the First Strategic Arms Limitation Talks* (Garden City: Doubleday, 1980), 455–456.

4. Lawrence Freedman, *The Evolution of Nuclear Strategy*, 3rd ed. (Basingstoke, UK: Palgrave Macmillan, 2003), 333.

5. Colin S. Gray, *The Soviet-American Arms Race* (Lexington, MA: Lexington Books, 1976), 181–188.

6. Donald G. Brennan, "Strategic Alternatives: I," *New York Times*, May 24, 1971, 31.

7. Freedman, *Evolution of Nuclear Strategy*, 72–85; John Lewis Gaddis, *Strategies of Containment: A Critical Appraisal of American National Security Strategy During the Cold War*, 2nd ed. (New York: Oxford University Press, 2005), 125–161; Fred Kaplan, *The Wizards of Armageddon*, 2nd ed. (Stanford, CA: Stanford University Press, 1991), 174–184.

8. Freedman, *Evolution of Nuclear Strategy*, 131–136; Gregg Herken, *Counsels of War*, 2nd. ed. (New York: Oxford University Press, 1987), 111–134; Kaplan, *Wizards*, 144–173.

9. Freedman, *Evolution of Nuclear Strategy*, 215–231; Gaddis, *Strategies of Containment*, 197–234; Kaplan, *Wizards*, 248–306.

10. Freedman, *Evolution of Nuclear Strategy*, 232–242; Kaplan, *Wizards*, 315–327, 343–355; Herken *Counsels of War*, 187–203.

11. Freedman, *Evolution of Nuclear Strategy*, 332, 338–339; Herken, *Counsels of War*, 242–247. This is the assumption in policy literature today. See, for example, Christopher A. Ford, "Anything But Simple: Arms Control and Strategic Stability," in *Strategic Stability: Contending Interpretations*, eds. Elbridge A. Colby and Michael S. Gerson (Carlisle, PA: Strategic Studies Institute and U.S. Army War College, 2013), 221.

12. Desmond Ball, *Politics and Force Levels: The Strategic Missile Program and the Kennedy Administration* (Berkeley: University of California Press, 1980), 232–278.

13. Morton H. Halperin, "The Decision to Deploy the ABM: Bureaucratic and Domestic Politics in the Johnson Administration," *World Politics* 25, no. 1 (October 1972): 62–95; Ernest J. Yanarella, *The Missile Defense Controversy: Technology in Search of a Mission*, 2nd ed. (Lexington: University Press of Kentucky, 2002), 3–6, 223–228.

14. Garthoff, *Détente*, 167–170, 208, 211, 216–219; Smith, *Doubletalk*, 222–246, 453–473.

15. Richard Nixon, "Address at the Air Force Academy Commencement Exercises in Colorado Springs, Colorado," June 4, 1969, *The American Presidency Project*, University of California, Santa Barbara (hereafter APP), eds. John Woolley and Gerhard Peters, accessed March 25, 2017, http://www.presidency.ucsb.edu/ws/?pid=2081.

16. Gavin, *Nuclear Statecraft*, 104–119. For detailed studies of Nixon's attempts to use nuclear weapons as a "useful tool," including nuclear alerts and "limited" use; see Terry Terriff, *The Nixon Administration and the Making of U.S. Nuclear Strategy* (Ithaca, NY: Cornell University Press, 1995); William Burr, "The Nixon Administration, the 'Horror Strategy,' and the Search for Limited Nuclear Options, 1969–1972," *Journal of Cold War Studies* 7, no. 3 (Summer 2005): 34–78; Kaplan, *Wizards*, 356–380; Freedman, *Evolution of Nuclear Strategy*, 355–377; William Burr and Jeffrey Kimball, *Nixon's Nuclear Specter: The Secret Alert of 1969, Madman Diplomacy, and the Vietnam War* (Lawrence: University Press of Kansas, 2015); Jeremi Suri and Scott D. Sagan, "The Madman Nuclear Alert: Secrecy, Signaling, and Safety in October 1969," *International Security* 27, no. 4 (Spring 2003): 150–183; Nina Tannenwald, *The Nuclear Taboo: The United States and the Non-Use of Nuclear Weapons Since 1945* (Cambridge, UK: Cambridge University Press, 2007), 227–240.

17. Richard Nixon, "Address to a Joint Session of the Congress on Return from Austria, the Soviet Union, Iran, and Poland," June 1, 1972, APP, accessed March 25, 2017, http://www.presidency.ucsb.edu/ws/?pid=3450; Richard M. Nixon, *RN: The Memoirs of Richard Nixon* (New York: Grosset and Dunlap, 1978), 617–618.

18. McGeorge Bundy, *Danger and Survival: Choices About the Bomb in the First Fifty Years* (New York: Random House, 1988), 461–462; Robert S. McNamara, *Blundering Into Disaster: Surviving the First Century of the Nuclear Age* (New York: Parthenon, 1986), 44–45.

19. Robert S. McNamara, "The Military Role of Nuclear Weapons: Perceptions and Misperceptions," *Foreign Affairs* 62, no. 1 (Fall 1983): 62.

20. Herken, *Counsels of War,* 200–202.

21. The "double game" may remind readers of Robert D. Putnam's logic of two-level games. However, accounting for the dynamic between public demands and private doubts and constraints rather than domestic and foreign constraints, this explanatory framework is substantially different. See: Robert D. Putnam, "Diplomacy and Domestic Politics: The Logic of Two-Level Games," *International Organization* 42, no. 3 (Summer 1988): 427–460.

22. Marc Trachtenberg, *A Constructed Peace: The Making of the European Settlement, 1945–1963* (Princeton, NJ: Princeton University Press, 1999); Gavin, *Nuclear Statecraft*, 30–74, 104–119; Matthew Jones, *After Hiroshima: the United States, Race and Nuclear Weapons in Asia, 1945–1965* (Cambridge, UK: Cambridge University Press, 2010).

23. For examples of this debate, see Matthew Kroenig, "Nuclear Superiority and the Balance of Resolve: Explaining Nuclear Crisis Outcomes," *International Organization* 67, no. 1 (January 2013): 141–171; Todd S. Sechser and Matthew Fuhrmann, "Crisis Bargaining and Nuclear Blackmail," *International Organization* 67, no.1 (January 2013): 173–195; Matthew Kroenig, "Debating the Benefits of Nuclear Superiority for Crisis Bargaining, Part I," comment on Sechser and Fuhrmann, *Duck of Minerva Blog*, March 23, 2013, accessed March 25, 2017, http://duckofminerva.dreamhosters.com/?p=16003; Todd Sechser and Matthew Fuhrmann, "Debating the Benefits of Nuclear Superiority for Crisis Bargaining, Part II," comment on Kroenig, *Duck of Minerva Blog*, March 25, 2013, accessed March 24, 2017, http://duckofminerva.dreamhosters.com/?p=16008; Todd Sechser and Matthew Fuhrmann, "Debating the Benefits of Nuclear Superiority for Crisis Bargaining,

Part III," *Duck of Minerva Blog*, March 28, 2013, accessed March 25, 2017, http://duckofminerva.com/2013/03/debating-the-benefits-of-nuclear-superiority-part-iii.html; Matthew Kroenig, "Debating the Benefits of Nuclear Superiority for Crisis Bargaining, Part IV," *Duck of Minerva Blog*, March 29, 2013, accessed March 24, 2017, http://duckofminerva.com/2013/03/debating-the-benefits-of-nuclear-superiority-for-crisis-bargaining-part-iv.html.

CHAPTER 1

1. Deborah Shapley, *Promise and Power: The Life and Times of Robert McNamara* (Boston, MA: Little, Brown, 1993), 92–93; John F. Kennedy, "Inaugural Address," January 20, 1961, APP, accessed March 24, 2017, http://www.presidency.ucsb.edu/ws/?pid=8032.
2. Christopher A. Preble, "'Who Ever Believed in the "Missile Gap"?': John F. Kennedy and the Politics of National Security." *Presidential Studies Quarterly* 33, no. 4 (December 2003): 821–826.
3. "Excerpts of Remarks of Senator John F. Kennedy at Rock Island, Illinois," October 24, 1960, APP, accessed March 25, 2017, http://www.presidency.ucsb.edu/ws/index.php?pid=74195.
4. Vladislav A. Zubok, *A Failed Empire: The Soviet Union in the Cold War from Stalin to Gorbachev* (Chapel Hill: University of North Carolina Press, 2007), 131.
5. Preble, "'Who Ever Believed in the "Missile Gap"?,'" 806; "Speech of Senator John F. Kennedy, American Legion Convention, Miami Beach, FL," October 18, 1960, APP, accessed March 25, 2017, http://www.presidency.ucsb.edu/ws/index.php?pid=74096.
6. Kaplan, *Wizards*, 249–250.
7. Leonard McCombe, "A Valuable Batch of Brains," *Life*, May 11, 1959, 101–107.
8. Bruce Kuklick, *Blind Oracles: Intellectuals and War from Kennan to Kissinger* (Princeton, NJ: Princeton University Press, 2006), 61–62.
9. Henry M. Jackson to John F. Kennedy, "The Secretary of Defense, Certain Key Posts in Defense, and the Chairman of the AEC," December 6, 1960, Jackson, Henry M., December 1960 to June 1962, Box 30, Special Correspondence, President's Office Files (hereafter POF), John F. Kennedy Presidential Library (hereafter JFKL). The admiration was mutual. Nitze described Jackson as "my kind of Democrat – clear-headed, tough-minded, liberal in the best tradition of the party but not in the least naïve about the hard issues." Quoted in Strobe Talbott, *The Master of the Game: Paul Nitze and the Nuclear Peace* (New York: Knopf, 1988), 78.
10. For accounts of how Kennedy wooed McNamara, see: Shapley, *Promise and Power*, 83–89; Robert S. McNamara Oral History Interview, April 4, 1964, Oral History Collection, JFKL.
11. David Halberstam, *The Best and the Brightest* (New York: Random House, 1972), 217.
12. Tom J. Farer, "McNamara: The Glacial Technocrat," *The Nation*, November 11, 1968, 501–503, available from the author on request.
13. Robert S. McNamara Oral History Interview, April 4, 1964, JFKL.
14. Halberstam, *Best and the Brightest*, 216–217.
15. Shapley, *Promise and Power*, 58–80; Kaplan, *Wizards*, 252.
16. Kaplan, *Wizards*, 252; Alain C. Enthoven and K. Wayne Smith, *How Much is Enough? Shaping the Defense Program, 1961–1969*, 2nd ed. (Santa Monica, CA: RAND Corp., 2005), 33; Charles J. Hitch and Roland N. McKean, *The*

Economics of Defense in the Nuclear Age (Cambridge, MA: Harvard University Press, 1960), v.

17. Enthoven and Smith, *How Much*, 13–16, 22; Yanarella, *Missile Defense Controversy*, 48–49.

18. Enthoven and Smith, *How Much*, 33–38, 61–62.

19. Enthoven and Smith, *How Much*, 65–66.

20. Henry S. Rowen to McGeorge Bundy, "Basic National Security Policy," May 22, 1961, attachment, Military Policy Basic National Security Policy, 1/61-5/61, Box 374, Carl Kaysen Files, National Security Files (hereafter NSF), JFKL.

21. Carl Kaysen, "Memorandum of Conversation with Mr. Henry Rowen Deputy Assistant Secretary of Defense for International Security Affairs," May 25, 1961, May 27, 1961, Military Policy Basic National Security Policy, 1/61–5/61, Box 374, Carl Kaysen Files, NSF, JFKL.

22. Gaddis, *Strategies of Containment*, 218.

23. Rowen to Bundy, "Basic National Security Policy," May 22, 1961, attachment, JFKL.

24. Carl Kaysen to John F. Kennedy, December 9, 1961, Department of Defense – Defense Budget FY 1963 11/61–12/61, Box 275, Departments and Agencies (hereafter D&A), NSF, JFKL.

25. Charles Hitch to Service Secretaries, "Instruction Number I," May 13, 1961, Budget Guidance and Planning Memoranda, 1960–1961, Box 9, Papers of Alain Enthoven, Lyndon Baines Johnson Library. Emphasis is Hitch's.

26. Gaddis, *Strategies of Containment*, 199; David Milne, *America's Rasputin: Walt Rostow and the Vietnam War* (New York: Hill and Wang, 2008), 117.

27. Robert S. McNamara to John F. Kennedy, "Recommended Department of Defense FY '63 Budget and 1963–67 Program," October 6, 1961, Department of Defense Recommended FY '63 Budget, Box 275, D&A, NSF, JFKL.

28. McNamara to Kennedy, "Recommended Department of Defense FY '63 Budget and 1963-67 Program," October 6, 1961, JFKL. McNamara mentioned the possibility of building up to 1,200 Minutemen in his statements to Congress. Robert S. McNamara, "Statement Before the Senate Subcommittee on Department of Defense Appropriations the Fiscal Year 1963–67 Defense Program and 1963 Defense Budget," February 14, 1962, NH00439, *U.S. Nuclear History: Nuclear Arms and Politics in the Missile Age, 1955–1968* (hereafter *USNH*), ed. William Burr, Digital National Security Archive (hereafter DNSA).

29. David Coleman, "Camelot's Nuclear Conscience," *Bulletin of Atomic Scientists*, 62 (May/June 2006): 45.

30. Maxwell D. Taylor to Robert S. McNamara, "Preliminary Comments on the Department of Defense FY '63 Budget and 1963-67 Program," October 14, 1961, Department of Defense Defense Budget FY 1963 1/61–10/61, Box 275, D&A, NSF, JFKL.

31. David Bell to John F. Kennedy, "FY 1963 Defense Budget Issues," November 13, 1961, Department of Defense—Defense Budget FY 1963 11/61/12/61, Box 275, D&A, NSF, JFKL.

32. Security Resources Panel of the Science Advisory Committee, "Deterrence and Survival in the Nuclear Age, November 7, 1957," in "The Master of the Game: Paul H. Nitze and U.S. Cold War Strategy from Truman to Reagan," *National Security Archive Electronic Briefing Book No. 139* (hereafter *NSAEBB 139*), eds. William Burr and Robert Wampler, accessed March 25, 2017, http://nsarchive.gwu.edu/NSAEBB/NSAEBB139/; Donald R. Baucom, *The Origins of*

SDI, 1944–1983 (Lawrence: University Press of Kansas, 1993), 9, 11; David L. Snead, *The Gaither Committee, Eisenhower, and the Cold War* (Columbus: Ohio State University Press, 1999), 144.

33. Security Resources Panel of the Science Advisory Committee, "Deterrence and Survival in the Nuclear Age," November 7, 1957, *NSAEBB 139*.

34. "The President's Science Advisory Committee, Report of the AICBM Panel," May 21, 1959, NH01357, *USNH*, DNSA.

35. Robert S. McNamara to John F. Kennedy, "Review of FY 1961 and FY 1962 Military Programs and Budgets," February 21, 1961, Department of Defense Review of FY 61 and FY 62 Military Programs and Budgets, 2/21/61, Box 273, D&A, NSF, JFKL.

36. McNamara to Kennedy, "Review of FY 1961 and FY 1962 Military Programs and Budgets," February 21, 1961, JFKL; Robert S. McNamara to John F. Kennedy, "Appendix II: Program for Deployment of Nike Zeus," September 30, 1961, Defense Budget FY 1963 11/61–12/61, Box 275, D&A, NSF, JFKL.

37. Robert S. McNamara to John F. Kennedy, "Review of FY 1961 and FY 1962 Military Programs and Budgets, Attachment No.1: Strategic and Continental Air Defense Proposals," February 21, 1961, Department of Defense Review of FY 61 and FY 62 Military Programs and Budgets, 2/21/61, Box 273, D&A, NSF, JFKL.

38. McNamara to Kennedy, " Appendix II: Program for Deployment of Nike Zeus," September 30, 1961, JFKL.

39. Robert Jervis, *The Meaning of the Nuclear Revolution: Statecraft and the Prospect of Armageddon* (Ithaca, NY: Cornell University Press, 1989), 196.

40. George H. Decker, "The Military Aspects of the Cold War," June 8, 1961, Army 10/61–12/61, Box 269, D&A, NSF, JFKL.

41. Jervis, *Meaning of the Nuclear Revolution*, 201.

42. Maxwell D. Taylor to John F. Kennedy, "Nike-Zeus Program, FY 1963 Budget," November 22, 1961, Department of Defense—Defense Budget FY 1963 11/61–12/61, Box 275, D&A, NSF, JFKL.

43. Yanarella, *Missile Defense Controversy*, 61–65.

44. "Memorandum of Conference with the President," February 6, 1961, Conferences with the President Joint Chiefs of Staff 1/61–2/61, Box 345, Chester V. Clifton Files, NSF, JFKL.

45. Yanarella, *Missile Defense Controversy*, 62.

46. Bell to Kennedy, "FY 1963 Defense Budget Issues," November 13, 1961, JFKL.

47. McNamara to Kennedy, "FY '63 Budget and 1963-67 Program," October 6, 1961, JFKL.

48. Yanarella, *Missile Defense Controversy*, 29–32.

49. Theodore Sorensen to John F. Kennedy, "Defense Message and Task Force Reports," March 9, 1961, Department of Defense General 3/61, Box 273, D&A, NSF, JFKL.

50. Bell to Kennedy, "FY 1963 Defense Budget Issues," November 13, 1961, JFKL; David Bell to McGeorge Bundy, "Status of 1963 Defense Budget," December 9, 1961, Department of Defense—Defense Budget FY 1963 11/61–12/61, Box 275, D&A, NSF, JFKL.

51. "Memorandum for the President," December 9, 1961, Department of Defense Defense Budget FY 1963 11/61–12/61, Box 273, D&A, NSF, JFKL.

52. "U.S. vs Soviet Missile Strength," February 20, 1961, Department of Defense Review of FY 61 and FY 62 Military Programs and Budgets 2/21/61, Box 273, D&A, NSF, JFKL.

53. Andreas Wenger, *Living With Peril: Eisenhower, Kennedy, and Nuclear Weapons* (Lanham, MD: Rowman and Littlefield, 1997), 242–243.

54. Carl Kaysen to McGeorge Bundy, "Secretary McNamara's Memorandum on the Defense Budget dated October 6, 1961," November 13, 1961, Department of Defense Defense Budget FY 1963 11/61–12/61, Box 275, D&A, NSF, JFKL; McGeorge Bundy to Theodore Sorensen, "Defense Message," March 13, 1961, Department of Defense General 3/61, Box 273, D&A, NSF, JFKL.

55. U. Alexis Johnson to Dean Rusk, "Department of Defense FY '63 Budget," November 8, 1961, NH00435, *USNH*, DNSA.

56. Trachtenberg, *Constructed Peace*, 322.

57. Campbell Craig, *Destroying the Village: Eisenhower and Thermonuclear War* (New York: Columbia University Press, 1998), 130–131.

58. John F. Kennedy, "Radio and Television Report to the American People on the Berlin Crisis," July 25, 1961, APP, accessed March 25, 2017, http://www.presidency.ucsb.edu/ws/?pid=8259.

59. Craig, *Destroying the Village*, 135.

60. Craig, *Destroying the Village*, 134–135.

61. Trachtenberg, *Constructed Peace*, 323–324.

62. Michael R. Beschloss, *The Crisis Years: Kennedy and Khrushchev, 1961–1963* (New York: Edward Burlingame, 1991), 327; Aleksandr Fursenko and Timothy Naftali, *Khrushchev's Cold War: The Inside Story of an American Adversary* (New York: Norton, 2006), 399.

63. Roswell L. Gilpatric, "Address before the Business Council at the Homestead, Hot Springs, Virginia," October 21, 1961, in "First Strike Options and the Berlin Crisis: New Documents from the Kennedy Administration," *National Security Archive Electronic Briefing Book No.56* (hereafter *NSAEBB 56*), ed. William Burr, accessed March 25, 2017, http://nsarchive.gwu.edu/NSAEBB/NSAEBB56/.

64. Fred Kaplan, "JFK's First Strike Plan," *The Atlantic*, October 2001, accessed March 24, 2017, http://www.theatlantic.com/magazine/archive/2001/10/jfks-first-strike-plan/376432/. For documents related to this discussion, see *NSAEBB 56*.

65. Beschloss, *Crisis Years*, 328–330.

66. Craig, *Destroying the Village*, 149–150.

67. Lawrence Freedman, *Kennedy's Wars: Berlin, Cuba, Laos, and Vietnam* (New York: Oxford University Press, 2000), 82–83; Beschloss, *Crisis Years*, 328–330.

68. "Outline for Talk to NSC, January 18, 1962," January 17, 1962, *The Cuban Missile Crisis, 1962*, eds. Lawrence Chang and Peter Kornbluh, DNSA.

69. "Summary of President Kennedy's Remarks to the 496th meeting of the National Security Council," January 18, 1962, in *Foreign Relations of the United States, 1961–1963, Volume VIII, National Security Policy*, ed. David W. Mabon (Washington, DC: United States Government Printing Office, 1996) 238–242.

70. McGeorge Bundy, "To Cap the Volcano," *Foreign Affairs* 40, no.1 (October 1969): 1–20; Dean Rusk, Robert McNamara, George Ball, Roswell Gilpatric, Theodore Sorensen, and McGeorge Bundy, "The Lessons of the Cuban Missile Crisis," *Time*, September 27, 1982, 85; Bundy, *Danger and Survival*, 445–453, 461–462.

71. Marc Trachtenberg, "The Influence of Nuclear Weapons in the Cuban Missile Crisis," *International Security* 10, no. 1 (Summer, 1985): 152, 155–156.

72. "Friday, October 19, 1962, Meeting with the Joint Chiefs of Staff on the Cuban Missile Crisis," in *The Presidential Recordings: John F. Kennedy: The Great Crises, Volume Two, September–October 21, 1962*, eds. Timothy Naftali and Philip Zelikow (New York: Norton, 2001), 580.

73. "Meeting with Congressional Leadership, Monday, October 22, 1962," in *The Presidential Recordings: John F. Kennedy: The Great Crises, Volume Three, October 22–28, 1962*, eds. Philip Zelikow and Ernest R. May (New York: Norton, 2001), 72;Sheldon M. Stern, *The Cuban Missile Crisis in American Memory: Myths Versus Reality* (Stanford, CA: Stanford University Press, 2012), 167–168.

74. "Meeting with Congressional Leadership, Monday, October 22, 1962," in *The Great Crises*, Vol. 3, 72.

75. "Friday, October 19, 1962, Meeting with the Joint Chiefs of Staff on the Cuban Missile Crisis," in *The Great Crises*, Vol. 2, 583–584.

76. "Friday, October 19, 1962, Meeting with the Joint Chiefs of Staff on the Cuban Missile Crisis," in *The Great Crises*, Vol. 2, 581.

77. "Meeting with Congressional Leadership, Monday, October 22, 1962," in *The Great Crises*, Vol. 3, 169.

78. "Friday, October 19, 1962, Meeting with the Joint Chiefs of Staff on the Cuban Missile Crisis," in *The Great Crises*, Vol. 2, 585.

79. "Meeting with Congressional Leadership, Monday, October 22, 1962," in *The Great Crises*, Vol. 3, 89.

80. Stern, *The Cuban Missile Crisis in American Memory*, 156.

81. "Friday, October 19, 1962, Meeting with the Joint Chiefs of Staff on the Cuban Missile Crisis," in *The Great Crises*, Vol. 3, 590, 594; Stern, *The Cuban Missile Crisis in American Memory*, 165.

82. "Friday, October 19, 1962, Meeting with the Joint Chiefs of Staff on the Cuban Missile Crisis," in *The Great Crises*, Vol. 3, 597–598.

83. Trachtenberg, "Influence of Nuclear Weapons," 145.

84. Stern, *The Cuban Missile Crisis in American Memory*, 64–66.

85. Aleksandr Fursenko and Timothy Naftali, *"One Hell of a Gamble": Khrushchev, Castro, Kennedy, and the Cuban Missile Crisis, 1958–1964* (New York: W.W. Norton, 1997), 282–283.

86. Trachtenberg, "Influence of Nuclear Weapons," 155.

87. Schelling Study Group, "A Report on Strategic Developments Over the Next Decade for the Inter-Agency Panel," October 12, 1962, Nuclear Energy Matters, Inter-Agency Panel and the Schelling Study Group Report, 10/12/62, Box 376, Carl Kaysen Files, NSF, JFKL.

88. "Meeting on the Defense Budget," December 5, 1962, Tapes 65 Part 3 and 66 Part 1, Meetings, Presidential Recordings, POF, JFKL. All the recordings cited are also available at the Miller Center of Public Affairs, Presidential Recordings Program, accessed March 24, 2017, http://millercenter.org/presidentialrecordings; Kuklick, *Blind Oracles*, 114;James G. Blight and Janet M. Lang, *The Fog of War: Lessons from the Life of Robert S. McNamara* (Lanham, MD: Rowman and Littlefield, 2005), 84–85.

89. Wenger, *Living with Peril*, 307.

90. Stern, *The Cuban Missile Crisis in American Memory*, 54–67.

91. "Draft Memorandum from Secretary of Defense McNamara to President Kennedy," November 20, 1962, in *FRUS 1961–1963*, Vol. 8, 393–397; McNamara to Kennedy, "Appendix II: Plan for Deployment of Nike Zeus," September 30, 1961, JFKL.

92. "Draft Memorandum from Secretary of Defense McNamara to President Kennedy," November 20, 1962, in *FRUS 1961–1963*, Vol. 8, 393–394.

93. "Draft Memorandum from Secretary of Defense McNamara to President Kennedy," November 20, 1962, in *FRUS 1961–1963*, Vol. 8, 393.

94. "Daily Report to Secretary of Defense," June 27, 1962, Department of Defense (B) Joint Chiefs of Staff General, 1962–1963, Box 276, D&A, NSF, JFKL.

95. Henry S. Rowen to McGeorge Bundy, "Basic National Security Policy," May 22, 1961, attachment, Military Policy Basic National Security Policy, 1/61-5/61, Box 374, Carl Kaysen Files, NSF, JFKL.

96. "Editorial Comment on Cuba Accord," *New York Times*, October 30, 1962, 17.

97. C.L. Sulzberger "Mr. K's Own 'Huckster's Approach'," *New York Times*, October 29, 1962, 28.

98. Asa McKercher, "Steamed Up: Domestic Politics, Congress, and Cuba, 1959–1963," *Diplomatic History* 38, no. 3 (August 2014): 599–627.

99. Tom Wicker, "Khrushchev Reply Buoys Democrats," *New York Times*, October 29, 1962, 20.

100. Stewart Alsop, "McNamara Thinks about the Unthinkable," *The Saturday Evening Post*, 235, no. 43, December 1, 1962, 18; Stewart Alsop, "Our New Strategy: Alternatives to Total War," *The Saturday Evening Post*, 235, no. 43, December 1, 1962, 13–17.

101. Herken, *Counsels of War*, 169.

102. "The State of Our Defense," *Washington Post*, February 1, 1963, 10.

103. John G. Norris, "McNamara Bares Shift in Defense," *Washington Post*, January 31, 1963, A1; Jack Raymond, "Air Force Assails Strategic Plans," *New York Times*, February 1, 1963, 1, 3.

104. McGeorge Bundy, "Notes on Read-Through of the McNamara Papers at 2142 Tracey Place, June 20-21, 1984," Folder 11, Box 2, Series 1, Robert S. McNamara Papers, Manuscripts Division, Library of Congress.

105. Kuklick, *Blind Oracles*, 107–109; Gavin, *Nuclear Statecraft*, 30–56; Kaplan, *Wizards*, 283–285.

106. Robert S. McNamara, "Speech to NATO Council, Athens," May 5, 1962, in *U.S. Nuclear Strategy: A Reader*, eds. Philip Bobbitt, Lawrence Freedman, and Gregory F. Treverton (Basingstoke, UK: Macmillan, 1989), 211. McNamara used a similar line in his Ann Arbor speech. See: "Excerpts From Address by McNamara," *New York Times*, June 17, 1962, 26, available from the author on request.

107. Kaplan, *Wizards*, 316.

108. Wenger, *Living with Peril*, 241.

109. "Memorandum from Kaysen to President Kennedy," January 5, 1962, in *Foreign Relations of the United States, 1961–1963, Volumes VII/VIII/IX, Microfiche Supplement, Arms Control; National Security; Foreign Economic Policy*, eds. Evans Gerakas, David W. Mabon, David S. Patterson, William S. Sanford, Jr., and Carolyn B. Yee (Washington, DC: United States Government Printing Office, 1997), Document 74.

110. "Paper Prepared for President Kennedy," undated, in *Foreign Relations of the United States, 1961–1963, Volume VII, Arms Control and Disarmament*, eds. David W. Mabon and David S. Patterson (Washington, DC: United States Government Printing Office, 1995), 177–180.

111. "Letter from the Director of Defense Research and Engineering (Brown) to President Kennedy," December 12, 1961, in *FRUS 1961–1963*, Vol. 7, 266.

112. Twining Committee to the Chief of Staff U.S. Air Force, "Military Implications of U.S. and Soviet Nuclear Testing," March 4, 1963, Nuclear Weapons–Twining Committee Report to Chief of Staff of U.S. Air Force: Military Implications of U.S and Soviet Nuclear Testing, 3/4/63, Box 302, Subject Files, NSF, JFKL.

113. "Report of Ad Hoc Panel on Nuclear Testing," July 21, 1961, in *FRUS 1961–1963*, Vol. 7, 108.

114. "Report of Ad Hoc Panel on Nuclear Testing," July 21, 1961, 108–109.

115. "Atomic Energy Commission Chairman Glenn Seaborg, Journal Entry for September 5, 1961," in "The Making of the Limited Test Ban Treaty, 1958–1963," *National Security Archive Electronic Briefing Book No.94* (hereafter *NSAEBB 94*), eds. William Burr and Hector L. Montford, accessed March 25, 2017, http://nsarchive.gwu.edu/NSAEBB/NSAEBB94/. Burr and Montford make a similar point in their introduction.

116. Richard Reeves, *President Kennedy: Profile of Power* (New York: Simon and Schuster, 1993), 252.

117. "Memorandum of Conversation," May 23, 1961, in *FRUS 1961–1963*, Vol. 7, 73.

118. "Memorandum of the 497th Meeting of the National Security Council," February 27, 1962, in *FRUS 1961–1963*, Vol. 7, 332–333.

119. Yanarella, *Missile Defense Controversy*, 95–96.

120. "Editorial Note," in *FRUS 1961–1963*, Vol. 7, 600–601.

121. "Memorandum From the Deputy Secretary of Defense (Gilpatric) to President Kennedy," undated, in *FRUS 1961–1963*, Vol. 7, 312, 315.

122. Yanarella, *Missile Defense Controversy*, 97.

123. Yanarella, *Missile Defense Controversy*, 98.

124. Trachtenberg, *Constructed Peace*, 384–388; "The President's News Conference," August 1, 1963, APP, accessed March 25, 2017, http://www.presidency.ucsb.edu/ws/?pid=9366.

125. "Addendum to the 20 December 1962 Report of the NSAM 205 Committee," August 15, 1963, in *FRUS 1961–1963, Vols. VII/VIII/IX, Microfiche Supplement*, Document 219.

126. Mikhail Pervov, *Sistemy raketno-kosmicheskoi oborony Rossii sozdavalis' tak*, 2nd ed. (Moscow: Aviarius-XXI, 2004), 111.

127. William W. Kaufmann, *The McNamara Strategy* (New York: Harper and Row, 1964), 157.

128. "The President's News Conference," August 1, 1963, APP, accessed March 25, 2017, http://www.presidency.ucsb.edu/ws/?pid=9366.

129. Reeves, *President Kennedy*, 555.

130. "Meeting on the Nuclear Test Ban Treaty with Senators Mansfield and Dirksen," September 9, 1963, Tape 109.2, Presidential Recordings, POF, JFKL.

131. Kaufmann, *McNamara Strategy*, 159.

132. John F. Kennedy, "Letter to Senate Leaders Restating the Administration's Views on the Nuclear Test Ban Treaty," September 11, 1963, APP, accessed March 25, 2017, http://www.presidency.ucsb.edu/ws/?pid=9403.

133. "The President's News Conference," August 20, 1963, APP, accessed March 25, 2017, http://www.presidency.ucsb.edu/ws/?pid=9374.

134. *109 Congressional Record*, September 16, 1963, 17051; *109 Congressional Record*, September 10, 1963, 16613; *109 Congressional Record*, September 19, 1963, 17587.

135. Andreas Wenger and Marcel Gerber, "John F. Kennedy and the Limited Test Ban Treaty: A Case Study of Presidential Leadership," *Presidential Studies Quarterly* 29, no. 2 (June 1999): 478.

136. "Statement of the Position of the Joint Chiefs of Staff on the Three-Environment Nuclear Test Ban Treaty," August 12, 1963, *NSAEBB 94*.

137. "Secretary McNamara's Conversation with Chancellor Adenauer," July 31, 1963, *NSAEBB 94*.

138. "Telegram from the Department of State to the Embassy in Germany," August 6, 1963, in *FRUS 1961–1963*, Vol. 7, 870–871.

139. "Memorandum of Conversation," July 8, 1963, in *FRUS 1961–1963*, Vol. 7, 776.

140. Bundy, *Danger and Survival*, 554; John F. Kennedy, "Remarks Prepared for Delivery at the Trade Mart in Dallas," November 22, 1963, APP, accessed March 25, 2017, http://www.presidency.ucsb.edu/ws/?pid=9539; John F. Kennedy, "Remarks Intended for Delivery to the Texas Democratic State Committee in the Municipal Auditorium in Austin," November 22, 1963, APP, accessed March 25, 2017, http://www.presidency.ucsb.edu/ws/?pid=9540.

141. "Summary Record of the 517th Meeting of the National Security Council," September 12, 1963, in *FRUS 1961–1963*, Vol. 8, 499–500.

142. "Meeting on the Defense Budget," December 5, 1962, JFKL.

143. Bundy, *Danger and Survival*, 554.

144. Wenger, *Living With Peril*, 241.

145. Glenn T. Seaborg, *Kennedy, Khrushchev and the Test Ban* (Berkeley: University of California Press, 1981), 297–298.

146. David Kaiser, "Men and Policies: 1961–1969," in *The Diplomacy of the Crucial Decade: American Foreign Relations During the 1960s*, ed. Diane B. Kunz (New York: Columbia University Press, 1994), 37.

147. Andrew Preston, *The War Council: McGeorge Bundy, the NSC, and Vietnam* (Cambridge, MA: Harvard University Press, 2006), 55.

148. "Meeting on the Defense Budget," December 5, 1962, JFKL.

149. "Meeting on the Defense Budget," December 5, 1962, JFKL; "Summary Record of the 517th Meeting of the National Security Council," September 12, 1963, in *FRUS 1961–1963*, Vol. 8, 500–501.

CHAPTER 2

1. Julian E. Zelizer, *The Fierce Urgency of Now: Lyndon Johnson, Congress, and the Battle for the Great Society* (New York: Penguin Press, 2015), 62; Robert Dallek, *Flawed Giant: Lyndon Johnson and His Times, 1961–1973* (New York: Oxford University Press, 1998), 49.

2. Shapley, *Promise and Power*, 273–275.

3. Randall Bennett Woods, *Prisoners of Hope: Lyndon B. Johnson, the Great Society, and the Limits of Liberalism* (New York: Basic Books, 2016), 16, 24–25; Zelizer, *Fierce Urgency of Now*, 63–4; Randall Bennett Woods, *LBJ: Architect of American Ambition* (New York: Free Press, 2006), 558.

4. Robert A. Caro, *The Years of Lyndon Johnson: The Passage of Power* (New York: Knopf, 2012), 466–475; Dallek, *Flawed Giant*, 71–72; Irving Bernstein, *Guns or Butter: The Presidency of Lyndon Johnson* (New York: Oxford University Press, 1996), 27–32; Zelizer, *Fierce Urgency of Now*, 76–77.

5. Caro, *Passage of Power*, 478.

6. Lyndon Johnson-Robert McNamara Telcon, 17:03, December 7, 1963, K6312.05 Program Number (hereafter PNO) 3, Recordings and Transcripts of Conversations and Meetings (hereafter RTCM), Lyndon Baines Johnson Library (hereafter, LBJL). All recordings cited are also available at Presidential Recordings Program, Miller Center of Public Affairs, University of Virginia,

accessed March 25, 2017, https://millercenter.org/the-presidency/
secret-white-house-tapes.

7. Lyndon Johnson, "Annual Budget Message to the Congress, Fiscal Year 1965," January 21, 1964, APP, accessed March 25, 2017, http://www.presidency.ucsb.edu/ws/index.php?pid=26013; Bernstein, *Guns or Butter*, 34–35.

8. Caro, *Passage of Power*, 478.

9. Lyndon Johnson-Robert McNamara Telcon, 15:40, January 6, 1964, WH6401.06 #1195, RTCM, LBJL.

10. Lyndon Johnson-Dick West Office Conversation, 11:50, September 21, 1964, WH6409.12 #5625, RTCM, LBJL.

11. Lyndon Johnson-Robert McNamara Telcon, 14:00, January 2, 1964, WH6401.03 #1149, RTCM, LBJL.

12. Lyndon Johnson-Walter Heller Telcon, 13:40, December 14, 1963, K6312.08 PNO 39, RTCM, LBJL; Lyndon Johnson-Walter Heller Telcon, 12:00, December 23, 1963, K6312.15 PNO 1, RTCM, LBJL; John Dumbrell, *President Lyndon Johnson and Soviet Communism* (Manchester, UK: Manchester University Press, 2004), 61.

13. Robert McNamara to Lyndon Johnson, "Recommended FY 1965-FY 1969 Strategic Retaliatory Forces," December 6, 1963, The Office of the Secretary of Defense and Joint Staff (hereafter OSD/JS) Freedom of Information Act (hereafter FOIA) Requester Service Center, accessed March 25, 2016, http://www.dod.mil/pubs/foi/Reading_Room/Homeland_Defense/333.pdf.

14. McNamara to Johnson, "Recommended FY 1965-1969 Strategic Retaliatory Forces," December 6, 1963, OSD/JS FOIA Requester Service Center.

15. McNamara to Johnson, "Recommended FY 1965-1969 Strategic Retaliatory Forces," December 6, 1963, OSD/JS FOIA Requester Service Center.

16. Robert McNamara to John F. Kennedy, "Recommended FY 1965-FY 1969 Continental Air and Missile Defense Forces," November 14, 1963, Defense Budget—1965 Sec.2, Box 15, Agency File (hereafter AF), National Security Files (hereafter NSF), LBJL; McNamara to Johnson, "Recommended FY 1965-1969 Strategic Retaliatory Forces," December 6, 1963, OSD/JS FOIA Requester Service Center.

17. Carl Kaysen to McGeorge Bundy, Covering Note and "Comment on DOD Draft Memorandum: Strategic Striking Forces," October 25, 1963, Defense Budget—1965 Sec. 2, Box 15, AF, NSF, LBJL.

18. McNamara to Johnson, "Recommended FY 65-69 Strategic Retaliatory Forces," December 6, 1963, OSD/JS FOIA Requester Service Center.

19. Robert McNamara to Lyndon Johnson, "Recommended FY 1966-1970 Programs for Strategic Offensive Forces, Continental Air and Missile Defense Forces, and Civil Defense," December 3, 1964, OSD/JS FOIA Requester Service Center, accessed March 25, 2017, http://www.dod.mil/pubs/foi/Reading_Room/Homeland_Defense/326.pdf.

20. "State-Defense Discussion on Defense Budget and Five Year Force Structure," May 27, 1964, NH01405, *USNH*, DNSA.

21. McNamara to Kennedy, "Recommended FY 1965-FY 1969 Continental Air and Missile Defense Forces," November 14, 1963, LBJL.

22. Lawrence S. Kaplan, Ronald D. Landa, and Edward J. Drea, *History of the Office of the Secretary of Defense, The McNamara Ascendancy, 1961–1965* (Washington, DC: Historical Office, Office of the Secretary of Defense, 2006), 141;Robert

David Johnson, *Congress and the Cold War* (New York: Cambridge University Press, 2006), 87, 144–145, 159–160.

23. Gilbert C. Fite, *Richard B. Russell, Jr., Senator from Georgia* (Chapel Hill: University of North Carolina Press, 1991), 425–426.

24. Lloyd A. Free and Hadley Cantril, *The Political Beliefs of Americans; A Study of Public Opinion* (New Brunswick, NJ: Rutgers University Press, 1967), 51–59, 65, 83–86, 90.

25. William Smith to McGeorge Bundy, "FY 65 Budget Discussions," November 22, 1963, Defense Budget—Sec. 2, Box 15, AF, NSF, LBJL.

26. Kaysen to Bundy, Covering Note and "Comment on DOD Draft Memorandum: Strategic Striking Forces," October 25, 1963, LBJL.

27. Dallek, *Flawed Giant*, 131, 175–176; Dumbrell, *Lyndon Johnson and Soviet Communism*, 60.

28. Lyndon Johnson-Chalmers Roberts Telcon, 15:00, August 15, 1964, WH6408.22 #4962, RTCM, LBJL.

29. Editorial, "Our Defense: A Crucial Issue for Candidates," *Life*, September 25, 1964, 10; Lyndon Johnson-Dick West Office Conversation, 11:50 September 21, 1964, WH6409.12 #5625, RTCM, LBJL.

30. Kaplan, Landa, and Drea, *The McNamara Ascendancy*, 494, 497; Lyndon Johnson, "Annual Message to the Congress on the State of the Union," January 4, 1965, APP, accessed March 25, 2017, http://www.presidency.ucsb.edu/ws/?pid=26907; Woods, *LBJ*, 559–560.

31. Fredrik Logevall, *Choosing War: The Lost Chance for Peace and the Escalation of the War in Vietnam* (Berkeley: University of California Press, 1999), 196–206, 333–375.

32. Woods, *Prisoners of Hope*, 240.

33. Lyndon Johnson-Robert McNamara Telcon, 10:10 December 22, 1965, WH6512.04 #9327, RTCM, LBJL; Donald F. Kettl, "The Economic Education of Lyndon Johnson: Guns, Butter, and Taxes," in *The Johnson Years, Volume Two: Vietnam, the Environment, and Science*, ed. Robert A. Divine (Lawrence: University Press of Kansas, 1987), 54–78; Bernstein, *Guns or Butter*, 358–378; Shapley, *Promise and Power*, 367–376.

34. McNamara to Kennedy, "Recommended FY 1965-FY 1969 Continental Air and Missile Defense Forces," November 14, 1963, LBJL.

35. Dee Garrison, *Bracing for Armageddon: Why Civil Defense Never Worked* (New York: Oxford University Press, 2006), 134. Garrison believes that McNamara conspired with Senator Henry Jackson, in charge of funding civil defense, in order to hobble ABM's chances. However, given Jackson's well-known enthusiasm for nuclear programs, this seems unlikely. See: Edward Geist, *Armageddon Insurance: Civil Defense in the United States and the Soviet Union* (unpublished manuscript, April 22, 2016), PDF file, 254, n. 566.

36. Kenneth D. Rose, *One Nation Underground: The Fallout Shelter in American Culture* (New York: New York University Press, 2001), 2.

37. Edward Zuckerman, *The Day After World War III* (New York: Viking, 1984), 140.

38. Rose, *One Nation Underground*, 202.

39. Geist, *Armageddon Insurance*, 12, 251–255.

40. Rose, *One Nation Underground*, 206.

41. John F. Kennedy, "Radio and Television Report to the American People on the Berlin Crisis," July 25, 1961, APP, accessed March 25, 2017, http://www.presidency.ucsb.edu/ws/?pid=8259.

42. "Memo of Conference, LBJ Ranch, Texas," December 22, 1964, JCS Filed by the LBJ Library, Box 29, AF, NSF, LBJL.

43. "Memo of Conference, LBJ Ranch, Texas," December 22, 1964, LBJL.

44. McNamara to Johnson, "Recommended FY 65-69 Strategic Retaliatory Forces," December 6, 1963, OSD/JS FOIA Requester Service Center.

45. Hardening is a process by which missiles are placed in a concrete silo and buried in the ground in order to protect them from the huge pressure and heat generated by a nuclear blast.

46. McNamara to Johnson, "Recommended FY 65-69 Strategic Retaliatory Forces," December 6, 1963, OSD/JS FOIA Requester Service Center.

47. McNamara to Johnson, "Recommended FY 65-69 Strategic Retaliatory Forces," December 6, 1963, OSD/JS FOIA Requester Service Center.

48. John McCone and the United States Intelligence Board (hereafter USIB), "National Intelligence Estimate (hereafter NIE) 11-8-62: Soviet Capabilities for Long-Range Attack," July 6, 1962, Central Intelligence Agency (hereafter CIA) Freedom of Information Act (hereafter FOIA) Electronic Reading Room, accessed March 25, 2017, http://www.foia.cia.gov/sites/default/files/document_conversions/89801/DOC_0000267773.pdf; John McCone and USIB, NIE 11-8-63: Soviet Capabilities for Strategic Attack, October 18, 1963, CIA FOIA Reading Room, accessed March 25, 2017, http://www.foia.cia.gov/sites/default/files/document_conversions/89801/DOC_0000267776.pdf; John McCone & USIB, Soviet Capabilities for Strategic Attack, October 8, 1964, accessed March 25, 2017, http://www.foia.cia.gov/sites/default/files/document_conversions/89801/DOC_0000267908.pdf.

49. David Engerman, *Know Your Enemy: The Rise and Fall of America's Soviet Experts* (New York: Oxford University Press, 2009), 180–232. For Parsons' contribution to modernization theory, see Michael E. Latham, *Modernization as Ideology: American Social Science and "Nation Building" in the Kennedy Era* (Chapel Hill: University of North Carolina Press, 2000), 31–35.

50. John McCone and USIB, "NIE 11-4-64: Main Trends in Soviet Military Policy," April 22, 1964, CIA FOIA Reading Room, accessed March 27, 2017, http://www.foia.cia.gov/sites/default/files/document_conversions/89801/DOC_0000267778.pdf.

51. Robert McNamara, "Statement Before the Senate Subcommittee on Department of Defense Appropriations, the Fiscal Year 1963–67 Defense Program and 1963 Defense Budget," February 14, 1962, NH00439, *USNH*, DNSA.

52. Robert McNamara, "Statement Before a Joint Session of the Senate Armed Services Committee and the Senate Subcommittee on Department of Defense Appropriations on the Fiscal Year 1965–69 Defense Program and 1965 Defense Budget," February 3, 1964, NH00451, *USNH*, DNSA.

53. Hal Brands, "Progress Unseen: U.S. Arms Control Policy and the Origins of Détente, 1963–1968," *Diplomatic History* 30, no. 2 (April 2006), 253–255.

54. Jones, *After Hiroshima*, 401–449.

55. McNamara to Kennedy, "Recommended FY 1965-FY 1969 Continental Air and Missile Defense Forces," November 14, 1963, LBJL.

56. "Memo of Conference, LBJ Ranch, Texas," December 22, 1964, LBJL.

57. Robert McNamara to Lyndon Johnson, "Recommended FY 68-72 Strategic Offensive and Defensive Forces," November 9, 1966, OSD/JS FOIA Requester Service Center, accessed March 25, 2017, http://www.dod.mil/pubs/foi/Reading_Room/Homeland_Defense/318.pdf.

58. Dumbrell, *Lyndon Johnson and Soviet Communism*, 77.

59. CIA Office of Current Intelligence, "Special Report: The Top Military Men in Communist China," December 11, 1964, CIA FOIA Reading Room, accessed March 25, 2017, http://www.foia.cia.gov/sites/default/files/document_conversions/89801/DOC_0001197456.pdf.

60. Richard Helms and USIB, "NIE 13-9-65: Communist China's Foreign Policy," May 5, 1965, CIA FOIA Reading Room, accessed March 25, 2017, http://www.foia.cia.gov/sites/default/files/document_conversions/89801/DOC_0001085117.pdf.

61. Jones, *After Hiroshima*, 402–404; James Peck, *Washington's China: The National Security World, the Cold War, and the Origins of Globalism* (Amherst: University of Massachusetts Press, 2006) 195–197.

62. Richard Helms and USIB, "Communist China's Foreign Policy," May 5, 1965, CIA FOIA Reading Room; CIA Directorate of Intelligence (hereafter DI), "Peiping's Views on 'Revolutionary War,'" December 14, 1964, CIA FOIA Reading Room, accessed March 27, 2017, http://www.foia.cia.gov/sites/default/files/document_conversions/89801/DOC_0001231436.pdf.

63. CIA DI, "Peiping's Views on 'Revolutionary War,'" December 14, 1964, CIA FOIA Reading Room.

64. CIA Office of National Estimates to Richard Helms, "Use of Nuclear Weapons in the Vietnam War," March 18, 1966, CIA FOIA Reading Room, accessed March 25, 2017, http://www.foia.cia.gov/sites/default/files/document_conversions/89801/DOC_0001166479.pdf.

65. Richard Helms and USIB, "NIE 13-2-66: Communist China's Advanced Weapons Program," July 1, 1966, CIA FOIA Reading Room, accessed March 25, 2017, http://www.foia.cia.gov/sites/default/files/document_conversions/89801/DOC_0001160120.pdf.

66. John McCone and USIB, "NIE 13-2-65: Communist China's Advanced Weapons Program," January 27, 1965, CIA FOIA Reading Room, accessed March 25, 2017, http://www.foia.cia.gov/sites/default/files/document_conversions/89801/DOC_0001090197.pdf.

67. "Memo of Conference, LBJ Ranch, Texas," December 22, 1964, LBJL.

68. Jones, *After Hiroshima*, 448–449; "Draft Memorandum from Secretary of Defense McNamara to President Johnson," November 3, 1965, in *Foreign Relations of the United States, 1964–1968, Volume III, Vietnam, June–December 1965*, eds. David C. Humphrey, Edward C. Keefer, and Louis J. Smith (Washington, DC: United States Government Printing Office, 1996), 514–528.

69. Jennifer G. Mathers, "A Fly in Outer Space: Soviet Ballistic Missile Defence During the Khrushchev Period," *Journal of Strategic Studies* 21, no. 2 (June 1998): 31–59; Jennifer G. Mathers, *The Russian Nuclear Shield from Stalin to Yeltsin* (Basingstoke, UK: Palgrave Macmillan, 2000).

70. Pervov, *Sistemy sozdavalis' tak*, 175–181.

71. John McCone and USIB, "NIE 11-3-64: Soviet Air and Missile Defense Capabilities Through Mid-1970," December 16, 1964, CIA FOIA Reading Room, accessed March 25, 2017, http://www.foia.cia.gov/sites/default/files/document_conversions/89801/DOC_0000278465.pdf.

72. McNamara to Johnson, "Recommended FY 65-69 Strategic Retaliatory Forces," December 6, 1963, OSD/JS FOIA Requester Service Center.

73. Lawrence Freedman, *U.S. Intelligence and the Soviet Strategic Threat*. 2nd ed. (Basingstoke, UK: Palgrave, 1986), 86–96; Halperin, "Decision to Deploy the ABM," 84.

74. Richard Helms and USIB, "Memorandum to Holders of NIE 11-8-64," May 10, 1965, CIA FOIA Reading Room, accessed March 25, 2017, http://www.foia.cia.gov/sites/default/files/document_conversions/89801/DOC_0000267911.pdf; Richard Helms and USIB, "NIE 11-8-65: Soviet Capabilities for Strategic Attack," October 7, 1965, CIA FOIA Reading Room, accessed March 25, 2017, http://www.foia.cia.gov/sites/default/files/document_conversions/89801/DOC_0000267912.pdf.

75. Richard Helms and USIB, "NIE 11-8-66: Soviet Capabilities for Strategic Attack," October 20, 1966, CIA FOIA Reading Room, accessed March 25, 2017, http://www.foia.cia.gov/sites/default/files/document_conversions/89801/DOC_0000267915.pdf.

76. "Letter from Secretary of State Rusk to Secretary of Defense McNamara," December 1, 1966, in *Foreign Relations of the United States, 1964–1968, Volume X, National Security Policy*, ed. David S. Patterson (Washington, DC: United States Government Printing Office, 2002), 453–454.

77. Cyrus Vance to Lyndon Johnson, December 10, 1966, OSD/JS FOIA Requester Service Center, accessed March 25, 2017, http://www.dod.mil/pubs/foi/Reading_Room/Homeland_Defense/1001.pdf.

78. Yanarella, *Missile Defense Controversy*, 134.

79. *111 Congressional Record*, May 12, 1965, 10366.

80. Nathaniel Davis to Walt Rostow, "ABMs and Politics," April 14, 1967, Filed by LBJ Library, Files of Nathaniel Davis, NSF, LBJL; Yanarella, *Missile Defense Controversy*, 125.

81. McNamara to Johnson, "Recommended FY 68-72 Strategic Offensive and Defensive Forces," November 9, 1966, OSD/JS FOIA Requester Service Center.

82. Yanarella, *Missile Defense Controversy*, 134.

83. Shapley, *Promise and Power*, 391.

84. Yanarella, *Missile Defense Controversy*, 116–117; George C. Wilson, "Congress Shows the Spirit of '66 in Writing Defense Budget Bill," *Washington Post*, October 17, 1966, A4; Vance to Johnson, December 10, 1966, OSD/JS FOIA Requester Service Center.

85. "Draft Notes of Meeting," December 6, 1966, in *FRUS, 1964–1968*, Vol. 10, 459–464.

86. Vance to Johnson, December 10, 1966, OSD/JS FOIA Requester Service Center.

87. Lyndon Johnson-Robert McNamara Telcon, 18:40, January 4, 1967, WH6071.01 #11307, RTCM, LBJL.

88. Vance to Johnson, December 10, 1966, OSD/JS FOIA Requester Service Center.

89. Vance to Johnson, December 10, 1966, OSD/JS FOIA Requester Service Center.

90. Record of Meeting with President Johnson, January 4, 1967, in *FRUS 1964–1968*, Vol. 10, 526–531.

91. Lyndon Johnson-Robert McNamara Telcon, 18:40, January 4, 1967, WH6071.01 #11307, RTCM, LBJL.

92. Lyndon Johnson-William McC.Martin Telcon, 12:36, December 12, 1966, WH6612.02 #11126, RTCM, LBJL.

93. Lyndon Johnson-George Mahon Telcon, 15:14, August 22, 1966, WH6608.12 #10628, RTCM, LBJL.

94. Lyndon Johnson-Everett Dirksen Telcon, 19:54, January 4, 1967, WH6701.01 #11310, RTCM, LBJL.

95. Halperin, "Decision to Deploy the ABM," 85.

96. Dallek, *Flawed Giant*, 353, 369–371. Fulbright came out against the war publicly in January 1966. Randall Bennett Woods, *Fulbright: A Biography* (Cambridge, UK: Cambridge University Press, 1995), 397–402.

97. Lyndon Johnson-William Fulbright Telcon, 17:30, October 11, 1966, WH6610.04 #10941, RTCM, LBJL.

98. Henry Owen to Walt Rostow, June 15, 1966, Non-Vietnam April-July 1966, Box 15, Files of Walt W. Rostow, NSF, LBJL.

99. Owen to Rostow, June 15, 1966, LBJL.

100. Walt Rostow to Lyndon Johnson, June 15, 1966, Non-Vietnam April-July 1966, Box 15, Files of Walt W. Rostow, NSF, LBJL.

101. Gavin, *Nuclear Statecraft*, 120–133; McNamara, *Blundering Into Disaster*, 95–96; Jervis, *Meaning of the Nuclear Revolution*, 74–106.

102. "Memorandum of Conversation," December 7, 1966, in *Foreign Relations of the United States, 1964–1968, Volume XI, Arms Control and Disarmament*, eds. Evans Gerakas, David S. Patterson, and Caroline B. Yee (Washington, DC: United States Government Printing Office, 1997), 405–407.

103. Lyndon Johnson, "Annual Budget Message to the Congress, Fiscal Year 1968," January 24, 1967, APP, accessed March 25, 2017, http://www.presidency.ucsb.edu/ws/index.php?pid=28150.

CHAPTER 3

1. Brands, "Progress Unseen," 253–285; John Prados, "The Prague Spring and SALT: Arms Setbacks in 1968," in *The Foreign Policies of Lyndon Johnson: Beyond Vietnam*, ed. H.W. Brands (College Station: Texas A&M University Press, 1999), 19–36. See also Glenn T. Seaborg and Benjamin S. Loeb, *Stemming the Tide: Arms Control in the Johnson Years* (Lexington, MA: Lexington Books, 1987), 440–443 for an early version of this view.

2. Dumbrell, *Lyndon Johnson and Soviet Communism*, 78–86.

3. Lyndon Johnson, "Message to the 18-Nation Disarmament Conference in Geneva," January 21, 1964, APP, accessed March 25, 2017, http://www.presidency.ucsb.edu/ws/index.php?pid=26009#axzz1t3aK9F3w.

4. John McCone and USIB, "NIE 11-8-63: Soviet Capabilities for Strategic Attack," October 18, 1963, CIA FOIA Reading Room, accessed March 25, 2017, http://www.foia.cia.gov/sites/default/files/document_conversions/89801/DOC_0000267776.pdf; McNamara to Johnson, "Recommended FY 1965-FY 1969 Strategic Retaliatory Forces," December 6, 1963, OSD/JS FOIA Requester Service Center.

5. "Memorandum of Conversation," February 13, 1964, in *FRUS 1964–1968*, Vol. 11, 20.

6. "Memorandum of Conversation," February 13, 1964, in *FRUS 1964–1968*, Vol. 11, 20.

7. CIA, "Soviet Economic Problems Multiply," January 9, 1964, CIA FOIA Reading Room, accessed June 3, 2017, https://www.cia.gov/library/readingroom/docs/CIA-RDP66B00403R000500080004-3.pdf.

8. CIA DI, "Soviet Strategic Interest in Limited Disarmament," March 6, 1964, CIA FOIA Reading Room, accessed March 25, 2017, http://www.foia.cia.gov/sites/default/files/document_conversions/89801/DOC_0000499819.pdf.

9. "Memorandum of Conversation," February 13, 1964, *FRUS 1964–1968*, Vol. 11, 20.

10. Zelizer, *Fierce Urgency of Now*, 257–265, 271; Woods, *Prisoners of Hope*, 299.

11. "Memorandum from Acting Secretary of State Katzenbach to the President's Special Assistant (Rostow)," December 10, 1966, in *FRUS 1964–1968,* Vol. 11, 408; "Memorandum from Director of Central Intelligence Helms to the President's Special Assistant (Rostow)," December 10, 1966, in *FRUS 1964–1968,* Vol. 11, 411–417; Walt Rostow to Lyndon Johnson, "Soviet reaction to U.S. Deployment of Nike-X, Postures A or B," December 10, 1966, Walt Rostow, Vol 16, Dec 1–13, 1966 [1 of 3], Box 11 [2 of 2], Memos to the President, NSF, LBJL.

12. Foy Kohler to Walt Rostow, "Statement re Possible Soviet Reaction to U.S. Deployment of ABMs," December 10, 1966, Walt Rostow, Vol. 16, Dec. 1–13, 1966 [1 of 3], Box 11 [2 of 2], Memos to the President, NSF, LBJL.

13. William Raborn and USIB, "NIE 11-7-66: Trends in Soviet General Policies," April 28, 1966, CIA FOIA Reading Room, accessed March 25, 2017, http://www.foia.cia.gov/sites/default/files/document_conversions/89801/DOC_0000273216.pdf.

14. "Memorandum From Director of Central Intelligence Helms to the President's Special Assistant (Rostow)," December 10, 1966, in *FRUS 1964–1968,* Vol. 11, 417.

15. Kohler to Rostow, "Statement re Possible Soviet Reaction to U.S. Deployment of ABMs," December 10, 1966, LBJL; Raborn and USIB, "NIE 11-7-66: Trends in Soviet General Policies," April 26, 1966, CIA FOIA Reading Room.

16. "Letter from President Johnson to Chairman Kosygin," January 21, 1967, in *FRUS 1964–1968,* Vol. 11, 431–432.

17. "Memorandum of Conversation: British Discussions with the Soviets on ABM," February 27, 1967, USSR, ABM Negotiations (III) 1/67–9/68, Box 231, Country File (hereafter CF), NSF, LBJL; Dean Rusk to American Embassy London, American Embassy Moscow, "Exchange of Messages Between Secretary and British Foreign Secretary Brown on ABM Systems," February 3, 1967, ABM I, 1966–67, Box 1, Files of Spurgeon Keeny, NSF, LBJL.

18. Dana Adams Schmidt, "Kosygin is Cool to Missiles Curb," *New York Times,* February 10, 1967, 1, 6.

19. Walt Rostow to Lyndon Johnson, February 18, 1967, Kosygin [2 of 7], Box 10, Files of Walt W. Rostow (hereafter FWR), NSF, LBJL; "Message from the Embassy in the Soviet Union to the Department of State," February 18, 1967, in *FRUS 1964–1968,* Vol. 11, 442–444.

20. "Oral Statement Delivered to the Ambassador to the Soviet Union (Thompson)," February 28, 1967, in *FRUS 1964–1968,* Vol. 11, 452.

21. "Letter from Chairman Kosygin to President Johnson," February 27, 1967, in *FRUS 1964–1968,* Vol. 11, 450–451.

22. Foy Kohler to Nicholas Katzenbach, "ABM Discussion with the Russians," February 15, 1967, USSR, ABM Negotiations (II) 1/67–9/68, Box 231, CF, NSF, LBJL.

23. Nathaniel Davis to Walt Rostow, "The Soviets on ABMs," March 1, 1967, USSR ABM Negotiations (II) 1/67–9/68, Box 231, CF, NSF, LBJL.

24. Walt Rostow to Lyndon Johnson, "Draft Instruction to Ambassador Thompson on U.S.-Soviet Strategic Weapons Talks," March 17, 1967, ABM I 1966–67, Box 1, Files of Spurgeon Keeny, NSF, LBJL.

25. Kohler to Katzenbach, "ABM Discussion with the Russians," February 15, 1967, LBJL.

26. Lyndon Johnson-William Fulbright Telcon, 22:57, June 19, 1967, WH6706.01 #11908, RTCM, LBJL.

27. Lyndon Johnson-Everett Dirksen Telcon, 22:45, June 22, 1967, WH6706.02 #11913, RTCM, LBJL; Lyndon Johnson-William Fulbright Telcon, 22:57, June 19, 1967, WH6706.01 #11909, RTCM, LBJL.

28. "Memorandum of Conversation," June 23, 1967, in *Foreign Relations of the United States, 1964–1968, Volume XIV, Soviet Union*, eds. David C. Humphrey and Charles S. Sampson (Washington, DC: United States Government Printing Office, 2001), 516, 519.

29. Anatoly Dobrynin, *In Confidence: Moscow's Ambassador to Six Cold War Presidents, 1962–1986* (New York: Times Books, 1995), 165–166.

30. "Memorandum of Conversation," June 23, 1967, in *FRUS 1964–1968*, Vol. 14, 529–30.

31. "Memorandum of Conversation," June 23, 1967, in *FRUS 1964–1968*, Vol. 14, 518.

32. Lyndon B. Johnson, *The Vantage Point: Perspectives of the Presidency, 1963–1969* (New York: Holt, Rinehart and Winston, 1971), 483.

33. "Memorandum of Conversation," June 23, 1967, in *FRUS 1964–1968*, Vol. 14, 530.

34. Dobrynin, *In Confidence*, 165.

35. "Memorandum of Conversation," September 12, 1967, in *FRUS 1964–1968*, Vol. 10, 607.

36. Dean Rusk, *As I Saw It*, ed. Daniel S. Papp (New York: W.W. Norton, 1990), 350.

37. Lyndon Johnson-Dwight Eisenhower Telcon, 21:44, June 25, 1967, WH6706.02 #11914 & #11915, RTCM, LBJL.

38. Aleksandr' G. Savel'yev and Nikolai N. Detinov, *The Big Five: Arms Control Decision-Making in the Soviet Union*, ed. Gregory Varhall, trans. Dmitri Trenin (Westport, CT: Praeger, 1995), 2–7; Georgii Arbatov, *Chelovek sistemy* (Moscow: Vagrius, 2002), 252–253.

39. "Draft Notes of Meeting," December 6, 1966, in *FRUS 1964–1968*, Vol. 10, 461.

40. Gennady Gorelik, *The World of Andrei Sakharov: A Russian Physicist's Path to Freedom*, trans. Antonina W. Bouis (New York: Oxford University Press, 2005), 263–268; "Pis'mo Sakharova v Politbiuro TsK KPSS ot 21 iiulia 1967 goda," and attachments, Gennady Gorelik Personal Website, accessed March 25, 2017, http://ggorelik.narod.ru/ADS68/ADS_AMB_TsK_670721.htm. Own translation.

41. "Pis'mo Sakharova v Politbiuro TsK KPSS ot 21 iiulia 1967 goda" and attachments, Gorelik Personal Website; Gorelik, *The World of Andrei Sakharov*, 267.

42. Pervov, *Sistemy sozdavalis' tak*, 205–208.

43. Gorelik, *The World of Andrei Sakharov*, 268–269.

44. David Holloway, *The Soviet Union and the Arms Race*, 2nd ed. (New Haven, CT: Yale University Press, 1984), 44–45; Steven J. Zaloga, *The Kremlin's Nuclear Sword: The Rise and Fall of Russia's Strategic Nuclear Forces, 1945–2000* (Washington, DC: Smithsonian Institution Press, 2002), 118–119.

45. Fursenko and Naftali, *Khrushchev's Cold War*, 537.

46. *XXIII s'ezd Kommunisticheskoi partii Sovetskogo Soiuza, 29 marta-8 aprelia 1966 goda: Stenograficheskii otchet* (Moscow: Politizdat, 1966), 44.

47. Leonid Brezhnev, "O politike Sovetksogo Soiuza v sviazi s agressiei Izrailia na Blizhnem Vostoke," June 20, 1967, Fond 2 Opis' 3 Delo 65, 68–69, *Plenumy Tsentral'nogo Komiteta Kommunisticheskoi partii Sovetsogo Soiuza, 1941–1990: iz fondov Rossiiskogo gosudarstevennogo arkhiva noveishei istorii* (Woodbury, CT: Research Publications, 2001).

48. Leonid Brezhnev, "O politike Sovetksogo Soiuza v sviazi s agressiei Izrailia na Blizhnem Vostoke," 68; *XXIII s'ezd Kommunisticheskoi partii Sovetskogo Soiuza, 29 marta-8 aprelia 1966 goda*, 43.

49. Savel'yev and Detinov, *Big Five*, 1–4; Arkady N. Shevchenko, *Breaking With Moscow* (New York: Knopf, 1985), 329.

50. Zaloga, *Kremlin's Nuclear Sword*, 101–103; Zubok, *Failed Empire*, 205. Good overviews of the place of military industry within Soviet politics are: Irina V. Bystrova, *Sovetskii voenno-promyshlennyi kompleks: problemy stanovleniia i razvitiia (1930–1980-e gody)* (Moscow: Institut rossiiskoi istorii RAN, 2006); Christopher Davis, "The Defence Sector in the Economy of a Declining Superpower: Soviet Union and Russia, 1965–2000," *University of Oxford Department of Economics Discussion Paper Series* 8 (April 2000).

51. Lyndon Johnson-William Fulbright Telcon, 22:57 June 19, 1967, WH6706.01 #11909, RTCM, LBJL.

52. "Memorandum of Conversation," June 23, 1967, in *FRUS 1964–1968*, Vol. 14, 529.

53. Konstantin Zalesskii, *Kto Est' Kto v Istorii SSSR 1953–1991gg.* (Moscow: Veche, 2010), 302.

54. "Memorandum of Conversation," June 23, 1967, in *FRUS 1964–1968*, Vol. 14, 529.

55. Zubok, *Failed Empire*, 204.

56. "News Conference of Honorable Robert S. McNamara Secretary of Defense and Deputy Secretary of Defense Cyrus R. Vance," February 15, 1967, Defense, Dept of, Vol. IV 6/66 (1 of 2), Box 12, Agency File (hereafter AF), NSF, LBJL.

57. Herken, *Counsels of War*, 200–203.

58. "Draft Notes of Meeting," December 6, 1966, in *FRUS 1964–1968*, Vol. 10, 461–462, 464.

59. McGeorge Bundy to Robert McNamara, April 7, 1967, Memcons—No NATO, Volume II, Sec 5, Box 134, Records of Robert S. McNamara, RG 200, National Archives and Records Administration, College Park, MD.

60. Nathaniel Davis to Walt Rostow, "ABMs and Politics," April 14, 1967, Filed by LBJ Library, Box 1, Files of Nathaniel Davis, NSF, LBJL.

61. George C. Wilson, "Johnson Building Case for Reduction Of Nuclear Margin," *Washington Post*, April 9, 1967, A1, A22.

62. "Message from the Embassy in the Soviet Union to the Department of State," February 18, 1967, in *FRUS, 1964–1968*, Vol. 11, 442–444.

63. Herken, *Counsels of War*, 201.

64. Dean Rusk to Lyndon Johnson, June 24, 1967, USSR [Glassboro Memcons], Box 295, Country File, Addendum (hereafter CF/A), NSF, LBJL; Dumbrell, *Lyndon Johnson and Soviet Communism*, 124–125.

65. Walt Rostow to Lyndon Johnson, August 2, 1967, USSR ABM Negotiations (II) 1/67–9/68, Box 231, CF, NSF, LBJL.

66. Robert A. Divine, "Lyndon Johnson and Strategic Arms Limitation," in *The Johnson Years, Volume Three: LBJ at Home and Abroad*, ed. Robert A. Divine (Lawrence: University Press of Kansas, 1994), 255. McNamara was so embarrassed by the anti-China section of his announcement that he moved it to the appendix of a collected series of his speeches, issued shortly after his resignation from the Department of Defense. See Robert S. McNamara, *The Essence of Security: Reflections in Office* (New York: Harper and Row, 1968), 163–166.

67. Spurgeon Keeny to Walt Rostow, "McNamara Speech," August 29, 1967, ABM II Deployment Decision; McNamara's Speech of 9/18/67, Box 1, Files of Spurgeon Keeny, NSF, LBJL.

68. Robert McNamara to Lyndon Johnson, August 19, 1967, Defense, Department of Vol. V., August, 1967 (2 of 2), Box 12, AF, NSF, LBJL.

69. "Text of McNamara Speech on Anti-China Missile Defense and U.S. Nuclear Strategy," *New York Times*, September 19, 1967, 18.

70. David Bruce to Dean Rusk, "UK Reaction to ABM Announcement," September 22, 1967, ABM I 1966–67, Box 1, Files of Spurgeon Keeny, NSF, LBJL.

71. Ball, *Politics and Force Levels*, 103–104, 273–274.

72. Kaufmann, *McNamara Strategy*, 152.

73. "Meeting on the Defense Budget," December 5, 1962, Tape 65 Part 1 and Tape 65 Part 2, Presidential Recordings, POF, JFKL.

74. Spurgeon Keeny to Walt Rostow, "Change (?) in ABM Deployment Plans," October 3, 1967, USSR ABM Negotiations (I) 1/67-9/68, Box 231, CF, NSF, LBJL.

75. Spurgeon Keeny to Walt Rostow, "Meeting with Secretary McNamara on FY 69 Budget," November 17, 1967, Defense Meeting w/ Secretary McNamara on FY 69 Budget, Box 18, AF, NSF, LBJL.

76. Zelizer, *Fierce Urgency of Now*, 278–283.

77. "Conversation between Mr. Walt Rostow and Gen. Volkov during Luncheon given by President Johnson for Chairman Kosygin of the USSR and his Delegation," June 23, 1967, USSR, [Glassboro Memcons] 6/67, Box 295, CF/A, NSF, LBJL.

78. "Obsuzhdenie doklada 'Ob aktual'nykh problemakh mezhdunarodnogo polzheniia i o bor'be KPSS za splochennost' mirnogo kommunisticheskogo dvizheniia,'" April 9, 1968, Fond 2, Opis' 3, Delo 96, 13, *Plenumy Tsentral'nogo Komiteta Kommunisticheskoi partii Sovetsogo Soiuza.*

79. Of all of Johnson's advisers, National Security Advisor Walt Rostow was the most articulate advocate of bombing as a way to halt Vietnamese modernization. See Milne, *America's Rasputin*, 131–157.

80. Shapley, *Promise and Power*, 418–424; Milne, *America's Rasputin*, 192–193.

81. Shapley, *Promise and Power*, 428–430.

82. Shapley, *Promise and Power*, 429, 436–437.

83. Dallek, *Flawed Giant*, 529.

84. Divine, "Johnson and Strategic Arms Limitation," 261.

85. "Memorandum From the Deputy Under Secretary of State for Political Affairs (Bohlen) to Secretary of State Rusk," April 5, 1968, in *FRUS 1964–1968*, Vol. 11, 565.

86. Dean Rusk to Lyndon Johnson, April 26, 1968, Strategic Missile Talks [1 of 3], Box 11, FWR, NSF, LBJL; Edward J. Drea, *Secretaries of Defense Historical Series, McNamara, Clifford, and the Burdens of Vietnam* (Washington, DC: Historical Office, Office of the Secretary of Defense, 2011), 337.

87. "Record of Meeting," July 29, 1968, in *FRUS 1964–1968*, Vol. 14, 669.

88. "Record of Meeting of Executive Committee of Principals," July 8, 1968, in *FRUS 1964-1968*, Vol. 9, 634–635; John Newhouse, *Cold Dawn: The Story of SALT* (New York: Holt, Reinhart and Winston, 1973), 126–130.

89. Rusk, *As I Saw It*, 350.

90. "Memorandum from the Ambassador to the Soviet Union (Thompson) to Secretary of State Rusk," August 30, 1968, in *FRUS 1964–1968*, Vol. 11, 713–714.

91. Arms Control and Disarmament Agency (ACDA), "Strategic Missile Talks Initial Presentation of U.S. Position," August 24, 1968, Strategic Arms Limitation Talks Basic Book, 25 Jan 1969, Box 6, Papers of Morton H. Halperin (hereafter PMH), LBJL; ACDA, Strategic Missile Talks Basic Position Paper, August 24, 1968, Strategic Arms Limitation Talks Basic Book, 25 Jan 1969, Box 6, PMH, LBJL; Divine, "Johnson and Strategic Arms Limitation," 266–268.

92. "Memorandum of Conversation," September 20, 1968, in *FRUS 1964–1968*, Vol. 14, 719.

93. Jeremi Suri, "Lyndon Johnson and the Global Disruption of 1968," in *Looking Back at LBJ: White House Politics in a New Light*, ed. Mitchell B. Lerner (Lawrence: University Press of Kansas, 2004), 66–69.

94. Lyndon Johnson-Richard Nixon Telcon, 23:22 August 20, 1968, WH6808.01 #13309, RTCM, LBJL. Johnson had, of course, made great political capital from his hearings of the Senate Preparedness Subcommittee after the launching of Sputnik. See Robert A. Caro, *The Years of Lyndon Johnson: Master of the Senate* (New York: Alfred A. Knopf, 2002), 1020–1030.

95. Clark Clifford, "Address at the National Press Club, Washington, DC," September 5, 1968, Kosygin—Talks with the Soviet Union [3], Box 22, Papers of Clark Clifford (hereafter PCC), LBJL.

96. Clark Clifford and Richard Holbrooke, *Counsel to the President: A Memoir* (New York: Random House, 1991), 560; Drea, *McNamara, Clifford, and the Burdens of Vietnam*, 342–343; October 7, 1968, George Elsey's Notes of Secretary of Defense Clark Clifford's Morning Staff Conferences, May 1968–January 1969, Box 1, Papers of George M. Elsey [VanDeMark Transcripts], LBJL; Paul Warnke to Clark Clifford, "Strategic Missile Talks," April 22, 1968, Dr. Halperin's Chron File, Apr–May 1968 [1 of 2], Box 2, PMH, LBJL; Paul Warnke to Clark Clifford, "Talks with the Soviets on Limiting Strategic Offensive and Defense Systems," October 8, 1968, Kosygin—Talks with the Soviet Union [3], PCC, LBJL; Paul Warnke to Clark Clifford, "Strategic Talks," October 23, 1968, Kosygin—Talks with Soviet Union [3], PCC, LBJL; Clark Clifford to Lyndon Johnson, "Strategic Talks with the Soviets," November 27, 1968, Dr. Halperin Chron File, Aug–Dec 1968 [1 of 2], Box 3, PMH, LBJL.

97. Walt Rostow to Lyndon Johnson, November 14, 1968, [Non-Vietnam: October-December 1968] [2 of 2], Box 16, FWR, NSF, LBJL.

98. Undated handwritten note, Strategic Missile Talks [3 of 3], Box 11, FWR, NSF, LBJL; Message from the Soviet Government to President-elect Nixon, December 18, 1968, in *FRUS 1964–1968*, Vol. 14, 788–789, n.1.

99. Dean Rusk to Lyndon Johnson, "Proposed Joint Statement of Agreed Objectives and Principles Affecting the Limitation and Subsequent Reduction in Strategic Armaments," December 18, 1968, Soviet Union—Talks on Reduction of Strategic Nuclear Weapons, Box 17, PCC, LBJL; Clark Clifford to Dean Rusk, "Soviet Memorandum on Strategic Arms Limitation and attached statement," undated, Soviet Union—Talks on Reduction of Strategic Nuclear Weapons, Box 17, PCC, LBJL; "Joint Statement of Agreed Objectives and Principles Affecting the Limitation and Subsequent Reduction in Strategic Armaments," January 13, 1969, Soviet Union—Talks on Reduction of Strategic Nuclear Weapons, Box 17, PCC, LBJL.

100. Hugh Sidey, *A Very Personal Presidency: Lyndon Johnson in the White House* (New York: Atheneum, 1968), 260.

101. Bernstein, *Guns and Butter*, 527.

102. "Draft Notes of Meeting," December 6, 1966, in *FRUS 1964–1968*, Vol. 10, 462.

103. Joseph Califano to Walt Rostow, August 27, 1967, Defense, Department of Vol. V August, 1967 [2 of 2], Box 12, AF, NSF, LBJL.

104. Johnson, *Congress and the Cold War*, 148; Yanarella, *Missile Defense Controversy*, 153.

105. December 13, 1968, December 17, 1968, George Elsey's Notes of Secretary of Defense Clark Clifford's Morning Staff Conferences, May 1968–January 1969, Box 1, Papers of George M. Elsey [VanDeMark Transcripts], LBJL; "Times Readers Have Their Say: Bainbridge, Too, Unsuitable for Missiles," *Seattle Times*, January 5, 1969, 10; Yanarella, *Missile Defense Controversy*, 149–152.

106. Divine, "Johnson and Strategic Arms Limitation," 240, 266–268.

107. Fite, *Richard B. Russell, Jr*, 461.

108. Warnke to Clifford, "Strategic Missile Talks," April 22, 1968, LBJL.

109. Bernstein, *Guns or Butter*, 527.

110. Dumbrell, *Lyndon Johnson and Soviet Communism*, 85.

111. Thomas Alan Schwartz, "Lyndon Johnson and Europe: Alliance Politics, Political Economy, and 'Growing Out of the Cold War,'" in *The Foreign Policies of Lyndon Johnson: Beyond Vietnam*, ed. H.W. Brands (College Station: Texas A&M University Press, 1999), 37–60; Thomas Alan Schwartz, *Lyndon Johnson and Europe: In the Shadow of Vietnam* (Cambridge, MA: Harvard University Press, 2003), 205–222.

CHAPTER 4

1. Mario Del Pero, *The Eccentric Realist: Henry Kissinger and the Shaping of American Foreign Policy* (Ithaca, NY: Cornell University Press, 2010), 17–20.

2. Richard Nixon, "Inaugural Address," January 20, 1969, APP, accessed March 26, 2017, http://www.presidency.ucsb.edu/ws/?pid=1941.

3. Keith L. Nelson, *The Making of Détente: Soviet-American Relations in the Shadow of Vietnam* (Baltimore, MD: Johns Hopkins University Press, 1995), 80.

4. Jussi M. Hanhimäki, *The Flawed Architect: Henry Kissinger and American Foreign Policy* (New York: Oxford University Press, 2004), 39; Robert Dallek, *Nixon and Kissinger: Partners in Power* (New York: Harper Collins, 2007), 137.

5. Rick Perlstein, *Nixonland: The Rise of a President and the Fracturing of America* (New York: Scribner, 2008), 298–300; Sarah Katherine Mergel, *Conservative Intellectuals and Richard Nixon* (New York: Palgrave Macmillan, 2010), 12–27.

6. "Notes of National Security Council (NSC) Meeting," February 14, 1969, in *Foreign Relations of the United States, 1969–1976, Volume XXXIV, National Security Policy, 1969–1972*, ed. M. Todd Bennett (Washington: United States Government Printing Office, 2012), 18; Gavin, *Nuclear Statecraft*, 104–119.

7. In 1967 the total number of Soviet ICBMs stood at 769. By 1968 it had grown to 1,010 and by 1969 to 1,220. See Zaloga, *Kremlin's Nuclear Sword*, 241. Zaloga's appendices are an invaluable guide to quantitative and qualitative trends in Soviet nuclear forces during this period.

8. "Notes of NSC Meeting," February 14, 1969, in *FRUS, 1969–1976*, Vol. 34, 20; Gavin, *Nuclear Statecraft*, 111–2.

9. "The President's News Conference," January 27, 1969, APP, accessed March 26, 2017, http://www.presidency.ucsb.edu/ws/index.php?pid=1942.

10. Alexander Butterfield to John Ehrlichman and Henry Kissinger, June 16, 1969, Memos/ John Ehrlichman (June 1969), Box 50, H.R. Haldeman, Staff Member

and Office Files (hereafter SMOF), White House Special Files (hereafter WHSF), Richard Nixon Presidential Library (hereafter NPL), Yorba Linda, California.

11. "Minutes of Review Group Meeting," May 29, 1969, in *FRUS 1969–1976*, Vol. 34, 115.

12. "Memorandum of Conversation," January 2, 1969, in *Foreign Relations of the United States, 1969–1976, Volume XII, Soviet Union, January 1969–October 1970*, ed. Erin R. Mahan (Washington, DC: United States Government Printing Office, 2006), 1–4.

13. Theodore Shabad, "Soviet Tells U.S. That It is Ready for Missile Talks," *New York Times*, January 21, 1969, 1, 2.

14. "Memorandum of Conversation," January 2, 1969, in *FRUS 1969–1976*, Vol. 12, 2; "The President's News Conference," January 27, 1969, APP.

15. "Notes of NSC Meeting," February 14, 1969, 22.

16. Gavin, *Nuclear Statecraft*, 105.

17. "Letter From President Nixon to Chairman of the Council of Ministers of the Soviet Union Kosygin," March 26, 1969, in *FRUS 1969–1976*, Vol. 12, 99.

18. Theodore Shabad, "Soviet Tells U.S. That It is Ready for Missile Talks," *New York Times*, January 21, 1969, 1, 2; "Memorandum from Presidential Assistant Kissinger to President Nixon," February 18, 1969, in *Soviet-American Relations: The Détente Years, 1969–1972*, eds. David C. Geyer and Douglas E. Selvage (Washington, DC: United States Government Printing Office, 2007), 19–20.

19. "Memorandum From The President's Assistant for National Security Affairs (Kissinger) to President Nixon," June 13, 1969, in *FRUS 1969–1976*, Vol. 12, 180.

20. "Henry Kissinger to Richard Nixon, Modified Sentinel System," March 5, 1969, ABM—Memoranda (March 1969) (2 of 2), Box 843, ABM/MIRV, National Security Council Files (hereafter NSC Files), NPL.

21. "Minutes of National Security Council Meeting," February 19, 1969, in *FRUS 1969–1976*, Vol. 34, 28.

22. Johnson, *Congress and the Cold War*, 148.

23. Senate Vote #469, June 24, 1968, "To Amend a Committee Amendment in the Nature of a Substitute for H.R. 16703," accessed March 26, 2017, *govtrack*, https://www.govtrack.us/congress/votes/90-1968/s469.

24. Yanarella, *Missile Defense Controversy*, 151.

25. Senate Vote #469, June 24, 1968; Senate Vote #54, August 6, 1969, "To amend S. 2546," *govtrack*, accessed March 26, 2017, https://www.govtrack.us/congress/votes/91-1969/s54.

26. John W. Finney, "Senate Defeats a Move to Delay Sentinel System," *New York Times*, June 25, 1968, 1.

27. Senate Vote #469, June 24, 1968; Senate Vote #54, August 6, 1969.

28. A good early overview of local scientists' role in suburban protests against ABM can be found in Anne Hessing Cahn, "Scientists and the ABM" (PhD diss., Massachusetts Institute of Technology, 1971), 70–77. The best recent account, focusing on grassroots activism around Boston, is Lily Geismer, *Don't Blame Us: Suburban Liberals and the Transformation of the Democratic Party* (Princeton, NJ: Princeton University Press, 2015), 134–138.

29. *Missile Defense Controversy*, 146–148; James Cameron, "From the Grass Roots to the Summit: The Impact of U.S. Suburban Protest on U.S. Missile Defence Policy, 1968–72," *The International History Review* 36, no. 2 (March 2014): 342–362.

30. Cameron, "Grass Roots to the Summit," 353–354; Adam Clymer, *Edward M. Kennedy: A Biography* (New York: William Morrow, 1999), 134–135; Burton Hersh, *Edward Kennedy: An Intimate Biography* (Berkeley, CA: Counterpoint, 2010), 328–335; William Beecher, "Sentinel Project Halted Pending Review," *New York Times*, February 7, 1969, 1–2.

31. John W. Finney, "Note to Senator Cooper by Aide Raised Doubts, and Battle Began," *New York Times*, February 9, 1969, 1, 64; Yanarella, *Missile Defense Controversy*, 152; December 13, 1968, George Elsey's Notes of Secretary of Defense Clark Clifford's Morning Staff Conferences, May 1968-January 1969, Box 1, Papers of George M. Elsey [VanDeMark Transcripts], LBJL.

32. Cameron, "Grass Roots to the Summit," 354–355; Yanarella, *Missile Defense Controversy*, 152; Warren Weaver Jr., "Dirksen Sees Close ABM Vote; Says He Has No Stand on Issue," *New York Times*, March 11, 1969, 30.

33. Cameron, "Grass Roots to the Summit," 354–355; Richard Nixon-Henry Kissinger Telcon, March 11, 1969 10:00pm, "The Kissinger Telcons," *National Security Archive Electronic Briefing Book No.123*, eds. Thomas Blanton and William Burr, accessed March 26, 2017, http://www.gwu.edu/~nsarchiv/NSAEBB/ NSAEBB123/.

34. Johnson, *Congress and the Cold War*, 152; Yanarella, *Missile Defense Controversy*, 155. On Fulbright's opposition, see Woods, *Fulbright*, 519–532.

35. "Memorandum From the President's Assistant for Congressional Relations (Harlow) to President Nixon," March 10, 1969, in *FRUS 1969–1976*, Vol. 34, 72–74.

36. "The President's News Conference," March 14, 1969, APP, accessed March 26, 2017, http://www.presidency.ucsb.edu/ws/?pid=1951.

37. "The President's News Conference," March 14, 1969, APP.

38. James Schlesinger to Henry Kissinger, "Presentation of the Prospective Sentinel Decision," March 6, 1969, ABM Memoranda (March 1969) (1 of 2), Box 843, ABM/MIRV, NSC Files, NPL.

39. James Keogh to Henry Kissinger, March 11, 1969, ABM System Vol. II (March 1969) (1 of 2), Box 840, ABM/MIRV, NSC Files, NPL.

40. "Minutes of National Security Council Meeting," February 19, 1969, *FRUS 1969–1976*, Vol. 34, 28.

41. "The President's News Conference," March 14, 1969, APP.

42. "Excerpts From Testimony on Antimissile System Before Foreign Relations Panel," *New York Times*, March 22, 1969, 17.

43. Warren Weaver Jr., "Fulbright Derides ABM As a 'Political Gimmick,'" *New York Times*, March 29, 1969, 1, 2.

44. "Congress Authorizes Controversial ABM Funds," *1969 Congressional Quarterly Almanac* (Washington, DC: Congressional Quarterly Inc., 1969), 263; For a full assessment of the role of software in the 1969 ABM debate, see Rebecca Slayton, *Arguments that Count: Physics, Computing, and Missile Defense, 1949–2012* (Cambridge, MA: The MIT Press, 2013), 109–131.

45. John W. Finney, "Fulbright Says Laird Uses Fear to Promote ABM," *New York Times*, March 22, 1969, 1, 16.

46. Patrick Buchanan to Richard Nixon, "EMK and ABM," March 19, 1969, Sentinel ABM System Vol. 1 2/11/69 (Feb-Apr 69), Box 843, ABM/MIRV, NSC Files, NPL; Alexander Haig to Henry Kissinger, Clearance for Release of Three Papers, April 30, 1969, Sentinel ABM System 4/1/69 (1 of 2), Box 844, ABM/MIRV, NSC Files, NPL. The divergence between domestic aides and the NSC is also covered

in Graham Spinardi, "The Rise and Fall of Safeguard: Anti-Ballistic Missile Technology and the Nixon Administration," *History and Technology* 26, no. 4 (December 2010): 317.

47. Alexander Butterfield to Henry Kissinger, April 9, 1969, Memos/Dr. (Henry) Kissinger (Apr '69), Box 50, H.R. Haldeman, SMOF, WHSF, NPL; Alexander Butterfield to Henry Kissinger, "Today's ABM Review for the President," April 14, 1969, Sentinel ABM System Vol. II 4/1/69–5/31/69 (2 of 2), Box 844, ABM/MIRV, NSC Files, NPL; Alexander Butterfield to Henry Kissinger, April 29, 1969, Sentinel ABM System Vol II 4/1/69–5/31/69 (1 of 2), Box 844, ABM/MIRV, NSC Files, NPL; "Background Briefing," May 2, 1969, Sentinel ABM System Vol. II 4/1/69–5/31/69 (1 of 2), Box 844, ABM/MIRV, NSC Files, NPL.

48. John W. Finney, "Administration Critics Say 'Intelligence Gap' Clouds ABM Issue," *New York Times*, June 1, 1969, 2.

49. *FRUS 1969–1976*, Vol. 34, 117, n.3.

50. Kirsten Lundberg, "The SS-9 Controversy: Intelligence as Political Football," Case C16-89-884.0, Kennedy School of Government, Harvard University, 1989, 16–17.

51. Robert E. Cushman and USIB, "Memorandum to Holders: National Intelligence Estimate Number 11-8-68: Soviet Strategic Attack Forces," June 23, 1969, CIA FOIA Reading Room, accessed March 26, 2017, http://www.foia.cia.gov/sites/default/files/document_conversions/89801/DOC_0000278487.pdf.

52. Good accounts of the expert debate over ABM can be found in Herken, *Counsels of War*, 229–241 and Freedman, *U.S. Intelligence and the Soviet Strategic Threat*, 129–152.

53. Albert Wohlstetter, "Supplement On Purported Proofs That The Minuteman Will Be Safe Without Further Protection," May 23, 1969, Sentinel ABM System Vol II 4/1/69–5/31/69 (1 of 2), Box 844, ABM/MIRV, NSC Files, NPL.

54. "Letters to the Editor of the *Times*: Safeguard Missile System is Evaluated by Two Scientists," *New York Times*, June 15, 1969, E17.

55. "Statement of Albert Wohlstetter, University of Chicago: The Role of the ABM in the 1970's," undated, NSC Files, Sentinel ABM System 4/1/69–5/31/69 (1 of 2), Box 844, ABM/MIRV, NSC Files, NPL.

56. Herken, *Counsels of War*, 229–241.

57. "The President's News Conference," March 14, 1969, APP.

58. Marshall D. Shulman, "The Effect of ABM on U.S. –Soviet Relations," in *ABM: An Evaluation of the Decision to Deploy an Antiballistic Missile System*, eds. Abram Chayes and Jerome B. Wiesner (New York: Harper and Row, 1969), 154–155.

59. "Minutes of Review Group Meeting," May 29, 1969, in *FRUS 1969–1976*, Vol. 34, 104–107.

60. Herken, *Counsels of War*, 236.

61. Bruce M. Russett, "The Revolt of the Masses: Public Opinion on Military Expenditures," in *Peace, War, and Numbers*, ed. Bruce M. Russett (Beverly Hills, CA: Sage, 1972), 306.

62. Richard Nixon, "Address at the Air Force Academy Commencement Exercises Colorado Springs, Colorado," June 4, 1969, APP, accessed March 26, 2017, http://www.presidency.ucsb.edu/ws/index.php?pid=2081.

63. Nixon, "Address at the Air Force Academy," June 4, 1969, APP; Perlstein, *Nixonland*, 390–391.

64. Perlstein, *Nixonland*, 391–392.

65. "Nation: Defending the Defenders," *Time*, June 13, 1969.

66. "Letter From Chairman of the Council of Ministers of the Soviet Union Kosygin to President Nixon," May 27, 1969, in *FRUS 1969–1976*, Vol. 12, 169.
67. "Memorandum from the President's Assistant for National Security Affairs (Kissinger) to President Nixon," May 28, 1969, in *FRUS 1969–1976*, Vol. 12, 167.
68. Hanhimäki, *Flawed Architect*, 46–48, 52–53, 94–95.
69. "Editorial Note," in *Foreign Relations of the United States, 1969–1976, Volume XXXII, SALT I, 1969–1972*, ed. Erin R. Mahan (Washington, DC: United States Government Printing Office, 2010), 39–40.
70. "The President's News Conference," June 19, 1969, APP, accessed March 26, 2017, http://www.presidency.ucsb.edu/ws/index.php?pid=2106.
71. "M'Intyre to Vote 'No' on Safeguard," *New York Times*, July 27, 1969, 26; Alexander Haig to Laurence Lynn, June 25, 1969, Sentinel ABM System Vol III 6/1/69, Box 844, ABM/MIRV, NSC Files, NPL; Untitled analysis of compromise, undated, Sentinel ABM System Vol III 6/1/69, Box 844, ABM/MIRV, NSC Files, NPL; Alexander Butterfield to Richard Nixon, "Safeguard Compromise," June 11, 1969, Sentinel ABM System, Vol III 6/1/69, Box 844, ABM/MIRV, NSC Files, NPL.
72. Haig to Lynn, June 25, 1969, NPL; Untitled analysis of compromise, undated, NPL.
73. Alexander Butterfield to Henry Kissinger, Bryce Harlow, and Herbert Klein, July 10, 1969, White House Action Memoranda 1969 (1 of 3), Box 5, Herbert Klein, SMOF, WHSF, NPL.
74. Warren Unna, "Prouty Switches to ABM," *Washington Post*, July 15, 1969, A1, A5; Johnson, *Congress and the Cold War*, 155–156.
75. Ken BeLieu to Richard Nixon, "Safeguard Status Report," July 13, 1969, (CF) ND Weapons-Ordnance-Munitions 7-1-69 to 10-31-69, Box 43, Confidential Files, 1969-1974, WHSF, NPL.
76. Johnson, *Congress and the Cold War*, 156.
77. "Nixon Wins Senate ABM Battle by One-Vote Margins," *Congressional Quarterly Weekly Report*, August 8, 1969, 1433–1444.
78. Richard Nixon to H.R. Haldeman, John Ehrlichman, Henry Kissinger, August 7, 1969, Sentinel ABM System Vol III 6/1/69, Box 844, ABM/MIRV, NSC Files, NPL.
79. Nixon to Haldeman, Ehrlichman, Kissinger, August 7, 1969, NPL.
80. "The ABM: Winners and Losers," *Washington Post*, August 7, 1969, A16.
81. Helmut Sonnenfeldt to Henry Kissinger, "Soviet Position on ABMs at Helsinki," January 20, 1970, VII 1/70 (1 of 2), Box 876, SALT, NSC Files, NPL.
82. Henry Kissinger to Richard Nixon, "FY 71 Safeguard Deployment Decision," undated, NSC Meeting 1/23/70 Safeguard (ABM) (1 of 2), Box H-026, Meeting Files, National Security Council Institutional Files, NPL.
83. Sonnenfeldt to Kissinger, "Soviet Position on ABMs at Helsinki," January 20, 1970, NPL.
84. "Report of the U.S. Delegation to the Preliminary Strategic Arms Limitation Talks," December 29, 1969, VII 1/70 (2 of 2), Box 876, SALT, NSC Files, NPL.
85. Office of the Secretary of Defense, "Memorandum on the Safeguard System," December 31, 1969, ABM System 1/70—Vol. III Memos and Misc (2 of 2), Box 840, ABM/MIRV, NSC Files, NPL.
86. "Memorandum From the Director of the Arms Control and Disarmament Agency (Smith) to President Nixon," January 21, 1970, in *FRUS 1969–1976*, Vol. 32, 174–176.

87. "Memorandum From the President's Assistant for National Security Affairs (Kissinger) to President Nixon," undated, in *FRUS 1969–1976*, Vol. 34, 443–444.

88. Kissinger to Nixon, "FY 71 Safeguard ABM Deployment Decision," undated, NPL; "Editorial Note," in *FRUS, 1969–1976*, Vol. 34, 439.

89. "Memorandum From the President's Assistant for National Security Affairs (Kissinger) to President Nixon," undated, in *FRUS 1969–1976*, Vol. 32, 444; Henry Kissinger, *White House Years* (Boston, MA: Little, Brown, 1979), 539.

90. "Memorandum From the President's Assistant for National Security Affairs (Kissinger) to President Nixon," undated, 445.

91. Garthoff makes this point regarding arms control in general in Garthoff, *Détente*, 170.

92. William Beecher, "Expansion of ABM to 3d Missile Site is Sought by Laird," *New York Times*, February 25, 1970, 1, 30.

93. Garthoff, *Détente*, 162–163; Kissinger, *White House Years*, 542.

94. "National Security Decision Memorandum 51," April 9, 1970, in *FRUS 1969–1976*, Vol. 32, 231–252; Garthoff, *Détente*, 154–162.

95. Kissinger, *White House Years*, 542, 547.

96. Garthoff, *Détente*, 162–163, n.43. Garthoff's argument has been reprised most recently in Eric Grynaviski, *Constructive Illusions: Misperceiving the Origins of International Cooperation* (Ithaca, NY: Cornell University Press, 2014), 93–97.

97. Kissinger, *White House Years*, 542.

98. "Report of the U.S. Delegation to the Preliminary Strategic Arms Limitation Talks," December 29, 1969, NPL; Robert Cushman and United States Intelligence Board, "Special National Intelligence Estimate 11-16-70: Soviet Attitudes Toward SALT," SE00442, in *The Soviet Estimate: U.S. Analysis of the Soviet Union, 1947-1991*, ed. John Prados, DNSA.

99. "Memorandum From the President's Assistant for National Security Affairs (Kissinger) to President Nixon," January 22, 1970, in *FRUS 1969–1976*, Vol. 32, 176–177, n.2.

100. "Evaluation of Possible Strategic Arms Control Agreements Between the United States and the Soviet Union," March 21, 1970, VII 1/70 (2 of 2), Box 876, SALT, NSC Files, NPL.

101. "Evaluation of Possible Strategic Arms Control Agreements," March 21, 1970, NPL.

102. "National Security Decision Memorandum 51," April 9, 1970, in *FRUS 1969–1976*, Vol. 32, 246–247. Kissinger had already told Soviet Ambassador Anatoly Dobrynin that Nixon believed "national technical means" (i.e. satellite surveillance without onsite inspections) would be sufficient for verification. See: "Memorandum of Conversation (USSR)," March 10, 1970, in *Détente Years*, 137–8.

103. Kissinger, *White House Years*, 540–541; Richard Nixon-Henry Kissinger Telcon, April 9, 1970, KA02551, *The Kissinger Telephone Conversations: A Verbatim Record of American Diplomacy, 1969–1977*, ed. William Burr, DNSA; Richard Nixon-Henry Kissinger Telcon, April 15, 1970, KA02599, *Kissinger Telephone Conversations*, DNSA.

104. "National Security Decision Memorandum 51," April 9, 1970, in *FRUS 1969–1976*, Vol. 32, 248; Melvin Laird to Richard Nixon, April 9, 1970, Vol. 7, January 1970, Box 876, SALT, NSC Files, NPL; Garthoff, *Détente*, 161–162.

105. "National Security Decision Memorandum 51," April 9, 1970, in *FRUS 1969–1976*, Vol. 32, 231.

106. Helmut Sonnenfeldt to Henry Kissinger, "Soviet 'Acceptance' of NCA Level for ABM Defense—Problem of Leak," April 27, 1970, SALT Talks II [Vienna] Vol. VIII, 4/9/70-/10/70 [1 of 2], Box 877, SALT, NSC Files, NPL.

107. Garthoff, *Détente*, 165; Royal B. Allison to General Wheeler and Admiral Moorer, June 29, 1970, SALT Talks [Vienna] X 6/13/70 to 6/30/70 [1 of 2], Box 878, SALT, NSC Files, NPL.

108. "Memorandum of Conversation," February 18, 1970, KT00098, *The Kissinger Transcripts: A Verbatim Record of American Diplomacy,* ed. William Burr, DNSA.

109. "Memorandum of Conversation," April 7, 1970, KT00115, *Kissinger Transcripts,* DNSA.

110. "Memorandum of Conversation," April 9, 1970, KT00118, *Kissinger Transcripts,* DNSA.

111. "Memorandum of Conversation (USSR)," April 10, 1970, in *Détente Years,* 146.

112. Stephen E. Ambrose, *Nixon, Volume Two: The Triumph of a Politician, 1962–1972* (New York: Simon and Schuster, 1989), 143; Richard Nixon, "Inaugural Address," January 20, 1969, APP, accessed March 26, 2017, http://www.presidency.ucsb.edu/ws/?pid=1941.

113. Kissinger, *White House Years,* 552. Good summaries of the frustrations experienced by Nixon and Kissinger in late 1969 and 1970 can be found in: Hanhimäki, *Flawed Architect,* 68–91; Dallek, *Nixon and Kissinger,* 168–244.

114. Richard M. Nixon, *In the Arena: A Memoir of Victory, Defeat, and Renewal* (New York: Simon and Schuster, 1990), 327.

115. "Memorandum of Conversation (USSR)," June 10, 1970, in *Détente Years,* 149.

116. "Memorandum of Conversation (U.S.)," June 10, 1970, in *Détente Years,* 155–156.

117. Richard Nixon-Henry Kissinger Telcon, June 11, 1970, KA03097, *Kissinger Telephone Conversations,* DNSA.

118. Kissinger, *White House Years,* 552.

119. Richard Nixon-Henry Kissinger Telcon, June 11, 1970, KA03097, DNSA.

120. "Memorandum of Conversation," June 23, 1970 KT00155, *Kissinger Transcripts,* DNSA.

121. H.R. Haldeman, *The Haldeman Diaries: Inside the Nixon White House* (New York: G.P. Putnam's, 1994), 177.

122. "Attachment: Aide-Memoire From the Soviet Union," undated, in *FRUS 1969–1976,* Vol. 12, 546–547.

123. Richard Nixon-Henry Kissinger Telcon, July 7, 1970, KA03264, *Kissinger Telephone Conversations,* DNSA.

124. "Memorandum of Conversation (USSR)," July 7, 1970, in *Détente Years,* 170.

125. Laurence Lynn to Henry Kissinger, "Possible SALT Agreements," July 1, 1970, Vol XIV, 7/1/70-7/19/70, Box 878, SALT, NSC Files, NPL; Laurence Lynn to Henry Kissinger, "SALT—Results of Verification Panel Meeting and Issues for President," July 1, 1970, Vol XI, 7/1/70-7/19/70, Box 878, SALT, NSC Files, NPL; Smith, *Doubletalk,* 146.

126. "Memorandum of Conversation (USSR)," July 9, 1970, in *Détente Years,* 175.

127. "Memorandum of Conversation (USSR)," September 25, 1970, in *Détente Years,* 195.

128. Savel'yev and Detinov, *Big Five,* 16.

129. Smith, *Doubletalk,* 150; Garthoff, *Détente,* 165.

130. Allison to Wheeler and Moorer, June 29, 1970, NPL.

131. Garthoff, *Détente,* 165.

132. Hanhimäki, *Flawed Architect*, 485–492; William P. Bundy, *A Tangled Web: The Making of Foreign Policy in the Nixon Presidency* (New York: Hill and Wang, 1998), 511.

CHAPTER 5

1. Nixon, *RN*, 497.
2. Nixon, *RN*, 522–525, 615; Kissinger, *White House Years*, 820–823, 1244–1245.
3. "Conversation Among President Nixon, the President's Assistant for National Security Affairs (Kissinger), and the Assistant to the President (Haldeman)," April 17, 1971, in *FRUS 1969–1976*, Vol. 32, 445.
4. Kissinger, *White House Years*, 820; Garthoff, *Détente*, 167, 211; Smith, *Doubletalk*, 233–234, 456–459.
5. Dallek, *Nixon and Kissinger*, 271.
6. "Memorandum of Conversation (U.S.)," October 22, 1970, in *Détente Years*, 227; "Memorandum of Conversation (USSR)," October 27, 1970, in *Détente Years*, 234.
7. "Memorandum of Conversation (U.S.)," October 22, 1970, in *Détente Years*, 224.
8. "Telegram From Foreign Minister Gromyko to the Central Committee of the Communist Party of the Soviet Union," October 26, 1970, in *Détente Years*, 213.
9. Christopher Lydon, "Polls on Election Found Accurate," *New York Times*, November 8, 1970, 39; Editorial,"Beyond the Election," *New York Times*, November 8, 1970, 12; Robert Mason, *Richard Nixon and the Quest for a New Majority* (Chapel Hill: University of North Carolina Press, 2004), 110.
10. Hal Sonnenfeldt to Henry Kissinger, "SALT: The Shaker is Running Out," December 5, 1970, SALT Talks (Helsinki) Vol XIII, Oct 70–Dec 70 [1 of 3], Box 879, SALT, NSC Files, NPL.
11. Smith, *Doubletalk*, 195.
12. "Memorandum from K. Wayne Smith and Helmut Sonnenfeldt of the National Security Council Staff to the President's Assistant for National Security Affairs (Kissinger)," December 11, 1970, in *FRUS 1969–1976*, Vol. 32, 376.
13. Nixon, *RN*, 497.
14. Haldeman, *Haldeman Diaries*, 223.
15. Dallek, *Nixon and Kissinger*, 274–275.
16. Dallek, *Nixon and Kissinger*, 278.
17. "Memorandum of Conversation (USSR)," December 22, 1970, in *Détente Years*, 247–248.
18. "Memorandum of Conversation (U.S.)," January 9, 1971, in *Détente Years*, 257–258. My own emphasis. Garthoff, *Détente*, 179.
19. "Memorandum of Conversation (USSR)," January 9, 1971, in *Détente Years*, 261.
20. "Issues Paper: NSC Meeting on Safeguard and SALT," January 27, 1971, NSC Meeting—Safeguard, January 27, 1971, Box H-030, National Security Council Institutional Files, NPL.
21. "Memorandum From the President's Assistant for National Security Affairs (Kissinger) to President Nixon," February 3, 1971, in *FRUS 1969–1976*, Vol. 34, 698–699.
22. Helmut Sonnenfeldt, handwritten note, undated, NSC Meeting—Safeguard, Box H-030, National Security Council Institutional Files, NPL.
23. William Beecher, "Nixon to Propose Option on 4th Site in Missile Shield," *New York Times*, February 26, 1971, 1, 9;William Beecher, "Laird Hints at Missile Threat But Asks Restrained Response," *New York Times*, March 10, 1971, 1, 7.

24. John W. Finney, "Senate Panel Limits Plans to Expand ABM System," *New York Times*, August 5, 1971, 11.

25. Kissinger, *White House Years*, 810–811; Editorial,"Russia's SALT Offer," *New York Times*, January 17, 1971, E14;"Muskie Assigned Key Senate Post," *New York Times*, March 4, 1971, 25.

26. "Conversation Among President Nixon, the President's Assistant for National Security Affairs (Kissinger), and the Assistant to the President (Haldeman)," April 17, 1971, *FRUS 1969–1976*, Vol. 32, 446.

27. "Conversation Among President Nixon, the President's Assistant for National Security Affairs (Kissinger), and the Assistant to the President (Haldeman)," April 17, 1971, *FRUS 1969–1976*, Vol. 32, 445.

28. Dallek, *Nixon and Kissinger*, 257–264; Kissinger, *White House Years*, 815.

29. "Conversation Among President Nixon, the President's Assistant for National Security Affairs (Kissinger), and the Assistant to the President (Haldeman)," April 17, 1971, in *FRUS 1969–1976*, Vol. 32, 445–447; Dallek, *Nixon and Kissinger*, 262–264.

30. "Editorial Note," in *FRUS 1969–1976*, Vol. 32, 429.

31. "Memorandum of Telephone Conversation (USSR)," December 24, 1970, in *Détente Years*, 250–251.

32. "Telegram from Ambassador Dobrynin to the Soviet Foreign Ministry," February 14, 1971, in *Détente Years*, 293–296.

33. "Memorandum of Conversation (USSR)," February 2, 1971, in *Détente Years*, 283.

34. "Memorandum of Conversation (U.S.)," February 22, 1971, in *Détente Years*, 299.

35. "Memorandum of Conversation (U.S.)," March 12, 1971, in *Détente Years*, 306.

36. "Memorandum of Conversation (USSR)," March 16, 1971, in *Détente Years*, 311.

37. Untitled Draft of American letter, May 12, 1971, SALT Jan 9–May 20 1971 [2 of 3], Box 78, Henry A. Kissinger Office Files, NPL.

38. "Memorandum of Conversation (U.S.)," May 12, 1971, in *Détente Years*, 352.

39. "Memorandum of Telephone Conversation (USSR)," May 11, 1971, in *Détente Years*, 349–351; "Transcript of Telephone Conversation (U.S.)," May 11, 1971, in *Détente Years*, 342–349.

40. "Memorandum of Telephone Conversation (USSR)," May 11, 1971, in *Détente Years*, 351.

41. "Memorandum of Conversation (USSR)," May 12, 1971, in *Détente Years*, 353.

42. "Text of Announcement on Accord," *New York Times*, May 21, 1971, 2.

43. Editorial, "Summit Accord on SALT," *New York Times*, May 21, 1971, 38.

44. "Editorial Note," in *FRUS 1969–1976*, Vol. 32, 429.

45. Henry Kissinger-Richard Nixon Telcon, May 21, 1971, KA05766, *Kissinger Telephone Conversations*, DNSA.

46. Henry Kissinger-Richard Nixon Telcon, May 21, 1971, KA05772, *Kissinger Telephone Conversations*, DNSA.

47. Henry Kissinger-William Fulbright Telcon, July 28, 1971 KA06187, *Kissinger Telephone Conversations*, DNSA.

48. Kissinger, *White House Years*, 820–821.

49. Richard Nixon to Alexei Kosygin, May 20, 1971, SALT Jan 9–May 20 1971 [3 of 3], Box 78, Henry A. Kissinger Office Files, NPL.

50. "Memorandum of Conversation (U.S.)," January 28, 1971, in *Détente Years*, 274; "Memorandum of Conversation (U.S.)," February 10, 1971, in *Détente Years*, 288; Garthoff, *Détente*, 179–180.

51. "Memorandum From the President's Assistant for National Security Affairs (Kissinger) to President Nixon," December 10, 1970, in *FRUS 1969-76*, Vol. 32, 373–374.

52. Garthoff, *Détente*, 180.

53. Kissinger, *White House Years*, 815.

54. "Memorandum of Conversation (U.S.)," April 26, 1971, in *Détente Years*, 332.

55. "Memorandum of Conversation (U.S.)," May 12, 1971, in *Détente Years*, 352.

56. Alexei Kosygin to Richard Nixon, May 20, 1971, SALT Jan 9–May 20 1971 [3 of 3], Box 78, Henry A. Kissinger Office Files, NPL. Translation and emphasis my own.

57. "SALT Public Statement and Letter, HS Comparison of 2 Language Texts," May 19, 1971, Exchange of Notes Between Dobrynin and Kissinger Vol. 1 (Part 1), Box 497, President's Trip Files, NSC Files, NPL.

58. Smith, *Doubletalk*, 250–251.

59. "Memorandum of Conversation (USSR)," March 16, 1971, in *Détente Years*, 312.

60. "Conversation Among President Nixon, the Chief of the Delegation to the Strategic Arms Limitation Talks (Smith), and the President's Deputy Assistant for National Security Affairs (Haig)," March 21, 1972, in *FRUS 1969–1976*, Vol. 32, 722.

61. Henry Kissinger-Richard Nixon Telcon, May 21, 1971, KA05766, *Kissinger Telephone Conversations*, DNSA.

62. Henry Kissinger-Henry Jackson Telcon, May 20, 1971, KA05756, *Kissinger Telephone Conversations*, DNSA.

63. Strom Thurmond, "The SALT Trap," *Human Events* 31, no. 24, 13, 477.

64. William Buckley, Jr., "The Patience of Mr. Nixon," *National Review* 23, no. 23, June 15, 1971, 669.

65. "Memorandum of Conversation," August 12, 1971, KT00330, *Kissinger Transcripts*, DNSA.

66. "Conversation Among President Nixon, the Chief of the Delegation to the Strategic Arms Limitation Talks (Smith), and the President's Deputy Assistant for National Security Affairs (Haig)," March 21, 1972, in *FRUS 1969–1976*, Vol. 32, 722.

67. Henry Kissinger-William Buckley, Jr. Telcon, July 28, 1971, KA06189, *Kissinger Telephone Conversations*, DNSA.

68. Henry Kissinger-Richard Nixon Telcon, May 21, 1971, KA05766, *Kissinger Telephone Conversations*, DNSA.

69. "Senate Armed Services Panel Cuts $1.2 Billion From Pentagon Budget," *Washington Post*, August 5, 1971, A1, A12.

70. Helmut Sonnenfeldt to Henry Kissinger, "Dobrynin's Comment on SALT to Senator Cooper," August 17, 1971, SALT Talks (Helsinki) Vol XVI-Aug 71, Box 881, SALT, NSC Files, NPL.

71. Smith, *Doubletalk*, 277.

72. "Memorandum of Conversation (U.S.)," June 21, 1971, in *Détente Years*, 386.

73. "Memorandum of Conversation (USSR)," June 30, 1971, in *Détente Years*, 393.

74. "Memorandum of Conversation (USSR)," July 31, 1971, in *Détente Years*, 421.

75. Smith, *Doubletalk*, 277.

76. Garthoff, *Détente*, 181–183.

77. Max Frankel, "Compromise Set: Scope and Shape of Possible Nuclear Accord Defined," *New York Times*, May 21, 1971, 1, 2; Michael Getler, "U.S. Goals Stress ABM, SS-9 Limits," *Washington Post*, May 21, 1971, A1, A8.

78. "Memorandum of Conversation (USSR)," June 30, 1971, in *Détente Years*, 394.
79. Melvin Laird to Henry Kissinger, "SALT—Next Steps," September 4, 1971, (Helsinki) Vol # 17 Sept–Dec 1971 [1 of 2], Box 882, SALT, NSC Files, NPL; "Memorandum From the Acting Chairman of the Joint Chiefs of Staff (Zumwalt) to Secretary of Defense Laird," July 31, 1971, in *FRUS 1969–1976*, Vol. 32, 581.
80. Melvin Laird to Richard Nixon, "SALT," September 15, 1971, (Helsinki) Vol # 17 Sep–Dec 1971 [1 of 2], Box 882, SALT, NSC Files, NPL.
81. "NSC Meeting on ABM," November 12, 1971, in *FRUS 1969–1976*, Vol. 32, 639–645.
82. Garthoff, *Détente*, 182–183.
83. An account of the often fitful early American approaches to the Chinese and Kissinger's secret visit can be found in Margaret MacMillan, *Seize the Hour: When Nixon Met Mao* (London: John Murray, 2007), 158–203.
84. Kissinger, *White House Years*, 837–839; MacMillan, *Seize the Hour*, 199; Hanhimäki, *Flawed Architect*, 147–148, 152–153; Garthoff, *Détente*, 263–274.
85. "Transcript of Telephone Conversation (U.S.)," July 15, 1971, in *Détente Years*, 399–400.
86. Kissinger, *White House Years*, 838.
87. "Memorandum of Conversation," July 29, 1971, in *Foreign Relations of the United States, 1969–1976, Volume XIII, Soviet Union, October 1970–October 1971*, ed. David C. Geyer (Washington, DC: United States Government Printing Office, 2011), 893–894; "Memorandum of Conversation," September 29, 1971, in *FRUS 1969–1976*, Vol. 13, 1034–1036.
88. "Telegram from Ambassador Dobrynin to the Soviet Foreign Ministry," July 17, 1971, in *Détente Years*, 401–402; James Cameron, "Moscow, 1972," in *Transcending the Cold War: Summits, Statecraft, and the Dissolution of Bipolarity in Europe*, eds. Kristina Spohr and David Reynolds (Oxford, UK: Oxford University Press, 2016), 74.
89. "Memorandum of Conversation (USSR)," August 17, 1971, in *Détente Years*, 433; Nixon, *RN*, 525; Cameron, "Moscow, 1972," 74.
90. "Memorandum of Conversation (U.S.)," March 1, 1972, in *Détente Years*, 595–596; "Memorandum of Conversation (USSR)," March 1, 1972, in *Détente Years*, 597. Kissinger makes a self-effacing reference to Acheson's saying in his foreword to *Détente Years*, x.
91. "Telegram From Ambassador Dobrynin to the Soviet Foreign Ministry," March 8, 1972, in *Détente Years*, 604.
92. "Telegram From Ambassador Dobrynin to the Soviet Foreign Ministry," March 8, 1972, in *Détente Years*, 604.
93. Jussi M. Hanhimäki, "An Elusive Grand Design," in *Nixon in the World: American Foreign Relations, 1969–1977*, eds. Fredrik Logevall and Andrew Preston (New York: Oxford University Press, 2008), 36–37.
94. "Conversation Between President Nixon and the President's Assistant for National Security Affairs (Kissinger)," January 3, 1972, in *FRUS 1969–1976*, Vol. 32, 660–662.
95. "Memorandum of Conversation (USSR)," January 21, 1972, in *Détente Years*, 564–565; "Memorandum of Conversation (U.S.)," February 15, 1972, in *Détente Years*, 587.
96. "Memorandum of Conversation (U.S.)," March 10, 1972, in *Détente Years*, 612.
97. "Memorandum of Conversation (USSR)," March 17, 1972, in *Détente Years*, 619; Robert G. Kaufman, *Henry M. Jackson: A Life in Politics* (Seattle: University of Washington Press, 2000), 223–241.

98. "Memorandum of Conversation," April 6, 1972, KT00463, *Kissinger Transcripts*, DNSA; Dallek, *Nixon and Kissinger*, 373.

99. Hanhimäki, *Flawed Architect*, 206–208; "Memorandum of Conversation (U.S.)," April 22, 1972, in *Détente Years*, 717–718.

100. "Memorandum From Presidential Assistant Kissinger to President Nixon," April 24, 1972, in *Détente Years*, 779. Emphasis in original.

101. "Memorandum of Conversation (U.S.)," April 23, 1972, in *Détente Years*, 746.

102. "Memorandum of Conversation (U.S.)," March 10, 1972, in *Détente Years*, 612.

103. "Conversation Among President Nixon, the President's Assistant for National Security Affairs (Kissinger), and the Assistant to the President (Haldeman)," March 9, 1972, in *FRUS 1969–1976*, Vol. 32, 693; Garthoff, *Détente*, 187.

104. "Memorandum of Conversation," April 22, 1972, in *Détente Years*, 717–718; Henry Kissinger to Richard Nixon, "Your Meeting with Ambassador Gerard Smith, Monday, May 1, 1972," May 1, 1972, SALT Talks (Helenski) (sic), Vol 18 May–Aug 1972 [2 of 3], Box 883, SALT, NSC Files, NPL; Garthoff, *Détente*, 188; Smith, *Doubletalk*, 370–378.

105. "Conversation Among President Nixon, Secretary of State Rogers, the President's Assistant for National Security Affairs (Kissinger), the President's Deputy Assistant for National Security Affairs (Haig), and the White House Press Secretary (Ziegler)," May 1, 1972, in *FRUS 1969–1976*, Vol. 32, 795–796.

106. "Memorandum of Conversation (USSR)," May 1, 1972, in *Détente Years*, 790.

107. "Memorandum of Conversation (USSR)," May 14, 1972, in *Détente Years*, 816–818.

108. Kissinger, *White House Years*, 1235.

109. Bernard Gwetzman, "Accord Expected to Offset Missile Totals and Power," *New York Times*, May 24, 1972, 1, 14; Richard Reeves, *President Nixon: Alone in the White House* (New York: Simon and Schuster, 2001), 489; Kissinger, *White House Years*, 1229–1242.

110. Smith, *Doubletalk*, 419–420.

111. Kissinger, *White House Years*, 1229–1242.

112. "Protocol to the Interim Agreement Between the United States and the Soviet Union," May 26, 1972, in *FRUS 1969–1976*, Vol. 32, 916; "Paper Prepared by the Verification Panel Working Group," June 7, 1972, in *FRUS 1969–1976*, Vol. 32, 940–941; Hedrick Smith, "Ceilings are Set," *New York Times*, May 27, 1972, 1, 8; Garthoff, *Détente*, 188. Nixon privately assured Brezhnev that "the United States had no plans" to exercise its right to build 54 new SLBMs in lieu of Titans. See: "Memorandum of Conversation," May 26, 1972, in *FRUS 1969-1976*, Vol. 32, 902, n.4.

113. Leonid Brezhnev, "Doklad 'O mezhdunarodnom polozhenii,'" May 19, 1972, Fond 2, Opis' 3, Delo 270, 51–3, *Plenumy Tsentral'nogo Komiteta Kommunisticheskoi partii Sovetsogo Soiuza*.

114. Laird to Kissinger, "SALT—Next Steps," September 4, 1971, NPL; Laird to Nixon, "SALT," September 15, 1971, NPL.

115. Smith, *Doubletalk*, 379–380.

116. Bernard Gwertzman, "Accord Expected to Offset Missile Totals and Power," *New York Times*, May 24, 1972, 14; Hedrick Smith, "Ceilings are Set," *New York Times*, May 28, 1972, 8.

117. "Background Use Only: Strategic Arms Limitation Agreements and National Security," June 13, 1972, SALT Materials [1 of 2], Box 79, Henry Kissinger Office Files, NSC Files, NPL.

118. "Conversation Among President Nixon, Members of the Republican Congressional Leadership, and Others," June, 13, 1972, in *FRUS 1969–1976*, Vol. 32, 945–950.

119. John W. Finney, "Squeeze Play on the Arms Issue," *New York Times*, June 11, 1972, E2.

120. Kaufman, *Henry M. Jackson*, 253–255.

121. Kaufman, *Henry M. Jackson*, 255–256.

122. "Text of McNamara Speech on Anti-China Missile Defense and U.S. Nuclear Strategy," *New York Times*, September 19, 1967, 18–19; Richard Nixon, "Address to a Joint Session of the Congress on Return from Austria, the Soviet Union, Iran, and Poland," June 1, 1972, APP, accessed March 26, 2017, http://www.presidency.ucsb.edu/ws/?pid=3450.

123. Kaufman, *Henry M. Jackson*, 255–257; Tad Szulc, "Nixon Signs Bill on Arms Accord," *New York Times*, October 1, 1972, 1.

124. John W. Finney, "Senate Approves Pact with Soviet on Missiles, 88–2," *New York Times*, August 4, 1972, 1.

125. For the interplay between domestic politics, Reagan's nuclear leadership and the Strategic Defense Initiative see Frances Fitzgerald, *Way Out There in the Blue: Reagan, Star Wars and the End of the Cold War* (New York: Simon and Schuster, 2000).

126. Kissinger, *White House Years*, 1255; Richard Nixon, "Address to a Joint Session of the Congress," June 1, 1972, APP.

127. Richard Nixon, "Address at the Air Force Academy," June 4, 1969, APP.

CONCLUSION

1. Bundy, *Danger and Survival*, 610–1.

2. Robert McNamara to McGeorge Bundy, November 12, 1984, Correspondence McNamara, Robert (2 of 2), Box 57, McGeorge Bundy Personal Papers, JFKL.

3. McGeorge Bundy to Robert McNamara, June 21, 1984, Folder 11, Box 2, Series I, Robert S. McNamara Papers, Library of Congress Manuscripts Division; McGeorge Bundy to Robert McNamara, November 29, 1984, Folder 11, Box 2, Series I, Robert S. McNamara Papers, Library of Congress Manuscripts Division.

4. Bundy to McNamara, November 29, 1984, McNamara Papers, Library of Congress.

5. Julian E. Zelizer, *Arsenal of Democracy: The Politics of National Security in America from World War II to the War on Terrorism* (New York: Basic Books, 2010), 506–7.

6. Adam Quinn, *H-Net*. Review of Colin Dueck, *The Obama Doctrine: American Grand Strategy Today* (New York: Oxford University Press, 2015), accessed March 26, 2017, http://www.h-net.org/reviews/showrev.php?id=44978.

7. Jervis, *The Meaning of the Nuclear Revolution*, 178–179, 191.

8. Jervis, *The Meaning of the Nuclear Revolution*, 191.

9. Marc Trachtenberg, *History and Strategy* (Princeton, NJ: Princeton University Press, 1991), 283–284.

10. Kroenig, "Nuclear Superiority and the Balance of Resolve," 141–171. Also see: Sechser and Fuhrmann, "Crisis Bargaining and Nuclear Blackmail," 173–195; Scott D. Sagan, Francis J. Gavin, Matthew Kroenig et al., "What We Talk about When We Talk About Nuclear Weapons," H-Diplo/ISSF Forum No.2, accessed March 26, 2017, http://issforum.org/ISSF/PDF/ISSF-Forum-2.pdf; Francis J. Gavin, Response to H-Diplo/ISSF Forum on "What We Talk About

When We Talk About Nuclear Weapons," accessed March 26, 2017, http:// issforum.org/ISSF/PDF/ISSF-Forum-2-Response.pdf.

11. Philip Zelikow, Review of Francis J. Gavin, *Nuclear Statecraft: History and Strategy in America's Atomic Age* (Ithaca, NY: Cornell University Press, 2012), in H-Diplo Roundtable, Vol. 15, no.1, accessed March 26, 2017, https://www.h-diplo.org/roundtables/PDF/Roundtable-XV-1.pdf.

12. Freedman, *Evolution of Nuclear Strategy*, 329.

13. Gavin, *Nuclear Statecraft*, 120–133; John Rosenberg, "The Quest Against Détente: Eugene Rostow, the October War, and the Origins of the Anti-Détente Movement," 1969–1976, *Diplomatic History* 39, no. 4 (October 2015), 720–744.

14. Freedman, *Evolution of Nuclear Strategy*, 335–338, 369–375; Gavin, *Nuclear Statecraft*, 120; Austin Long and Brendan Rittenhouse Green, "Stalking the Secure Second Strike: Intelligence, Counterforce, and Nuclear Strategy," *Journal of Strategic Studies* 38, no. 1–2 (February 2015), 38–73.

15. James Cameron, H-Diplo FRUS Review of *Foreign Relations of the United States, 1969–1976, Volume XXXV, National Security Policy, 1973–1976*, ed. M. Todd Bennett (Washington, DC: United States Government Printing Office, 2014), accessed March 26, 2017, https://networks.h-net.org/system/files/contributed-files/frus28.pdf.

16. Henry Kissinger, *Years of Upheaval* (Boston, MA: Little, Brown, 1982), 984; Cameron, H-Diplo Review of *FRUS 1969–1976*, Vol. 35.

17. Jimmy Carter, "Inaugural Address," January 20, 1977, APP, accessed March 26, 2017, http://www.presidency.ucsb.edu/ws/?pid=6575.

18. "Jimmy Carter's Controversial Nuclear Targeting Directive PD-59 Declassified," *National Security Archive Electronic Briefing Book No. 390*, ed. William Burr, accessed March 26, 2017, http://nsarchive.gwu.edu/nukevault/ebb390/.

19. Melvyn P. Leffler, *For the Soul of Mankind: The United States, the Soviet Union, and the Cold War* (New York: Hill and Wang, 2007), 394.

20. Leffler, *For the Soul of Mankind*, 399–400, 450; Zubok, *Failed Empire*, 301–302.

21. "ABM Treaty: Withdrawal Statement," December 11, 2001, Office of the Under Secretary of Defense for Technology, Acquisition, and Logistics, accessed March 26, 2017, http://www.acq.osd.mil/tc/treaties/abm/ABMwithdrawal.htm.

22. Brad Roberts, *The Case for U.S. Nuclear Weapons in the Twenty-First Century* (Stanford, CA: Stanford University Press, 2016), 106–175.

23. Barack Obama, "Remarks in Prague," April 5, 2009, APP, accessed March 26, 2017, http://www.presidency.ucsb.edu/ws/index.php?pid=85963&st=&st1=.

24. Josh Rogin, "Obama Plans Major Nuclear Policy Changes In His Final Months," *Washington Post*, July 10, 2016, accessed March 26, 2017, https://www.washingtonpost.com/opinions/global-opinions/obama-plans-major-nuclear-policy-changes-in-his-final-months/2016/07/10/fef3d5ca-4521-11e6-88d0-6adee48be8bc_story.html.

SOURCES

ARCHIVE COLLECTIONS
John F. Kennedy Presidential Library, Boston, Massachusetts.
    President's Office Files
    National Security Files
    McGeorge Bundy Personal Papers
    Oral History Collection

Lyndon Baines Johnson Presidential Library, Austin, Texas.
    National Security File
    Papers of Alain Enthoven
    Papers of Clark Clifford
    Papers of George M. Elsey [VanDeMark Transcripts]
    Papers of Morton H. Halperin
    Recordings and Transcripts of Conversations and Meetings
    Oral History Collection

Nixon Presidential Library, Yorba Linda, California.
    National Security Council Files
    National Security Council Institutional Files
    Henry A. Kissinger Office Files
    White House Special Files

National Archives and Records Administration, College Park, Maryland.
    Records of Robert S. McNamara, 1961–1968, RG 200

Library of Congress Manuscripts Division, Washington, DC.
    Robert S. McNamara Papers, 1934–2009

ONLINE AND PUBLISHED DOCUMENTS
XXIII s'ezd Kommunisticheskoi partii Sovetskogo Soiuza, 29 Marta-8 Aprelia 1966
    goda: Stenograficheskii otchet. Moscow: Politizdat, 1966.
Bennett, M. Todd, ed. *Foreign Relations of the United States, 1969–1976, Volume*
    XXIV, National Security Policy, 1969–1972. Washington, DC: United States
    Government Printing Office, 2012.
Burr, William, ed. "First Strike Options and the Berlin Crisis, September 1961: New
    Documents from the Kennedy Administration." *National Security Archive*

Electronic Briefing Book No.56. September 25, 2001. Accessed March 24, 2016. http://www.gwu.edu/~nsarchiv/NSAEBB/NSAEBB56/.

Burr, William, ed. "Jimmy Carter's Controversial Nuclear Targeting Directive PD-59 Declassified." *National Security Archive Electronic Briefing Book No. 390.* September 14, 2012. Accessed March 24, 2016. http://nsarchive.gwu.edu/nukevault/ebb390/.

Burr, William, ed. *The Kissinger Telephone Conversations: A Verbatim Record of U.S. Diplomacy.* Accessed March 23, 2017. Digital National Security Archive. http://nsarchive.chadwyck.com/.

Burr, William, ed. *U.S. Nuclear History: Nuclear Arms and Politics in the Missile Age, 1955–1968.* Accessed March 23, 2017. Digital National Security Archive. http://nsarchive.chadwyck.com.

Burr, William and Thomas Blanton, eds. "The Kissinger Telcons." May 26, 2004. National *Security Archive Electronic Briefing Book No.123.* Accessed March 26, 2017. http://www.gwu.edu/~nsarchiv/NSAEBB/NSAEBB123/.

Burr, William and Hector L. Montford, eds. "The Making of the Limited Test Ban Treaty, 1958–1963." August 8, 2003. *National Security Archive Electronic Briefing Book No.93.* Accessed March 24, 2017. http://www.gwu.edu/~nsarchiv/NSAEBB/NSAEBB94/index.htm.

Burr, William and Robert Wampler, eds. "The Master of the Game: Paul H. Nitze and U.S. Cold War Strategy from Truman to Reagan." October 7, 2004. *National Security Archive Electronic Briefing Book No. 139.* Accessed March 24, 2017. http://www.gwu.edu/~nsarchiv/NSAEBB/NSAEBB139/.

Central Intelligence Agency, Freedom of Information Act Electronic Reading Room. Accessed March 24, 2017. https://www.cia.gov/library/readingroom/.

Chang, Lawrence and Peter Kornbluh, eds. *The Cuban Missile Crisis, 1962.* Digital National Security Archive. Accessed March 24, 2017. http://nsarchive.chadwyck.com/.

Gerakas, Evans, David S., Mabon, David W. Patterson, William F. Sanford, Jr., and Carolyn B. Yee, eds. *Foreign Relations of the United States, 1961–1963 Volumes VII/VIII/IX, Microfiche Supplement, Arms Control; National Security; Foreign Economic Policy.* Washington, DC: United States Government Printing Office, 1997.

Gerakas, Evans, David S. Patterson, and Caroline B. Yee, eds. *Foreign Relations of the United States, 1964–1968, Volume XI, Arms Control and Disarmament.* Washington, DC: United States Government Printing Office, 1997.

Geyer, David C., ed. *Foreign Relations of the United States, 1969-1976, Volume XIII, Soviet Union, October 1970–October 1971.*Washington, DC: United States Government Printing Office, 2011.

Gorelik, Gennady. Personal Website. Accessed March 24, 2017. http://ggorelik.narod.ru/.

Govtrack.us. Accessed March 24, 2017. http://www.govtrack.us/.

Humphrey, David C., Edward C. Keefer, and Louis J. Smith, eds. *Foreign Relations of the United States, 1964–1968, Volume III, Vietnam, June–December 1965.* Washington, DC: United States Government Printing Office, 1996.

Humphrey, David C., and Charles S. Sampson, eds. *Foreign Relations of the United States, 1964–1968, Volume XIV, Soviet Union.* Washington, DC: United States Government Printing Office, 2001.

Mabon, David W., and David S. Patterson, eds. *Foreign Relations of the United States, 1961–1963, Volume VII, Arms Control and Disarmament.* Washington, DC: United States Government Printing Office, 1995.

Mabon, David W., ed. *Foreign Relations of the United States, 1961–1963, Volume VIII, National Security Policy*. Washington, DC: United States Government Printing Office, 1996.

Mahan, Erin R., ed. *Foreign Relations of the United States, 1969–1976, Volume XII, Soviet Union, January 1969–October 1970*. Washington, DC: United States Government Printing Office, 2006.

Mahan, Erin R., ed. *Foreign Relations of the United States, 1969–1976, Volume XXXII, SALT I, 1969–1972*. Washington, DC: United States Government Printing Office, 2010.

Meyer, David C. and Douglas E. Selvage, eds. *Soviet-American Relations: The Détente Years, 1969–1972*. Washington, DC: United States Government Printing Office, 2007.

Naftali, Timothy, Philip Zelikow, and Ernest R. May, eds. *The Presidential Recordings: John F. Kennedy: The Great Crises*. 3 vols. New York: Norton, 2001.

Office of the Secretary of Defense and Joint Staff Freedom of Information Act Requester Service Center. Accessed March 24, 2017. http://www.dod.mil/pubs/foi.

Office of the Under Secretary of Defense for Technology, Acquisition and Logistics. Accessed March 26, 2017. http://www.acq.osd.mil/.

Patterson, David S., ed. *Foreign Relations of the United States, 1964–1968, Volume X, National Security Policy*. Washington, DC: United States Government Printing Office, 2002.

Plenumy Tsentral'nogo Komiteta Kommunisticheskoi partii Sovetsogo Soiuza, 1941–1990: iz fondov Rossiiskogo gosudarstevennogo arkhiva noveishei istorii. Woodbury, CT: Research Publications, 2001.

Prados, John, ed. *The Soviet Estimate: U.S. Analysis of the Soviet Union, 1947–1991*. Accessed March 23, 2017. Digital National Security Archive. http://nsarchive.chadwyck.com.

Woolley, John and Gerhard Peters, eds. The American Presidency Project, University of California, Santa Barbara. Accessed March 24, 2017. http://www.presidency.ucsb.edu/.

NEWSPAPERS AND PERIODICALS

Congressional Quarterly Almanac
Congressional Quarterly Weekly Report
Congressional Record
Human Events
Life
National Review
New York Times
Scientific American
Seattle Times
Time
The Atlantic
The Nation
The Saturday Evening Post
Washington Post

BIBLIOGRAPHY

Allison, Graham, and Philip Zelikow. *Essence of Decision: Explaining the Cuban Missile Crisis.* 2nd ed. New York: Longman, 1999.

Ambrose, Stephen E. *Nixon, Volume Two: The Triumph of a Politician, 1962–1972.* New York: Simon and Schuster, 1989.

Arbatov, Georgii A. *Chelovek sistemy.* Moscow: Vagrius, 2002.

Ball, Desmond. *Politics and Force Levels: The Strategic Missile Program of the Kennedy Administration.* Berkeley: University of California Press, 1980.

Baucom, Donald R. *The Origins of SDI, 1944–1983.* Lawrence: University Press of Kansas, 1992.

Baylis, John, and John Garnett, eds. *Makers of Nuclear Strategy.* New York: St. Martin's Press, 1991.

Bernstein, Irving. *Guns or Butter: The Presidency of Lyndon Johnson.* New York: Oxford University Press, 1996.

Beschloss, Michael R. *The Crisis Years: Kennedy and Khrushchev, 1960–1963.* New York: Edward Burlingame, 1991.

Blight, James G., and Janet M Lang. *The Fog of War: Lessons from the Life of Robert S. McNamara.* Lanham, MD: Rowman and Littlefield, 2005.

Bobbitt, Philip, Lawrence Freedman, and Gregory F. Treverton, eds. *U.S. Nuclear Strategy: A Reader.* Basingstoke, UK: Macmillan, 1989.

Brands, H.W. *The Wages of Globalism: Lyndon Johnson and the Limits of American Power.* New York: Oxford University Press, 1995.

Brands, H.W., ed. *The Foreign Policies of Lyndon Johnson: Beyond Vietnam.* College Station: Texas A&M University Press, 1999.

Brands, Hal. "Progress Unseen: U.S. Arms Control Policy and the Origins of Détente, 1963–1968." *Diplomatic History* 30, no. 2 (April 2006): 253–285.

Bundy, McGeorge. *Danger and Survival: Choices About the Bomb in the First Fifty Years.* New York: Random House, 1988.

Bundy, McGeorge. "To Cap the Volcano." *Foreign Affairs* 40, no.1 (October 1969): 1–20.

Bundy, William P. *A Tangled Web: The Making of Foreign Policy in the Nixon Presidency.* New York: Hill and Wang, 1998.

Burr, William. "The Nixon Administration, the 'Horror Strategy,' and the Search for Limited Nuclear Options, 1969–1972." *Journal of Cold War Studies* 7, no. 3 (Summer 2005): 34–78.

Burr, William, and Jeffrey Kimball. *Nixon's Nuclear Specter: The Secret Alert of 1969, Madman Diplomacy, and the Vietnam War.* Lawrence: University Press of Kansas, 2015.

Burr, William, and Jeffrey Kimball. "Nixon's Secret Nuclear Alert: Vietnam War Diplomacy and the Joint Chiefs of Staff Readiness Test, October 1969." *Cold War History* 3, no. 2 (January 2003): 113–156.

Burr, William, and David Allen Rosenberg. "Nuclear Competition in the Era of Stalemate, 1963–1975." In *The Cambridge History of the Cold War Volume II: Crises and Détente.* Edited by Melvyn P. Leffler and Odd Arne Westad, 88–111. Cambridge, UK: Cambridge University Press, 2010.

Bystrova, Irina V. *Sovetskii voenno-promyshlennyi kompleks: problemy stanovleniia i razvitiia (1930-1980-e gody).* Moscow: Institut rossiiskoi istorii RAN, 2006.

Cahn, Anne Hessing. "Scientists and the ABM." PhD. diss., Massachusetts Institute of Technology, 1971.

Cahn, Anne Hessing. *Killing Détente: The Right Attacks the CIA.* University Park: Pennsylvania State University Press, 1998.

Cameron, James. "Moscow, 1972." *Transcending the Cold War: Summits, Statecraft, and the Dissolution of Bipolarity in Europe*. Edited by Kristina Spohr and David Reynolds, 67–91. Oxford, UK: Oxford University Press, 2016.

Cameron, James. "From the Grass Roots to the Summit: The Impact of U.S. Suburban Protest on U.S. Missile Defence Policy, 1968–72." *The International History Review* 36, no. 2 (March 2014): 342–362.

Cameron, James. H-Diplo FRUS Review of M. Todd Bennett, ed. *Foreign Relations of the United States, 1969-1976, Volume XXXV, National Security Policy, 1973–1976*. Washington: United States Government Printing Office, 2014. Accessed March 24, 2017. https://networks.h-net.org/system/files/contributed-files/frus28.pdf.

Caro, Robert A. *The Years of Lyndon Johnson: Master of the Senate*. New York: Alfred A. Knopf, 2002.

Caro, Robert A. *The Years of Lyndon Johnson: The Passage of Power*. New York: Knopf, 2012.

Carter, Ashton B., and David N. Schwartz, eds. *Ballistic Missile Defense*. Washington, DC: Brookings Institution, 1984.

Chayes, Abram, and Jerome B. Wiesner, eds. *ABM: An Evaluation of the Decision to Deploy an Antiballistic Missile System*. New York: Harper and Row, 1969.

Clearwater, John Murray. "Johnson, McNamara and the Birth of SALT." PhD diss., King's College London, 1996.

Clifford, Clark M., Richard Holbrooke. *Counsel to the President: A Memoir*. New York: Random House, 1991.

Clymer, Adam. *Edward M. Kennedy: A Biography*. New York: William Morrow and Company, 1999.

Cohen, Warren I., and Nancy Bernkopf Tucker, eds. *Lyndon Johnson Confronts the World: American Foreign Policy, 1963–1968*. New York: Cambridge University Press, 1994.

Coleman, David. "Camelot's Nuclear Conscience." *Bulletin of Atomic Scientists* 62, no. 3 (May 2006): 40–44.

Craig, Campbell. *Destroying the Village: Eisenhower and Thermonuclear War*. New York: Columbia University Press, 1998.

Dallek, Robert. *An Unfinished Life: John F. Kennedy, 1917–1963*. Boston, MA: Little, Brown. 2003.

Dallek, Robert. *Flawed Giant: Lyndon Johnson and His Times, 1961–1973*. New York: Oxford University Press, 1998.

Dallek, Robert. *Nixon and Kissinger: Partners in Power*. New York: Harper Collins, 2007.

Davis, Christopher. "The Defense Sector in the Economy of a Declining Superpower: Soviet Union and Russia, 1965-2000." *University of Oxford Department of Economics Discussion Paper Series* 8 (April 2000).

Del Pero, Mario. *The Eccentric Realist: Henry Kissinger and the Shaping of American Foreign Policy*. Ithaca, NY: Cornell University Press, 2010.

Divine, Robert A. "Lyndon Johnson and Strategic Arms Limitation." In *The Johnson Years, Volume Three: LBJ at Home and Abroad*. Edited by Robert A. Divine, 239–279. Lawrence: University Press of Kansas, 1994.

Dobrynin, Anatoly. *In Confidence: Moscow's Ambassador to Six Cold War Presidents, 1962–1986*. New York: Times Books, 1995.

Drea, Edward J. *Secretary of Defense Historical Series, McNamara, Clifford, and the Burdens of Vietnam*. Washington, DC: Historical Office, Office of the Secretary of Defense, 2011.

Dumbrell, John. *President Lyndon Johnson and Soviet Communism*. Manchester, UK: Manchester University Press, 2004.

Edwards, Paul N. *The Closed World: Computers and the Politics of Discourse in Cold War America*. Cambridge, MA: MIT Press, 1996.

Engerman, David. *Know Your Enemy: The Rise and Fall of America's Soviet Experts*. New York: Oxford University Press, 2009.

Enthoven, Alain C., and K. Wayne Smith. *How Much Is Enough? Shaping the Defense Program, 1961–1969*. 2nd ed. Santa Monica, CA: RAND Corp., 2005.

Fite, Gilbert C. *Richard Russell, Jr., Senator from Georgia*. Chapel Hill: University of North Carolina Press, 1991.

Fitzgerald, Frances. *Way Out There in the Blue: Reagan, Star Wars and the End of the Cold War*. New York: Simon and Schuster, 2000.

Ford, Christopher A. "Anything But Simple: Arms Control and Strategic Stability." In *Strategic Stability: Contending Interpretations*. Edited by Elbridge A. Colby and Michael S. Gerson, 201–270. Carlisle, PA: Strategic Studies Institute and U.S. Army War College Press, 2013.

Free, Lloyd A., and Hadley Cantril. *The Political Beliefs of Americans; A Study of Public Opinion*. New Brunswick, NJ: Rutgers University Press, 1967.

Freedman, Lawrence. *U.S. Intelligence and the Soviet Strategic Threat*. 2nd ed. Basingstoke, UK: Macmillan, 1986.

Freedman, Lawrence. *Kennedy's Wars: Berlin, Cuba, Laos, and Vietnam*. New York: Oxford University Press, 2000.

Freedman, Lawrence. *The Evolution of Nuclear Strategy*. 3rd ed. Basingstoke, UK: Palgrave Macmillan, 2003.

Fursenko, Aleskandr, and Timothy Naftali. *Khrushchev's Cold War: The Inside Story of an American Adversary*. New York: Norton, 2006.

Fursenko, Aleksandr, and Timothy Naftali. *"One Hell of a Gamble": Khrushchev, Castro, and Kennedy, 1958–1964*. New York: W.W. Norton & Co., 1997.

Gaddis, John Lewis. *Strategies of Containment: A Critical Appraisal of American National Security Policy During the Cold War*. 2nd ed. New York: Oxford University Press, 2005.

Garrison, Dee. *Bracing for Armageddon: Why Civil Defense Never Worked*. New York: Oxford University Press, 2006.

Garthoff, Raymond L. *Détente and Confrontation: American Foreign Relations from Nixon to Reagan*. 2nd ed. Washington: Brookings Institution, 1994.

Gavin, Francis J. *Nuclear Statecraft: History and Strategy in America's Atomic Age*. Ithaca, NY: Cornell University Press, 2012.

Gavin, Francis J. Response to H-Diplo/ISSF Forum on "What We Talk About When We Talk About Nuclear Weapons." Accessed March 26, 2017. http://issforum.org/ISSF/PDF/ISSF-Forum-2-Response.pdf.

Geismer, Lily. *Don't Blame Us: Suburban Liberals and the Transformation of the Democratic Party*. Princeton, NJ: Princeton University Press, 2015.

Geist, Edward. *Armageddon Insurance: Civil Defense in the United States and the Soviet Union*. Unpublished manuscript, last modified April 22, 2016, PDF file.

Gorelik, Gennady. *The World of Andrei Sakharov: A Russian Physicist's Path to Freedom*. Translated by Antonina W. Bouis. New York: Oxford University Press, 2005.

Gray, Colin S. *The Soviet-American Arms Race*. Lexington, MA: Lexington Books, 1976.

Greenberg, David. *Nixon's Shadow: The History of an Image*. New York: W.W. Norton, 2003.

Grynaviski, Eric. *Constructive Illusions: Misperceiving the Origins of International Cooperation*. Ithaca, NY: Cornell University Press, 2014.

Halberstam, David. *The Best and the Brightest*. New York: Random House, 1972.

Haldeman, H.R. *The Haldeman Diaries: Inside the Nixon White House*. New York: G.P. Putnam's, 1994.

Halperin, Morton H. *Bureaucratic Politics and Foreign Policy*. Washington, DC: Brookings Institution, 1974.

Halperin, Morton H. "The Decision to Deploy the ABM: Bureaucratic and Domestic Politics in the Johnson Administration." *World Politics* 25, no. 1 (October 1972): 62–95.

Hanhimäki, Jussi M. *The Flawed Architect: Henry Kissinger and American Foreign Policy*. New York: Oxford University Press, 2004.

Heefner, Gretchen. *The Missile Next Door: The Minuteman in the American Heartland*. Cambridge, MA: Harvard University Press, 2012.

Herken, Gregg. *Counsels of War*. 2nd ed. New York: Oxford University Press, 1987.

Hersh, Burton. *Edward Kennedy: An Intimate Biography*. Berkeley, CA: Counterpoint, 2010.

Hitch, Charles J. and Roland N. McKean. *The Economics of Defense in the Nuclear Age*. Cambridge, MA: Harvard University Press, 1960.

Hoff, Joan. *Nixon Reconsidered*. New York: Basic Books, 1994.

Holloway, David. *The Soviet Union and the Arms Race*. 2nd ed. New Haven, CT: Yale University Press, 1984.

Hymans, Jacques E.C., Austin Long, Leopoldo Nuti, et al. Roundtable Review of Francis J. Gavin, *Nuclear Statecraft: History and Strategy in America's Atomic Age*, Ithaca, NY: Cornell University Press, 2012. H-Diplo Roundtables, Vol. 15, no.1. Accessed March 26, 2017. https://www.h-diplo.org/roundtables/PDF/Roundtable-XV-1.pdf.

Isaacson, Walter. *Kissinger: A Biography*. New York: Simon and Schuster, 1992.

Jervis, Robert. *The Meaning of the Nuclear Revolution: Statecraft and the Prospect of Armageddon*. Ithaca, NY: Cornell University Press, 1989.

Johnson, Lyndon B. *The Vantage Point: Perspectives of the Presidency, 1963–1969*. New York: Holt, Rinehart, and Winston, 1971.

Johnson, Robert David. *Congress and the Cold War*. New York: Cambridge University Press, 2006.

Jones, Matthew. *After Hiroshima: The United States, Race and American Nuclear Weapons in Asia, 1945–1965*. Cambridge, UK: Cambridge University Press, 2010.

Kaiser, David. *American Tragedy: Kennedy, Johnson, and the Origins of the Vietnam War*. Cambridge, MA: Belknap Press of Harvard University Press, 2000.

Kaiser, David. "Men and Policies: 1961–1969." In *The Diplomacy of the Crucial Decade: American Foreign Relations During the 1960s*. Edited by Diane B. Kunz, 11–41. New York: Columbia University Press, 1994.

Kaplan, Fred. *The Wizards of Armageddon*. 2nd ed. Stanford, CA: Stanford University Press, 1991.

Kaplan, Lawrence S., Ronald D. Landa and Edward J. Drea. *History of the Office of the Secretary of Defense, The McNamara Ascendancy 1961–1965*. Washington, DC: Historical Office, Office of the Secretary of Defense, 2006.

Kaufman, Robert G. *Henry M. Jackson: A Life in Politics*. Seattle: University of Washington Press, 2000.

Kaufmann, William W. *The McNamara Strategy*. New York: Harper and Row, 1964.

Kettl, Donald F. "The Economic Education of Lyndon Johnson: Guns, Butter, and Taxes." In *The Johnson Years, Volume Two: Vietnam, the Environment, and Science*. Edited by Robert A. Divine, 54–78. Lawrence: University Press of Kansas, 1987.

Kimball, Jeffrey. *Nixon's Vietnam War*. Lawrence: University Press of Kansas, 1998.

Kissinger, Henry A. *American Foreign Policy: Three Essays*. New York: Norton, 1969.

Kissinger, Henry A. *Nuclear Weapons and Foreign Policy*. New York: Harper, 1957.

Kissinger, Henry A. *White House Years*. Boston, MA: Little, Brown, 1979.

Kissinger, Henry A. *Years of Upheaval*. Boston, MA: Little, Brown, 1982.

Kroenig, Matthew. "Nuclear Superiority and the Balance of Resolve: Explaining Nuclear Crisis Outcomes." *International Organization* 67, no. 1 (January 2013): 141–171.

Kroenig, Matthew, Todd Sechser, and Matthew Fuhrmann. "Debating the Benefits of Nuclear Superiority for Crisis Bargaining." Parts I-IV. *Duck of Minerva Blog*. Accessed March 24, 2017. http://duckofminerva.com/2013/03/debating-the-benefits-nuclear-superiority-for-crisis-bargaining-part-i.html.

Kuklick, Bruce. *Blind Oracles: Intellectuals and War from Kennan to Kissinger*. Princeton, NJ: Princeton University Press, 2006.

Latham, Michael E. *Modernization as Ideology: American Social Science and "Nation Building" in the Kennedy Era*. Chapel Hill: University of North Carolina Press, 2000.

Leffler, Melvyn P. *For the Soul of Mankind: The United States, the Soviet Union, and the Cold War*. New York: Hill and Wang, 2007.

Lerner, Mitchell B. "'Trying to Find the Guy Who Invited Them': Lyndon Johnson, Bridge Building, and the End of the Prague Spring." *Diplomatic History* 32, no. 1 (January 2008): 77–103.

Lindsay, James M., and Michael E. O'Hanlon. *Defending America: The Case for Limited National Missile Defense*. Washington, DC: Brookings Institution Press, 2001.

Lindsay, James M. , and Michael E. O'Hanlon "Missile Defense After the ABM Treaty." *Washington Quarterly* 25, no. 3 (Summer 2002): 163–176.

Logevall, Fredrik. *Choosing War: The Lost Chance for Peace and the Escalation of the War in Vietnam*. Berkeley: University of California Press, 1999.

Logevall, Fredrik and Andrew Preston, eds. *Nixon in the World: American Foreign Relations, 1969–1977*. New York: Oxford University Press, 2008.

Long, Austin, and Brendan Rittenhouse Green. "Stalking the Secure Second Strike: Intelligence, Counterforce, and Nuclear Strategy." *Journal of Strategic Studies* 38, no. 1–2 (February 2015): 38–73.

Lumbers, Michael. *Piercing the Bamboo Curtain: Tentative Bridge-Building to China During the Johnson Years*. Manchester, UK: Manchester University Press, 2008.

Lundberg, Kirsten. "The SS-9 Controversy: Intelligence as Political Football." Case C16-89-884.0, Kennedy School of Government, Harvard University, 1989.

Mackenzie, Donald A. *Inventing Accuracy: A Historical Sociology of Missile Guidance*. Cambridge, MA: MIT Press, 1990.

Mackenzie, G. Calvin, and Robert Weisbrot. *The Liberal Hour: Washington and the Politics of Change in the 1960s*. New York: Penguin Press, 2008.

MacMillan, Margaret. *Seize the Hour: When Nixon Met Mao*. London: John Murray, 2007.

Maddock, Shane J. *Nuclear Apartheid: The Quest for American Atomic Supremacy from World War II to the Present*. Chapel Hill: University of North Carolina Press, 2010.

Mason, Robert. *Richard Nixon and the Quest for a New Majority*. Chapel Hill: University of North Carolina Press, 2004.

Mathers, Jennifer G. "A Fly in Outer Space: Soviet Ballistic Missile Defense During the Khrushchev Period." *Journal of Strategic Studies* 21, no. 2 (June 1998): 31–59.

Mathers, Jennifer G. *The Russian Nuclear Shield from Stalin to Yeltsin*. Basingstoke, UK: Palgrave Macmillan, 2000.

McKercher, Asa. "Steamed Up: Domestic Politics, Congress, and Cuba, 1959–1963." *Diplomatic History* 38, no. 3 (June 2014): 599–627.

McMahon, Robert J. "Bernath Lecture: Credibility and World Power: Exploring the Psychological Dimension in Postwar American Diplomacy." *Diplomatic History* 15, no. 4 (October 1991): 455–471.

McNamara, Robert S. *Blundering into Disaster: Surviving the First Century of the Nuclear Age*. New York: Parthenon, 1987.

McNamara, Robert S. *The Essence of Security: Reflections in Office*. New York: Harper and Row, 1968.

McNamara, Robert S. "The Military Role of Nuclear Weapons: Perceptions and Misperceptions." *Foreign Affairs* 62, no. 1 (Fall 1983): 59–80.

McNamara, Robert S. *In Retrospect: The Tragedy and Lessons of Vietnam*. New York: Times Books, 1995.

Mergel, Sarah Katherine. *Conservative Intellectuals and Richard Nixon*. New York: Palgrave Macmillan, 2010.

Milne, David. *America's Rasputin: Walt Rostow and the Vietnam War*. New York: Hill and Wang, 2008.

Nelson, Keith L. *The Making of Détente: Soviet-American Relations in the Shadow of Vietnam*. Baltimore, MD: Johns Hopkins University Press, 1995.

Newhouse, John. *Cold Dawn: The Story of SALT*. New York: Holt, Rinehart and Winston, 1973.

Nixon, Richard M. *In the Arena: A Memoir of Victory, Defeat, and Renewal*. New York: Simon and Schuster, 1990.

Nixon, Richard M. *RN: The Memoirs of Richard Nixon*. New York: Grosset and Dunlap, 1978.

Peck, James. *Washington's China: The National Security World, the Cold War, and the Origins of Globalism*. Amherst: University of Massachusetts Press, 2006.

Perlstein, Rick. *Nixonland: The Rise of a President and the Fracturing of America*. New York: Scribner, 2008.

Pervov, Mikhail. *Sistemy raketno-kosmicheskoi oborony Rossii sozdavalis' tak*. 2nd ed. Moscow: Aviarus-XXI, 2004.

Podvig, Pavel L. "Protivoraketnaia oborona kak factor strategicheskikh vzaimootnoshenii SSSR/Rossii i SSha v 1945-2003gg." PhD. diss., Institute of Global Economics and International Relations, Russian Academy of Sciences, 2004.

Preble, Christopher A. *John F. Kennedy and the Missile Gap*. DeKalb: Northern Illinois University Press, 2004.

Preble, Christopher A. "'Who Ever Believed in the "Missile Gap"?': John F. Kennedy and the Politics of National Security." *Presidential Studies Quarterly* 33, no. 4 (December 2003): 801–826.

Preston, Andrew. *The War Council: McGeorge Bundy, the NSC, and Vietnam*. Cambridge, MA: Harvard University Press, 2006.

Putnam, Robert D. "Diplomacy and Domestic Politics: The Logic of Two-Level Games." *International Organization* 42, no. 3 (Summer 1988): 427–460.

Quinn, Adam. *H-Net*. Review of Colin Dueck, *The Obama Doctrine: American Grand Strategy Today*. New York: Oxford University Press, 2015. Accessed March 24, 2017. http://www.h-net.org/reviews/showrev.php?id=44978.

Reeves, Richard. *President Kennedy: Profile of Power*. New York: Simon and Schuster, 1993.

Reeves, Richard. *President Nixon: Alone in the White House*. New York: Simon and Schuster, 2001.

Roberts, Brad. *The Case for U.S. Nuclear Weapons in the Twenty-First Century*. Stanford, CA: Stanford University Press, 2016.

Rose, Kenneth D. *One Nation Underground: The Fallout Shelter in American Culture*. New York: New York University Press, 2001.

Rosenberg, John. "The Quest Against Détente: Eugene Rostow, the October War, and the Origins of the Anti-Détente Movement, 1969–1976." *Diplomatic History* 39, no. 4 (October 2015): 720–744.

Rusk, Dean. *As I Saw It*. Edited by Daniel S. Papp. New York: W.W. Norton, 1990.

Russett, Bruce M. "The Revolt of the Masses: Public Opinion on Military Expenditures." In *Peace War and Numbers*. Edited by Bruce M. Russett, 299–319. Beverly Hills, CA: Sage, 1973.

Sagan, Scott, D., Francis J. Gavin, Matthew Kroenig, et al. "What We Talk About When We Talk About Nuclear Weapons." H-Diplo/ISSF Forum No.2. Accessed March 24, 2017. http://issforum.org/ISSF/PDF/ISSF-Forum-2.pdf.

Savel'yev, Aleksandr' G., and Nikolai N. Detinov. *The Big Five: Arms Control Decision-Making in the Soviet Union*. Edited by Gregory Varhall. Translated by Dmitri Trenin. Westport, CT: Praeger, 1995.

Schlesinger, Arthur M. Jr., *A Thousand Days: John F. Kennedy in the White House*. Boston, MA: Houghton Mifflin, 1965.

Schwartz, Thomas Alan. *Lyndon Johnson and Europe: In the Shadow of Vietnam*. Cambridge, MA: Harvard University Press, 2003.

Seaborg, Glenn T. *Kennedy, Khrushchev, and the Test Ban*. Berkeley: University of California Press, 1981.

Seaborg, Glenn T., and Benjamin S. Loeb. *Stemming the Tide: Arms Control in the Johnson Years*. Lexington, MA: Lexington Books, 1987.

Sechser, Todd S., and Matthew Fuhrmann. "Crisis Bargaining and Nuclear Blackmail." *International Organization* 67, no. 1 (January 2013): 173–195.

Shapley, Deborah. *Promise and Power: The Life and Times of Robert McNamara*. Boston, MA: Little, Brown, 1993.

Shevchenko, Arkady N. *Breaking With Moscow*. New York: Knopf, 1985.

Sidey, Hugh. *A Very Personal Presidency: Lyndon Johnson in the White House*. New York: Atheneum, 1968.

Siniver, Asaf. *Nixon, Kissinger, and U.S. Foreign Policy Making: The Machinery of Crisis*. Cambridge, UK: Cambridge University Press, 2008.

Slayton, Rebecca. *Arguments that Count: Physics, Computing, and Missile Defense, 1949–2012*. Cambridge, MA: The MIT Press, 2013.

Smith, Gerard C. *Doubletalk: The Story of the First Strategic Arms Limitation Talks*. Garden City, NJ: Doubleday, 1980.

Snead, David L. *The Gaither Committee, Eisenhower, and the Cold War*. Columbus: Ohio State University Press, 1999.

Sorensen, Theodore C. *Kennedy*. New York: Harper and Row, 1965.

Spinardi, Graham. "The Rise and Fall of Safeguard: Anti-Ballistic Missile Technology and the Nixon Administration." *History and Technology* 26, no. 4 (December 2010): 313–334.

Stein, Jonathan B. *From H-Bomb to Star Wars: The Politics of Strategic Decision Making.* Lexington, MA: Lexington, 1984.

Stern, Sheldon M. *The Cuban Missile Crisis in American Memory: Myths Versus Reality.* Stanford, CA: Stanford University Press, 2012.

Suri, Jeremi. *Henry Kissinger and the American Century.* Cambridge, MA: Belknap Press of Harvard University Press, 2007.

Suri, Jeremi. "Lyndon Johnson and the Global Disruption of 1968." In *Looking Back at LBJ: White House Politics in a New Light,* edited by Mitchell B. Lerner, 53–77. Lawrence: University Press of Kansas, 2005.

Suri, Jeremi. *Power and Protest: The Global Disruption of 1968 and the Rise of Détente.* Cambridge, MA: Harvard University Press, 2003.

Suri, Jeremi, and Scott D. Sagan. "The Madman Nuclear Alert: Secrecy, Signaling, and Safety in October 1969." *International Security* 27, no. 4 (Spring 2003): 150–183.

Suri, Jeremi, and Andreas Wenger. "At the Crossroads of Diplomatic and Social History: the Nuclear Revolution, Dissent, and Détente." *Cold War History* 1, no.3 (April 2003): 1–42.

Talbott, Strobe. *The Master of the Game: Paul Nitze and the Nuclear Peace.* New York: Knopf, 1988.

Tammen, Ronald L. *MIRV and the Arms Race: An Interpretation of Defense Strategy.* New York: Praeger, 1973.

Tannenwald, Nina. *The Nuclear Taboo: The United States and the Non-Use of Nuclear Weapons Since 1945.* Cambridge, UK: Cambridge University Press, 2007.

Taubman, William. *Khrushchev: The Man and His Era.* New York: Norton, 2003.

Teller, Edward. *Better a Shield Than a Sword: Perspectives on Peace and Technology.* New York: Free Press, 1987.

Terriff, Terry. *The Nixon Administration and the Making of U.S. Nuclear Strategy.* Ithaca, NY: Cornell University Press, 1995.

Trachtenberg, Marc. *A Constructed Peace: The Making of the European Settlement, 1945–1963.* Princeton, NJ: Princeton University Press, 1999.

Trachtenberg, Marc. *History and Strategy.* Princeton, NJ: Princeton University Press, 1991.

Trachtenberg, Marc. "The Influence of Nuclear Weapons in the Cuban Missile Crisis." *International Security* 10, no. 1 (Summer 1985): 137–163.

Wang, Zuoyue. *In Sputnik's Shadow: The President's Science Advisory Committee and Cold War America.* New Brunswick, NJ: Rutgers University Press, 2008.

Wenger, Andreas. *Living With Peril: Eisenhower, Kennedy, and Nuclear Weapons.* Lanham, MD: Rowman and Littlefield, 1997.

Wenger, Andreas, and Marcel Gerber. "John F. Kennedy and the Limited Test Ban Treaty: A Case Study in Presidential Leadership." *Presidential Studies Quarterly* 29, no. 2 (June 1999): 460–487.

Woods, Randall Bennett. *Fulbright: A Biography.* Cambridge, UK: Cambridge University Press, 1995.

Woods, Randall Bennett. *LBJ: Architect of American Ambition.* New York: Free Press, 2006.

Woods, Randall Bennett. *Prisoners of Hope: Lyndon B. Johnson, the Great Society, and the Limits of Liberalism.* New York: Basic Books, 2016.

Yanarella, Ernest J. *The Missile Defense Controversy: Technology in Search of a Mission*. 2nd ed. Lexington: University Press of Kentucky, 2002.

York, Herbert F. *Making Weapons, Talking Peace: A Physicist's Odyssey from Hiroshima to Geneva*. New York: Basic Books, 1987.

Zalesskii, Konstantin. *Kto est' kto v istorii SSSR 1953–1991gg*. Moscow: Veche, 2010.

Zaloga, Steven J. *The Kremlin's Nuclear Sword: The Rise and Fall of Russia's Strategic Nuclear Forces, 1945–2000*. Washington, DC: Smithsonian Institution Press, 2002.

Zelizer, Julian E. *Arsenal of Democracy: The Politics of National Security in America from World War II to the War on Terrorism*. New York: Basic Books, 2010.

Zelizer, Julian E. *The Fierce Urgency of Now: Lyndon Johnson, Congress, and the Battle for the Great Society*. New York: Penguin, 2015.

Zubok, Vladislav A. *A Failed Empire: The Soviet Union in the Cold War From Stalin to Gorbachev*. Chapel Hill: University of North Carolina Press, 2007.

Zuckerman, Edward. *The Day After World War III*. New York: Viking, 1984.

INDEX

ABM systems (antiballistic missile systems). *See also* ABM Treaty

"ABM gap" debate (1960s) and, 71–72, 74–75

aboveground nuclear testing and the development of, 38–43, 72

arms control negotiations and, 8–10, 74–75, 86–89, 101–2, 109, 111, 115, 119, 121, 124–35, 138–51, 158

arms race potential regarding, 2, 34, 82, 108, 124

assured destruction doctrine and, 58, 69–71, 92

bureaucratic and domestic political factors in deployment of, 4, 8–10, 23, 58, 118–19, 128–29

China cited as impetus for developing, 4, 66, 68–69, 74, 94–96, 114–15

civil defense programs and, 60–62

Congress and, 23, 54–55, 71–73, 75, 80, 83, 104, 112–17, 119–26, 129, 140–41, 143, 149–51, 158, 162, 164, 166

costs of, 21, 45, 73–74, 82, 84–88, 104

Eisenhower administration and, 20–21

first strikes potentially nullified by, 1–2, 88–89

Gaither Report (1957) and, 20–21

Galosh system and, 111

ICBM launch site protection as goal for, 96, 114, 126, 140, 150

ICBMs as impetus for creating, 20–21, 39, 68, 114

Johnson administration and, 3–4, 8, 50, 54–55, 58, 62–64, 66, 68, 71–75, 77–78, 80, 82–87, 94–96, 104, 112–13, 127, 163–64

Kennedy administration and, 3, 13, 21, 23–24, 33–34, 37–38, 41, 44, 48, 72, 163–64

Limited Test Ban Treaty and, 41–42, 45, 72

McNamara and, 3, 8, 13, 21–24, 33–34, 41–42, 50, 54, 60, 62–64, 66, 68–72, 74–75, 77, 84, 87, 93–96, 104, 124

MIRVs and, 44, 92–93

mutual assured destruction doctrine and, 1–2, 77

National Command Authorities (NCAs) and, 127, 129, 133–34, 137, 140, 143, 145, 153

Nike-Hercules system and, 20–21

Nike-X system and, 34, 37, 42, 45, 66

Nike-Zeus system and, 21–24, 34, 37, 39–40, 45, 54–55

Nixon administration and, 8–9, 108–9, 111–35, 137–51, 153, 158–60, 166

"rogue states" as possible reason for, 169

Safeguard system, 108, 114–18, 121–26, 128–29, 134, 137, 140–41, 143, 149–50, 158–60, 167

Sakharov on, 88–89

SALT I talks and, 9–10, 109, 111, 124–35, 138–51, 158

Sentinel system and, 95–96, 102, 104, 112–15

Soviet development of, 21–22, 42, 69–71, 75, 84, 87–89, 92–93, 101, 111, 125, 127–28

"System A" (Soviet prototype) and, 69

Taran (Soviet prototype) and, 69

technical complexities involved in, 21, 39–42, 66, 82, 86–87, 89, 117–18

Teller on, 42–43

US domestic opposition to, 104, 108, 112–16, 120–21, 126, 128, 134, 137, 140, 149, 164

ABM Treaty (Antiballistic Missile Treaty, 1972). *See also* SALT I accords
Congressional approval of, 160
critics of, 2
defensive arms race nullified by, 2, 159
détente doctrine and, 1, 160
mutual assured destruction (MAD) doctrine and, 1–2, 4
mutual vulnerability doctrine and, 2
US withdrawal (2002) from, 9, 169
Acheson, Dean, 15, 25, 153
Adenauer, Konrad, 44
Ad Hoc Panel on Nuclear Testing (Panofsky Panel), 39–40
Agnew, Spiro, 123
Aiken, George, 112
Allen, James B., 160
Alsop, Stewart, 36
Anderson, Clinton P., 123
Anderson, George, 30
Anderson, Robert B., 51
antiballistic missiles. *See* ABM systems
anti-ICBM (AICBM) Panel of the President's Science Advisory Committee, 21, 39
Arbatov, Georgii, 88
Arms Control and Disarmament Agency (ACDA; US government agency), 88, 99–100, 128, 151
Ashbrook, John M., 157
assured destruction doctrine. *See also* mutual assured destruction (MAD) doctrine
ABM systems and, 58, 69–71, 92
China and, 66–67
Johnson administration and, 3, 7, 52–53, 56, 58, 62–64, 69–71, 78–81, 90, 92–93, 95, 104–5
McNamara and, 7–8, 52–53, 58, 62–64, 66–67, 69–73, 77, 79–81, 92, 104–5, 159
mutual vulnerability doctrine and, 8, 95
Nixon administration and, 159
rational superiority doctrine and, 58
SALT I accords and, 159
Soviet Union and, 62–64, 69, 72–73, 77–80, 90, 92–93, 104
survival of first strike as criterion under, 3, 7–8, 52–53
aboveground nuclear testing, 38–45
Atlas ICBM missiles, 24
Atomic Energy Commission, 38–40, 100

B-1 bomber, 159, 168
Backfire bomber (Soviet Union), 167
Ball, Desmond, 4
Bay of Pigs invasion (Cuba, 1961), 35
Bell, David, 20, 23–24
Berlin crisis (1961)
Acheson's advice during, 25
backchannel negotiations during, 28
Berlin Wall constructed during, 26
deterrence doctrine and, 12
Khrushchev and, 25–26, 28
US nuclear superiority during, 7, 13, 26, 28, 103, 162
The Best and the Brightest (Halberstam), 16
Bohlen, Charles, 100
bombers
ABM systems as means of protecting, 114
B-1 bombers and, 159, 168
Backfire bomber (Soviet Union) and, 167
Chinese air force and, 68
first strike doctrine and, 27
Johnson's proposed budget cuts regarding, 52
McNamara's criticism of spending on, 53
Soviet development of, 2, 167
US advantage in, 101
Brandt, Willy, 31
Breech, Ernest R., 17
Brennan, Donald, 2
Brezhnev, Leonid I., 90, 155–56, 158
Brooke, Edward, 112
Brooks, Overton, 23
Brown, Harold, 39–40
Buchanan, Pat, 116
Buckley, James L., 160
Buckley Jr., William F., 148–49
Bundy, McGeorge
ABM systems and, 24
Cuban missile crisis and, 32
on difficulty of "telling the truth" regarding nuclear strategy, 92, 161–62, 164, 168–69
Dobrynin and, 92
mutual assured destruction (MAD) doctrine and, 6
nuclear superiority doctrine and, 24, 28, 46, 92, 161–62
Reagan administration nuclear buildup opposed by, 161
Butterfield, Alexander, 116, 122
Byrd, Harry, 51, 55

Cambodia invasion (1970), 131, 152
Cantril, Hadley, 55–56
Carter, Jimmy, 167–69
Castro, Fidel, 31
Central Intelligence Agency (CIA)
    arms control negotiations and, 100, 128
    China analyzed by, 67–68, 94
    Soviet economy analyzed by, 81
    Soviet missile systems analyzed by,
        70–71, 73, 81–82, 116–17
    Soviet Politburo analyzed by, 83
Chelomey, Vladimir N., 69
China
    air force of, 68
    assured destruction doctrine and, 66–67
    first-strike capabilities and, 68
    Great Leap Forward collectivization
        program in, 67
    ICBMs and, 66, 68, 94
    Kissinger's visit (1971) to, 145, 152–53
    Limited Test Ban Treaty and, 41
    Nixon administration's opening of
        relations with, 130–31, 149, 152–54,
        166
    Nixon administration's relations prior to
        opening of, 115, 121
    nuclear program in, 41, 66
    ping pong diplomacy with United States
        and, 152
    Soviet Union and, 67, 125
    Taiwan and, 66–67
    twenty-first century diplomacy
        and, 169–70
    US ABM systems and, 4, 66, 68–69, 74,
        94–96, 114–15
    US intelligence estimates
        regarding, 67–68
    Vietnam War and, 67–68, 98, 121
Church, Frank, 141
Churchill, Winston, 115
civil defense programs, 60–62
Civil Rights Act of 1964, 55
Clifford, Clark M.
    arms control negotiations with Soviet
        Union and, 100, 102–3, 105
    McNamara replaced as secretary of
        defense by, 99
    Vietnam War and, 99, 102
Congress
    ABM systems and, 23, 54–55, 71–73, 75,
        80, 83, 104, 112–17, 119–26, 129,
        140–41, 143, 149–51, 158, 162, 164, 166

ABM Treaty and, 160
    arms control negotiations and, 9, 83,
        129, 136, 141, 145, 147–51, 156–60
    civil defense programs and, 60–61
    Civil Rights Act of 1964 and, 55
    Cuban missile crisis and, 29–31, 35, 37
    defense budget for 1963 and, 19–20,
        22–24, 34
    defense budget for 1964 and, 34
    defense budget for 1965 and, 50–51,
        51–52, 54, 56
    defense budget for 1966 and, 58
    defense budget for 1967 and, 59
    defense budget for 1969 and, 97
    Johnson administration and, 50–51, 58,
        62, 71–73, 75, 92–93, 104, 112
    Kennedy administration and, 23–24,
        28–31, 35, 37, 42–44
    Limited Test Ban Treaty and, 42–44
    midterm elections of 1966 and, 82
    midterm elections of 1970 and, 138
    Nixon administration and, 8–9,
        112–17, 119–23, 127, 140–41, 143,
        145.147–48, 150–51, 157–59, 164
    Nixon's address (June 1, 1972) to, 5, 159
    nuclear superiority doctrine and, 43, 56,
        71, 92–93, 104–5, 165
    SALT I accords and, 9, 160
    SALT I talks and, 129, 136, 141, 145,
        147–51, 156–59
    Southern Democrats in, 35, 51, 54–55
    tax cut (1964) and, 50–51
    Tonkin Gulf Resolution (1964) and, 59
    Vietnam War and, 59, 75, 98, 104
containment doctrine
    domestic legislative action and,
        50, 55, 58
    Jackson's run for president (1972)
        and, 155
    Johnson administration and, 50,
        55, 58
    Nixon administration and, 107, 120,
        148, 164
    Vietnam War and, 148
Cooper, John Sherman, 104, 112,
    123, 149–50
Craig, Campbell, 25
Crimea invasion (Russian Federation,
    2014), 170
Cuban missile crisis (1962)
    air strike against Cuba discussed
        during, 30–32

Cuban missile crisis (1962) (*cont.*)
   assured destruction doctrine in
      wake of, 62
   backchannel negotiations during, 28, 32
   Bay of Pigs invasion (1961) and, 35
   Berlin as source of concern
      during, 30–31
   Congress and, 29–31, 35, 37
   discovery of Soviet missiles in Cuba
      and, 29
   fear of Soviet strike on United States
      during, 31
   Joint Chiefs of Staff and, 29–31
   Khrushchev and, 30–32, 35
   mutual assured destruction doctrine
      and, 77
   Nixon on, 5
   nuclear testing policies in aftermath
      of, 40–41
   press responses to, 35
   quarantine strategy implemented
      during, 29–30
   Turkey missile ultimatum during,
      31–32, 35
   U-2 aircraft downed over Cuba
      during, 32–33
   US nuclear superiority during, 5–7,
      13, 29–33, 36, 47, 73, 90, 96, 103,
      162, 165
Czechoslovakia invasion (1968), 101–2,
   120, 160

Dallek, Robert, 57
Da Nang landing (1965) of, 59
Danger and Survival (Bundy), 161
Davis, Nathaniel, 72, 85, 92, 100, 105
Decker, George H., 22–23, 27
Defense Department (DoD)
   ABM development and, 70, 104, 114,
      116–18, 125–26
   arms control negotiations and, 74, 100,
      102–3, 128
   defense budget for 1963 and, 19–20,
      22–24, 34
   defense budget for 1964 and, 34
   defense budget for 1965 and, 50–51, 54
   defense budget for 1966 and, 58
   defense budget for 1967 and, 59
   defense budget for 1969 and, 97
   Eisenhower administration and, 17
   Johnson administration and, 11, 100,
      102–3

   Kennedy administration and, 11,
      17–19, 22, 25, 45
   Nixon administration and, 114, 116–18,
      125–26, 128–29, 151
   nuclear testing policies and,
      38–39, 41, 45
   Planning Programming Budgeting
      System (PPBS) and, 17–18, 24, 96
   SALT I talks and, 128–29, 151, 156
   systems analysis and, 17–18
   Vietnam War strategy and, 98
détente doctrine
   ABM Treaty and, 1, 160
   arms control negotiations and, 10,
      47–48, 76, 103, 107, 160, 162, 165
   criticisms of, 72, 166, 168
   Czechoslovakia invasion (1968) as threat
      to, 101
   Germany as key factor in, 9–10
   Johnson administration and, 8, 48,
      75–76, 165
   Kennedy administration and, 47–48
   Limited Test Ban Treaty and, 38, 44
   military spending pressures as
      factor in, 65
   Moscow Summit (1972) and, 1
   Nixon and, 47, 136, 162
   right-wing challenges to, 149
   SALT I accords (1972) and, 160, 162
deterrence doctrine
   ABM systems and, 22–23, 33, 119
   assured destruction doctrine and, 159
   Eisenhower's "New Look" doctrine and, 2
   first strikes and, 36, 46
   McNamara and, 35–36
   mutual assured destruction (MAD)
      doctrine and, 5
   mutual deterrence concept and,
      35–36, 71
   nuclear testing and, 39–40
   rational superiority doctrine and, 21–22
   Soviet nuclear advantage as challenge
      to, 166
   Soviet understandings of, 87
Detinov, Nikolai, 87, 90
Dirksen, Everett, 43, 113
Dobrynin, Anatoly
   ABM systems and, 132, 142–44, 147,
      149–51, 153
   arms control negotiations and, 9,
      77–78, 108–9, 111, 121–22, 130–36,
      138–40, 142–44, 146–47, 149–57

Bundy and, 92
Cuban missile crisis and, 32
Czechoslovakia invasion (1968) and, 101
Kissinger's backchannel negotiations
    during SALT I with, 9, 108–9, 111,
    130–35, 139–40, 142–44, 146,
    154–55, 157
Kissinger's China visit (1971) and,
    152–53
May 20 Agreement (1971) and, 143–44,
    146–47, 149–51, 153
Middle East diplomacy and, 142
Moscow Summit (1972) and, 153–54
Muskie visit to Moscow (1971) and, 142
Rogers's meeting (1969) with, 121–22
SALT I talks and, 9, 108–9, 111,
    130–36, 138–40, 142–44, 146–47,
    149–51, 153–57
SLBMs and, 146, 151, 154–56
Thompson's meeting (1966) with, 77–78
Vietnam War and, 121
Douglas-Home, Alec, 81
Dulles, John Foster, 2
Dumbrell, John, 105

East Germany, 9, 25. *See also* Berlin crisis
    (1961)
The Economics of Defense in the Nuclear Age
    (Hitch), 17
Eisenhower, Dwight D.
    ABM systems and, 4, 20–21
    civil defense program and, 60
    defense budgeting and, 20
    Department of Defense and, 17
    Johnson's discussions regarding Soviet
        Union with, 87
    Khrushchev's demands in Berlin and, 25
    massive retaliation doctrine and,
        2, 18, 56
    on the "military-industrial complex," 100
    "missile gap" charges against
        administration of, 13–14,
        48, 72
    moratorium on nuclear tests
        (1958) by, 38
    New Look strategy of, 2
    rational superiority doctrine
        and, 57
    Sputnik satellite launch (1957)
        and, 2–3, 7
Ellsberg, Daniel, 27–28
Elsey, George, 102

Enthoven, Alain, 17–19, 54
Evans, Stan, 149

Farer, Tom J., 16
Federal Republic of Germany (FRG)
    ABM systems and, 37
    détente policies and, 9–10
    Limited Test Ban Treaty and, 41, 44, 47
first strikes
    ABM systems as response to problem of,
        1–2, 89
    assured destruction doctrine as response
        to problem of, 3, 7–8, 52–53
    bombers and, 27
    China as potential initiator of, 68
    countermeasures against, 81
    deterrence doctrine and, 46
    Joint Chiefs of Staff and, 48
    mutual assured destruction (MAD)
        doctrine as response to, 1
    mutual deterrence and, 36
    nuclear testing and, 39
    Soviet Union's ability to survive, 46,
        63, 148
    Soviet Union's probabilities of
        succeeding in, 116–18
    Sputnik satellite launch (1957)
        and, 3
    US ability to survive and counter,
        26–27, 34–35, 52–53, 56, 167
    US period of nuclear superiority and,
        8, 26–27
flexible response doctrine (Kennedy), 3,
    18–19, 110
Flood, Daniel, 23
Fong, Hiram, 43
Ford, Gerald R., 167
Ford II, Henry, 17
forward-based systems (FBS), 132,
    138, 146
France, 25, 37, 156
Free, Lloyd, 55–56
Freedman, Lawrence, 166
freeze proposals
    ICBMs as subject of, 140, 143, 145–46,
        151, 158
    Johnson administration and, 80–82, 85,
        95, 100–101
    May 20 Agreement (1971), 143–46,
        151, 159
    MIRVs as means of
        circumventing, 158–59

freeze proposals (*cont.*)
  Nixon administration and, 140, 143,
    145–47, 151, 154–56, 158–59
  nuclear superiority doctrine and, 81, 85
  SLBMs as subject of, 146, 151, 154–56
  Soviet ABM development as
    threat to, 71
Fulbright, J. William
  ABM systems and, 112, 114
  détente doctrine and, 75–76
  Johnson's discussions about Kosygin
    (1967) with, 85–86
  Kissinger and, 145
  Nonproliferation Treaty (1968) and, 114
  Vietnam War and, 75

Gaither Report (1957), 20–21
Galosh ABM system (Soviet Union), 111
Garthoff, Raymond L., 4, 127–28, 146
Gavin, Francis J., 9, 111
Geist, Edward, 61
German Democratic Republic (GDR), 9, 25.
  See also Berlin crisis (1961)
Gilpatric, Roswell, 26–28
Glassboro Summit (1967)
  ABM systems discussed at, 86–87,
    124, 127
  Johnson and, 86–87, 89–90, 93–94,
    124, 127
  Kosygin and, 85–87, 89, 93, 124, 127
  McNamara and, 85–87
  Middle East peace discussed at, 93–94
  modernization theory discussed at, 97
  Vietnam War talks discussed at, 93–94
Goldwater, Barry, 56–57
Gorbachev, Mikhail, 168
Gore Sr., Albert, 114, 116, 121, 141
Great Britain, 25, 38, 156
Great Leap Forward (China), 67
Great Society programs (Johnson
    administration)
  budget measures designed to protect,
    62, 97, 112
  cost of, 82
  fear of Great Depression as motivation
    for, 76
  inflationary pressures in United States
    and, 75
  initial impetus behind, 49–50
  Johnson's national security policies and,
    7, 10, 50, 55, 58–59, 77, 103–4
Grechko, Andrei, 90

Griffiths, Marsha, 61
Gromyko, Andrei, 76, 84, 138
Gulf of Tonkin Incident and Resolution
    (1964), 57, 59

Halberstam, David, 16
Haldeman, H.R. "Bob," 132, 139, 141–42
Halperin, Morton, 4, 110
Harlow, Bryce, 114, 116, 122
Harriman, Averell, 43–45
Hart, Philip, 104, 123
Healey, Denis, 95–96
Heller, Walter, 52
Helms, Richard, 71, 116–17
Herken, Gregg, 93, 118–19
Hiss, Alger, 121
Hitch, Charles, 17, 19
Hotel-class ballistic missile submarines
    (Soviet Union), 157–58
Hughes, Harold, 141
Human Events magazine, 148–49
Humphrey, Hubert, 43, 109, 141

ICBMs (intercontinental ballistic missiles).
    See also specific missiles
  ABM systems as means of protecting
    launch sites of, 114, 126, 140, 150
  ABM systems as response to threat from,
    21, 39, 68, 114
  China's development of, 66, 68, 94
  efforts to "harden and disperse" holdings
    in, 63, 72, 81
  freeze proposals regarding, 140, 143,
    145–46, 151, 158
  Kennedy's buildup in, 3–4, 13, 20,
    23–24, 52–53, 95
  MIRVs and, 6, 91–92
  "missile gap" favoring Soviets as
    1960 election topic, 13–14, 72,
    107, 162
  redundancy in US efforts to build, 17
  SALT I talks and, 9, 127, 129, 140,
    145–46, 151, 155–58
  Soviet buildup (1960s) and advantage
    (early 1970s) in, 3, 5, 8–9, 17, 20, 63,
    71–73, 80–82, 89, 93, 95, 107, 109–11,
    148–49, 158, 166–67
  Soviet deficit (early 1960s) in, 24, 148
  US intelligence estimates regarding
    Soviet holdings in, 63, 70–71, 95
  US vulnerability to Soviet strike by, 14
Inkeles, Alex, 64

intercontinental ballistic missiles.
  See ICBMs
Interim Agreement on the Limitation of
    Strategic Offensive Arms (1972), 1, 5,
    136, 158–60. *See also* SALT I accords
Intermediate-Range Nuclear Forces (INF)
    Treaty (1987), 168

Jackson, Henry "Scoop"
  ABM systems and, 55, 61, 104, 113,
    122–23, 126, 140, 159, 166
  civil defense spending and, 60–61
  containment doctrine and, 155
  Interim Agreement on the Limitation
    of Strategic Offensive Arms (1972)
    and, 160
  Nitze and, 15
  presidential election of 1972 and, 155
  SALT I talks and, 147–48, 159, 166–67
Jervis, Robert, 22, 77, 163
Johnson, Harold, 46, 48
Johnson, Lyndon B.
  ABM systems and, 3–4, 8, 50, 54–55,
    58, 62–64, 66, 68, 71–75, 77–78,
    80, 82–87, 94–96, 104, 112–13,
    127, 163–64
  arms control negotiations and, 5–6,
    77–89, 91–94, 99–106, 124, 127,
    162, 165
  ascendancy to presidency (1963) by, 49
  assured destruction doctrine and, 3, 7,
    52–53, 56, 58, 62–64, 69–71,
    78–81, 90, 92–93, 95, 104–5
  China policy and, 67–68, 94–95
  civil defense programs and, 62
  Civil Rights Act of 1964 and, 55
  defense budget for 1965 and,
    51–52, 54, 56
  defense budget for 1966 and, 58
  defense budget for 1967 and, 59
  defense budget for 1969 and, 97
  Department of Defense and, 11,
    100, 102–3
  détente doctrine and, 8, 48,
    75–76, 165
  Eighteen Nation Disarmament
    Conference (1964) and, 80
  Eisenhower's discussions regarding
    Soviet Union with, 87
  Glassboro Summit (1967) and, 86–87,
    89–90, 93–94, 124, 127
  on Goldwater, 57

Great Society programs and, 7, 10,
    49–50, 55, 58–59, 62, 75–77, 82,
    97, 104, 112, 162
inflation as political problem for, 75
Joint Chiefs of Staff and, 11, 51–52, 54,
    62, 71, 73, 100–101, 105
Khrushchev and, 86
Kosygin and, 83–86, 90, 93, 100
Middle East peace proposal (1967) of, 93
midterm elections of 1966 and, 82
MIRVs and, 92–93
mutual assured destruction (MAD)
    doctrine and, 6, 77
Nixon's conversations (1968)
    with, 101–2
Nonproliferation Treaty and, 10, 65, 79,
    100, 114
nuclear superiority and, 7–10, 48,
    50, 54, 56–58, 64–65, 77, 79–82,
    84–85, 92–93, 95–96, 99, 103–6, 110,
    161–65, 170
Outer Space Treaty (1967) and, 65
presidential election of 1964 and, 56–57
Six Day War (1967) and, 87
Soviet invasion of Czechoslovakia (1968)
    and, 102
State of the Union address (1965) by, 58
tax cut (1964) and, 50–51
tax surcharge (1968) and, 97, 104, 112
Vietnam War and, 8, 10, 50, 58–59, 68,
    73, 75–77, 79–80, 82, 86,
    97–99, 101–3, 106, 162–63
withdrawal from presidential election of
    1968 by, 99
Johnson, U. Alexis, 24
Joint Chiefs of Staff (JCS)
  ABM systems development and, 71,
    73–74, 126, 134
  arms control negotiations and, 100–101,
    105, 128, 134, 151
  civil defense programs and, 62
  Cuban missile crisis and, 29–31
  defense budget of 1965 and, 51–52, 54
  first strike doctrine and, 48
  Johnson administration and, 11, 51–52,
    54, 62, 71, 73, 100–101, 105
  Kennedy administration and, 11, 27,
    29–31, 39–40, 43–45, 48
  Limited Test Ban Treaty and, 43–44
  MIRVs and, 128
  Nixon administration and, 126, 128, 134,
    151, 156

Joint Chiefs of Staff (JCS) (*cont.*)
  nuclear testing policies and, 39–40, 44
  SALT I talks and, 151, 156
  SLBMs and, 151, 156
Jones, Matthew, 9, 68
Jupiter missiles in Turkey controversy
  (1962), 32, 35

Kaiser, David, 47
Kaplan, Fred, 37
Katzenbach, Nicholas, 82, 94
Kaysen, Carl
  on ABM system development, 38, 41
  Basic National Security Policy and, 18
  Berlin crisis and, 28
  concerns about nuclear force reductions
    expressed by, 56
  on Defense Department budget for
    1963, 19–20
  first strike doctrine and, 27
  on McNamara's strategic doctrine and
    budgeting, 53–54
  nuclear superiority assumptions
    questioned by, 24
Keeny, Spurgeon, 94, 96–97
Kennedy, Edward, 113, 123, 154
Kennedy, John F.
  ABM systems and, 3, 13, 21, 23–24,
    33–34, 37–38, 41, 44, 48, 72, 163–64
  assassination of, 10, 45–47, 49
  Basic National Security Policy
    and, 18–19
  Berlin crisis and, 12–13, 25–26, 28,
    30–31, 41, 103, 162
  China policy and, 41, 67
  civil defense program and, 60–61
  Congress and, 23–24, 28–31, 35,
    37, 42–44
  Cuban missile crisis and, 5–6, 12,
    29–32, 35, 47, 62, 77, 90, 96,
    164–65
  defense budget for 1963 and, 19–20
  Defense Department and, 11, 17–19,
    22, 25, 45
  "defense intellectuals" and, 14–15
  first strike doctrine and, 27
  flexible response doctrine and, 3, 18–19
  ICBM buildup under, 3–4, 13, 20, 23–24,
    52–53, 95
  inaugural address (1961) by, 12
  Joint Chiefs of Staff and, 11, 27, 29–31,
    39–40, 43–45, 48

Limited Test Ban Treaty (LTBT) and, 13,
  38, 42–45, 47, 56, 72, 95–96, 132
mutual assured destruction (MAD)
  doctrine and, 6
North Atlantic Treaty Organization
  and, 37
nuclear superiority and, 6–10, 12–13,
  18–19, 22, 24, 26–33, 35–37, 40,
  43–48, 55, 73, 90, 92, 95–96, 105,
  110, 161–62, 164–65, 170
nuclear testing policies and, 40
presidential election of 1960 and, 3, 7,
  13–14, 72, 107, 162
presidential election of 1964 planning
  by, 6–7, 45–47
rational superiority doctrine and, 6–7,
  19, 35, 37–38, 42, 45–48, 54, 57, 96
strategic arms limitation accords'
  impossibility under, 5–6
tax cut promised for 1964 by, 50–51
Vienna Summit (1961) and, 24–25
Vietnam War and, 162
Kennedy, Robert F., 28, 32
Kent State shootings (1970), 131
Keogh, Jim, 115
Khrushchev, Nikita
  ABM systems and, 69
  Berlin crisis and, 25–26, 28
  Cuban missile crisis and, 30–32, 35
  Johnson and, 86
  ouster of, 69, 89–90
  on Soviet capacity to strike United
    States, 14
  Twenty-Second Congress of the
    Communist Party of the Soviet Union
    speech by, 26
  Vienna Summit and, 25
Killian, James, 74
Kissinger, Henry
  ABM systems and, 9, 115–16, 119,
    121–28, 140–44, 149–51, 153
  arms control negotiations and, 9, 108–9,
    111, 115, 119, 121, 124–25, 130–35,
    139–40, 142–44, 146, 154–55, 157
  backchannel negotiations with Dobrynin
    during SALT I and, 9, 108–9, 111,
    130–35, 139–40, 142–44, 146,
    154–55, 157
  China trip (1971) by, 145, 152–53
  Fulbright and, 145
  May 20 Agreement (1971) and, 137,
    143–51, 153, 159

Middle East diplomacy and, 142
MIRVs and, 129
Muskie visit to Moscow (1971) and, 142
"peace rhetoric of 1972" disparaged
    by, 160
SALT I talks and, 9, 124–25, 127–29,
    136–51, 153, 156–57, 159
SLBMs and, 151, 154–57
Vietnam War and, 111
Kistiakowsky, George, 74
Klein, Herb, 122
Kohler, Foy D., 83–85, 100, 105
Kopechne, Mary Jo, 123
Kosygin, Alexei
ABM systems and, 84, 87–88, 127
arms control negotiations and, 83–90,
    93, 100, 102, 106, 111, 121, 124, 127
as chairman of Council of Ministers, 83
Glassboro Summit (1967) and, 85–87,
    89, 93, 124, 127
Johnson and, 83–86, 90, 93, 100
McNamara criticized by, 84, 90
Middle East and, 85, 87, 121
military background of, 91
Nixon and, 111, 121
Nonproliferation Treaty and, 100
Vietnam War and, 121

Laird, Melvin
executive branch control of information
    and, 119
Safeguard ABM system and, 116–18, 158
SALT I talks and, 151, 158–59
Sentinel ABM system halted (1969)
    by, 113
on SLBMs, 151
support for post-SALT military programs
    and, 159
Lamb, Charles, 87
LeMay, Curtis, 30–31, 48, 54
Limited Test Ban Treaty (LTBT, 1963)
ABM systems and, 41–42, 45, 72
aboveground nuclear tests banned
    under, 38, 45, 72
China's nuclear program and, 41
Congress and, 42–44
domestic political windfall from, 132
Federal Republic of Germany and,
    41, 44, 47
Harriman as lead negotiator for, 43–45
nuclear superiority doctrine and, 13,
    42–45, 47, 56, 95–96

Lin Biao, 67
Long, Russell, 51
Lovett, Robert, 15

MAD. *See* mutual assured destruction
    (MAD) doctrine
Manatos, Mike, 104
Mao Zedong, 1, 67
massive retaliation doctrine, 2, 18
May 20 Agreement (1971)
ABM systems and, 143–51, 153
as basis for final SALT I talks, 136
criticisms of, 148–49
détente policies reflected in, 162
forward-based systems discussed in, 146
inspection and verification provisions
    in, 145
offensive and defensive weapons
    delinked in, 137, 143–45, 147–48,
    150–51, 153, 159
presidential election of 1972 as an
    impetus for, 137
press reviews of, 144
SLBMs and, 151
McCone, John, 32
McConnell, John, 73–74
McCormack, John, 23
McGovern, George, 43, 141
McIntyre, Thomas, 122
McNamara, Robert S.
ABM programs and, 3, 8, 13, 21–24,
    33–34, 41–42, 50, 54, 60, 62–64, 66,
    68–72, 74–75, 77, 84, 87, 93–96,
    104, 124
Adenauer's meeting (1963) with, 44
arms control negotiations and, 85–88,
    90, 93, 100, 102, 106
assured destruction doctrine and, 7–8,
    52–53, 58, 62–64, 66–67, 69–73, 77,
    79–81, 92, 104–5, 159
Berlin crisis and, 103
China policy and, 66–69, 94–96
"China speech" (1967) and,
    95–96, 190n66
civil defense programs and, 60–62
Cuban missile crisis and, 103
defense budget for 1963 and, 19–20,
    22–24, 34
defense budget for 1964 and, 34
defense budget for 1965 and, 51–52, 54
defense budget of 1966 and, 58
defense budget of 1967 and, 59

McNamara, Robert S. (*cont.*)
defense budget for 1969 and, 96–97
on divisions with Soviet leadership, 65
executive branch control of information
and, 119
first strike doctrine and, 27, 36
flexible response doctrine and, 3
Ford Motor Company and, 15–17
Glassboro Summit (1967) and, 85–87
Halberstam on, 16
Kosygin's criticism of, 84, 90
Limited Test Ban Treaty and, 42–45
MIRVs and, 6, 91–93
mutual assured destruction (MAD)
doctrine and, 6
on mutual deterrence concept, 35–36
on NATO's nuclear forces, 36–37
Nike-Zeus ABM system and, 21
North Atlantic Council speech
(1962) by, 36
nuclear superiority and, 8, 22, 33,
35–37, 43–44, 46–48, 50, 64–65,
79–80, 90, 92–93, 95–96, 99, 103,
105, 161–62, 165
nuclear testing policies and, 40–41
policy continuity following Kennedy
assassination and, 49
rational superiority doctrine and, 42,
51, 79, 96
Reagan administration nuclear buildup
opposed by, 161
Senate Armed Services Committee
testimony (August 1967) by, 98–99
SLBM buildup under, 20
on Soviet ABM systems, 21–22
tactical nuclear weapons in
Europe and, 6
technocratic approach of, 15–18
University of Michigan commencement
speech (1962) by, 36
on US ability to survive and counter
Soviet nuclear attack, 52
Vietnam War and, 68, 73, 96–99, 102
on Western Europe's conventional
militaries, 37
World Bank appointment of, 99
Miller, George, 23
Minuteman missiles
ABM systems designed to protect, 74,
96, 117–18, 125–26, 140, 150
assured destruction theory and, 52–53
cost of, 82

defense budget for 1965 and, 54
hardening launch sites of, 81, 117
Kennedy administration buildup in, 14,
20, 23–24, 26
Minuteman III ICBM missile and, 91
Soviet SS-9 missiles as potential threat
to, 116–17, 166–67
US ICBM superiority in late 1960s
and, 81
MIRVs (multiple independently targetable
reentry vehicles)
ABM systems and, 44, 92–93
arms control negotiations and, 101–2,
111, 127–29, 158–59
arms race potential regarding, 108
McNamara and, 6, 91–93
military-technical advantages of, 91–92
Minuteman III ICBMs and, 91
Nixon administration and, 111, 129, 152,
158–59, 166
nuclear superiority doctrine and, 93, 166
SALT I talks and, 127–29, 158–59
SLBMs and, 6, 91–92, 152
Soviet development of, 117–18, 159, 167
US advantage in, 158–59
missile defense systems. *See* ABM systems
"missile gap"
Eisenhower administration blamed for,
13–14, 48, 72
Kennedy's 1960 election and, 13–14, 72,
107, 162
Sputnik launch as impetus for
discussions of, 7, 13
modernization theory, 64, 97
Moore, Jr., Barrington, 64
Moorer, Thomas, 156
Morse, Richard, 23
Moscow Summit (1972), 1, 5, 136,
152–53, 157
multiple independently targetable reentry
vehicles. *See* MIRVs
Mundt, Karl, 23
Muskie, Edmund, 141–42
mutual assured destruction (MAD)
doctrine
ABM systems and, 1–2, 77
ABM Treaty and, 1–2, 4
as alternative to nuclear superiority
doctrine, 163
criticisms of, 2, 77
Cuban missile crisis and, 77
deterrence doctrine and, 5

first strike advantages nullified under, 1
Johnson administration and, 6, 77
Kennedy administration and, 6
McNamara and, 77
Nixon administration and, 4–5, 9
SALT I accords and, 5
mutual vulnerability doctrine, 2, 4, 8,
95, 165
MX ICBM missile, 168

National Air Defense Forces (Soviet Union),
88
National Command Authorities (NCAs).
See under ABM systems
National Review magazine, 148–49
National Security Council (NSC)
ABM systems and, 119
Kennedy administration and, 29, 46
Nixon administration and, 116, 119,
123–24
Review Group (1969) and, 119
NATO. *See* North Atlantic Treaty
Organization (NATO)
New Look strategy (Eisenhower), 2
New START treaty, 169–70
Nike-Hercules ABM system, 20–21
Nike-X ABM system
aboveground test ban and, 45
McNamara's advocacy for, 34, 42,
45, 54, 66
"minor power" as potential target for, 66
rational superiority doctrine and, 37
Nike-Zeus ABM system
aboveground test ban and, 45
authorization of, 21–22
Congressional proponents of, 23, 55
defense budget of 1963's dropping
of, 24, 34
defense budget of 1964 and, 34, 55
cost of, 21
McNamara's evaluations of, 34, 54
military proponents for, 34
rational superiority doctrine and, 37
technical complexities involved in,
21, 39–40
testing (1962) of, 34
US Army as proponent of, 22, 23
Nitze, Paul H., 15, 27
Nixon, Richard M.
ABM systems and, 8–9, 108–9,
111–35, 137–51, 153, 158–60, 166
ABM Treaty (1972) and, 1, 5, 9, 136

Air Force Academy commencement
speech (1969) by, 120–21, 124
arms control negotiations and, 102–3,
107–8, 110–12, 115, 121–22, 124–34,
138–44, 146–47, 149–51, 153–60,
162, 166–68
assured destruction doctrine and, 159
Cambodia War (1970) and, 131, 152
China summit (1972) and, 1, 107, 153
Congressional elections of 1970 and, 138
containment doctrine and, 107, 120,
148, 164
on Cuban missile crisis, 5
détente policies and, 47, 136, 162
Dobrynin and, 155
inaugural address (1969) of, 107, 130
Interim Agreement on the Limitation
of Strategic Offensive Arms (1972)
and, 1, 5
Johnson's conversations (1968)
with, 101–2
Joint Chiefs of Staff and, 126, 128, 134,
151, 156
Kissinger's backchannel negotiations
with Dobrynin during SALT I talks
and, 9, 108–9, 111, 130–35, 139–40,
142–44, 146, 154–55, 157
Kosygin and, 111, 121
"madman theory" of, 5
May 20 Agreement (1971) and, 137,
143–47, 149
Middle East diplomacy and, 139
Moscow Summit (1972) and, 1, 5, 107,
136, 152
mutual assured destruction (MAD)
theory and, 4–5, 9
mutual vulnerability doctrine and, 165
on "new isolationists," 120
nuclear superiority doctrine and, 8,
107–10, 159–60, 164, 167, 170
presidential election of 1960 and, 13,
107, 109
presidential election of 1968 and,
102, 109
presidential election of 1972 and, 4, 10,
137, 139, 143, 154, 160
SALT I accords and, 4–5, 166–67
SALT I talks and, 2, 4, 9, 79, 108–9, 111,
122, 124–34, 137–47, 149–51, 153–60,
162, 166–68
US-Soviet summit as goal of, 130–32,
137–38, 142

Nixon, Richard M. (*cont.*)
  Vietnam War and, 5, 9, 103, 108,
    110–12, 120–21, 124, 130, 134,
    137–39, 141, 148, 155, 163
Nonproliferation Treaty (NPT, 1968), 10,
    65, 79, 100, 113–14
North American Air Defense Command
    (NORAD), 23
North Atlantic Treaty Organization (NATO)
  Goldwater on, 57
  Limited Test Ban Treaty and, 44, 47
  nuclear forces of, 36–37
  nuclear superiority doctrine and,
    47–48, 56, 64, 110
  US missiles in Turkey and, 32
  Western Europe's conventional
    militaries and, 37, 56, 110
North Vietnam. *See* Vietnam War
nuclear deterrence. *See* deterrence
Nuclear Nonproliferation Treaty.
    See Nonproliferation Treaty
nuclear superiority doctrine
  arms control negotiations and, 79–85,
    89, 92, 105–6
  Berlin crisis (1961) and, 7, 13, 26, 28,
    103, 162
  Congress and, 43, 56, 71, 92–93,
    104–5, 165
  costs of maintaining, 11, 53–54
  Cuban missile crisis (1962) and, 5–7,
    13, 29–33, 36, 47, 73, 90, 96, 103,
    162, 165
  doubts regarding advantages of, 24,
    27–28, 31–33, 35, 46, 103, 108,
    161–64, 169–70
  Johnson administration and, 7–10, 48,
    50, 54, 56–58, 64–65, 77,
    79–82, 84–85, 92–93, 95–96, 99,
    103–6, 110, 161–65, 170
  Kennedy administration and, 6–10,
    12–13, 18–19, 22, 24, 26–33, 35–37,
    40, 43–48, 55, 73, 90, 92, 95–96, 105,
    110, 161–62, 164–65, 170
  Limited Test Ban Treaty and, 13,
    42–45, 47, 56, 95–96
  McNamara and, 8, 22, 33, 35–37, 43–44,
    46–48, 50, 64–65, 79–80, 90, 92–93,
    95–96, 99, 103, 105, 161–62, 165
  MIRVs and, 93, 166
  mutual assured destruction doctrine
    and, 77

Nixon administration and, 8, 107–10,
    159–60, 164, 167, 170
North Atlantic Treaty Organization
    (NATO) and, 47–48, 56, 64, 110
nuclear testing policies and, 39–40
Obama administration and, 169
SALT I accords (1972) and, 159
Soviet perceptions regarding, 90
US public opinion regarding, 55–56
Vietnam War and, 45
Western Europe and, 44

Obama, Barack, 11, 169–70
Operation Rolling Thunder (Vietnam
    War), 59
Outer Space Treaty (1967), 65
Owen, Henry, 76

Packard, David, 110
Panofsky, Wolfgang, 39–40, 116
Paris peace negotiations (Vietnam War),
    102, 131
Parsons, Talcott, 64
People's Republic of China. *See* China
Percy, Charles, 112
Perlstein, Rick, 121
ping pong diplomacy (United States and
    China), 152
Pittman, Steuart L., 60–61
Planning Programming Budgeting System
    (PPBS), 17–18, 24, 96
Polaris submarines, 14, 20, 24, 26, 152
The Political Beliefs of Americans (Free and
    Cantril), 55–56
Poseidon SLBM missile, 91, 152
Potsdam Agreement (1945), 25
Prague Spring (1968), 101
Presidential Directive (PD)-59 (Carter
    administration), 168
President's Science Advisory Committee
    (PSAC), 21, 39, 74
Preston, Andrew, 47
Prouty, Winston, 122, 124
Putnam, Robert D., 173n31

Quinn, Adam, 163

RAND (Research and Development)
    Corporation
  Basic National Security Policy and, 18
  "defense intellectuals" and, 14–15

rational superiority doctrine and, 35, 37, 39, 47
Sputnik launch (1957) and, 15
systems analysis and, 17
US Air Force and, 14–15
Rathjens, George, 117–18, 166–67
rational superiority doctrine. *See also* nuclear superiority doctrine
arms control negotiations and, 80
assured destruction doctrine and, 58
Berlin crisis (1961) and, 27
critiques of, 46–47, 96
defining features of, 6
deterrence doctrine and, 21–22
domestic political factors and, 51
Eisenhower administration and, 57
Johnson administration and, 50–51, 57, 79–80, 108
Kennedy administration and, 6–7, 19, 35, 37–38, 42, 45–48, 54, 57, 96
Limited Test Ban Treaty and, 38–45
McNamara and, 42, 51, 79, 96
RAND Corporation and, 35, 37, 39, 47
Reagan, Ronald, 109, 160–61, 168–69
Republican National Committee, 72
Reykjavik Summit (1986), 168
Rivers, Mendel, 55
Roberts, Chalmers, 57
Rogers, William, 121–22, 156
Rostow, Walt
ABM systems and, 82
on China's foreign policy, 94
Cuban missile crisis and, 32
Glassboro Summit (1967) and, 97, 100
on Johnson administration's strategic outlook, 76
on possible arms control negotiations (1968), 102
Vietnam bombing debate (1967) and, 98
Rowen, Henry S., 18
Rusk, Dean
arms control negotiations and, 81, 87, 100–101, 105
Cuban missile crisis and, 32
Czechoslovakia invasion (1968) and, 101
Douglas-Home's meeting with, 81
first strike doctrine and, 27
Kennedy administration nuclear forces buildup and, 24

on Kosygin's views of nuclear strategy, 87
on Soviet ICBM buildup, 71
Russell, Richard
ABM system development and, 55, 73, 114, 122–23
arms control negotiations and, 105
Civil Rights Act of 1964 opposed by, 55
Cuban missile crisis and, 29–30
Limited Test Ban Treaty and, 43
as Senate Armed Services Committee chairman, 29, 55, 105, 113
Russian Federation, 169–70

Safeguard antiballistic missile system
arms control negotiations and, 115, 125, 128–29, 143, 150, 158
Congress and cuts to, 121–26, 140–41, 149–50, 159
McIntyre Amendment (1969) regarding, 122
Nixon administration decision to halt (1971), 141
Nixon's announcement (1969) of, 114–15, 160
Phase II of, 126
SALT I talks and, 125, 128–29, 143, 150, 158
Soviet responses to development of, 118–19
technical complexities involved in, 117–18
US domestic opposition to, 108, 115–16, 121, 126, 128, 134, 137, 140
Sakharov, Andrei, 88–89
SALT I accords (Strategic Arms Limitation Accords, 1972)
Congress and, 129, 136, 141, 145, 147–51, 156–59
criticisms of, 157, 166–67
détente doctrine and, 160, 162
Interim Agreement on the Limitation of Strategic Offensive Arms and, 1, 5, 136, 158–60
mutual assured destruction (MAD) doctrine and, 5
mutual vulnerability doctrine and, 4
Nixon's speech to Congress (June 1, 1972) following, 159
nuclear superiority doctrine and, 159

SALT I talks (Strategic Arms Limitation
Talks, 1969–72)
ABM systems and, 9–10, 109, 111,
124–35, 138–51, 158
backchannel negotiations between
Kissinger and Dobrynin during, 9,
108–9, 111, 130–35, 139–40, 142–44,
146, 154–55, 157
forward-based systems (FBS) discussed
at, 132, 138, 146
ICBMs and, 9, 127, 129, 140, 145–46,
151, 155–58
inspection and verification provisions
discussed at, 127–29, 145
May 20 Agreement (1971) and, 136–37,
143–51, 154, 159, 162
MIRVs and, 127–29, 158–59
mutual assured destruction (MAD)
doctrine accepted in, 2, 4
opening (1969) of, 124
Protocol to the Interim Agreement
(1972) and, 157–58
SLBMs and, 9, 129, 140, 145–46,
151, 154–58
Vietnam War and, 111–12
SALT II talks, 168
Savel'yev, Aleksandr, 87, 90
Schelling, Thomas C., 32–33
Schlesinger, James, 115
Seaborg, Glenn, 40, 47
Semenov, Vladimir, 124–25, 138, 140, 143
Sentinel antiballistic missile system
arms control negotiations and, 102
Chinese ICBMs presented as reason
for, 95–96
Congressional vote to delay (1968), 112
domestic opposition to, 104, 113–14
Laird's halting (1969) of, 113
McNamara's speech (1967)
announcing, 95
Minuteman silo protection and, 96
Nixon administration's move away
(1969) from, 114–15
Shapley, Deborah, 73
Shelest, Petro, 97
Shelter Incentive Program, 60
shelters. See civil defense programs
Shoup, David, 31
Shulman, Marshall, 118–19
Sino-Soviet split, 67
Six Day War (Middle East, 1967), 85, 87,
93, 121

SLBMs (submarine-launched ballistic
missiles). See also specific missiles
arms control negotiations regarding, 9,
101, 129, 140, 145–46, 151, 154–58
defensive measures against, 53
freeze proposals regarding, 146,
151, 154–56
Kennedy and McNamara's buildup
in, 20, 24
MIRVs and, 6, 91–92, 152
SALT I talks and, 9, 129, 140, 145–46,
151, 154–58
Soviet buildup (1960s) and advantage
(early 1970s) in, 5, 9, 63, 107, 111,
151–52, 157
Smith, Gerard, 4, 125, 143, 149, 154, 156
Smith, K. Wayne, 138
Smith, Margaret Chase, 123
Smith, William, 56
Sonnenfeldt, Helmut, 119, 138, 140, 147
Sorensen, Theodore, 23–24
Southern Democrats in US Congress, 35,
51, 54–55
South Vietnam. See Vietnam War
Soviet Union
ABM systems developed by, 21–22, 42,
69–71, 75, 84, 87–89, 92–93, 101, 111,
125, 127–28
arms control negotiations and, 2, 4, 9,
77–89, 91–95, 99–111, 115, 121–22,
124–34, 138–44, 146–47, 149–51,
153–54, 156–60, 162, 165–68
assured destruction doctrine and,
62–64, 69, 72–73, 77–80, 90,
92–93, 104
atomic bomb first tested (1949) by, 2
Berlin crisis and, 25–26, 28
CIA analysis of, 70–71, 73,
81–83, 116–17
Cuban missile crisis and, 29–32, 35
Czechoslovakia invaded (1968) by, 101
economy of, 81, 88–90, 97
General Staff and Military Industrial
Commission in, 89
Glassboro Summit (1967) and, 86–90,
93–94, 97–98, 124, 127, 132
ICBM buildup (1960s) and advantage
(early 1970s) and, 3, 5, 8–9, 17, 20, 63,
71–73, 80–82, 89, 93, 95, 107, 109–11,
148–49, 158, 166–67
Limited Test Ban Treaty and, 13, 38,
41–44, 47, 56, 72, 79, 95–96

May 20 Agreement (1971) and, 136–37, 143–51, 154, 159, 162

military spending levels in, 64–65, 83, 89

Ministry for General Machine-Building in, 90

Ministry of Foreign Affairs (MFA) in, 88, 110–11, 133

modernization theory and, 64, 97

National Air Defense Forces in, 88

Nonproliferation Treaty and, 10, 65, 100, 114

nuclear tests (1962) by, 40, 42

Outer Space Treaty and, 65

SALT I talks and, 2, 4, 9, 79, 108–9, 111, 124–34, 138–44, 146–47, 149–51, 153–54, 156–60, 162, 166–68

Sino-Soviet split and, 67

SLBM buildup (1960s) and advantage (early 1970s) by, 5, 9, 63, 107, 111, 151–52, 157

Sputnik satellite launch (1957) and, 2–3, 7, 13, 15, 47, 109–10

Twenty-Third Congress of the Communist Party (1966) and, 90

US ABM systems and, 74, 114–15, 118–19

US nuclear targeting strategy regarding, 52–53

Vietnam War and, 93–94, 99, 108, 111–12, 121

Sputnik satellite launch (Soviet Union, 1957)

Eisenhower administration response to, 2–3, 7

"missile gap" discussions following, 7, 13

RAND Corporation predictions regarding, 15

Soviet technological prowess vindicated by, 2–3, 109

US anxiety regarding, 7, 13, 47, 109–10

SS-9 missiles (Soviet Union), 116–17, 129, 145, 151

SSBNs (nuclear-powered ballistic missile submarines), 151, 156–57, 159

Stennis, John, 43, 98, 113–14, 122, 147

Stern, Sheldon M., 31

Strategic Air Command, 25, 117

Strategic Arms Limitation Accords (1972). See SALT I accords (Strategic Arms Limitation Accords)

Strategic Arms Limitation Talks. See SALT I talks (Strategic Arms Limitation Talks)

Strategic Arms Reduction Treaties (START treaties, 1991–92), 168

Strategic Defense Initiative (SDI), 160, 168

submarines. See SLBMs (submarine-launched ballistic missiles)

Suslov, Mikhail, 88–89

Symington, Stuart, 55

"System A" (Soviet ABM system), 69

Taiwan, 66–67

Taran (Soviet ABM system), 69

Taylor, Maxwell D., 20, 22, 27, 29, 33

Teller, Edward, 39–40, 42, 117

test ban. See Limited Test Ban Treaty (LTBT, 1963)

Thompson, Llewellyn "Tommy," 32, 77–78, 84, 86, 101

Thurmond, Strom, 23, 55, 71, 98, 109, 148–49

Titan ICBM missiles, 158

Tonkin Gulf Incident and Resolution (1964), 57, 59

Tower, John, 123

Trachtenberg, Marc, 9, 29

Trident SLBM missile, 152, 159, 168

Turkey, 32, 35

Ulam, Stanislaw, 39–40

underground nuclear testing, 40, 42–44

United Kingdom. See Great Britain

United States Air Force (USAF)

competition with US Army to build ballistic missiles and, 17

estimates regarding Soviet ABM capabilities and, 70

first strikes and, 27

Minuteman missiles and, 23

MIRVs and, 91

Nike-X ABM system and, 34

nuclear superiority doctrine and, 36

nuclear testing policies and, 39

RAND Corporation and, 14–15

United States Intelligence Board (USIB), 64–65

Ustinov, Dmitri, 90

Vance, Cyrus, 71, 74

Vienna Summit (1961), 24–25

Vietnam War

bombing pause (1965–66) in, 73

China and, 67–68, 98, 121

containment doctrine and, 148

Vietnam War (*cont.*)
  costs of, 82
  Da Nang landing (1965) and, 59
  Easter Offensive (1972) and, 155
  inflationary pressures in United States
    and, 75
  Johnson administration and, 8, 10, 50,
    58–59, 68, 73, 75–77, 79–80, 82, 86,
    97–99, 101–3, 106, 162–63
  Kennedy administration and, 162
  Laos campaign (1971) and, 141
  McNamara and, 68, 73, 96–99, 102
  Nixon administration and, 5, 9, 103, 108,
    110–12, 120–21, 124, 130, 134,
    137–39, 141, 148, 155, 163
  North Vietnam bombed during, 58–59,
    73, 93–94, 97–99, 101, 131
  nuclear superiority doctrine and, 45
  Operation Rolling Thunder bombing
    campaign and, 59
  Paris peace negotiations (1968)
    and, 102, 131
  peace talk proposals and, 93–94, 100,
    108, 124
  South Vietnam's support from United
    States in, 50, 58, 68, 80, 82, 99, 103,
    139, 141
  Soviet Union and, 93–94, 99, 108,
    111–12, 121

Tet Offensive (1968) and, 99
Tonkin Gulf Incident and Resolution
  (1964) during, 57, 59
US defeat in, 166
Vietnamization strategy and, 99
Vinson, Carl, 55
Volkov, Vladimir, 97

Warnke, Paul, 94, 102, 105
Warren Air Force Base (Wyoming), 140
West Germany. *See* Federal Republic of
  Germany
Westmoreland, William, 98
Wheeler, Earle, 31, 62, 73, 126
Whiteman Air Force Base (Missouri),
  125–27, 140
Why England Slept (Kennedy,
  John F.), 35
Wiesner, Jerome, 113, 116
Williams, John, 123
Wohlstetter, Albert, 15, 117, 166–67

Yahya Khan, Agha Muhammad, 152
Yanarella, Ernest, 4
Yom Kippur War (Middle East,
  1973), 166

Zelikow, Philip, 165
Zuckert, Eugene, 54